ANGER AT WORK

Elizabeth E. Van Voorhees, PhD, Psychologist, Durham Veterans Affairs Medical Center and Assistant Professor, Department of Psychiatry and Behavioral Sciences, and Duke University Medical Center, Durham, NC, United States

Chloe A. Wilson, PhD, Industrial-Organizational Psychology Graduate Student, Department of Psychology, Clemson University, Clemson, SC, United States

Acknowledgments

We thank our colleagues at the Walter Reed Army Institute of Research and Phoenix Australia–Centre for Posttraumatic Mental Health for their support in putting together this volume. In particular, we thank Kelly Toner and Belinda Pacella for their technical assistance. We also recognize those who serve or have served in high-risk occupations, including first responders and military personnel, for their dedication, professionalism, and sacrifice. We hope that this volume can facilitate efforts to provide effective support for members of these essential occupations.

WHY ANGER MATTERS

An Introduction

AMY B. ADLER AND DAVID FORBES

Anger is a normal human emotion. It can signal response to difficulty, injustice, and frustration. It can highlight the need to address serious shortfalls at work or in society, energize calls for social change, and motivate people to action. However, problematic anger—anger that is elevated, prolonged, and destructive—can not only fail to serve a useful purpose but also interfere with effective functioning and contribute to distress in those with problematic anger and those around them. It can also cost an organization. For example, one study estimated that dealing with conflict in the U.S. workplace cost approximately $359 billion a year in employee time (CPP Inc., 2008). Not only can problematic anger potentially reduce morale, suppress productivity, and increase employee turnover, there is emerging consensus that it can take a toll on an individual's physical and psychological health. There is also emerging consensus that problematic anger is relatively prevalent. For example, in a

---

Material has been reviewed by the Walter Reed Army Institute of Research. There is no objection to its presentation and/or publication. The opinions or assertions contained herein are the private views of the author, and are not to be construed as official, or as reflecting true views of the Department of the Army or the Department of Defense.

https://doi.org/10.1037/0000244-001
Anger at Work: Prevention, Intervention, and Treatment in High-Risk Occupations, A. B. Adler and D. Forbes (Editors)

large survey study of U.S. military personnel and military veterans, one in six exceeded the established cutoff on a measure of problematic anger (Adler et al., 2020). Problematic anger is not simply a reflection of other mental health problems but can occur independent of disorders such as posttraumatic stress disorder, depression, and alcohol abuse (Adler et al., 2020) and may reflect transdiagnostic biases and distortions in information processing (Owen, 2011). The prevalence of problematic anger, its association with distress, impact on interpersonal relationships, and disruption of decision making (Angie et al., 2011) have significance for job performance.

HIGH-RISK OCCUPATIONS

Although job performance is critical across a range of industries, in the context of high-risk occupations, job performance can mean the difference between life and death. These high-risk occupations require employees to operate under high-stakes conditions. Typified by occupations such as the military, policing, and firefighting, high-risk occupations include a range of jobs in which employees routinely place their lives on the line or work to rescue the lives of others. The lessons learned about problematic anger from these occupations are important because they occur in a context that may amplify the role of problematic anger. Thus, these lessons have the potential to chart a path forward for how employees, clinicians, supervisors, and senior management can address problematic anger before it undermines the mission of these organizations or causes distress in individuals, teams, and families.

This volume is designed to recognize the importance of problematic anger by pulling together key lessons from a range of disciplines. These disciplines, including clinical, organizational, and cognitive perspectives, often exist in parallel, although there is much that can be gained from considering the advances made in each of these areas. Across chapters, the authors in this volume offer a summary of key points and description of implications regarding how this information can be applied. In bringing voices from across these disciplines together in one volume, our goal is to help support this crossover and the development of a transdisciplinary approach to addressing problematic anger.

THE NATURE OF HIGH-RISK OCCUPATIONS

High-risk occupations differ culturally from other occupations in ways that are important to consider (see Table 1 for a summary). First, these high-risk occupations typically operate with an underlying psychological contract in

TABLE 1. Unique Characteristics of High-Risk Occupations

Characteristic	Description
Psychological contract	Individuals accept the danger inherent in the occupation and in exchange expect adequate training, equipment, and leadership, as well as support for themselves and their family if they are injured.
Close bonds	The shared experience of facing a common threat forges a strong connection between teammates that can create an intense sense of loyalty within the group.
Multilevel leadership	Organizations are defined by strong hierarchies that reinforce the importance of leaders in the health and well-being of team members.
Mission focused	Team members are dedicated to the mission, deriving their core values and identity from their work.
Encountering threat	As part of their work, individuals are trained to encounter potentially traumatic events and are prepared for multiple and repeated threats.
Heightened activation	In preparing for threats, individuals may develop reactions that reflect heightened physiological activation or hypervigilance.

which the elements of danger are considered in the context of a commitment to the employee by the organization (Adler & Castro, 2013; Adler & Sowden, 2018). That is, individuals are willing to risk their lives to perform a particular mission, and in exchange they expect that they will receive adequate training, equipment, and leadership to perform under these conditions. They also expect that if they are to be hurt or killed during their job, the organization will support them in dealing with their injury, and where fatal, the families they leave behind.

Second, the shared experience of operating under these difficult conditions creates a strong bond across members of these occupations. This bond can be reflected at the individual level (in terms of battle buddies in the military or partners in policing) and at the team or unit level. This bond is important for helping provide mutual support based on a common understanding of the threats that these individuals face and the fact that they rely on one another for their survival. Indeed, these bonds can create a perspective reflecting an ingroup and outgroup dynamic. This dynamic can both strengthen the sense of connection within the team and challenge the sense of connection beyond that team, which under extreme conditions can potentially result in unrestricted loyalty to the group or alienation from the larger civilian community but which otherwise can serve as an important source of support.

Third, these occupations are multilevel and typically organized around a strong hierarchical structure. The multilevel nature of this structure implies that anger can be understood not only in terms of changes within individuals over time or between individuals but also in terms of differences across teams and in terms of the organization's culture and climate as a whole (Ashkanasy & Dorris, 2017). In high-risk occupations, this structure is an efficient way to direct teams and communicate, and it elevates the significant role of leaders throughout the organization. These leaders are usually nested within a larger hierarchy and have tremendous influence on the health, well-being, and functioning of their subordinate employees. Thus, understanding the role of leaders is essential to understanding the experience of employees working in high-risk occupations.

Fourth, individuals working within high-risk occupations typically share a sense of dedication to the mission and derive meaning from the work. These jobs are more than simply a way to earn a living; they represent an individual's identity and define their core values of service. Thus, violations of this identity or core value (see Phelps et al., Chapter 3, this volume) present a potentially traumatic event that can set off a cascade of difficulties with emotion regulation in general and problematic anger in particular.

Fifth, individuals operating in high-risk occupations may be confronted with potentially traumatic events as part of their occupational responsibilities. Rather than react to a specific unexpected event, these employees are trained for these potentially traumatic events, and to some degree even expect them. For example, in the military, even though combat-related events may occur suddenly and without warning, they are not wholly unexpected. Indeed, they may not even be completely unwelcome, as they present an opportunity to use one's training, test one's mettle, and perform one's duty in support of the larger team. This context, however, means that understanding the mental health sequelae of these events requires considering that they are not necessarily due to a discrete event; rather they may represent a series of events. This occupational context suggests that prevention, assessment, and treatment for trauma-related mental health should consider the circumstances of symptom emergence and the nature of the traumatic events.

Finally, individuals in these high-risk occupations may experience symptoms prior to being directly exposed to an occupationally related traumatic event (Adler & Castro, 2013). For example, although irritability may be a symptom of posttraumatic mental health problems, it may result from a heightened level of chronic physiological activation consistent with what is needed in the occupation rather than direct exposure to trauma. Problematic anger may also result from inconsistent sleep schedules because of shift work or operating under restricted sleep conditions (Hisler & Krizan, 2017). Thus, heightened irritability or problematic anger may reflect training that results

Cassiello-Robbins, C., & Barlow, D. H. (2016). Anger: The unrecognized emotion in emotional disorders. *Clinical Psychology: Science and Practice, 23*(1), 66–85. https://doi.org/10.1111/cpsp.12139

CPP, Inc. (2008, July). *Workplace conflict and how business can harness it to thrive* (Global Human Capital Report). https://www.cpp.com/pdfs/CPP_Global_Human_Capital_Report_Workplace_Conflict.pdf

Fernandez, E., & Johnson, S. L. (2016). Anger in psychological disorders: Prevalence, presentation, etiology and prognostic implications. *Clinical Psychology Review, 46*, 124–135. https://doi.org/10.1016/j.cpr.2016.04.012

Hisler, G., & Krizan, Z. (2017). Anger tendencies and sleep: Poor anger control is associated with objectively measured sleep disruption. *Journal of Research in Personality, 71*, 17–26. https://doi.org/10.1016/j.jrp.2017.08.009

Kassinove, H., & Sukhodolsky, D. G. (1995). Anger disorders: Basic science and practice issues. *Issues in Comprehensive Pediatric Nursing, 18*(3), 173–205. https://doi.org/10.3109/01460869509087270

Lloyd, D., Nixon, R. D. V., Varker, T., Elliott, P., Perry, D., Bryant, R. A., Creamer, M., & Forbes, D. (2014). Comorbidity in the prediction of Cognitive Processing Therapy treatment outcomes for combat-related posttraumatic stress disorder. *Journal of Anxiety Disorders, 28*(2), 237–240. https://doi.org/10.1016/j.janxdis.2013.12.002

Martin, L. A., Neighbors, H. W., & Griffith, D. M. (2013). The experience of symptoms of depression in men vs women: Analysis of the National Comorbidity Survey Replication. *JAMA Psychiatry, 70*(10), 1100–1106. https://doi.org/10.1001/jamapsychiatry.2013.1985

Owen, J. M. (2011). Transdiagnostic cognitive processes in high trait anger. *Clinical Psychology Review, 31*(2), 193–202. https://doi.org/10.1016/j.cpr.2010.10.003

PART I FOUNDATIONS

1 AN OVERVIEW OF ANGER

A Common Emotion With a Complicated Backstory

JEFFREY M. OSGOOD AND PHILLIP J. QUARTANA

KEY POINTS

- The literature describing anger is extant, predates modern scientific research, and extends to early philosophical thought.
- Anger may occur in reaction to a perceived hostile situation and is quelled or intensified through a combination of biological, physiological, cognitive, psychological, motivational, and sociocultural factors.
- Anger is unique among negative emotions, as it is associated with approach motivation. Unlike other negative emotions (e.g., sadness), anger can be a powerful motivator to take action.

(continues)

Material has been reviewed by the Walter Reed Army Institute of Research. There is no objection to its presentation and/or publication. The opinions or assertions contained herein are the private views of the authors and are not to be construed as official or as reflecting true views of the Department of the Army or the Department of Defense.

https://doi.org/10.1037/0000244-002
Anger at Work: Prevention, Intervention, and Treatment in High-Risk Occupations, A. B. Adler and D. Forbes (Editors)

KEY POINTS (*Continued*)

- Stable individual differences in the tendency to become angry (trait anger) and individual difference in the expression of anger (trait anger management) are associated with a host of outcomes in the areas of judgment and decision making, health, pain sensitivity, and occupational behavior.
- The stresses and challenges of high-risk occupations may create environments prone to foster anger and vulnerable to the negative consequences thereof.

When asked to describe his character named Anger from Disney's film *Inside Out*, comedian and voice actor Lewis Black remarked, "Anger is all about getting the job done. . . . He only does it because he really cares though" (Pixar, 2015). Anger is unique because it is the lone negative emotional state that is approach motivated. Unlike fear, sadness, and worry, anger compels one to act, to get even, to come out on top (Harmon-Jones et al., 2011). The approach-motivation aspect of anger is borne out in behavioral and psychophysiological data (Carver & Harmon-Jones, 2009). Like positive emotions, which are also fundamentally approach motivated, anger can be useful in the right context. For example, anger can facilitate persuasion in political, consumer, and business communications when used adeptly (Adam & Brett, 2015; Walter et al., 2019). Of course, anger and aggression often have negative individual, interpersonal, and societal consequences. However, some evidence suggests that volitional attempts to suppress anger can also have deleterious consequences for one's health and well-being (Julkunen, 1996). In short, anger is complicated, and attempts to understand and conceptualize it have been a part of philosophical, clinical, and scientific inquiry for centuries. The complicated nature of anger may be particularly relevant in high-risk occupations. As we identify at several points in this chapter, high-risk occupational settings often combine the ingredients for anger with heightened stakes for the inappropriate expression of anger and aggression.

Anger is a ubiquitous and unique negative emotion that has been tied to manifold physiological, psychological, clinical, and social outcomes. Anger is experienced by everyone. A large sample of adults reported experiencing an average of 7.3 episodes of anger per week (Averill, 1983). It can manifest as feelings of irritation to feelings of rage. Aggression, the primary behavioral corollary of anger, can range from subtle to extreme. Predictions of when one will become angry, how angry one will become, and ultimately whether one will act upon that anger are immensely complicated. There is an interweaving of biological, physiological, cognitive, psychological, motivational, and sociocultural factors.

In this chapter, we outline conceptualizations of anger and aggression. We then discuss the cornerstone role for individual differences in the tendency to become angry, or trait anger, in the context of predicting anger and its behavioral corollaries. We summarize four modern theoretical models of trait anger and aggression: (a) the integrative cognitive model (ICM; Wilkowski & Robinson, 2010), (b) general aggression model (GAM; Anderson & Bushman, 2002), (c) transdiagnostic model (Owen, 2011), and (d) triple imbalance model (van Honk et al., 2010). To conclude, we present examples of workplace anger and aggression, as well as anger in judgment and decision making.

ANGER: CONCEPTUALIZATIONS PAST AND PRESENT

Ancient Greeks and Romans observed the ease with which people are angered. Those who had what was called "choleric temperament" were defined by some combination of being aggressive, selfish, excitable, and impulsive (Kalachanis & Michailidis, 2015; Lester, 1990). Roman poet Horace proclaimed that anger is temporary madness (Lindebaum & Gabriel, 2016). Seneca argued that anger is inherently counterproductive and should be avoided even in warfare and sporting competitions (Kemp & Strongman, 1995). This perspective may be attributable to the tendency for ancient thinkers to conflate the emotion of anger with acts of extreme or overt aggression. For instance, Aristotle defined anger as "a desire, accompanied by pain, for a perceived revenge, on account of a perceived slight on the part of people who are not to slight one or one's own" (Braund & Most, 2004, p. 100). Similarly, Homeric Greek poetry contains many terms in place of anger, but most poems describe anger principally as a mentally distressing reaction to perceived wrongdoing and as part of an impelling force in revenge (Braund & Most, 2004). Over time, Western philosophical thought has largely adopted the notion that anger is harmful and/or socially unacceptable and should be subdued (Braund & Most, 2004; Potegal & Novaco, 2010). These characterizations, which were made largely on the basis of anecdotes and not through any scientific experimentation or analysis, are actually broadly well-aligned with more modern conceptualizations of individual differences in anger. Indeed, in the 1980s, Spielberger and colleagues (1988) introduced what remains to this day the most influential state–trait theory of anger. In short, *state anger* is a transient reaction that ranges from mild annoyance or irritation to outright rage. *Trait anger* reflects more enduring individual differences in the tendency to experience state anger in the context of provocation, in terms of frequency, intensity, and duration. These two components act additively and interactively to determine the intensity, duration, and frequency of anger and aggression.

Literary depictions of anger have mirrored the philosophical winds surrounding the emotion. Hera cursed Heracles with blind rage that caused him to murder his family. The typically measured and rational Othello murdered his beloved Desdemona out of jealous anger in the classic Shakespearean play. This pattern remains evident in modern times. For instance, in the popular Marvel Comics series *The Incredible Hulk*, the calm and intelligent scientist Bruce Banner is transformed into an uncontrollable Hulk of rage when he is provoked to anger.

The traditional view in pop psychology is also generally that anger is a dangerous emotion, one that should at most times be kept in check. In fact, society tends to view anger and aggression as signs of trouble, danger, and destruction. The self-help industry has capitalized on public concerns about anger. A simple search on Amazon.com for "anger management self-help books" yields more than 2,000 results. The view of anger as "pent up" has given rise to the widespread pop belief that finding nonviolent ways to release aggressive energy (e.g., physical exercise) is important to prevent anger from reaching uncontrollable levels. Indeed, our vernacular contains popular phrases that imply this perspective (e.g., "blow off steam").

Building on these notions, some studies have shown that bottling anger can yield painful short-term consequences (Burns, Quartana, & Bruehl, 2008). Burns and colleagues (2007) showed that healthy young adults who were asked to suppress their emotional responses and thoughts about their emotions during anger provocation had increased negative emotional and physical responses to acute pain. Among chronic pain patients, holding back emotional expression during anger provocation has also been linked to exaggerated muscle tension and increased clinical pain severity (Burns et al., 2006; Burns, Holly, et al., 2008).

The link between anger suppression and pain may be particularly prescient for workers in certain high-risk occupations. Many high-risk jobs (e.g., military, police, firefighters, emergency medical technicians) involve stressful situations that can engender anger as well as a high incidence of chronic pain in the workforce (Carleton et al., 2017; Hauret et al., 2010). This link underscores the importance of preparing workers in high-risk occupations to use prosocial and effective anger-regulation strategies.

Other research paradoxically suggests that venting anger can cause more harm than good. Social psychologist Brad Bushman (2002) conducted a classic experiment in which college undergraduates were angered with criticizing feedback on a personal essay ostensibly from another study participant (actually prepared by the experimenter). Study participants were randomly assigned to a rumination, control, or distraction condition. Those in the rumination condition followed the age-old advice of venting anger by hitting a punching bag as hard and as many times as they wanted for 15 minutes while viewing a picture of the "other participant" whom they believed had criticized their essay. They were also instructed to think about the person who had insulted their work. Participants in the distraction condition still hit the punching bag but were asked to think about becoming physically fit. Participants in the control condition simply waited for 15 minutes without further instructions. Later, participants completed a mood questionnaire and had the opportunity to harass their criticizer with unpleasant tones via headphones during a subsequent task. Contrary to popular belief, those who "vented" their anger by hitting a punching bag while viewing and imagining their provocateur reported being the most angry on mood measures after the fact and administered the loudest and longest duration or noise blasts during the subsequent task. In other words, those who vented their anger for 15 minutes were more angry and aggressive than those who were distracted or received no intervention at all. This study tested only one type of venting (physical aggression); thus, it remains unclear whether other forms of venting might have produced different results.

The ruminative effects of venting anger may impact workers in high-risk occupations in particular (e.g., military, police), given the combination of high stress and high stakes in their jobs. Limited research suggests venting may be a common technique used by this population. For instance, venting anger was a common coping strategy reported in a survey of police officers in the United Kingdom (Pedersen et al., 2012). Unfortunately, such coping strategies may be associated with burnout (Padyab et al., 2016). In comparison, structured debriefings and counseling can reduce anger following stressful work events (Leonard & Alison, 1999). However, venting in high-risk occupations is underresearched and likely confounded with the experience of greater anger and stress. Thus, more research is needed to determine the extent to which venting anger is used and how it affects occupational and health outcomes.

If we can take anything away from the history of the conceptualization of anger, it is that anger is a complicated construct. Anger has uncommon characteristics that make it difficult to categorize with other emotions. Whether anger or aggression are acceptable, useful, harmful, or helpful depends upon an interweaving of person-level and contextual factors, both enduring and transient. This complexity is evident in modern theoretical conceptualizations of trait anger and aggression, to which we now turn.

TRAIT ANGER: A GENERAL FRAMEWORK FOR UNDERSTANDING ANGER AND AGGRESSION

Variance in state anger and aggression is most robustly accounted for when personality is considered (Wilkowski & Robinson, 2010). Indeed, trait anger is particularly important in the context of workplace aggression (Hershcovis et al., 2007). Perceived provocation seems to be key to the importance of trait anger in predicting state anger and aggression. The absence of provocation tends to yield less robust associations between trait variables and state anger and aggression outcomes (Bettencourt et al., 2006). The literature on trait anger highlights the critical nature of trait constructs but also the importance of considering them not in isolation but in the presence of key contextual factors, perceived or otherwise (more on this later). We term this a Trait × Situation framework. It is tantamount to notions of diathesis—stress most commonly espoused in the abnormal and health psychology literatures.

Why is trait anger so critical to understanding anger? Research from several areas suggests that trait anger accelerates reactivity effects in response to a common stimulus set across a variety of relevant domains (e.g., social exclusion/rejection, being insulted). This finding lays the foundation by which we can underscore potential mechanisms that drive the link between trait constructs and state outcomes. For instance, trait anger is associated with heightened pain sensitivity, particularly during acute anger (Bruehl et al., 2006). It is hypothesized that this relationship is due to dysfunctional endogenous opioid analgesic systems (Bruehl et al., 2011). In addition to physiological reactivity, high trait anger is associated with cognitive biases that can facilitate anger. For example, high trait anger is associated with attentional biases toward hostile stimuli, increased hostile attributional bias when judging the intentions of other people, and increased rumination (Wilkowski & Robinson, 2008; for a detailed discussion of cognitive bias, see Arad & Bar-Haim, Chapter 9, this volume). The relationship between trait anger and hostile attributional bias may be especially relevant to high-risk teams (e.g., military, emergency medical technicians) that often work under conditions that already put a strain on making judgments related to social cognition in ways that intensify cognitive biases (e.g., poor sleep).

Not all individuals with the same level of trait anger will express their anger the same way. Indeed, the inner experience of emotion is not always strongly correlated with its associated behavioral outcome (Kennedy-Moore & Watson, 1999). *Trait anger management* refers to individual differences in how people manage their expression. The most used framework for trait anger management in the literature comes from the work of Spielberger and colleagues (1988), who distinguished between *anger-out* (the tendency to express anger outwardly) and *anger-in* (the tendency to bottle up anger).

The majority of the work in this area has relied on self-report measures of anger expression tendencies (Spielberger & Reheiser, 2003).

Whether self-report data accurately capture objective behavioral expression styles is not well known. However, in one study, Jasinski and colleagues (2016) acutely angered research participants using a computer maze task and then coded participants' anger during a 4-minute postprovocation opportunity that participants had to express their feelings. The Anger-Out/Expression scale correlated with behavioral anger expression. The Anger-In/Suppression scale did not correlate with any behavioral index of anger expression.

MEASUREMENT OF TRAIT ANGER

The theoretical frameworks that predict individual differences in the experience and expression of anger are only as useful as the instruments available to assess these constructs. In general, most scientists have relied on one of two methods: self-report questionnaires and ecological momentary assessments.

Self-Report Questionnaire

A multitude of self-report measures exist for anger and its various subconstructs (Spielberger & Reheiser, 2010). By a wide margin, the most used assessment of trait anger and anger expression is from the State–Trait Anger Expression Inventory (STAXI), originally introduced by Spielberger and his associates in the 1980s (Spielberger, 1988). The original scale included subscales tapping trait anger, anger-out, anger-in, and anger control. The instrument includes items such as, "When I get frustrated, I feel like hitting someone" and "I am hot-headed." A revised version, called STAXI-2 (Spielberger et al., 1999), includes additional subscales for anger control and state anger. The STAXI and STAXI-2 have been validated across many populations, and languages display good psychometric properties (Etzler et al., 2014). They continue to be highly popular tools for both researchers and clinicians to assess anger (Eckhardt et al., 2004).

Ecological Momentary Assessment

Conceptually, the trait versus state distinction is clear. However, assessment of these distinct facets of anger and aggression is difficult using retrospective self-report questionnaires. Responses may be influenced too heavily by contextual factors, and the specificity of trait emotion-specific scales has been called into question (Edmondson et al., 2013). The STAXI considers state anger and trait anger as distinct constructs. However, some have argued that anger may exist along on a continuum from state-like to trait-like (Chaplin et al., 1988). It is difficult to capture this continuum using one-shot measures of trait anger and anger expression. Questionnaires force respondents into responses referring to "right now" or "in general" and do not allow for empirical partitioning of sources of systematic variance across state and trait anger components.

Ecological momentary assessment (EMA) can perhaps provide a more nuanced picture of state anger, trait anger, and aggression. EMA involves assessing anger periodically (e.g., every 30 minutes) throughout an extended measurement window (e.g., 24 hours). This approach is often accomplished using a diary or mobile app; questions ask respondents how they feel in their current situation. EMA allows for partitioning of variance into state- and trait-like components. State components are derived from within-person variance, whereas trait components are derived from between-person variance (Bauer, 2011). Edmondson et al. (2013) showed that the majority of variance in EMA reports of anger was attributable to trait-like (between-person) individual differences. Unexpectedly, the estimate of trait-like variance did not correlate strongly with traditional trait measures of hostility. The authors of the study suggested that this finding could have arisen because the EMA questions do not assess the broad content domain of single-setting self-report scales. EMA appears to offer a more valid assessment of how individuals actually experience anger in their normal daily lives as opposed to asking respondents to theorize about how angry they think they are in general. Thus, EMA could offer an opportunity for researchers to assess state and trait aspects of anger across a variety of ecologically valid settings and produce more externally valid results but would be more costly than traditional self-report measures.

The availability of so many measures of trait and state anger, including those just mentioned, has spawned much research on the nature of anger. Further, the ease of use and wide-reaching validation of some self-report measures have resulted in anger being measured across a broad range of psychological research. As both an impetus for and consequence of this research, several prominent theoretical frameworks have arisen to organize our knowledge of anger and aggression.

MODELS OF ANGER AND AGGRESSION

We present four models of anger and aggression. These models share the notion that enduring and stable differences in core patterns of thought and motivation processes, such as attributional biases and approach motivation, are drivers of individual differences in anger and aggression. They differ with respect to the weight given to particular processes in the cognitive and motivational domains. Some models are also more focused on the role of additional factors, such as genetics and physiological and sociocultural mediators and moderators. The literature contains numerous models of anger and aggression. It is beyond the scope of this chapter to review them all, but the models discussed in this section ought to provide the reader with a primer.

Integrative Cognitive Model

At its core, the ICM suggests that anger is the result of exaggerated hostile interpretations of perceived hostile stimuli and perceived provocations (Wilkowski & Robinson, 2010). This model is predominantly concerned with predictions of *reactive aggression*, that is, aggression that is in response to a provocation. This is opposed to another type of aggression, *proactive aggression*, which has received significantly less empirical attention and refers to aggression used in the service of obtaining an instrumental goal (Hubbard et al., 2010).

Overall, ICM attempts to explain anger and aggression as the result of interacting cognitive processes when the individual is presented with a hostile situation. The ICM considers a number of cognitive processes; however, these processes can be broadly organized into three groups: hostile interpretations, ruminative attention, and effortful control. The first of these is a biased and hostile-leaning interpretation of a situation or stimulus input. Those who tend toward higher levels of anger and aggression have automatic interpretation biases that lean toward hostile attributions. For instance, individuals with high trait anger displayed stronger hostile attributional bias. *Hostile attributional bias* is the tendency to attribute hostile intent to the actions of others, particularly when contextual and social cues are ambiguous (Pornari & Wood, 2010). Further, high-trait-anger individuals often display attentional biases toward hostile cues in their environment (Wilkowski et al., 2007). Second, the ICM proposes that ruminative processes follow the interpretation bias, which leads to an amplification of the intensity of anger and/or more enduring anger response. Ample data support a link between ruminative processes and amplified emotional response (see Wilkowski & Robinson, 2008).

As a final function, the model proposes that anger and aggression are more likely when the ability or motivation to control anger or aggression using effortful self-regulation techniques is low. Individuals with high trait anger are theorized to have dispositional low motivation or capacity to self-regulate anger and aggression. The ICM proposes three viable pathways whereby effortful regulation of anger can effectively curb a response to a perceived hostile action: reappraisal, distraction, and suppression (Denson et al., 2012; Gross, 2002). The ICM suggests that effortful control processes are dynamic and not fixed. That is, activated hostile thoughts do not always trigger self-regulatory cognitive responses, particularly for those with higher levels of trait anger. It has been suggested that motivation to exert effortful control over anger and aggression is limited (Stucke & Baumeister, 2006). This limitation can contribute to anger and aggressive responding. For instance, lab studies suggest that state-level variations in motivation to use effortful control significantly alter aggressive responding to provocation (Osgood & Muraven, 2016). On the one hand, this last point may be particularly relevant to high-stress workplaces, as certain job stressors (time pressure, work demands) can deplete one's motivation to use self-control (Germeys & De Gieter, 2018; Prem et al., 2016). On the other hand, high self-control can buffer against the effect of high trait anger on workplace deviance following provocation (Restubog et al., 2010).

In sum, the ICM suggests that interpretation and attributional biases ignite an angry response and that effortful cognitive control processes are not appropriately engaged among individuals who report higher levels of trait anger. Thus, assuming the same situational event, both low- and high-trait-anger individuals might display anger and some form of behavioral aggression, but the former will be able to engage in some form of effortful top-down cognitive control process to curtail the initial response.

General Aggression Model

The GAM considers social, cognitive, developmental, and biological factors related to anger and aggression (Anderson & Bushman, 2002). The model borrows from extant and more domain-specific theories in an attempt to link disparate models into a more unifying framework. At the broadest level, the GAM suggests that anger and aggression is driven by *knowledge structures*, which include attitudes, perceptual/attention patterns, expectation schema, and behavioral repertoires. Knowledge structures are developed over time through experience and become automatized with repeated practice. In this sense, becoming automatized is similar to the notion of automatic processes discussed in the context of the ICM (Wilkowski & Robinson, 2010). The knowledge structures result in automatic and well-learned processes that take over following provocation (Allen & Anderson, 2017).

The model divides processes into those that are proximate and distal. Distal processes include biological and environmental determinants, which feed into and ultimately drive personality characteristics. The distal processes thus overlay and influence each component of the proximate processes described in the next section. Biological determinants include, but are not limited to, hormonal components, executive function difficulties, genetic contributions, and low arousal (Anderson & Carnagey, 2004). Determinants of an environmental nature include things such as cultural norms, early childhood experiences, group conflict, and exposure to media violence (Anderson & Carnagey, 2004).

The cornerstone of the GAM lies in the variety of proximate determinants of anger and aggression. There are three stages of proximal determinants: inputs, routes (affect, cognition, and arousal), and outcomes (Allen & Anderson, 2017). The first stage—*inputs*—outlines how individual and situational factors interact to affect the likelihood of anger and aggression. Individual factors are stable individual differences that influence how a person generally responds to a situation. This is essentially the notion of a disposition or trait anger (Anderson & Bushman, 2002). A number of individual-level factors have been identified as risk factors for aggression within the GAM framework (e.g., hostile attribution bias, narcissistic personality characteristics, high neuroticism, sociocultural acceptance for aggression, positive attitudes for aggression, moral justification of violence). Situation factors are typically associated with anger and aggressive responses, such as social rejection, intoxication, provocation, violent media, pain, and hot temperatures (Allen & Anderson, 2017).

Routes are passages through which the individual and situational factors exert their influence. There are three main routes: affect, cognition, and arousal. These routes are not mutually exclusive and can influence one another. For instance, when someone is angry, hostile cognitions are more readily accessible (cognitive route) and arousal may be high (arousal route). Moreover, cognition and arousal can work together to foster more robust affective responses to a given situation (Allen & Anderson, 2017). The ordering of activation of these internal routes does not matter. Affect in the GAM includes the influence of inputs on moods and emotions; cognition refers to conscious thoughts and unconscious cognitive processes (e.g., attention biases). Arousal is the final route. Arousal can affect the likelihood of anger or aggression by fostering misattribution processes, strengthening action tendencies, and creating a subjectively aversive state (Anderson & Bushman, 2002).

The final stage of proximate determinants is outcomes. In the GAM, *outcomes* may include three phases: appraisal processes, decision processes, and aggressive outcomes. Immediately following a provocation, the individual begins the appraisal stage. At this stage, before selecting a behavioral response, the individual makes an immediate appraisal of the situation that occurs in a predominantly automatic fashion and is influenced by the three routes just described, as well as by distal determinants at the person and environmental levels. Part of the immediate appraisal process includes goal and intention information, which can result in appraising an action as hostile, becoming angry, wanting to get even, and considering a specific intention or action (e.g., yelling at someone). When the routes are consistent with an angry state, a person is more likely to appraise a situation in a manner that will lead to an aggressive response. Following an immediate appraisal is the decision stage. There is a decision on how to act, and there is an opportunity for reappraisal processes to modulate this decision. Finally, an aggressive action (may) occur. According to the model, once an action has been carried out, it will influence the situation and therefore trigger the process anew. Elements of this model have been validated in the context of pain, intimate partner violence, domestic violence, and personality disorders (Allen & Anderson, 2017).

Although the GAM is theorized to apply to aggression across domains, it may inform how certain aspects of high-risk occupations could relate to anger and aggression. In particular, activities in high-risk occupations may be associated with heightened arousal, which can increase the propensity for anger and aggression, according to the GAM. Further, some high-risk occupations (e.g., military operations, medical emergencies) involve activities that must occur in situations that involve rapid decision making with incomplete information. This ambiguity can lead to heightened cognitive and attentional biases, which influence anger and aggression.

To summarize, the GAM proposes that processes determine how person and situation variables influence affect, arousal, and cognition, which in turn influence appraisals, decisions, reappraisals, and eventual actions. Distal processes are in the background and influence each element of the proximate processes. Over time, reinforcement of aggression following the input, route, and outcomes stage lead to stable knowledge structures, which result in varying degrees of what can be considered trait anger or aggressiveness.

Transdiagnostic Model of Trait Anger

This model was developed to help understand how individual differences in trait anger are aligned with transdiagnostic cognitive processes that have been identified as fundamental and shared in common across primary *DSM-IV-TR* Axis I disorders (Owen, 2011). The processes that trait anger and transdiagnostic processes share appear to be evident in selective attention, memory, recurrent negative thinking, and reasoning.

Cognitive models of psychopathology focus on biased internal and external information processing as key determinants of risk for psychological difficulties. Information-processing biases lead to maladaptive physiological, psychological, cognitive, and motivational responses to a variety of situational inputs (Williams et al., 1988). Importantly, shared aberrations in common cognitive processes result in a number of disorders, hence the term *transdiagnostic*. This model contrasts with models that have traditionally focused on specific information processing abnormalities and their relation to specific disorders. Harvey et al. (2004) were the first to systematically delineate a number of specific types of information-processing biases, cognitive processes, and behavioral patterns that are actually shared across a number of Axis I disorders. It is important to note that the Harvey et al. study was restricted to Axis I psychopathology. Thus, Harvey et al. did not consider anger, because heightened anger was not a central diagnostic feature of any Axis I disorders, even though anger can be a symptom of a number of disorders (Novaco, 2010). Owen (2011) presented evidence that the processes common to various psychopathological outcomes are evident for trait anger, suggesting that trait anger may be a relevant risk factor for clinical psychological disorders. In fact, research among combat veterans and active component soldiers has shown that anger is indeed found in those who suffer from stress-related and anxiety disorders (Jakupcak et al., 2007).

There is substantial evidence that the transdiagnostic cognitive processes identified by Harvey et al. (2004) are evident for those with higher versus lower trait anger. For example, trait anger is associated with selective attention toward hostile stimuli (van Honk, Tuiten, de Haan, et al., 2001), bias to recall anger-themed autobiographical memories (Hung & Bryant, 2016), and increased rumination (Wilkowski & Robinson, 2010). These findings collectively suggest that trait anger may be a risk factor for negative psychological outcomes and provide a priori points of access for interventions that can alleviate cognitive aberrations common to both anger problems and psychiatric disturbances.

Triple Imbalance Theory of Aggression

The triple imbalance theory of aggression attempts to bridge disparate literatures concerning the psychobiological basis of aggression (van Honk et al., 2010). At the root of this model is a hormonal balance between testosterone and cortisol, each of which is involved in hypothalamic–pituitary–gonadal and hypothalamic–pituitary–adrenal axis regulation, which has been linked to anger, impulsiveness, and aggression (Hermans et al., 2008). In general, the model argues that an imbalance of greater testosterone to cortisol drives an imbalance at the subcortical level and may even impede the ability of top-down cortical–subcortical down-regulation of reactionary and reflexive angry and aggressive responses to provocation.

The triple imbalance theory of aggression is rooted in core assumptions of the triple balance hypothesis (van Honk et al., 2010), an evolutionary psychobiological framework that states that well-being is contingent on the ability to effectively respond to environmental rewards and punishments with socially appropriate approach- or withdrawal-related behaviors. The proper balance between approach and withdrawal actions in the context of rewards and punishments determines healthy versus unhealthy outcomes (Ressler, 2004). The triple imbalance model hypothesizes three types of imbalance: subcortical, subcortical–cortical, and cortical imbalance hypotheses (see Figure 1.1). For each, hormonal imbalances induce motivational derivatives and influence bottom-up and top-down regulation of responses to anger-provoking stimuli. The subcortical balance is accounted for by cortisol and testosterone. The cortical–subcortical balance refers to the prefrontal cortex-mediated top-down modulation of subcortically generated emotional responses. In particular, the prefrontal cortex exhibits lateralized electrical activity hypothesized to represent specialized activity for regulating relative avoidance–approach balance. It appears that avoidance or withdrawal motivations are mediated by the right prefrontal cortex, whereas approach motivation and emotions, to include aggression, are localized in the left prefrontal cortex (Amodio et al., 2004). The balance between left and right cortices is termed the *cortical balance*.

The first of the three components of the triple imbalance theory is the *subcortical imbalance hypothesis*. In this hypothesis, subcortical balance is a ratio of testosterone (anger inducing) and cortisol (anger mitigating). In general, findings suggest that a higher ratio of testosterone to cortisol is associated with greater anger and aggression. Administration of exogenous testosterone has been linked to exaggerated cardiac acceleration in response to threatening faces but not for fear or happy faces (van Honk, Tuiten, Hermans, et al., 2001). Data using functional magnetic resonance imaging showed activation to angry and not happy facial expressions in the amygdala, hypothalamus, brainstem, and orbitofrontal cortex. Salivary testosterone and cortisol were also assessed, and a higher ratio of testosterone to cortisol predicted significant neural activation of the hypothalamus and amygdala in response to angry but not happy facial expressions (see van Honk et al., 2010). Administration of testosterone has also been linked to exaggerated neural responses of an aggression network during viewing of angry or threatening faces compared with other emotional expressions (Hermans et al., 2008).

The second of the three components of the triple imbalance hypothesis is the *cortical–subcortical imbalance hypothesis*, in which testosterone is understood to decrease coupling between subcortical and cortical regions

FIGURE 1.1. Triple Imbalance Hypothesis of Reactive Aggression

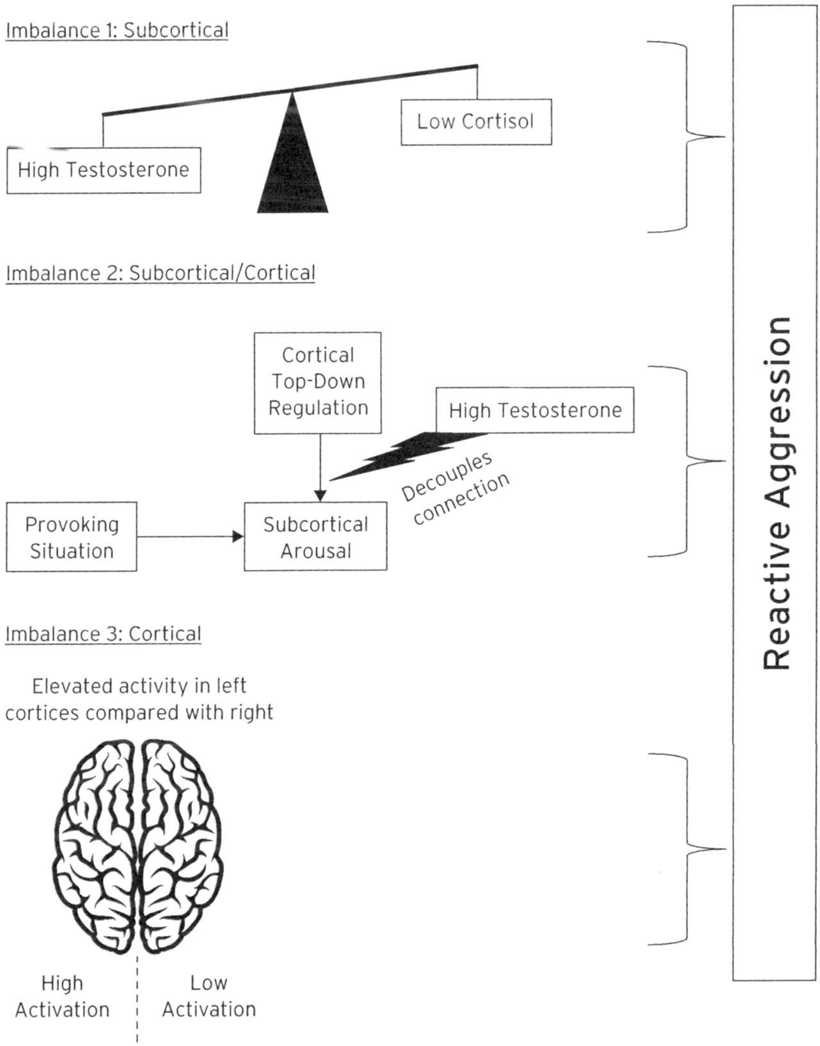

(van Honk et al., 2010). This decoupling is important as top-down cortical regulation of more reactive subcortically mediated emotional responses may be a defining feature of those lower versus higher in anger and aggression tendencies. Essentially, a breakdown of cortical top-down control over subcortical activity, combined with strong subcortical activation in neural aggression networks, sets the stage for stronger and more lasting anger and aggressive response.

The final component of the triple imbalance hypothesis posits that cortical balance involves transitions from reflexive and hormonally mediated behavior to thoughtful and controlled cognitively mediated behavior (van Honk et al., 2010). The role of the prefrontal cortex in mediating approach versus fear behaviors can be captured by measurement of EEG asymmetries (Davidson, 2004; Davidson et al., 2000). Left-sided dominance is predictive of increased behavioral approach and reward. Resting-state asymmetries in cortical activity are correlated with individual differences in approach and withdrawal behaviors. Higher resting left dominance has been associated with measurements of trait anger and anger expression, as well as with acute aggression following provocation (van Honk et al., 2010). Experimental behavioral manipulation of cortical asymmetry using unilateral hand contractions showed that when the right hand was contracted, counteraggression in an experimental provocation paradigm was more robust (Peterson et al., 2008). Relatedly, transcranial magnetic stimulation can locally decrease neural excitability (Hallett, 2007). transcranial magnetic stimulation–induced reductions of right cortical excitability resulted in reduced bias for fearful facial expressions, and reductions in left neural excitability led to reduced memory for angry faces (Schutter et al., 2008). It is hypothesized that cortical imbalance, whereby there is greater left than right neural activation, is a neurobiological basis for individual differences in trait anger and aggression.

Summary of Reviewed Anger and Aggression Models

The four models just described provide a primer on theories of anger and aggression. Reviewing these models illustrates how scientific theorizing on anger across the discipline shares certain underlying factors despite approaching the topic from different perspectives. In Figure 1.2, we present a graphic that combines common elements of many models. Typically, a hostile situation initiates the pathway to anger and reactive aggression. This could be external (e.g., a coworker makes a rude remark) or internal (e.g., an employee recalls a memory of an upsetting event). This could also be social (e.g., an insult) or nonsocial (e.g., a frustrating error message on a printer). Biases in attention and interpretation of information affect whether a hostile situation will be noticed and how it will be interpreted. For example, attentional biases might cause an employee to be hyperaware of perceived slights. Similarly, interpretation biases might cause an employee to interpret the slight as intentionally hurtful. This leads to initial levels of anger. Self-regulation and emotional thinking (i.e., rumination) interact to either reduce or intensify the initial experience of anger. For example, an employee may stew over the slight (ruminate), thereby increasing anger.

FIGURE 1.2. **Unified Model of Anger at Work**

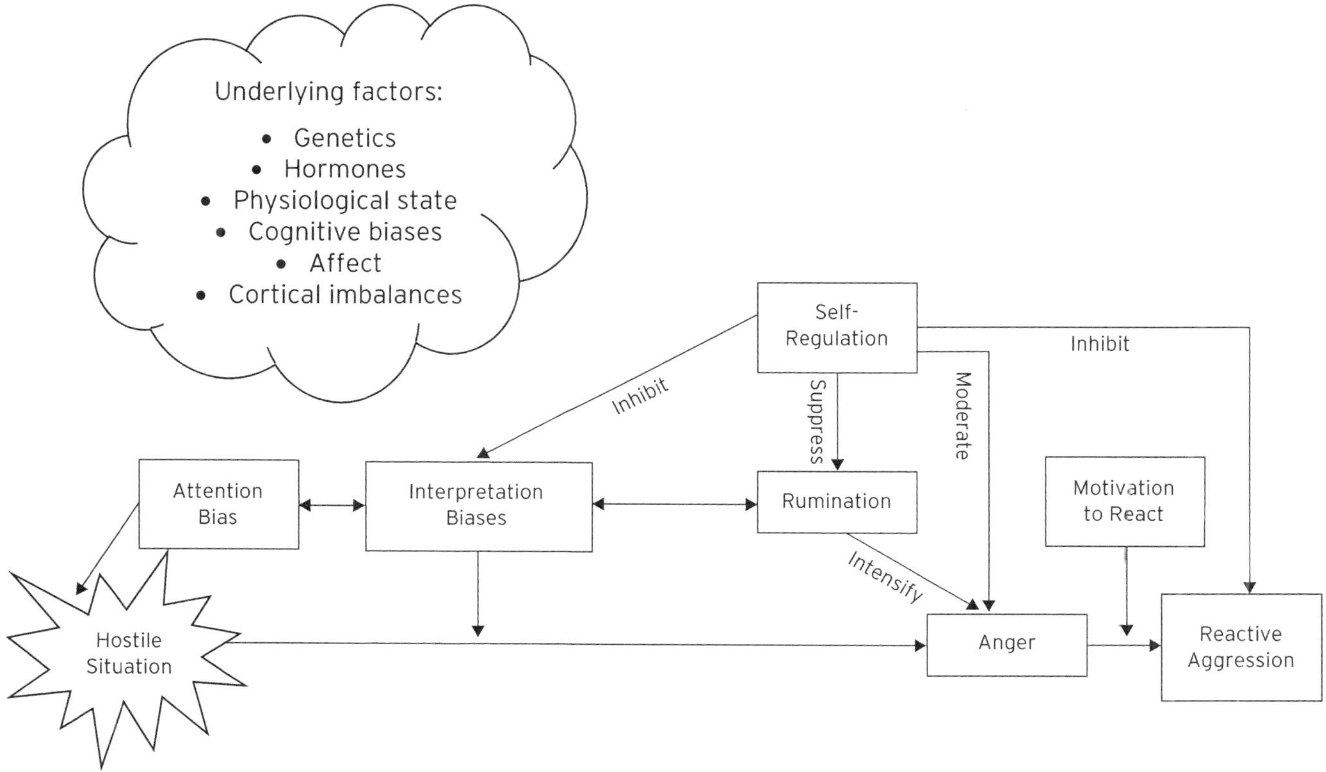

On the other hand, the individual may use effortful self-regulation to change their interpretation of the event (e.g., use cognitive reappraisal) or inhibit anger-provoking thoughts with self-control. Indeed, anger does not always lead to reactive aggression; however, given sufficient motivation to react and lacking inhibitory self-regulation, reactive aggression occurs. Throughout the entire process, state- and trait-level differences in underlying factors and applications of self-regulation techniques (e.g., effortful control) can modulate the cognitive, emotional, and behavioral reactions to the hostile situation.

In the next two sections, we pivot from theoretical modeling of anger to observe how anger plays out in more practical terms in the workplace as well as in judgment and decision making.

WORKPLACE AGGRESSION

Life in organizations is replete with potential reasons for individuals to become angry. Anger can motivate retributive aggression against organizations, coworkers, and even clients (Osgood, 2017). However, important individual differences and situational variables predict when this anger will occur and when it will translate into behavior (see Gibson & Callister, 2010). We highlight three of the most notable moderators of this link here.

First, trait anger moderates the relationship between provocation and aggression (Buss & Perry, 1992). Thus, it follows that trait anger would moderate the relationship between state anger and behavior at work. Indeed, trait anger is associated with greater expression of anger at work. For instance, it is associated with greater counterproductive workplace behaviors (Spector & Fox, 2002). Critically, Domagalski and Steelman (2005) found that trait anger moderated the relationship between the experience and expression anger at work. Second, the empirical evidence overwhelmingly supports that both men and women experience the same amount of anger at work (Frost & Averill, 1982; Gibson et al., 2009; Simon & Nath, 2004). However, expressing anger is normatively less acceptable for women (e.g., Brescoll, 2016; Radke et al., 2016). Correspondingly, women are less likely to exhibit aggression at work (Hershcovis et al., 2007). Finally, many organizations are designed hierarchically. As such, individuals within organizations occupy different levels of status and power. Research suggests that individuals with lower status tend to experience more anger, and more intense anger, in the workplace and yet are significantly less likely to express this anger than their higher status colleagues (see Domagalski & Steelman, 2007). A popular explanation for these effects is that higher status members' position gives them more freedom to express their feelings without concern for negative repercussions (Ridgeway & Johnson, 1990). To date, few studies have considered how any of these moderators interact with one another to affect the anger–behavior relationship at work. In one of these few studies, Domagalski and Steelman (2007) found an interaction of gender and organizational status on the expression of anger in the workplace. They found that low-status men were more likely than low-status women to express anger directly to high-status members.

Given the strong relationship between trait anger and aggression, employers may seek to screen for trait anger and/or related constructs when hiring in order to reduce workplace violence and aggression (see Day & Catano, 2006). Indeed, personality screenings are a common practice for certain high-risk occupations, such as police officers and emergency workers (Lough & Treuer, 2013; Marshall et al., 2017). Evidence shows that scores on constructs such as hostility predict problematic aggression on the job (Castora et al., 2003; Koepfler et al., 2012). However, the literature is less clear on the predictive utility of preemployment trait anger screenings on workplace aggression, as far fewer studies have investigated preemployment trait anger specifically.

ANGER, JUDGMENT, AND DECISION MAKING

One critical area of occupational life that is heavily impacted by anger is the ability to form judgments and engage in effective decision making. Anger has myriad effects on judgment and decision making (see Lambert et al., 2019; Litvak et al., 2010). Individual and situational variables moderate this relationship. It goes beyond the scope of this chapter to review this literature in its entirety, but we discuss some relevant research here.

A popular paradigm through which to consider the effects of anger on judgment and decision making is the appraisal tendency framework (ATF; Lerner & Keltner, 2000). This model views anger as arising from experiencing a harm to the self that is attributable to another person, particularly when the self still has the ability to affect the situation. This emotional reaction produces changes in cognitive and motivational tendencies that carry over into subsequent situations. Specifically, anger produces biases toward heuristic, attributional, and hostile appraisals of situations and the behavior of others (Lerner & Tiedens, 2006). In other words, when people are angry, they are more likely to engage in heuristic-based decision making, overestimate their abilities, underestimate risk, and attribute hostile intent to the actions of other people (see Lerner & Tiedens, 2006). These biases carry over into subsequent situations while the individual is still angry.

The intuitive style of thinking engendered by anger has implications for workplace decision making. For example, laboratory studies suggest that anger affects perception of risk and alters level of commitment in management decisions. In one study, participants who were asked to make mock hiring decisions perceived less risk in their decisions when angry (Tsai & Young, 2010). Further, angrier decision makers were more likely to reaffirm their decisions when new information suggested that their chosen job candidate underperformed relative to alternatives after hiring. In other words, angry decision makers underestimated risk and were less able or less willing to admit they had made a mistake in their hiring decisions.

The effect of anger on decision making may be especially important in high-risk occupations. In one study, police volunteers completed questionnaires on decision-making style (intuitive vs. reflective) and on individual differences in tendency to control anger (Brown & Daus, 2015). Then they read two scenarios describing interactions with suspects (a motorist stopped for speeding and a domestic violence dispute in which the suspect approached the officer holding a sharp object). They were given a range of choices on how to respond along a continuum of force (with shooting the suspect on the far end of the continuum). Police officers with the combination of intuitive decision-making style and a low propensity to control anger were the most likely to choose to shoot the domestic violence suspect. No effect was found for the speeding motorist scenario. In another example of a high-stakes decision, mock jurors in a lab study were more likely to determine guilt and suggest harsher sentences when reviewing capital offense cases if their evidence packet was accompanied with gruesome photographs of the case despite no other changes in evidence (Bright & Goodman-Delahunty, 2006). This effect was mediated by between-group differences in anger. Given the implications of anger for decision making, it is important for organizational leaders to consider how to promote effective decision making even in anger-provoking contexts.

Several lab-based studies suggest that the simplified cognitive processing underlying the effects of anger on decision making can be counteracted by increasing accountability for decisions (Osgood & Muraven, 2016). For example, participants in one lab study were asked to review fictional tort cases and decide punitive attributions and punishments following either an anger- or neutral priming activity (Lerner et al., 1998). Furthermore, a subset of participants were told that their decision would be evaluated by an expert who would ask them to explain their decisions during an interview following the study. Angry participants generally used less complex judgment processes (e.g., engaged with less available information) and administered harsher sentences than nonangry participants. However, this between-group difference in anger was significantly attenuated for the subset of participants who believed they would need to explain their decisions to an expert. Put another way, angry decision makers may still engage in thoughtful decision making if they are reminded that they will be held accountable for their actions.

Despite a strong literature on anger and individual decision making, current research is incomplete on the effect of anger on group-level decision making. To date, most research on emotions and collective decision making has focused on positive versus negative group affect (see Barsade & Knight, 2015). Within this literature, the findings are contradictory. Multiple studies report that positive affect improves group creativity, information sharing/elaboration, and the quality of group decisions (e.g., Bramesfeld & Gasper, 2008; Grawitch et al., 2003). However, other studies have found that negative group affect leads to greater information sharing, information building, and higher quality group decisions (e.g., Kooij-de Bode et al., 2010; van Knippenberg et al., 2010). Relatedly, increasing arousal may affect group decision making. In one study, increasing arousal (requiring teams to stand rather than sit while working—arousal was also measured via wrist-worn sensors) led to more creative decision making, more information sharing, and better idea building by the group (Knight & Baer, 2014). It is likely that the effect of negative affect and arousal on group decision making is moderated by variables that have not yet been adequately modeled (Barsade & Knight, 2015). Negative affect and high arousal are key components of anger, so it is possible that some of the patterns observed in the group affect literature would apply to anger; however, targeted research is needed.

Although ATF remains a popular model, there have been empirical challenges to the traditional notion that anger increases heuristic decision making. For instance, Moons and Mackie (2007) found that angry participants were actually better at distinguishing strong versus weak arguments and exhibited less heuristic decision making than neutral mood controls.

Notwithstanding these challenges, researchers have documented situational and dispositional factors that moderate the effect of anger on subsequent appraisal tendencies as described by the ATF. For example, disgust interacts with anger to predict moral outrage in response to moral transgressions (sexual assault and funeral picketing; Salerno & Peter-Hagene, 2013). That is, anger results in more moral outrage when accompanied by disgust (see also Phelps et al., Chapter 3, this volume, for an in-depth discussion of moral injury).

Situational factors can moderate motivational consequences of anger on decision making as well. For example, anger (but not fear or anxiety) in response to perceiving the mistreatment of an ingroup member by an outgroup member increases desire to take action against the outgroup only if the ingroup is perceived as more powerful than the outgroup (Gordijn et al., 2001; Mackie et al., 2000). In other words, anger and ingroup power interact to predict desire to retaliate against an outgroup. Several individual difference variables have also been identified that moderate the relationship between anger and judgment and decision making. For instance, trait aggressiveness (Tiedens & Linton, 2001) and emotion regulation style (Kligyte et al., 2013) moderate the role of anger in heuristic use and ethical decision making, respectively. Thus, as has been the case with many topics discussed in this chapter, the relationship between anger, judgment, and decision making is nuanced, complex, and requires further research.

CONCLUSION

The overview of anger provided in this chapter illustrates the intricacy and nuance of a common emotional experience. We have attempted to counteract the risk of being unable to see the forest for the trees by providing a unified model of anger and reactive aggression (Figure 1.2) that synthesizes common threads from various models of anger. However, even this model is complex and does not fully capture all of the popular models in the literature. Our focus in this chapter has been primarily on anger and aggression in response to hostile situations and provocations, and we have tried to address the individual-level experience of anger. However, a robust literature exists on anger as a group-level phenomenon (for a discussion of anger operating at the team level, see O'Neill, Chapter 4, this volume).

This chapter emphasizes the need of additional research into anger despite centuries of inquiry and decades of scientific research in this area. In particular, the extant literature has understudied how additional variables moderate the relationship between anger at work and perpetrating aggression against coworkers. Although strides have been made in this area, most research on anger and aggression at work focuses on the perspective of the victim rather than the perpetrator. This is particularly true for psychological moderators such as sleep. Recent investigations suggest that sleep may interact with trait anger to predict workplace aggression (Osgood et al., 2021), but more work is needed. Similarly, the effect of anger and aggression in the workplace on third-party observers is understudied.

Although further research is needed, the current literature reveals that anger is a common emotional experience tied to a host of physiological, psychological, clinical, and social outcomes. Anger is also unique among the negative valence emotions as it is associated with increased approach motivation. This places anger in a class of its own as a negative emotion that serves primarily to overcome frustrations and respond to threatening, hostile situations in order to protect the interests of the self. In this way, anger is also unusually social compared with other negative emotions. Insightfully, many personifications of anger in popular media (e.g., Grumpy from *Snow White and the Seven Dwarfs*, Anger from *Inside Out*) are often as much (or more) at odds with characters representing other negative emotions as they are with positive emotions. Assuredly, the ubiquity of anger and its impact on our behavior and decision making guarantee that anger will remain an influential, if unwelcome, coworker for many and a topic of inquiry for years to come.

IMPLICATIONS

- Organizational leader development programs should consider including lessons or trainings concerning the potential impact of anger on decision making.
- Preemployment personality screening for trait hostility may reduce aggression on the job site.
- Training for employees in positions of high stress and high risk (e.g., police, military) should include instruction on effective and efficient methods to understand and manage anger.
- Training employees to positively manage anger may also help improve chronic and acute pain, which are common for workers in high-stress and high-risk occupations.

REFERENCES

Adam, H., & Brett, J. M. (2015). Context matters: The social effects of anger in cooperative, balanced, and competitive negotiation situations. *Journal of Experimental Social Psychology*, *61*, 44–58. https://doi.org/10.1016/j.jesp.2015.07.001

Allen, J. J., & Anderson, C. A. (2017). General aggression model. In P. Roessler, C. A. Hoffner, & L. van Zoonen (Eds.), *The international encyclopedia of media effects* (pp. 1–15). John Wiley & Sons. https://doi.org/10.1002/9781118783764.wbieme0078

Amodio, D. M., Shah, J. Y., Sigelman, J., Brazy, P. C., & Harmon-Jones, E. (2004). Implicit regulatory focus associated with asymmetrical frontal cortical activity. *Journal of Experimental Social Psychology*, *40*(2), 225–232. https://doi.org/10.1016/S0022-1031(03)00100-8

Anderson, C. A., & Bushman, B. J. (2002). Human aggression. *Annual Review of Psychology, 53*(1), 27–51. https://doi.org/10.1146/annurev.psych.53.100901.135231

Anderson, C. A., & Carnagey, N. L. (2004). Violent evil and the general aggression model. In A. Miller (Ed.), *The social psychology of good and evil* (pp. 168–192). Guilford Press.

Averill, J. R. (1983). Studies on anger and aggression. Implications for theories of emotion. *The American Psychologist, 38*(11), 1145–1160. https://doi.org/10.1037/0003-066X.38.11.1145

Barsade, S. G., & Knight, A. P. (2015). Group affect. *Annual Review of Organizational Psychology and Organizational Behavior, 2*(1), 21–46. https://doi.org/10.1146/annurev-orgpsych-032414-111316

Bauer, D. J. (2011). Evaluating individual differences in psychological processes. *Current Directions in Psychological Science, 20*(2), 115–118. https://doi.org/10.1177/0963721411402670

Bettencourt, B. A., Talley, A., Benjamin, A. J., & Valentine, J. (2006). Personality and aggressive behavior under provoking and neutral conditions: A meta-analytic review. *Psychological Bulletin, 132*(5), 751–777. https://doi.org/10.1037/0033-2909.132.5.751

Bramesfeld, K. D., & Gasper, K. (2008). Happily putting the pieces together: A test of two explanations for the effects of mood on group-level information processing. *The British Journal of Social Psychology, 47*(2), 285–309. https://doi.org/10.1348/000712607X218295

Braund, S., & Most, G. W. (Eds.). (2004). *Ancient anger: Perspectives from Homer to Galen* (Vol. 32). Cambridge University Press. https://doi.org/10.1017/CBO9780511482120

Brescoll, V. L. (2016). Leading with their hearts? How gender stereotypes of emotion lead to biased evaluations of female leaders. *The Leadership Quarterly, 27*(3), 415–428. https://doi.org/10.1016/j.leaqua.2016.02.005

Bright, D. A., & Goodman-Delahunty, J. (2006). Gruesome evidence and emotion: Anger, blame, and jury decision-making. *Law and Human Behavior, 30*(2), 183–202. https://doi.org/10.1007/s10979-006-9027-y

Brown, S. G., & Daus, C. S. (2015). The influence of police officers' decision-making style and anger control on responses to work scenarios. *Journal of Applied Research in Memory and Cognition, 4*(3), 294–302. https://doi.org/10.1016/j.jarmac.2015.04.001

Bruehl, S., Burns, J. W., Chung, O. Y., & Chont, M. (2011). Interacting effects of trait anger and acute anger arousal on pain: The role of endogenous opioids. *Psychosomatic Medicine, 73*(7), 612–619. https://doi.org/10.1097/PSY.0b013e318227cb88

Bruehl, S., Chung, O. Y., & Burns, J. W. (2006). Anger expression and pain: An overview of findings and possible mechanisms. *Journal of Behavioral Medicine, 29*(6), 593–606. https://doi.org/10.1007/s10865-006-9060-9

Burns, J. W., Bruehl, S., & Quartana, P. J. (2006). Anger management style and hostility among patients with chronic pain: Effects on symptom-specific physiological reactivity during anger- and sadness-recall interviews. *Psychosomatic Medicine, 68*(5), 786–793. https://doi.org/10.1097/01.psy.0000238211.89198.e4

Burns, J. W., Holly, A., Quartana, P., Wolff, B., Gray, E., & Bruehl, S. (2008). Trait anger management style moderates effects of actual ("state") anger regulation on symptom-specific reactivity and recovery among chronic low back pain patients. *Psychosomatic Medicine, 70*(8), 898–905. https://doi.org/10.1097/PSY.0b013e3181835cb7

Burns, J. W., Quartana, P. J., & Bruehl, S. (2007). Anger management style moderates effects of emotion suppression during initial stress on pain and cardiovascular responses during subsequent pain-induction. *Annals of Behavioral Medicine*, *34*(2), 154–165. https://doi.org/10.1007/BF02872670

Burns, J. W., Quartana, P. J., & Bruehl, S. (2008). Anger inhibition and pain: Conceptualizations, evidence and new directions. *Journal of Behavioral Medicine*, *31*(3), 259–279. https://doi.org/10.1007/s10865-008-9154-7

Bushman, B. J. (2002). Does venting anger feed or extinguish the flame? Catharsis, rumination, distraction, anger, and aggressive responding. *Personality and Social Psychology Bulletin*, *28*(6), 724–731.

Buss, A. H., & Perry, M. (1992). The aggression questionnaire. *Journal of Personality and Social Psychology*, *63*(3), 452–459. https://doi.org/10.1037/0022-3514.63.3.452

Carleton, R. N., Afifi, T. O., Turner, S., Taillieu, T., El-Gabalawy, R., Sareen, J., & Asmundson, G. J. G. (2017). Chronic pain among public safety personnel in Canada. *Canadian Journal of Pain*, *1*(1), 237–246. https://doi.org/10.1080/24740527.2017.1410431

Carver, C. S., & Harmon-Jones, E. (2009). Anger is an approach-related affect: Evidence and implications. *Psychological Bulletin*, *135*(2), 183–204. https://doi.org/10.1037/a0013965

Castora, K., Brewster, J., & Stoloff, M. (2003). Predicting aggression in police officers using the MMPI-2. *Journal of Police and Criminal Psychology*, *18*(1), 1–8. https://doi.org/10.1007/BF02802602

Chaplin, W. F., John, O. P., & Goldberg, L. R. (1988). Conceptions of states and traits: Dimensional attributes with ideals as prototypes. *Journal of Personality and Social Psychology*, *54*(4), 541–557. https://doi.org/10.1037/0022-3514.54.4.541

Davidson, R. J. (2004). What does the prefrontal cortex "do" in affect: Perspectives on frontal EEG asymmetry research. *Biological Psychology*, *67*(1–2), 219–234. https://doi.org/10.1016/j.biopsycho.2004.03.008

Davidson, R. J., Putnam, K. M., & Larson, C. L. (2000). Dysfunction in the neural circuitry of emotion regulation—A possible prelude to violence. *Science*, *289*(5479), 591–594. https://doi.org/10.1126/science.289.5479.591

Day, A. L., & Catano, V. M. (2006). Screening and selecting out violent employees. In E. K. Kelloway, J. Barling, & J. J. Hurrell, Jr. (Eds.), *Handbook of workplace violence* (pp. 549–577). Sage Publications. https://doi.org/10.4135/9781412976947.n24

Denson, T. F., Moulds, M. L., & Grisham, J. R. (2012). The effects of analytical rumination, reappraisal, and distraction on anger experience. *Behavior Therapy*, *43*(2), 355–364. https://doi.org/10.1016/j.beth.2011.08.001

Domagalski, T. A., & Steelman, L. A. (2005). The impact of work events and disposition on the experience and expression of employee anger. *Organizational Analysis*, *13*(1), 31–52. https://doi.org/10.1177/0893318906295681

Domagalski, T. A., & Steelman, L. A. (2007). The impact of gender and organizational status on workplace anger expression. *Management Communication Quarterly*, *20*(3), 297–315. https://doi.org/10.1177/0893318906295681

Eckhardt, C., Norlander, B., & Deffenbacher, J. (2004). The assessment of anger and hostility: A critical review. *Aggression and Violent Behavior*, *9*(1), 17–43. https://doi.org/10.1016/S1359-1789(02)00116-7

Edmondson, D., Shaffer, J. A., Chaplin, W. F., Burg, M. M., Stone, A. A., & Schwartz, J. E. (2013). Trait anxiety and trait anger measured by ecological momentary assessment and their correspondence with traditional trait questionnaires. *Journal of Research in Personality*, *47*(6), 843–852. https://doi.org/10.1016/j.jrp.2013.08.005

Etzler, S. L., Rohrmann, S., & Brandt, H. (2014). Validation of the STAXI-2: A study with prison inmates. *Psychological Test and Assessment Modeling*, *56*(2), 178–194.

Frost, W. D., & Averill, J. R. (1982). Differences between men and women in the everyday experience of anger. In J. R. Averill (Ed.), *Anger and aggression* (pp. 281–316). Springer.

Germeys, L., & De Gieter, S. (2018). A diary study on the role of psychological detachment in the spillover of self-control demands to employees' ego depletion and the crossover to their partner. *European Journal of Work and Organizational Psychology*, *27*(1), 140–152. https://doi.org/10.1080/1359432X.2017.1417259

Gibson, D. E., & Callister, R. R. (2010). Anger in organizations: Review and integration. *Journal of Management*, *36*(1), 66–93.

Gibson, D. E., Schweitzer, M. E., Callister, R. R., & Gray, B. (2009). The influence of anger expressions on outcomes in organizations. *Negotiation and Conflict Management Research*, *2*(3), 236–262. https://doi.org/10.1111/j.1750-4716.2009.00039.x

Gordijn, E. H., Wigboldus, D., & Yzerbyt, V. (2001). Emotional consequences of categorizing victims of negative outgroup behavior as ingroup or outgroup. *Group Processes & Intergroup Relations*, *4*(4), 317–326. https://doi.org/10.1177/1368430201004004002

Grawitch, M. J., Munz, D. C., Elliott, E. K., & Mathis, A. (2003). Promoting creativity in temporary problem-solving groups: The effects of positive mood and autonomy in problem definition on idea-generating performance. *Group Dynamics*, *7*(3), 200–213. https://doi.org/10.1037/1089-2699.7.3.200

Gross, J. J. (2002). Emotion regulation: Affective, cognitive, and social consequences. *Psychophysiology*, *39*(3), 281–291. https://doi.org/10.1017/S0048577201393198

Hallett, M. (2007). Transcranial magnetic stimulation: A primer. *Neuron*, *55*(2), 187–199. https://doi.org/10.1016/j.neuron.2007.06.026

Harmon-Jones, C., Schmeichel, B. J., Mennitt, E., & Harmon-Jones, E. (2011). The expression of determination: Similarities between anger and approach-related positive affect. *Journal of Personality and Social Psychology*, *100*(1), 172–181. https://doi.org/10.1037/a0020966

Harvey, A. G., Watkins, E., & Mansell, W. (2004). *Cognitive behavioural processes across psychological disorders: A transdiagnostic approach to research and treatment*. Oxford University Press.

Hauret, K. G., Jones, B. H., Bullock, S. H., Canham-Chervak, M., & Canada, S. (2010). Musculoskeletal injuries: Description of an under-recognized injury problem among military personnel. *American Journal of Preventive Medicine*, *38*(1, Suppl.), S61–S70. https://doi.org/10.1016/j.amepre.2009.10.021

Hermans, E. J., Ramsey, N. F., & van Honk, J. (2008). Exogenous testosterone enhances responsiveness to social threat in the neural circuitry of social aggression in humans. *Biological Psychiatry*, *63*(3), 263–270. https://doi.org/10.1016/j.biopsych.2007.05.013

Hershcovis, M. S., Turner, N., Barling, J., Arnold, K. A., Dupré, K. E., Inness, M., LeBlanc, M. M., & Sivanathan, N. (2007). Predicting workplace aggression: A meta-analysis. *The Journal of Applied Psychology*, *92*(1), 228–238. https://doi.org/10.1037/0021-9010.92.1.228

Hubbard, J. A., McAuliffe, M. D., Morrow, M. T., & Romano, L. J. (2010). Reactive and proactive aggression in childhood and adolescence: Precursors, outcomes, processes, experiences, and measurement. *Journal of Personality, 78*(1), 95–118. https://doi.org/10.1111/j.1467-6494.2009.00610.x

Hung, L., & Bryant, R. A. (2016). Autobiographical memory in the angry self. *PLOS ONE, 11*(3), e0151349. https://doi.org/10.1371/journal.pone.0151349

Jakupcak, M., Conybeare, D., Phelps, L., Hunt, S., Holmes, H. A., Felker, B., Klevens, M., & McFall, M. E. (2007). Anger, hostility, and aggression among Iraq and Afghanistan War veterans reporting PTSD and subthreshold PTSD. *Journal of Traumatic Stress, 20*(6), 945–954. https://doi.org/10.1002/jts.20258

Jasinski, M. J., Lumley, M. A., Latsch, D. V., Schuster, E., Kinner, E., & Burns, J. W. (2016). Assessing anger expression: Construct validity of three emotion expression-related measures. *Journal of Personality Assessment, 98*(6), 640–648. https://doi.org/10.1080/00223891.2016.1178650

Julkunen, J. (1996). Suppressing your anger: Good manners, bad health? In C. D. Spielberger & I. G. Sarason (Eds.), *Stress and emotion* (Vol. 16, pp. 227–240). Taylor & Francis.

Kalachanis, K., & Michailidis, I. E. (2015). The Hippocratic view on humors and human temperament. *European Journal of Social Behaviour, 2*(2), 1–5.

Kemp, S., & Strongman, K. T. (1995). Anger theory and management: A historical analysis. *The American Journal of Psychology, 108*(3), 397–417. https://doi.org/10.2307/1422897

Kennedy-Moore, E., & Watson, J. C. (1999). *Emotions and social behavior. Expressing emotion: Myths, realities, and therapeutic strategies.* Guilford Press.

Kligyte, V., Connelly, S., Thiel, C., & Devenport, L. (2013). The influence of anger, fear, and emotion regulation on ethical decision making. *Human Performance, 26*(4), 297–326. https://doi.org/10.1080/08959285.2013.814655

Knight, A. P., & Baer, M. (2014). Get up, stand up: The effects of a non-sedentary workspace on information elaboration and group performance. *Social Psychological & Personality Science, 5*(8), 910–917. https://doi.org/10.1177/1948550614538463

Koepfler, J., Brewster, J., Stoloff, M., & Saville, B. (2012). Predicting police aggression: Comparing traditional and non-traditional prediction models. *Journal of Police and Criminal Psychology, 27*(2), 141–149. https://doi.org/10.1007/s11896-012-9101-y

Kooij-de Bode, H. J., Van Knippenberg, D., & Van Ginkel, W. P. (2010). Good effects of bad feelings: Negative affectivity and group decision-making. *British Journal of Management, 21*(2), 375–392. https://doi.org/10.1111/j.1467-8551.2009.00675.x

Lambert, A. J., Eadeh, F. R., & Hanson, E. J. (2019). Anger and its consequences for judgment and behavior: Recent developments in social and political psychology. *Advances in Experimental Social Psychology, 59*, 103–173. https://doi.org/10.1016/bs.aesp.2018.12.001

Leonard, R., & Alison, L. (1999). Critical incident stress debriefing and its effects on coping strategies and anger in a sample of Australian police officers involved in shooting incidents. *Work and Stress, 13*(2), 144–161. https://doi.org/10.1080/026783799296110

Lerner, J. S., Goldberg, J. H., & Tetlock, P. E. (1998). Sober second thought: The effects of accountability, anger, and authoritarianism on attributions of responsibility. *Personality and Social Psychology Bulletin, 24*(6), 563–574. https://doi.org/10.1177/0146167298246001

Lerner, J. S., & Keltner, D. (2000). Beyond valence: Toward a model of emotion-specific influences on judgement and choice. *Cognition & Emotion, 14*(4), 473–493. https://doi.org/10.1080/026999300402763

Lerner, J. S., & Tiedens, L. Z. (2006). Portrait of the angry decision maker: How appraisal tendencies shape anger's influence on cognition. *Journal of Behavioral Decision Making, 19*(2), 115–137. https://doi.org/10.1002/bdm.515

Lester, D. (1990). Galen's four temperaments and four-factor theories of personality: A comment on "Toward a four-factor theory of temperament and/or personality." *Journal of Personality Assessment, 54*(1), 423–426. https://doi.org/10.1207/s15327752jpa5401&2_40

Lindebaum, D., & Gabriel, Y. (2016). Anger and organization studies: From social disorder to moral order. *Organization Studies, 37*(7), 903–918. https://doi.org/10.1177/0170840616640848

Litvak, P. M., Lerner, J. S., Tiedens, L. Z., & Shonk, K. (2010). Fuel in the fire: How anger impacts judgment and decision-making. In M. Potegal, G. Stemmler, & C. Spielberger (Eds.), *International handbook of anger* (pp. 287–310). Springer. https://doi.org/10.1007/978-0-387-89676-2_17

Lough, J., & Treuer, K. V. (2013). A critical review of psychological instruments used in police officer selection. *Policing, 36*(4), 737–751.

Mackie, D. M., Devos, T., & Smith, E. R. (2000). Intergroup emotions: Explaining offensive action tendencies in an intergroup context. *Journal of Personality and Social Psychology, 79*(4), 602–616.

Marshall, R. E., Milligan-Saville, J. S., Mitchell, P. B., Bryant, R. A., & Harvey, S. B. (2017). A systematic review of the usefulness of pre-employment and pre-duty screening in predicting mental health outcomes amongst emergency workers. *Psychiatry Research, 253*, 129–137. https://doi.org/10.1016/j.psychres.2017.03.047

Moons, W. G., & Mackie, D. M. (2007). Thinking straight while seeing red: The influence of anger on information processing. *Personality and Social Psychology Bulletin, 33*(5), 706–720. https://doi.org/10.1177/0146167206298566

Novaco, R. W. (2010). Anger and psychopathology. In M. Potegal, G. Stemmler, & C. Spielberger (Eds.), *International handbook of anger* (pp. 465–497). Springer. https://doi.org/10.1007/978-0-387-89676-2_27

Osgood, J. M. (2017). Is revenge about retributive justice, deterring harm, or both? *Social and Personality Psychology Compass, 11*(1), e12296. https://doi.org/10.1111/spc3.12296

Osgood, J. M., & Muraven, M. (2016). Does counting to ten increase or decrease aggression? The role of state self-control (ego-depletion) and consequences. *Journal of Applied Social Psychology, 46*(2), 105–113. https://doi.org/10.1111/jasp.12334

Osgood, J. M., Yates, H. K., Adler, A. B., Dyches, K. D., & Quartana, P. J. (2021). Tired and angry: Sleep, mental health, and workplace relational aggression. *Military Psychology, 33*(2), 80–91. https://doi.org/10.1080/08995605.2021.1897490

Owen, J. M. (2011). Transdiagnostic cognitive processes in high trait anger. *Clinical Psychology Review, 31*(2), 193–202. https://doi.org/10.1016/j.cpr.2010.10.003

Padyab, M., Backteman-Erlanson, S., & Brulin, C. (2016). Burnout, coping, stress of conscience and psychosocial work environment among patrolling police officers. *Journal of Police and Criminal Psychology, 31*(4), 229–237. https://doi.org/10.1007/s11896-015-9189-y

Pedersen, S., Burnett, S., Smith, R., & Neill, A. (2012). Motivations for police blogging and how fear of being 'outed' can force a blogger to cease. *Association of Internet*

Researchers Selected Papers of Internet Research, 2, 1–18. https://journals.uic.edu/ojs/index.php/spir/article/view/8219

Peterson, C. K., Shackman, A. J., & Harmon-Jones, E. (2008). The role of asymmetrical frontal cortical activity in aggression. *Psychophysiology, 45*(1), 86–92.

Pixar. (2015, May 15). *Meet Lewis Black as Anger in Inside Out* [Video]. YouTube. https://youtu.be/1DtMdRhtlfk

Pornari, C. D., & Wood, J. (2010). Peer and cyber aggression in secondary school students: The role of moral disengagement, hostile attribution bias, and outcome expectancies. *Aggressive Behavior, 36*(2), 81–94. https://doi.org/10.1002/ab.20336

Potegal, M., & Novaco, R. W. (2010). A brief history of anger. In M. Potegal, G. Stemmler, & C. Spielberger (Eds.), *International handbook of anger* (pp. 9–24). Springer. https://doi.org/10.1007/978-0-387-89676-2_2

Prem, R., Kubicek, B., Diestel, S., & Korunka, C. (2016). Regulatory job stressors and their within-person relationships with ego depletion: The roles of state anxiety, self-control effort, and job autonomy. *Journal of Vocational Behavior, 92*, 22–32. https://doi.org/10.1016/j.jvb.2015.11.004

Radke, H. R., Hornsey, M. J., & Barlow, F. K. (2016). Barriers to women engaging in collective action to overcome sexism. *American Psychologist, 71*(9), 863–874. https://doi.org/10.1037/a0040345

Ressler, N. (2004). Rewards and punishments, goal-directed behavior and consciousness. *Neuroscience and Biobehavioral Reviews, 28*(1), 27–39. https://doi.org/10.1016/j.neubiorev.2003.10.003

Restubog, S. L. D., Garcia, P. R. J. M., Wang, L., & Cheng, D. (2010). It's all about control: The role of self-control in buffering the effects of negative reciprocity beliefs and trait anger on workplace deviance. *Journal of Research in Personality, 44*(5), 655–660. https://doi.org/10.1016/j.jrp.2010.06.007

Ridgeway, C., & Johnson, C. (1990). What is the relationship between socioemotional behavior and status in task groups? *American Journal of Sociology, 95*(5), 1189–1212. https://doi.org/10.1086/229426

Salerno, J. M., & Peter-Hagene, L. C. (2013). The interactive effect of anger and disgust on moral outrage and judgments. *Psychological Science, 24*(10), 2069–2078. https://doi.org/10.1177/0956797613486988

Schutter, D. J., Hofman, D., & Van Honk, J. (2008). Fearful faces selectively increase corticospinal motor tract excitability: A transcranial magnetic stimulation study. *Psychophysiology, 45*(3), 345–348. https://doi.org/10.1111/j.1469-8986.2007.00635.x

Simon, R. W., & Nath, L. E. (2004). Gender and emotion in the United States: Do men and women differ in self-reports of feelings and expressive behavior? *American Journal of Sociology, 109*(5), 1137–1176. https://doi.org/10.1086/382111

Spector, P. E., & Fox, S. (2002). An emotion-centered model of voluntary work behavior: Some parallels between counterproductive work behavior and organizational citizenship behavior. *Human Resource Management Review, 12*(2), 269–292. https://doi.org/10.1016/S1053-4822(02)00049-9

Spielberger, C. D. (1988). *Manual for the State–Trait Anger Expression Scale (STAXI)*. Psychological Assessment Resources.

Spielberger, C. D., Krasner, S. S., & Solomon, E. P. (1988). The experience, expression, and control of anger. In M. P. Janisse (Ed.), *Individual differences, stress, and health psychology* (pp. 89–108). Springer.

Spielberger, C. D., & Reheiser, E. C. (2003). Measuring anxiety, anger, depression, and curiosity as emotional states and personality traits with the STAI, STAXI, and STPI. *Comprehensive Handbook of Psychological Assessment, 2*, 70–86.

Spielberger, C. D., & Reheiser, E. C. (2010). The nature and measurement of anger. In M. Potegal, G. Stemmler, & C. Spielberger (Eds.), *International handbook of anger* (pp. 403–412). Springer.

Spielberger, C. D., Sydeman, S. J., Owen, A. E., & Marsh, B. J. (1999). Measuring anxiety and anger with the State–Trait Anxiety Inventory (STAI) and the State–Trait Anger Expression Inventory (STAXI). In M. E. Maruish (Ed.), *The use of psychological testing for treatment planning and outcomes assessment* (pp. 993–1021). Lawrence Erlbaum Associates.

Stucke, T. S., & Baumeister, R. F. (2006). Ego depletion and aggressive behavior: Is the inhibition of aggression a limited resource? *European Journal of Social Psychology, 36*(1), 1–13. https://doi.org/10.1002/ejsp.285

Tiedens, L. Z., & Linton, S. (2001). Judgment under emotional certainty and uncertainty: The effects of specific emotions on information processing. *Journal of Personality and Social Psychology, 81*(6), 973–988. https://doi.org/10.1037/0022-3514.81.6.973

Tsai, M. H., & Young, M. J. (2010). Anger, fear, and escalation of commitment. *Cognition and Emotion, 24*(6), 962–973. https://doi.org/10.1080/02699930903050631

van Honk, J., Harmon-Jones, E., Morgan, B. E., & Schutter, D. J. (2010). Socially explosive minds: The triple imbalance hypothesis of reactive aggression. *Journal of Personality, 78*(1), 67–94. https://doi.org/10.1111/j.1467-6494.2009.00609.x

van Honk, J., Tuiten, A., de Haan, E., vann de Hout, M., & Stam, H. (2001). Attentional biases for angry faces: Relationships to trait anger and anxiety. *Cognition and Emotion, 15*(3), 279–297. https://doi.org/10.1080/02699930126112

van Honk, J., Tuiten, A., Hermans, E., Putman, P., Koppeschaar, H., Thijssen, J., Verbaten, R., & van Doornen, L. (2001). A single administration of testosterone induces cardiac accelerative responses to angry faces in healthy young women. *Behavioral Neuroscience, 115*(1), 238–242. https://doi.org/10.1037/0735-7044.115.1.238

van Knippenberg, D., Kooij-de Bode, H. J., & van Ginkel, W. P. (2010). The interactive effects of mood and trait negative affect in group decision making. *Organization Science, 21*(3), 731–744. https://doi.org/10.1287/orsc.1090.0461

Walter, N., Tukachinsky, R., Pelled, A., & Nabi, R. (2019). Meta-analysis of anger and persuasion: An empirical integration of four models. *Journal of Communication, 69*(1), 73–93. https://doi.org/10.1093/joc/jqy054

Wilkowski, B. M., & Robinson, M. D. (2008). The cognitive basis of trait anger and reactive aggression: An integrative analysis. *Personality and Social Psychology Review, 12*(1), 3–21. https://doi.org/10.1177/1088868307309874

Wilkowski, B. M., & Robinson, M. D. (2010). The anatomy of anger: An integrative cognitive model of trait anger and reactive aggression. *Journal of Personality, 78*(1), 9–38. https://doi.org/10.1111/j.1467-6494.2009.00607.x

Wilkowski, B. M., Robinson, M. D., Gordon, R. D., & Troop-Gordon, W. (2007). Tracking the evil eye: Trait anger and selective attention within ambiguously hostile scenes. *Journal of Research in Personality, 41*(3), 650–666. https://doi.org/10.1016/j.jrp.2006.07.003

Williams, J. M. G., Watts, F. N., MacLeod, C., & Mathews, A. (1988). *Cognitive psychology and emotional disorders*. John Wiley & Sons.

2 ANGER AS AN OCCUPATIONAL HEALTH CHALLENGE FOR EMPLOYEES IN HIGH-RISK OCCUPATIONS

THOMAS W. BRITT, CHLOE A. WILSON, ERIC B. ELBOGEN, ELIZABETH E. VAN VOORHEES, AND KIRSTEN DILLON

KEY POINTS

- Although anger has frequently been examined among employees in high-risk occupations, the lack of a standardized measure of anger makes examining its prevalence difficult.
- Anger is associated with a number of dysfunctional outcomes, but the expression of anger can be adaptive when addressing sources of injustice in the workplace.
- Anger is a frequent consequence of exposure to traumatic events among employees in high-risk occupations and is intensified through hostile appraisals of threatening stimuli.
- The experience of anger problems is associated with certain secondary problems for employees through negative effects of different areas of mental function.

(continues)

https://doi.org/10.1037/0000244-003
Anger at Work: Prevention, Intervention, and Treatment in High-Risk Occupations, A. B. Adler and D. Forbes (Editors)

KEY POINTS (*Continued*)

- Research on anger among employees in high-risk occupations has largely failed to examine how organizational culture influences the relationship between anger and other outcomes.

The study of workplace violence and aggression has surged in recent years, perhaps driven by highly publicized incidents of workplace aggression involving homicide committed by disgruntled employees (Geck et al., 2017; Hershcovis et al., 2007). Exposure to this workplace violence has been examined in occupations including health care worker, law enforcement, and bus driver (Geoffrion et al., 2017; Hershcovis et al., 2007). However, research in these areas focuses almost exclusively on how violence enacted by patients, customers, and prisoners is related to stress and burnout, and the research is virtually silent about anger (Hershcovis et al., 2007). Likewise, research on public safety professions, such as military, law enforcement, and firefighter, primarily emphasizes posttraumatic stress disorder (PTSD) rather than anger per se.

There are many studies of workplace violence in higher risk occupations, but relatively few look at the role of workplace anger. Despite this gap, some studies are beginning to document the prevalence of anger and its importance in understanding the health of individuals working in high-risk occupations. We are aware of only a few studies that examine the prevalence of anger among employees in a high-risk occupation: Worthen et al. (2014) found that self-reported anger problems were common among male (53.0%, n = 1,036) and female (51.3%, n = 257) service members in a sample of Reserve Component personnel. Booth et al. (2017) completed an event-contingent anger diary over a period of 4 working weeks. These authors found that 50% of the sample of employees, which included both managers and nonmanagers, disclosed anger-causing events at some point during the 4 weeks. As we discuss in greater detail in our section on the measurement of anger, the use of a wide variety of anger measures has hindered the estimation of anger prevalence in the workforce and a comparison of how occupations differ in the prevalence of anger.

A focus on workplace anger in different occupations is critical, given the role that anger can play in workplace aggression (Inness et al., 2008) and the mental health of employees (Meffert et al., 2008). Anger also has the potential to disrupt team functioning, which can have high-stakes consequences given the importance of cohesion in high-risk occupations (Britt & McFadden, 2012). This chapter first addresses how anger in the workplace has been conceptualized and assessed among employees in general. The chapter then highlights workplace anger in high-risk occupations. Much of the research on anger as a problematic response to workplace stressors has been conducted with military personnel, but research has also been conducted with police officers, medical professionals, and bus drivers. Common themes from these high-risk occupations are identified and discussed.

CONCEPTUALIZATION OF ANGER IN THE WORKPLACE

Anger in the workplace has been conceptualized in different ways. Organizational researchers interested in anger as a predictor of workplace aggression have often examined *trait anger*, which is defined as a predisposition to respond to a variety of provocations with hostility (Spielberger, 1999). In a meta-analysis of the predictors of workplace aggression, Hershcovis et al. (2007) found that trait anger emerged as a significant predictor of both aggression directed toward other individuals (interpersonal aggression) and aggression directed toward the organization (e.g., stealing, sabotage). Inness et al. (2008) examined trait anger and trait aggression as predictors of aggression toward a supervisor, peer, or subordinate. The authors found that trait anger was predictive of aggression toward a subordinate, especially when organizational sanctions for acting aggressively were low.

Other organizational researchers have examined anger as an outcome of perceived victimization or injustice at work. Studies examining anger as an emotion typically posit that anger is a result of being treated unfairly or perceiving an injustice has occurred (Bies et al., 1997). Aquino et al. (2004) examined employee expression of anger in response to being victimized by coworkers and found that the relationship between victimization and anger expression was stronger among employees reporting a higher hostile attributional bias and norms that supported confrontation.

In addition to examining anger as a predictor and outcome, occupational health researchers have also examined anger as a moderator. Sliter et al. (2011) examined trait anger as a moderator of the relationships between different forms of interpersonal conflict (customer and coworker) and employee outcomes (task performance, burnout, and physical health symptoms). The authors found that trait anger potentiated the relationships between (a) customer interpersonal conflict and employee burnout and (b) customer interpersonal conflict and employee physical health. The relationships between conflict and outcomes was stronger among employees higher in trait anger.

Although most of the research in organizational settings has highlighted the negative consequences of workplace anger, other researchers have noted that the experience and expression of anger can have beneficial effects for employees and organizations (Geddes et al., 2020). Geddes and Callister (2007) developed the dual threshold model of workplace anger to specify those conditions when experiencing and expressing workplace anger would have beneficial consequences. This model states that once employees experience anger in the workplace, that anger can be suppressed, expressed, or deviant. Suppressed anger occurs when organizational norms do not condone talking about anger and the employee is required to suppress anger. Expressed anger occurs when organizational norms allow employees to describe why they feel angry so that the cause of the anger can potentially be addressed. Deviant anger occurs when employees express their anger but the expressed anger is seen as inconsistent with organizational norms. Yelling at a coworker is an example of deviant anger.

According to Geddes and Callister (2007), the first threshold of *expression* involves whether organizational norms permit employees to talk openly about their anger. The second threshold of *impropriety* involves whether the expressed anger is viewed as passing what is appropriate to convey based on organizational norms. Organizations that have a wider space between the two thresholds provide employees greater latitude for expressing their anger so that it can be dealt with by the organization, resulting in positive outcomes for the employee and organization. In contrast, both suppressing anger and having expressed anger judged to be deviant result in negative outcomes. The impropriety threshold is consistent with research on how the inappropriate expression of emotions in the workplace can have negative consequences (Cheshin, 2020).

Geddes et al. (2020) reviewed evidence of the positive outcomes that can result from allowing anger to be expressed in the workplace, including providing important feedback to managers regarding the consequences of their actions, allowing for organizational change to address conditions causing anger among employees, and allowing employees to identify concerns regarding an organization violating moral standards. Researchers have argued that all emotions serve underlying functions (Gendolla, 2014) and that the experience and expression of anger can serve beneficial functions within an organization. Organizational norms encouraging the appropriate expression of anger may prevent the negative consequences that can come from suppressing anger or from being judged as deviant for voicing justifiable anger regarding specific conditions. Qualitative research has examined the extent to which leader expressions of anger may have positive consequences among military personnel, suggesting that followers report being more likely to correct mistakes following a military leader's expression of anger regarding poor performance (Lindebaum et al., 2016).

In summary, anger in the workplace has been examined as an individual difference predictor, as an outcome variable, and as a moderator. These different roles for workplace anger are not necessary problematic but rather illustrate the multiple ways that anger can affect employees in organizational settings. Furthermore, there is growing consensus that the experience and expression of anger in the workplace is not inevitably tied to dysfunctional outcomes but may also result in benefits for the employee and organization. The potential benefits of anger expression are further explored later in the chapter, when we examine anger in high risk occupations. In the next section of the chapter, we address how anger has been conceptualized among employees in diverse high-risk occupations.

ASSESSMENT OF ANGER IN THE WORKPLACE

In this section, we describe the most commonly used measures of anger in the workplace, including different indices of anger and accompanying cognitive, physiological, and behavioral symptoms stemming from anger. The most commonly used self-report assessments in the workplace are the State–Trait Anger Expression Inventory (STAXI-I; Spielberger, 1988) and its revised edition (STAXI-II; Spielberger, 1999), the Novaco Anger Scale (NAS; Novaco, 1994) and Novaco Anger Scale and Provocation Inventory (NAS-PI; Novaco, 2003), and the Multidimensional Anger Inventory (MAI; Siegel, 1986). These assessments have undergone numerous revisions addressing the dimensional framework, length, and response scales of the measures. Table 2.1 contains a summary of the common measures of anger in occupational settings, including the dimensions or subscales of these measures, and the occupational settings in which each anger measure was used (see also Osgood & Quartana, Chapter 1, this volume).

One of the ways that anger has been assessed is through individual differences in the frequency that it is experienced. Spielberger (1988, 1999) conceptualized trait anger as having two dimensions: anger temperament, which is the disposition to experience anger without specific provocation (e.g., being quick tempered), and anger reaction, which is the frequency with which angry feelings are experienced as a result of perceived unfair treatment from others. Measures to assess these dimensions include the State–Trait Anger Scale (Spielberger et al., 1983), the STAXI-I (Spielberger, 1988), and the STAXI-II (Spielberger, 1999). Trait-based variants of these scales have been used with military personnel (e.g., Bailie et al., 2015; Forbes et al., 2014), full-time employees from a variety of occupations (Ellis-Woroch, 2013), and disaster relief workers (S. Evans et al., 2006).

Other anger assessments have relied on assessing individuals based on situational descriptions and the extent to which the situation angers the

TABLE 2.1. Assessments of Anger Used in Occupational Settings

Assessment	Scale abbreviation	Reference	Dimension(s)	Purpose of assessment	Items	Populations studied using the scale
Anger Inventory	AI	Novaco (1974)	Unidimensional scale	Amount of anger provoked from a broad range of situations	80	Direct patient staff (Keyes & Dean, 1988)
Novaco Provocation Inventory	NPI	Novaco (1975, 1988)	Injustice-Unfairness Frustration-Clumsiness Physical Affronts	Amount of anger provoked from a broad range of situations	90 (80)	Police officers, military personnel, industrial workers, mental health workers (Bohl, 1991; Novaco, 1975, 1988)
Novaco Anger Scale	NAS	Novaco (1994)	Anger Arousal (4 subscales: Intensity, Duration, Somatic Tension, and Irritability) Cognitive Anger (4 subscales: Attentional Focus, Suspicion, Rumination, and Hostile Attitude) Behavioral Anger (4 subscales: Impulsive Reaction, Verbal Aggression, Physical Confrontation, Indirect Expression)	Physiological intensity and duration of anger symptoms as well as somatic tension and irritability Cognitive meditational aspects of anger process (e.g., the justification of anger) Chronic, confrontational, and inappropriate actions taken during the anger cycle (e.g., impulsive reactions)	48 (16 per dimension)	National Health Service employees (Jones et al., 1999); veterans (Mackintosh, Morland, Frueh, et al., 2014; Mackintosh, Morland, Kloezeman, et al., 2014; Novaco & Chemtob, 2002)

			Anger Intensity (5 subscales: Disrespectful Treatment, Unfairness Injustice, Frustrations/ Interruption, Annoying Traits, Irritations)	Intensity of anger across a range of potentially provocative situations	25		
The Novaco Anger Scale and Provocation Inventory	NAS-PI	Novaco (2003)	Anger (Arousal, Cognitive, Behavioral)	Revised version of Part A of NAS (Novaco, 1994)	60		
			Reactions to Provocative Events	Revised version of Part B of NAS (Novaco, 1994)	25		
Dimensions of Anger Reactions	DAR	Novaco (1975)	Unidimensional scale	Anger frequency, intensity, duration, and antagonism and anger's perceived impairment on work performance, social relationships, and health	7		Military personnel (Gonzalez et al., 2016; Hawthorne et al., 2006; Novaco et al., 2012; Shea et al., 2013)
Dimensions of Anger Reactions-Revised	DAR-5	Forbes et al. (2014)	Unidimensional scale	Revised version of DAR (Novaco, 1975)	5		Active duty military (Cash et al., 2018); veterans (Forbes et al., 2014)

(*continues*)

TABLE 2.1. Assessments of Anger Used in Occupational Settings (*Continued*)

Assessment	Scale abbreviation	Reference	Dimension(s)	Purpose of assessment	Items	Populations studied using the scale
State–Trait Anger Scale	STAS	Spielberger et al. (1983)	State Anger	Emotional experience to express anger	10	Navy recruits (Spielberger et al., 1983); bus drivers (Glasø et al., 2011)
			Trait Anger	Dispositional proneness to anger	10	
State–Trait Anger Expression Inventory	STAXI-I	Spielberger (1988)	State Anger	Psychological state or condition of subjective feelings of anger that vary in *intensity*	10	Active duty air force family members, spouses, and Department of Defense civilian employees (Linkh & Sonnek, 2003); police officers (Gerzina & Drummond, 2000; Leonard & Alison, 1999); veterans (Clark, 1994)
			Trait Anger (2 subscales: Angry Temperament and Angry Reaction)	Individual difference in *frequency* of anger as response to situations overtime	10	
			Anger Expression (3 subscales: Anger-In, Anger-Out, Anger-Control)	Anger directed toward other persons or objects (anger-out), anger suppression (anger-in), monitoring and prevent the outward expression of anger (anger-control)	24	

State–Trait Anger Expression Inventory II	STAXI-II	Spielberger (1999)	State Anger (3 subscales: Feeling Angry, Feeling Like Expressing Anger Verbally, and Feeling Like Expressing Anger Physically)	Revised version of STAXI-SAS (Spielberger, 1988)	15	Managerial, technical, and clerical personnel (Spielberger, 1999); military personnel (Bailie et al., 2015; Forbes et al., 2014; Mackintosh et al., 2014; Raab et al., 2013; Shea et al., 2013); retail, wholesale, education, and health employment (Booth et al., 2017); full-time employees (Ellis-Woroch, 2013); disaster relief workers (S. Evans et al., 2006)
			Trait Anger (2 subscales: Angry Temperament and Angry Reaction)	Revised version of STAXI-TAS (Spielberger, 1988)	10	
			Anger Expression (3 subscales: Anger-In, Anger-Out, Anger-Control)	Revised version of STAXI-AX (Spielberger, 1988)	32	
Minnesota Multiphasic Personality Inventory-2 Anger Scale	MMPI-2	Graham (1993)	Anger and Aggressive Behavior	Assess the occurrence, frequency, and manner of expression of anger and hostility	16	National Guard soldiers (Arbisi et al., 2011); veterans (Clark, 1994)

(*continues*)

TABLE 2.1. Assessments of Anger Used in Occupational Settings (*Continued*)

Assessment	Scale abbreviation	Reference	Dimension(s)	Purpose of assessment	Items	Populations studied using the scale
Person Specific Anger Scale	–	Deffenbacher et al. (1986)	Anger Symptoms	Most salient physiological reactivity when angered	Self-generated list	Police officers (Gerzina & Drummond, 2000)
			Situational Anger	Degree of anger produced from ongoing situations of provoked anger	Self-generated situation	
			Severity of anger (3 indices: average daily rating, average rating for more than mild events [> 30], number of indicated rated [> 30])	Degree the most provocative situation of the day produced anger	Self-generated situation	
Multidimensional Anger Inventory	MAI	Siegel (1986)	Anger-arousal (frequency, duration, magnitude)	Reflects aspects of anger that include frequency, duration, and magnitude	11	Factory workers (Siegel, 1986); veterans (McFall et al., 1999); police officers (Gerzina & Drummond, 2000; Mearns & Mauch, 1998)
			Range of anger-eliciting situations	Measures the individual's anger as a result of different provocative scenarios	9	

			Hostile outlook	Combination of scenarios and items reflecting a general disdain for other people	6	
			Mode of anger expression (2 subscales: In, Out)	Reflect an individual's mode of expression	12	
Clinical Anger Scale	CAS	Snell et al. (1995)	Unidimensional scale	Severity of clinical anger symptomatology	21	Medical professionals (Faye et al., 2011);
Anger Reactions Questionnaire	AR	Thomas et al. (2010)	Unidimensional scale	Brief assessment of frequency of reactions of anger	4	Active duty soldiers (Adrian et al., 2019; J. L. Thomas et al., 2010)
McLinton Interpersonal Domain-Specific Anger Instrument	MIDAI	McLinton & Dollard (2013)	Overt hostility (5 scales: Family Members, Superiors, Coworkers, Subordinates, and Strangers) Covert Provocation (5 scales: Family Members, Superiors, Coworkers, Subordinates, and Strangers)	An individual's predisposition for interpersonal anger is relative to the social role of the target of that anger	60 (12 each dimension)	Full-time employees (McLinton & Dollard, 2013)

participant. For example, in the Anger Inventory (Novaco, 1974) and its later edition, the Novaco Provocation Inventory (Novaco, 1975, 1988), as well as the Range of Anger-Eliciting Situations dimension of the MAI (Siegel, 1986), participants read a list of situational descriptions and indicate how often they were angered by those specific situations. Similarly, for two of the dimensions of the Person Specific Anger Scale (Deffenbacher et al., 1986), participants generate a list of situations that anger them on a daily basis and then rate the extent to which each situation produces anger. Situational provocations of anger have been assessed with direct patient staff (Keyes & Dean, 1988), police officers, military personnel, industrial workers, and mental health workers (Bohl, 1991; Novaco, 1975, 1988).

Another approach to the assessment of anger has involved self-reports of anger-related physiological responses or symptoms. In the Anger Arousal subscale of the NAS (Novaco, 1994) and in the NAS-PI (Novaco, 2003), participants are asked to indicate how often they experienced certain symptoms or physiological reactions as a result of certain situations. The items are grouped into four subscales assessing the intensity, duration, somatic tension, and irritability symptoms resulting from the situations. Similarly, in the Dimensions of Anger (Novaco, 1975) and its shortened revised version (Forbes et al., 2014), participants rate not only the frequency and duration of anger but also the perceived impairment on work performance, social relationships, and well-being as a result of the anger experienced.

Other assessments of anger that capture the symptomatology of anger experiences are the state dimensions of the State–Trait Anger Scale (Spielberger et al., 1983), STAXI-I (Spielberger, 1988), STAXI-II (Spielberger, 1999), Anger Symptoms subscale of the Person Specific Anger Scale (Deffenbacher et al., 1986), anger-arousal dimension of the MAI (Siegel, 1986), Clinical Anger Scale (Snell et al., 1995), and the Anger Reactions Questionnaire (J. L. Thomas et al., 2010). Police officers (Gerzina & Drummond, 2000) and military personnel (Gonzalez et al., 2016; Hawthorne et al., 2006; Novaco et al., 2012; Shea et al., 2013) are two of the occupational specialties that have been assessed with these measures.

Fewer assessments of anger have measured the cognitive components of the experience of anger. Cognitive justifications and appraisals of anger have been assessed within the NAS and NAS-PI, with cognitive anger being grouped into the four dimensions of attentional focus, suspicion, rumination, and hostile attitude. Examples of cognitive components of anger include blaming others for frustration and being suspicious of others' intentions. National Health Service employees (Jones et al., 1999) and veterans (Mackintosh, Morland, Frueh, et al., 2014; Mackintosh, Morland, Kloezeman, et al., 2014; Novaco & Chemtob, 2002) have been assessed using these measures.

In addition to the physiological and cognitive aspects of anger, the behavioral implications of anger have been examined within some of the anger assessments. For example, both the NAS and the NAS-PI assess the confrontational and often inappropriate actions taken during experiences of anger. The behavioral components fall into the categories of impulsive reactions, verbal aggression, physical confrontation, and indirect expression of anger. Spielberger (1988, 1999) captured the behavioral outcomes of anger within the Anger Expression dimension of the STAXI-I and STAXI-II scales. Within the anger expression index, anger directed toward other persons or objects (anger-out), anger suppression (anger-in), and monitoring and preventing the outward expression of anger (anger-control) are examined. Other assessments have similar components, such as the Minnesota Multiphasic Personality Inventory–2 Anger scale (Graham, 1993), the Mode of Anger Expression dimension of the MAI (Siegel, 1986), and the McLinton Interpersonal Domain-Specific Anger Instrument (McLinton & Dollard, 2013).

Researchers have also gone beyond self-report measures and included observations and behavioral reports from peers, such as spouses and friends, adapting measures to reflect a targeted individual instead of themselves (Gerzina & Drummond, 2000). Furthermore, many studies do not limit anger assessment to a single measurement technique or scale but instead use subscales from multiple measures in a single study (e.g., Forbes et al., 2014; Gerzina & Drummond, 2000; Mackintosh, Morland, Frueh, et al., 2014; Shea et al., 2013).

Multiple reviews of the assessment of anger have been conducted, addressing the measures in depth and providing recommendations for future research (Eckhardt et al., 2004; Morland et al., 2012; Shahsavarani et al., 2015). Although researchers have called for the more uniform use of anger assessments, research is still characterized by the use of multiple anger assessment inventories, often with multiple revisions of a given inventory. This practice has prevented comparisons among different employee samples and contexts in terms of the prevalence of anger problems. Rather than a focus on the prevalence of anger within the workplace, researchers have focused on how anger is related to different antecedents and consequences, as well as the effectiveness of interventions designed to decrease symptoms of problematic anger. The next section of the chapter addresses these approaches among employees in high-risk occupations.

THE ROLE OF ANGER IN HIGH-RISK OCCUPATIONS

Anger is particularly important to examine in high-risk occupations, given research showing that anger-related problems frequently occur in these employees as a result of traumatic events encountered during the course of their work (Meffert et al., 2008; J. L. Thomas et al., 2010; Worthen et al., 2015), as well as the potential for anger to disrupt functioning and performance in close-knit teams. According to the *Diagnostic and Statistical Manual of Mental Disorders* (5th ed. [*DSM-5*]; American Psychiatric Association, 2013), traumatic events involve "actual or threatened death, serious injury, or sexual violence" (p. 271). Much of the research on anger in high-risk occupations has examined the experience of anger as a risk factor for mental health problems such as PTSD, as well as secondary effects on the employee and family. In this section of the chapter we first address the link between anger and other mental health outcomes, and then explanatory mechanisms linking trauma exposure to anger and mental health outcomes. We conclude this section of the chapter by considering whether the experience and expression of anger may ever be beneficial for employees in high-risk occupations.

The Link Between Anger and Other Outcomes

The majority of research examining anger in high-risk occupations has investigated how the traumatic events encountered by employees in these occupations are related to anger and other mental health problems. An overall model of how exposure to trauma is expected to affect anger and related problems is provided in Figure 2.1. This descriptive model was created

FIGURE 2.1. Overall Model Depicting the Relationships Between Trauma Exposure, Anger, and Additional Problems Among Employees in High-Risk Occupations

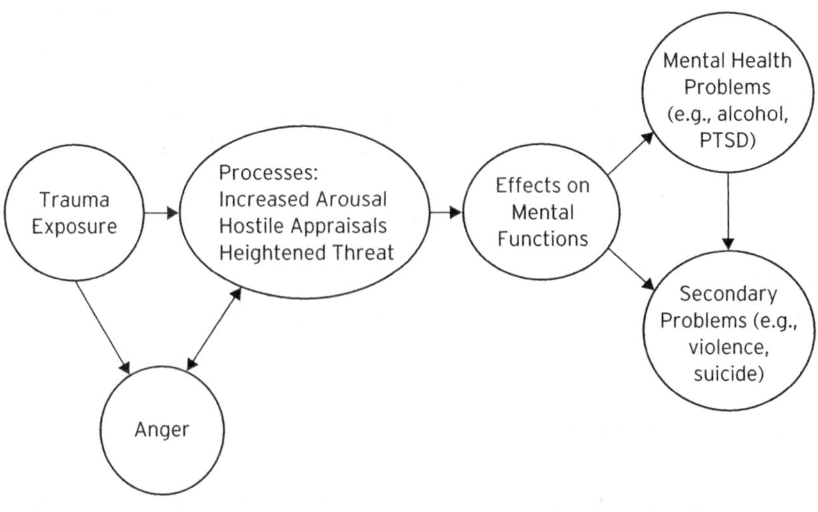

Note. PTSD = posttraumatic stress disorder.

specifically for the present chapter to address the relatively large amount of research in this area. This model starts with trauma exposure encountered by the employees and how this trauma affects the experience of both anger and processes that contribute to and follow from that experience. Proximal processes resulting from trauma exposure and anger include increased arousal, hostile appraisals of the causes of events, and an overall perception of a heightened threat. These processes then have negative effects on critical mental functions, including the direction of attention, emotional regulation, and motivation. Deficits in these mental functions are then hypothesized to predict the development of mental health problems that are ultimately related to secondary problems such as family violence and suicide. Our focus in this chapter is on anger as a response to traumatic events, but it is worth noting that there are multiple outcomes from exposure to trauma, including depression, PTSD, and other mental health problems (American Psychiatric Association, 2013).

Multiple studies have examined the role of anger in the development of PTSD among employees in high-risk occupations. Within these studies, anger has been found to play a role in the development, maintenance, and expression of PTSD. Research in this area has examined samples of first responders (e.g., law enforcement, firefighters, soldiers) by assessing them prior to training and then again months or years later. In a 2-year prospective study of firefighters, Heinrichs and colleagues (2005) found that pretraining high hostility and low self-efficacy accounted for 42% of the variance in PTSD symptoms measured 24 months later. Similarly, in a sample of soldiers, van Zuiden et al. (2011) found that predeployment high hostility and low self-directedness was associated with higher levels of PTSD symptoms 6 months after deployment to Afghanistan. Finally, in a study of police recruits, trait anger during training predicted PTSD symptoms 1 year later (Meffert et al., 2008). This study also found that PTSD symptoms at 1 year were associated with increased state anger, suggesting that anger may be both a vulnerability factor and a consequence of PTSD. These studies are critical because they demonstrate that trait anger and elevated levels of hostility have implications for how well members of high-risk professions will adjust to the demands of their occupation. In addition, health care workers treating patients during a pandemic such as the COVID-19 epidemic may experience anger over the fear of infection (as well as fear that their family members may get infected) or lack of adequate medical supplies, heightening intrusive thoughts, or hypervigilance.

Not only has meta-analytic research demonstrated a reliable association between PTSD and anger problems across samples of trauma-exposed individuals, but this relationship is especially pronounced in military veterans

(Olatunji et al., 2010; Orth & Wieland, 2006). In fact, difficulty controlling anger is the most commonly reported reintegration concern among combat veterans, with rates of self-reported anger problems among veterans, with PTSD topping out at 84% (Sayer et al., 2010). In a separate national survey of veterans as a whole, 61% of U.S. veterans reported experiencing difficulties controlling anger and 24% reported experiencing aggressive urges over a 2-year period (Sippel et al., 2016). In a large population-based study of postdeployment mental health concerns, up to 40% of Iraq War service members scoring above cutoff on a measure of PTSD reported recently becoming angry and engaging in physical aggression, with rates increasing from 3 to 12 months postdeployment (J. L. Thomas et al., 2010). Anger can also negatively impact PTSD treatment outcomes (see Morland et al., Chapter 8, this volume).

Besides being associated with PTSD as a whole, empirical research shows that violence and aggressive impulses are most consistently related to the hyperarousal cluster of symptoms of PTSD in military veterans (Elbogen et al., 2010; Taft et al., 2007). Consistent with these findings, one study found that veterans with PTSD and elevated anger and irritability were at increased risk of criminal justice involvement, whereas those with PTSD without high levels of anger and irritability were not (Elbogen et al., 2012). Researchers have found similar patterns with respect to violence in both veteran and nonveteran samples, such that PTSD with anger elevates risk of violence, whereas PTSD alone does not (Blakey et al., 2018; Novaco & Chemtob, 2015).

The role of alcohol misuse needs to be considered as well. One study of military veterans showed that the presence of both PTSD and alcohol misuse substantially elevated the risk of violence. However, what differentiated the risk of violence between veterans with PTSD alone and those with co-occurring alcohol misuse was the presence of higher anger symptoms (Elbogen et al., 2014).

The high prevalence of anger difficulty and resulting mental health problems among soldiers, veterans, and first responders has implications for adjustment in terms of mental health, work life, and personal relationships (see Figure 2.1). Most directly, higher levels of anger are associated with increases in aggressive behavior (Elbogen et al., 2010; Novaco & Chemtob, 2015; Wilk et al., 2015), including aggressive driving (Possis et al., 2014; Van Voorhees et al., 2018). Among veterans, problematic anger specifically has been found to be associated with negative psychosocial outcomes, including discord in family relationships (Galovski & Lyons, 2004), unemployment (Frueh et al., 1997), suicidal ideation (Wilks et al., 2019), and suicide risk (Rogers et al., 2017; see also Naifeh et al., Chapter 7, this volume).

Taken together, these studies document the high prevalence of anger in members of high-risk occupations such as first responders and military personnel, the link between anger and mental health problems like PTSD, and the importance of anger in understanding elevated risk of violence.

Explanatory Mechanisms Linking Trauma, Anger, and Other Related Outcomes

What explains the link between trauma, anger, and additional secondary problems among employees in high-risk occupations? The anger regulatory deficits model proposed by Chemtob and colleagues (1988) theorizes that anger in the context of PTSD is triggered when individuals adopt a "survival mode" of functioning. In this model, perceived threats trigger increased arousal, hostile appraisals, and hostile behaviors (Chemtob et al., 1988; Novaco et al., 2012; see Figure 2.1). This hostile response to threat, while protective and adaptive in combat situations, becomes maladaptive when individuals are no longer in danger. The model explains that this heightened sense of threat that develops as a result of combat training and PTSD may lead the veteran to misread ambiguous social situations and perceive others as having negative or hostile intentions, which will lead to an angry response. This same type of response may exist in other high-risk occupations. For example, police also likely experience a heightened sense of threat associated with potential violence from suspects in different scenarios; firefighters must remain vigilant to changes in a fire's dynamics that may signify an escalating threat (Sawhney et al., 2018); and paramedics must stay alert to violence when responding to drug overdoses (Maguire, 2018).

According to cognitive models of anger, individuals with problematic anger tend to construe ambiguous interpersonal interactions as hostile (Epps & Kendall, 1995). For example, when bumped by someone in a crowd, individuals with a predisposition toward anger may be more likely to attribute this incident to an act of aggression than a mistake (Wilkowski & Robinson, 2010). In fact, *hostile interpretation* of situations has been identified as the first step in the elicitation of anger and subsequent aggression in multiple models of anger and aggression (Bond et al., 2004; Dodge, 1980; Epps & Kendall, 1995; Hazebroek et al., 2001; Wenzel & Lystad, 2005; Wilkowski & Robinson, 2010). Hostile interpretation bias (see also Arad and Bar-Haim, Chapter 9, this volume) has been consistently linked to increased anger, starting with early work among aggressive children by Dodge (1980) and extending to adults as well (Bond et al., 2004; Epps & Kendall, 1995; Hazebroek et al., 2001; Wenzel & Lystad, 2005). Individuals who operate with a hostile interpretation bias are more likely to perceive threat and feel justified in sustaining their anger over time. Ultimately, this anger takes a toll on their ability to function.

Gaining a thorough understanding of what functioning entails is one way to better comprehend how anger can affect the functioning of employees in high-risk occupations. Addressing the sequalae of anger using a validated approach to functioning better maps the diverse ways that anger may ultimately harm the functioning of employees exposed to high levels of trauma. The *International Classification of Functioning, Disability and Health* (*ICF*) focuses on human functioning and provides a unified, standard language and framework that captures how people with a health condition function in their daily lives rather than focusing on their diagnosis or the presence or absence of disease. The links between anger, trauma, and secondary problems in high-risk occupations can be understood using four of the *ICF* domains that represent global and specific mental functions: Energy and Drive Functions, Shifting Attention, Emotional Functions, and Thought Functions.

Energy and Drive Functions

In the *ICF*, Energy and Drive Functions are defined as "general mental functions of physiological and psychological mechanisms that cause the individual to move towards satisfying specific needs and general goals in a persistent manner" (World Health Organization [WHO], 2001). As mentioned earlier, Chemtob and colleagues (1988) stated that aggression in PTSD is associated with an arousal regulation deficit, such that the inability to adequately regulate physiological arousal results in a priming toward anger and aggression in the presence of perceived threat (Beckham et al., 2000). Consistent with this formulation, the cardiovascular response to anger has been found to be exaggerated in individuals with PTSD, particularly in the presence of traumatic reminders (Vrana et al., 2009). Further, both PTSD and anger/hostility are associated with autonomic system dysregulation that may contribute to cardiovascular and metabolic disease (Dedert et al., 2010). The inability to maintain a state of physiological homeostasis impedes individuals from effectively functioning in terms of energy and drive.

The ability to maintain a physiological state consistent with productive goal pursuit is also shaped by the hyperarousal symptoms of PTSD, and these symptoms are specifically associated with aggression. In Vietnam War veterans, PTSD hyperarousal symptoms directly predicted aggression, numbing and avoidance symptoms were negatively associated with aggression, and reexperiencing symptoms had no direct relationship with aggression (Taft et al., 2007). In Iraq/Afghanistan War–era veterans, PTSD hyperarousal symptoms predicted aggressive impulses or urges, difficulty managing anger, and perceived problems controlling violent behavior even after the irritability symptom had been removed from analyses (Elbogen et al., 2010). The association between PTSD hyperarousal and aggression persists even after accounting for comorbid substance dependence, though the association may be complex (Savarese et al., 2001). Thus, hyperarousal appears to be implicated in understanding anger and aggression in military veterans, and a constant state of hyperarousal would ultimately deplete the resources that employees have to accomplish functional goals. Although less research has been conducted with others in high-risk occupations, the physiological link between hyperarousal and aggression would be expected to be present in these other occupations as well.

Shifting Attention

The *ICF* defines *shifting attention* as "mental functions that permit refocusing concentration from one stimulus to another" (WHO, 2001). Compared with healthy individuals without PTSD, individuals with PTSD demonstrate "attentional interference" to trauma-related stimuli, such that they have difficulty disengaging their attention from threat to efficiently engage in a relevant task (Pineles et al., 2007, 2009). This tendency to dwell upon threat may generalize beyond stimuli specifically associated with trauma. For example, a recent study used eye-tracking technology to examine the length of time that veterans with and without PTSD spent looking at fearful, disgusted, and happy faces. Results indicated that veterans with PTSD spent more time looking at fearful and disgusted expressions than at happy expressions, and this attention bias toward negative expressions distinguished veterans with PTSD from those without the disorder (Armstrong et al., 2013). Being unable to shift attention away from minor annoyances, as opposed to perseverating on the negative stimulus, may prompt an individual to dwell on perceived transgressions. Through rumination, these angry individuals may be less able to function effectively. In addition, sustained focus on negative stimuli may be a factor in the promotion of hostile attributional biases that increase the likelihood of more severe anger and aggression (Chemtob et al., 1988).

Emotional Functions

The *ICF* defines *emotional functions* as "specific mental functions related to the feeling and affective components of the processes of the mind," including the ability to express appropriate emotions, regulate emotions, and show the full range of emotions. Although PTSD was categorized as an anxiety or fear-based disorder in the *DSM-IV-TR* (American Psychiatric Association,

2000), research has suggested that the emotion of anger, as well as the ability to regulate the experience of anger, may also be fundamental to PTSD (Foa et al., 1995). For example, a meta-analysis found that although anger was elevated generally in anxiety disorders, severity of anger problems was greatest in PTSD, such that it distinguished it from all other anxiety disorders (Olatunji et al., 2010).

A series of studies have found that approximately half of the individuals who met full criteria for PTSD reported an emotion other than anxiety—such as anger, sadness, or disgust—as primary and that those with "nonanxiety" PTSD made less progress after exposure therapy than those for whom anxiety was central (Power & Fyvie, 2013). Similarly, a study of Vietnam combat veterans found that anger reactivity, but not anxiety reactivity, was associated with activation of a trauma memory in those with PTSD (Chemtob et al., 1988). Such findings most likely contributed to the removal of PTSD from the Anxiety Disorders section in the *DSM-5* (American Psychiatric Association, 2013) and its reclassification as a trauma and stressor-related disorder. This change was accompanied by a relatively greater emphasis on the expression of anger and aggression as PTSD symptoms (American Psychiatric Association, 2013).

Anger may be particularly salient for veterans with combat-related trauma. Anger is consistent with an approach or "fight" response to threat, and military training may cultivate anger as a part of the "survival mode" and as a means of combating feelings of guilt, vulnerability, and fear (Chemtob et al., 1988; Gerlock, 1994). Although anger is neither necessary nor sufficient for aggression, the presence of anger increases its likelihood (Chemtob et al., 1988). For example, anger has been found to mediate the association between PTSD and partner physical and psychological abuse (Taft et al., 2007), as well as between PTSD and family functioning (L. Evans et al., 2003). The experience of disproportionate anger in response to negative situations reflects the inability of employees to execute emotional functions and effectively regulate the emotion of anger, therefore exacerbating the link between anger and other mental health and secondary problems.

Thought Functions

The *ICF* defines *thought functions* as "specific mental functions related to the ideational component of the mind" (WHO, 2001). Individuals with PTSD have been found to be more likely to interpret ambiguous situations as threatening (Buckley et al., 2000) and to have information-processing biases toward negatively valenced emotional stimuli (Hayes et al., 2012). Attentional and information-processing biases in PTSD may interfere with memory and learning of safety cues and neutral stimuli, and slow processing relevant for goal-directed activity (Hayes et al., 2012). Both trait anger and experimentally induced anger are associated with processing biases of threat independent of trait anxiety, suggesting that anger may uniquely contribute to the information-processing disturbances observed in PTSD (Barazzone & Davey, 2009).

Anger-related cognitive schemas may be particularly salient in veterans with PTSD. Attentional and information-processing patterns that are shaped through military training and reinforced by combat can be maladaptive in a civilian setting (Morland et al., 2012). For example, an Iraq veteran may have survived multiple convoys by developing the capacity to quickly process and respond to minimal environmental data (e.g., a movement in her peripheral vision), matching these key stimuli with internally constructed patterns representing danger (e.g., an insurgent approaching the vehicle with a bomb), and reacting quickly and decisively with aggression (e.g., pulling her weapon). However, engaging in the "survival mode" pattern matching and responding in civilian life, divorced from the original context, is likely to increase risk and result in interpersonal conflict, damage to property, or legal conflict (Chemtob et al., 1988). To these individuals, though, negative outcomes function to confirm (rather than reduce) negative schemas that the world is dangerous and increase the probability of aggressive responding in the future.

In summary, a number of underlying processes are likely responsible for the relationships between trauma exposure, anger, mental health problems, and functional impairment in different domains. Much of the theory and research on these processes has used military personnel as participants, given the large number of service members who have been exposed to trauma as a result of the recent combat operations in Iraq and Afghanistan, as well as combat in Vietnam. Additional research is needed to determine the extent to which these different processes operate in employees exposed to trauma in other high-risk occupations.

Potential Benefits of Anger Expression in High-Risk Occupations

Virtually all the research conducted on anger in high-risk occupations, including the military, police officers, firefighters, and ambulance workers, has emphasized the negative effects of anger on the development of mental health problems and secondary effects on the employee and family members. Clearly, the traumatic events encountered by members of these occupations are capable of creating an anger that has a variety of dysfunctional consequences. Given the substantial evidence for the dysfunctional consequences of anger, addressing any beneficial effects of anger expression needs to be examined cautiously.

Importantly, much of the research examining the role of anger in the functioning of employees in high-risk occupations has taken a trait approach to assessing anger, implicitly assuming that exposure to trauma has the potential to affect trait anger in a way that results in additional negative consequences. Most of the research discussed in this chapter has also examined employee responses to anger without considering the organizational culture in which employees are embedded. Studies of military veterans involve personnel from a variety of civilian organizations, making it difficult to examine how organizational norms might influence the veteran's experience and expression of anger.

Studies of active duty military personnel and employees who are first responders have also typically focused on individual-level determinants and consequences of anger without considering how organizational norms within the unit shape the experience and expression of anger. Earlier in the chapter we discussed how the dual threshold model of Geddes and Callister (2007) addresses the organizational norms surrounding whether employees can express anger in the workplace and the extent to which anger can be expressed without being considered improper. Geddes et al. (2020) reviewed beneficial effects of employees being provided more space to discuss their experiences of anger and having the organization respond in a way that addresses sources of anger.

Within the context of anger experienced by employees in high-risk occupations, organizational norms supporting the expression of anger may buffer employees from the negative consequences identified in research discussed in this chapter. Geddes et al. (2020) discussed the large body of research documenting how the suppression of anger can result in negative consequences among employees and how organizational norms providing some space for expressing anger may help mitigate these negative consequences. Britt and McFadden (2012) noted that employees in high-risk occupations are typically embedded within highly cohesive units and that therefore these employees are highly responsive to the feedback and evaluation of their fellow unit members. It could be that employees who are able to express anger in a supportive environment may show fewer negative consequences than employees who suppress their experience of anger.

To our knowledge, research has not examined how organizational norms surrounding the experience and expression of anger influence the relationships between trauma exposure, anger, and mental health problems among employees in high-risk occupations. The extent to which employees are embedded within organizations characterized by an appropriate space for the expression of anger could serve as a moderator in the model described in Figure 2.1. For example, organizational norms for appropriate anger expression could buffer employees from the immediate consequences of trauma exposure, resulting in less anger experienced and potentially fewer hostile attributions for events that take place in the work environment. Additional research could also examine whether norms for the appropriate expression of anger within the organization has secondary benefits for the employee's evaluation of the organization, including greater perceived organizational support (Rhoades & Eisenberger, 2002) and psychosocial safety (Hall et al., 2010).

Finally, it may be important to consider how anger expression in different subgroups within an organization may be impacted by differential power among those groups. For example, women in the military may be in a disempowered position relative to men, both because there are fewer women in the military and because military culture tends to embrace traditional gender role norms and to value "masculine" qualities (Vogt et al., 2007). Research on anger expression in women and in racial minorities suggests that expression of anger from a disempowered position may be tolerated differently from expression of anger from those with higher status (Stevenson et al., 1997; S. A. Thomas & González-Prendes, 2009). Such differences in tolerance for anger expression may be particularly important to consider when trauma occurs within the context of the organization, such as in cases of military sexual trauma (Vogt et al., 2007) or institutionalized racism (McCluney et al., 2018).

FUTURE DIRECTIONS

A great deal of research has examined anger and its relationships with trauma exposure, mental health symptoms, and indices of functional impairment. The majority of this research has been completed with military personnel, with occasional studies involving employees in other high-risk occupations, including police officers, firefighters, and emergency medical technicians. Although some research has moved from a focus on the interrelationships between anger and other variables to the testing of theoretical mechanisms linking anger with important employee outcomes, more theory-guided research on anger in high-risk occupations is needed. The theoretical process described in Figure 2.1 was generated through an analysis of previous research among employees exposed to trauma, and one direction for future research is to examine whether the proposed theoretical model is supported in longitudinal investigations.

Additional areas for future research involve better clarifying anger-related concepts and using more real-time methods to assess anger experiences. Researchers need to clarify anger expression versus felt anger. Typically, we think of anger as the emotion and aggression as the act. However, the literature lacks consistency in how these anger-related concepts are conceptualized and assessed. Future research must also consider the measurement of anger in real time. Researchers typically use survey methods that are retrospective and rely on participants to think back to a certain time and reflect on the anger experience. However, this may not be the most effective way to understand the implications of anger. Experience sampling methods should be used with greater frequency to gain a better understanding of the proximal antecedents and consequences of anger episodes.

As mentioned in the last section of the chapter, future research should also better examine when and how anger expressions can be functional, especially in high-risk occupations. Conducting research on when anger expressions can have positive outcomes will require a closer examination of the organizational culture of high-risk occupations regarding how norms for anger expression influence how anger affects employee functioning. Studying teams will allow for an examination of how work units differ in anger expression norms (e.g., suppressing to legitimating) and how these norms influence individual and team functioning. These outcomes will likely depend on whether employee anger expressions do or do not match the prescriptions regarding anger displays in a given team or organization. In this regard, it may be important to consider how power, race, and gender interact to shape organizational norms around anger expression.

Finally, additional research is needed on how the experience and expression of anger among employees in high-risk occupations can spill over to colleagues or family members. In addition to the trauma-induced anger of these employees spilling over to others, many employees in high-risk occupations have emotional display rules characterized by stern, even angry, expressions when carrying out their job responsibilities. Research is needed to examine how this type of emotional labor (Grandey et al., 2015) affects those close to employees in high-risk occupations. Furthermore, organizations that provide the space for employees to express anger in the workplace may accrue a secondary benefit of less spillover anger to those close to the employee.

In summary, anger is only beginning to be examined as an occupational health challenge in high-risk occupations, and the majority of research on the predictors and consequences of anger in these occupations has been conducted with military personnel. Theory and research have also exclusively focused on the detrimental effects of anger among employees in high-risk occupations, neglecting the functional aspects that anger may display as an important emotion. It is our hope that the theory and research reviewed in the present chapter serve to motivate research investigating the multiple roles of anger in the functioning of employees in high-risk occupations.

IMPLICATIONS

- Researchers should use standard measures of state and trait anger to facilitate comparisons of anger prevalence and impact across occupations.
- Examine the possibility that expression of anger has beneficial effects under certain conditions for employees in high-risk occupations.
- Given the connection between trauma exposure and anger, employees and family members should be aware of the potential for anger and how best to respond in the face of anger.
- Study the organizational norms in high-risk occupations related to anger expression and examine whether these norms influence the relationship between anger and other outcomes.
- Conduct assessments of anger closer to when its experience actually occurred, rather than having employees reflect back to report on episodes of anger.

REFERENCES

Adrian, A. L., Skeiky, L., Burke, T. M., Gutierrez, I. A., & Adler, A. B. (2019). Sleep problems and functioning during initial training for a high-risk occupation. *Sleep Health*, *5*(6), 651–657. https://doi.org/10.1016/j.sleh.2019.06.009

American Psychiatric Association. (2000). *Diagnostic and statistical manual of mental disorders* (4th ed., text rev.).

American Psychiatric Association. (2013). *Diagnostic and statistical manual of mental disorders* (5th ed.). https://doi.org/10.1176/appi.books.9780890425596

Aquino, K., Douglas, S., & Martinko, M. J. (2004). Overt anger in response to victimization: Attributional style and organizational norms as moderators. *Journal of Occupational Health Psychology*, *9*(2), 152–164. https://doi.org/10.1037/1076-8998.9.2.152

Arbisi, P. A., Polusny, M. A., Erbes, C. R., Thuras, P., & Reddy, M. K. (2011). The Minnesota Multiphasic Personality Inventory–2 Restructured Form in National Guard soldiers screening positive for posttraumatic stress disorder and mild traumatic brain injury. *Psychological Assessment*, *23*(1), 203–214. https://doi.org/10.1037/a0021339

Armstrong, T., Bilsky, S. A., Zhao, M., & Olatunji, B. O. (2013). Dwelling on potential threat cues: An eye movement marker for combat-related PTSD. *Depression and Anxiety, 30*(5), 497–502. https://doi.org/10.1002/da.22115

Bailie, J. M., Cole, W. R., Ivins, B., Boyd, C., Lewis, S., Neff, J., & Schwab, K. (2015). The experience, expression, and control of anger following traumatic brain injury in a military sample. *The Journal of Head Trauma Rehabilitation, 30*(1), 12–20. https://doi.org/10.1097/HTR.0000000000000024

Barazzone, N., & Davey, G. C. (2009). Anger potentiates the reporting of threatening interpretations: An experimental study. *Journal of Anxiety Disorders, 23*(4), 489–495.

Beckham, J. C., Moore, S. D., & Reynolds, V. (2000). Interpersonal hostility and violence in Vietnam combat veterans with chronic posttraumatic stress disorder: A review of theoretical models and empirical evidence. *Aggression and Violent Behavior, 5*(5), 451–466. https://doi.org/10.1016/S1359-1789(98)00018-4

Bies, R. J., Tripp, T. M., & Kramer, R. M. (1997). At the breaking point: Cognitive and social dynamics of revenge in organizations. In R. Giacalone & J. Greenberg (Eds.), *Anti-social behavior in organizations* (pp. 18–36). Sage.

Blakey, S. M., Love, H., Lindquist, L., Beckham, J. C., & Elbogen, E. B. (2018). Disentangling the link between posttraumatic stress disorder and violent behavior: Findings from a nationally representative sample. *Journal of Consulting and Clinical Psychology, 86*(2), 169–178. https://doi.org/10.1037/ccp0000253

Bohl, N. (1991). The effectiveness of brief psychological interventions in police officers after critical incidents. In J. Reese, J. M. Horn, & C. Dunning (Eds.), *Critical incidents in policing: Revised* (pp. 31–38). U.S. Government Printing Office.

Bond, A. J., Verheyden, S. L., Wingrove, J., & Curran, H. V. (2004). Angry cognitive bias, trait aggression and impulsivity in substance users. *Psychopharmacology, 171*(3), 331–339.

Booth, J., Ireland, J. L., Mann, S., Eslea, M. J., & Holyoak, L. (2017). Anger expression and suppression in the workplace: Causes, characteristics and predictors. *International Journal of Conflict Management, 28*(3), 368–382. https://doi.org/10.1108/IJCMA-06-2016-0044

Britt, T. W., & McFadden, A. (2012). Understanding mental health treatment seeking in high stress occupations. In J. Houdmont, S. Leka, & R. Sinclair (Eds.), *Contemporary occupational health psychology: Global perspectives on research and practice* (pp. 57–73). Wiley-Blackwell Publishers. https://doi.org/10.1002/9781119942849.ch4

Buckley, T. C., Blanchard, E. B., & Neill, W. T. (2000). Information processing and PTSD: A review of the empirical literature. *Clinical Psychology Review, 20*(8), 1041–1065. https://doi.org/10.1016/S0272-7358(99)00030-6

Cash, R., Varker, T., McHugh, T., Metcalf, O., Howard, A., Lloyd, D., Costello, J., Said, D., & Forbes, D. (2018). Effectiveness of an anger intervention for military members with PTSD: A clinical case series. *Military Medicine, 183*(9–10), e286–e290. https://doi.org/10.1093/milmed/usx115

Chemtob, C. M., Roitblat, H. L., Hamada, R. S., Carlson, J. G., & Twentyman, C. T. (1988). A cognitive action theory of post-traumatic stress disorder. *Journal of Anxiety Disorders, 2*(3), 253–275. https://doi.org/10.1016/0887-6185(88)90006-0

Cheshin, A. (2020). The impact of non-normative displays of emotion in the workplace: How inappropriateness shapes the interpersonal outcomes of emotional displays. *Frontiers in Psychology, 11*, Article 6. https://doi.org/10.3389/fpsyg.2020.00006

Clark, M. E. (1994). Interpretive limitations of the MMPI-2 anger and cynicism content scales. *Journal of Personality Assessment, 63*(1), 89–96. https://doi.org/10.1207/s15327752jpa6301_7

Dedert, E. A., Calhoun, P. S., Watkins, L. L., Sherwood, A., & Beckham, J. C. (2010). Posttraumatic stress disorder, cardiovascular, and metabolic disease: A review of the evidence. *Annals of Behavioral Medicine, 39*(1), 61–78. https://doi.org/10.1007/s12160-010-9165-9

Deffenbacher, J. L., Demm, P. M., & Brandon, A. D. (1986). High general anger: Correlates and treatment. *Behaviour Research and Therapy, 24*(4), 481–489. https://doi.org/10.1016/0005-7967(86)90014-8

Dodge, K. A. (1980). Social cognition and children's aggressive behavior. *Child Development, 51*(1), 162–170. https://doi.org/10.2307/1129603

Eckhardt, C., Norlander, B., & Deffenbacher, J. (2004). The assessment of anger and hostility: A critical review. *Aggression and Violent Behavior, 9*(1), 17–43. https://doi.org/10.1016/S1359-1789(02)00116-7

Elbogen, E. B., Johnson, S. C., Newton, V. M., Straits-Troster, K., Vasterling, J. J., Wagner, H. R., & Beckham, J. C. (2012). Criminal justice involvement, trauma, and negative affect in Iraq and Afghanistan war era veterans. *Journal of Consulting and Clinical Psychology, 80*(6), 1097–1102. https://doi.org/10.1037/a0029967

Elbogen, E. B., Johnson, S. C., Wagner, H. R., Sullivan, C., Taft, C. T., & Beckham, J. C. (2014). Violent behaviour and post-traumatic stress disorder in US Iraq and Afghanistan veterans. *The British Journal of Psychiatry, 204*(5), 368–375. https://doi.org/10.1192/bjp.bp.113.134627

Elbogen, E. B., Wagner, H. R., Fuller, S. R., Calhoun, P. S., Kinneer, P. M., Beckham, J. C., & the Mid-Atlantic Mental Illness Research, Education, and Clinical Center Workgroup. (2010). Correlates of anger and hostility in Iraq and Afghanistan War veterans. *The American Journal of Psychiatry, 167*(9), 1051–1058. https://doi.org/10.1176/appi.ajp.2010.09050739

Ellis-Woroch, B. (2013). *A statistical examination of the relationship between workplace anger and hatred* [Unpublished doctoral dissertation]. Capella University.

Epps, J., & Kendall, P. C. (1995). Hostile attributional bias in adults. *Cognitive Therapy and Research, 19*(2), 159–178.

Evans, L., McHugh, T., Hopwood, M., & Watt, C. (2003). Chronic posttraumatic stress disorder and family functioning of Vietnam veterans and their partners. *Australian & New Zealand Journal of Psychiatry, 37*(6), 765–772.

Evans, S., Giosan, C., Patt, I., Spielman, L., & Difede, J. (2006). Anger and its association to distress and social/occupational functioning in symptomatic disaster relief workers responding to the September 11, 2001, World Trade Center disaster. *Journal of Traumatic Stress, 19*(1), 147–152. https://doi.org/10.1002/jts.20107

Faye, A., Kalra, G., Swamy, R., Shukla, A., Subramanyam, A., & Kamath, R. (2011). Study of emotional intelligence and empathy in medical postgraduates. *Indian Journal of Psychiatry, 53*(2), 140–144. https://doi.org/10.4103/0019-5545.82541

Foa, E. B., Riggs, D. S., Massie, E. D., & Yarczower, M. (1995). The impact of fear activation and anger on the efficacy of exposure treatment for posttraumatic stress disorder. *Behavior Therapy, 26*(3), 487–499. https://doi.org/10.1016/S0005-7894(05)80096-6

Forbes, D., Alkemade, N., Hopcraft, D., Hawthorne, G., O'Halloran, P., Elhai, J. D., McHugh, T., Bates, G., Novaco, R. W., Bryant, R., & Lewis, V. (2014). Evaluation of the Dimensions of Anger Reactions-5 (DAR-5) scale in combat veterans with posttraumatic stress disorder. *Journal of Anxiety Disorders, 28*(8), 830–835. https://doi.org/10.1016/j.janxdis.2014.09.015

Frueh, B. C., Henning, K. R., Pellegrin, K. L., & Chobot, K. (1997). Relationship between scores on anger measures and PTSD symptomatology, employment, and compensation-seeking status in combat veterans. *Journal of Clinical Psychology, 53*(8), 871–878. https://doi.org/10.1002/(SICI)1097-4679(199712)53:8<871::AID-JCLP12>3.0.CO;2-H

Galovski, T., & Lyons, J. A. (2004). Psychological sequelae of combat violence: A review of the impact of PTSD on the veteran's family and possible interventions. *Aggression and Violent Behavior, 9*(5), 477–501. https://doi.org/10.1016/S1359-1789(03)00045-4

Geck, C. M., Grimbos, T., Siu, M., Klassen, P. E., & Seto, M. C. (2017). Violence at work: An examination of aggressive, violent, and repeatedly violent employees. *Journal of Threat Assessment and Management, 4*(4), 210–229. https://doi.org/10.1037/tam0000091

Geddes, D., & Callister, R. R. (2007). Crossing the line(s): A dual threshold model of anger in organizations. *Academy of Management Review, 32*(3), 721–746. https://doi.org/10.5465/amr.2007.25275495

Geddes, D., Callister, R. R., & Gibson, D. E. (2020). A message in the madness: Functions of workplace anger in organizational life. *The Academy of Management Perspectives, 34*(1), 28–47. https://doi.org/10.5465/amp.2016.0158

Gendolla, G. H. E. (2014). Comment: Emotions are functional—so . . .? *Emotion Review, 6*(4), 317–318. https://doi.org/10.1177/1754073914534496

Geoffrion, S., Goncalves, J., Sader, J., Boyer, R., Marchand, A., & Guay, S. (2017). Workplace aggression against health care workers, law enforcement officials, and bus drivers: Differences in prevalence, perceptions, and psychological consequences. *Journal of Workplace Behavioral Health, 32*(3), 172–189. https://doi.org/10.1080/15555240.2017.1349611

Gerlock, A. A. (1994). Veterans' responses to anger management intervention. *Issues in Mental Health Nursing, 15*(4), 393–408. https://doi.org/10.3109/01612849409006916

Gerzina, M. A., & Drummond, P. D. (2000). A multimodal cognitive-behavioural approach to anger reduction in an occupational sample. *Journal of Occupational and Organizational Psychology, 73*(2), 181–194. https://doi.org/10.1348/096317900166976

Glasø, L., Bele, E., Nielsen, M. B., & Einarsen, S. (2011). Bus drivers' exposure to bullying at work: An occupation-specific approach. *Scandinavian Journal of Psychology, 52*(5), 484–493. https://doi.org/10.1111/j.1467-9450.2011.00895.x

Gonzalez, O. I., Novaco, R. W., Reger, M. A., & Gahm, G. A. (2016). Anger intensification with combat-related PTSD and depression comorbidity. *Psychological Trauma: Theory, Research, Practice, and Policy, 8*(1), 9–16. https://doi.org/10.1037/tra0000042

Graham, J. R. (1993). *MMPI-2 assessing personality and psychopathology*. Oxford University Press.

Grandey, A. A., Rupp, D., & Brice, W. N. (2015). Emotional labor threatens decent work: A proposal to eradicate emotional display rules. *Journal of Organizational Behavior, 36*(6), 770–785. https://doi.org/10.1002/job.2020

Hall, G. B., Dollard, M. F., & Coward, J. (2010). Psychosocial safety climate: Development of the PSC-12. *International Journal of Stress Management, 17*(4), 353–383. https://doi.org/10.1037/a0021320

Hawthorne, G., Mouthaan, J., Forbes, D., & Novaco, R. W. (2006). Response categories and anger measurement: Do fewer categories result in poorer measurement? Development of the DAR5. *Social Psychiatry and Psychiatric Epidemiology, 41*(2), 164–172. https://doi.org/10.1007/s00127-005-0986-y

Hayes, J. P., Vanelzakker, M. B., & Shin, L. M. (2012). Emotion and cognition interactions in PTSD: A review of neurocognitive and neuroimaging studies. *Frontiers in Integrative Neuroscience, 6*, Article 89. https://doi.org/10.3389/fnint.2012.00089

Hazebroek, J. F., Howells, K., & Day, A. (2001). Cognitive appraisals associated with high trait anger. *Personality and Individual Differences, 30*(1), 31–45. https://doi.org/10.1016/S0191-8869(00)00007-6

Heinrichs, M., Wagner, D., Schoch, W., Soravia, L. M., Hellhammer, D. H., & Ehlert, U. (2005). Predicting posttraumatic stress symptoms from pretraumatic risk factors: A 2-year prospective follow-up study in firefighters. *American Journal of Psychiatry, 162*(12), 2276–2286. https://doi.org/10.1176/appi.ajp.162.12.2276

Hershcovis, M. S., Turner, N., Barling, J., Arnold, K. A., Dupré, K. E., Inness, M., LeBlanc, M. M., & Sivanathan, N. (2007). Predicting workplace aggression: A meta-analysis. *The Journal of Applied Psychology, 92*(1), 228–238. https://doi.org/10.1037/0021-9010.92.1.228

Inness, M., Leblanc, M. M., & Barling, J. (2008). Psychosocial predictors of supervisor-, peer-, subordinate-, and service-provider-targeted aggression. *The Journal of Applied Psychology, 93*(6), 1401–1411. https://doi.org/10.1037/a0012810

Jones, J. P., Thomas-Peter, B. A., & Trout, A. (1999). Normative data for the Novaco Anger Scale from a non-clinical sample and implications for clinical use. *The British Journal of Clinical Psychology, 38*(4), 417–424. https://doi.org/10.1348/014466599163024

Keyes, J. B., & Dean, S. F. (1988). Stress inoculation training for direct contact staff working with mentally retarded persons. *Behavioral Interventions, 3*(4), 315–323. https://doi.org/10.1002/bin.2360030406

Leonard, R., & Alison, L. (1999). Critical incident stress debriefing and its effects on coping strategies and anger in a sample of Australian police officers involved in shooting incidents. *Work and Stress, 13*(2), 144–161. https://doi.org/10.1080/026783799296110

Lindebaum, D., Jordan, P. J., & Morris, L. (2016). Symmetrical and asymmetrical outcomes of leader anger expression: A qualitative study of army personnel. *Human Relations, 69*(2), 277–300. https://doi.org/10.1177/0018726715593350

Linkh, D. J., & Sonnek, S. M. (2003). An application of cognitive-behavioral anger management training in a military/occupational setting: Efficacy and demographic factors. *Military Medicine, 168*(6), 475–478. https://doi.org/10.1093/milmed/168.6.475

Mackintosh, M. A., Morland, L. A., Frueh, B. C., Greene, C. J., & Rosen, C. S. (2014). Peeking into the black box: Mechanisms of action for anger management treatment. *Journal of Anxiety Disorders, 28*(7), 687–695. https://doi.org/10.1016/j.janxdis.2014.07.001

Mackintosh, M. A., Morland, L. A., Kloezeman, K., Greene, C. J., Rosen, C. S., Elhai, J. D., & Frueh, B. C. (2014). Predictors of anger treatment outcomes. *Journal of Clinical Psychology, 70*(10), 905–913. https://doi.org/10.1002/jclp.22095

Maguire, B. J. (2018). Violence against ambulance personnel: A retrospective cohort study of national data from Safe Work Australia. *Public Health Research & Practice, 28*(1), e28011805. https://doi.org/10.17061/phrp28011805

McCluney, C. L., Schmitz, L. L., Hicken, M. T., & Sonnega, A. (2018). Structural racism in the workplace: Does perception matter for health inequalities? *Social Science & Medicine, 199*, 106–114. https://doi.org/10.1016/j.socscimed.2017.05.039

McFall, M. E., Wright, P. W., Donovan, D. M., & Raskind, M. (1999). Multidimensional assessment of anger in Vietnam veterans with posttraumatic stress disorder. *Comprehensive Psychiatry, 40*(3), 216–220. https://doi.org/10.1016/S0010-440X(99)90006-8

McLinton, S., & Dollard, M. F. (2013). How we look at others in anger: Development of the McLinton interpersonal domain-specific anger instrument (MIDAI). In M. G. Penrod & S. N. Paulk (Eds.), *Psychology of anger: New research* (pp. 1–26). Nova Science Publishers.

Mearns, J., & Mauch, T. G. (1998). Negative mood regulation expectancies predict anger among police officers and buffer the effects of job stress. *The Journal of Nervous and Mental Disease, 186*(2), 120–125. https://doi.org/10.1097/00005053-199802000-00008

Meffert, S. M., Metzler, T. J., Henn-Haase, C., McCaslin, S., Inslicht, S., Chemtob, C., Neylan, T., & Marmar, C. R. (2008). A prospective study of trait anger and PTSD symptoms in police. *Journal of Traumatic Stress, 21*(4), 410–416. https://doi.org/10.1002/jts.20350

Morland, L. A., Love, A. R., Mackintosh, M. A., Greene, C. J., & Rosen, C. S. (2012). Treating anger and aggression in military populations: Research updates and clinical implications. *Clinical Psychology: Science and Practice, 19*(3), 305–322. https://doi.org/10.1111/cpsp.12007

Novaco, R. W. (1974). *The effect of disposition for anger and degree of provocation on self-report and physiological measures of anger in various modes of provocation* [Unpublished manuscript]. Indiana University.

Novaco, R. W. (1975). *Anger control: The development and evaluation of an experimental treatment*. Lexington Books.

Novaco, R. W. (1988). Novaco Provocation Inventory. In M. Hersen & A. Bellack (Eds.), *Dictionary of dissent techniques* (pp. 315–317). Pergamon Press.

Novaco, R. W. (1994). Anger as a risk factor for violence among the mentally disordered. In J. Monahan & H. J. Steadman (Eds.), *The John D. and Catherine T. MacArthur Foundation series on mental health and development. Violence and mental disorder: Developments in risk assessment* (p. 21–59). The University of Chicago Press.

Novaco, R. W. (2003). *The Novaco Anger Scale and Provocation Inventory: NAS-PI* [Measurement instrument]. Western Psychological Services.

Novaco, R. W., & Chemtob, C. M. (2002). Anger and combat-related posttraumatic stress disorder. *Journal of Traumatic Stress, 15*(2), 123–132. https://doi.org/10.1023/A:1014855924072

Novaco, R. W., & Chemtob, C. M. (2015). Violence associated with combat-related posttraumatic stress disorder: The importance of anger. *Psychological Trauma: Theory, Research, Practice and Policy, 7*(5), 485–492. https://doi.org/10.1037/tra0000067

Novaco, R. W., Swanson, R. D., Gonzalez, O. I., Gahm, G. A., & Reger, M. D. (2012). Anger and postcombat mental health: Validation of a brief anger measure with U.S. soldiers postdeployed from Iraq and Afghanistan. *Psychological Assessment, 24*(3), 661–675. https://doi.org/10.1037/a0026636

Olatunji, B. O., Ciesielski, B. G., & Tolin, D. F. (2010). Fear and loathing: A meta-analytic review of the specificity of anger in PTSD. *Behavior Therapy, 41*(1), 93–105. https://doi.org/10.1016/j.beth.2009.01.004

Orth, U., & Wieland, E. (2006). Anger, hostility, and posttraumatic stress disorder in trauma-exposed adults: A meta-analysis. *Journal of Consulting and Clinical Psychology, 74*(4), 698–706. https://doi.org/10.1037/0022-006X.74.4.698

Pineles, S. L., Shipherd, J. C., Welch, L. P., & Yovel, I. (2007). The role of attentional biases in PTSD: Is it interference or facilitation? *Behaviour Research and Therapy, 45*(8), 1903–1913. https://doi.org/10.1016/j.brat.2006.08.021

Pineles, S. L., Vogt, D. S., & Orr, S. P. (2009). Personality and fear responses during conditioning: Beyond extraversion. *Personality and Individual Differences, 46*(1), 48–53. https://doi.org/10.1016/j.paid.2008.09.003

Possis, E., Bui, T., Gavian, M., Leskela, J., Linardatos, E., Loughlin, J., & Strom, T. (2014). Driving difficulties among military veterans: Clinical needs and current intervention status. *Military Medicine, 179*(6), 633–639. https://doi.org/10.7205/MILMED-D-13-00327

Power, M. J., & Fyvie, C. (2013). The role of emotion in PTSD: Two preliminary studies. *Behavioural and Cognitive Psychotherapy, 41*(2), 162–172. https://doi.org/10.1017/S1352465812000148

Raab, P. A., Mackintosh, M. A., Gros, D. F., & Morland, L. A. (2013). Influence of depression on state and trait anger in veterans with posttraumatic stress disorder. *Cognitive Therapy and Research, 37*(4), 673–679. https://doi.org/10.1007/s10608-012-9506-z

Rhoades, L., & Eisenberger, R. (2002). Perceived organizational support: A review of the literature. *The Journal of Applied Psychology, 87*(4), 698–714. https://doi.org/10.1037/0021-9010.87.4.698

Rogers, M. L., Kelliher-Rabon, J., Hagan, C. R., Hirsch, J. K., & Joiner, T. E. (2017). Negative emotions in veterans relate to suicide risk through feelings of perceived burdensomeness and thwarted belongingness. *Journal of Affective Disorders, 208*, 15–21. https://doi.org/10.1016/j.jad.2016.09.038

Savarese, V. W., Suvak, M. K., King, L. A., & King, D. W. (2001). Relationships among alcohol use, hyperarousal, and marital abuse and violence in Vietnam veterans. *Journal of Traumatic Stress, 14*(4), 717–732. https://doi.org/10.1023/A:1013038021175

Sawhney, G., Jennings, K. S., Britt, T. W., & Sliter, M. T. (2018). Occupational stress and mental health symptoms: Examining the moderating effect of work recovery strategies in firefighters. *Journal of Occupational Health Psychology, 23*(3), 443–456. https://doi.org/10.1037/ocp0000091

Sayer, N. A., Noorbaloochi, S., Frazier, P., Carlson, K., Gravely, A., & Murdoch, M. (2010). Reintegration problems and treatment interests among Iraq and Afghanistan combat veterans receiving VA medical care. *Psychiatric Services, 61*(6), 589–597. https://doi.org/10.1176/ps.2010.61.6.589

Shahsavarani, A. M., Noohi, S., Jafari, S., Hakimi Kalkhoran, M., & Hatefi, S. (2015). Assessment & measurement of anger in behavioral and social sciences: A systematic review of literature. *International Journal of Medical Reviews, 2*(3), 279–286.

Shea, M. T., Lambert, J., & Reddy, M. K. (2013). A randomized pilot study of anger treatment for Iraq and Afghanistan veterans. *Behaviour Research and Therapy, 51*(10), 607–613. https://doi.org/10.1016/j.brat.2013.05.013

Siegel, J. M. (1986). The Multidimensional Anger Inventory. *Journal of Personality and Social Psychology, 51*(1), 191–200. https://doi.org/10.1037/0022-3514.51.1.191

Sippel, L. M., Mota, N. P., Kachadourian, L. K., Krystal, J. H., Southwick, S. M., Harpaz-Rotem, I., & Pietrzak, R. H. (2016). The burden of hostility in US veterans: Results from the National Health and Resilience in Veterans Study. *Psychiatry Research, 243*, 421–430.

Sliter, M. T., Pui, S. Y., Sliter, K. A., & Jex, S. M. (2011). The differential effects of interpersonal conflict from customers and coworkers: Trait anger as a moderator. *Journal of Occupational Health Psychology, 16*(4), 424–440. https://doi.org/10.1037/a0023874

Snell, W. E., Jr., Gum, S., Shuck, R. L., Mosley, J. A., & Hite, T. L. (1995). The Clinical Anger Scale: Preliminary reliability and validity. *Journal of Clinical Psychology, 51*(2), 215–226. https://doi.org/10.1002/1097-4679(199503)51:2<215::AID-JCLP2270510211>3.0.CO;2-Z

Spielberger, C. D. (1988). *Manual for the State–Trait Anger Expression Scale (STAXI)*. Psychological Assessment Resources.

Spielberger, C. D. (1999). *State–Trait Anger Expression Inventory-2 (STAXI-2): Professional manual*. Psychological Assessment Resources.

Spielberger, C. D., Jacobs, G., Russell, S., & Crane, R. S. (1983). Assessment of anger: The State–Trait Anger Scale. In J. N. Butcher & C. D. Spielberger (Eds.), *Advances in personality assessment* (pp. 159–187). Lawrence Erlbaum Associates.

Stevenson, H. C., Reed, J., Bodison, P., & Bishop, A. (1997). Racism stress management: Racial socialization beliefs and the experience of depression and anger in African American youth. *Youth & Society, 29*(2), 197–222. https://doi.org/10.1177/0044118X97029002003

Taft, C. T., Kaloupek, D. G., Schumm, J. A., Marshall, A. D., Panuzio, J., King, D. W., & Keane, T. M. (2007). Posttraumatic stress disorder symptoms, physiological reactivity, alcohol problems, and aggression among military veterans. *Journal of Abnormal Psychology, 116*(3), 498–507. https://doi.org/10.1037/0021-843X.116.3.498

Thomas, J. L., Wilk, J. E., Riviere, L. A., McGurk, D., Castro, C. A., & Hoge, C. W. (2010). Prevalence of mental health problems and functional impairment among active component and National Guard soldiers 3 and 12 months following combat in Iraq. *Archives of General Psychiatry, 67*(6), 614–623. https://doi.org/10.1001/archgenpsychiatry.2010.54

Thomas, S. A., & González-Prendes, A. A. (2009). Powerlessness, anger, and stress in African American women: Implications for physical and emotional health. *Health Care for Women International, 30*(1–2), 93–113. https://doi.org/10.1080/07399330802523709

Van Voorhees, E. E., Moore, D. A., Kimbrel, N. A., Dedert, E. A., Dillon, K. H., Elbogen, E. B., & Calhoun, P. S. (2018). Association of posttraumatic stress disorder and traumatic brain injury with aggressive driving in Iraq and Afghanistan combat veterans. *Rehabilitation Psychology, 63*(1), 160–166. https://doi.org/10.1037/rep0000178

van Zuiden, M., Kavelaars, A., Rademaker, A. R., Vermetten, E., Heijnen, C. J., & Geuze, E. (2011). A prospective study on personality and the cortisol awakening response to predict posttraumatic stress symptoms in response to military deployment. *Journal of Psychiatric Research*, *45*(6), 713–719. https://doi.org/10.1016/j.jpsychires.2010.11.013

Vogt, D., Bruce, T. A., Street, A. E., & Stafford, J. (2007). Attitudes toward women and tolerance for sexual harassment among reservists. *Violence Against Women*, *13*(9), 879–900. https://doi.org/10.1177/1077801207305217

Vrana, S. R., Hughes, J. W., Dennis, M. F., Calhoun, P. S., & Beckham, J. C. (2009). Effects of posttraumatic stress disorder status and covert hostility on cardiovascular responses to relived anger in women with and without PTSD. *Biological Psychology*, *82*(3), 274–280.

Wenzel, A., & Lystad, C. (2005). Interpretation biases in angry and anxious individuals. *Behaviour Research and Therapy*, *43*(8), 1045–1054. https://doi.org/10.1016/j.brat.2004.02.009

Wilk, J. E., Quartana, P. J., Clarke-Walper, K., Kok, B. C., & Riviere, L. A. (2015). Aggression in US soldiers post-deployment: Associations with combat exposure and PTSD and the moderating role of trait anger. *Aggressive Behavior*, *41*(6), 556–565. https://doi.org/10.1002/ab.21595

Wilkowski, B. M., & Robinson, M. D. (2010). The anatomy of anger: An integrative cognitive model of trait anger and reactive aggression. *Journal of Personality*, *78*(1), 9–38. https://doi.org/10.1111/j.1467-6494.2009.00607.x

Wilks, C. R., Morland, L. A., Dillon, K. H., Mackintosh, M. A., Blakey, S. M., Wagner, H. R., Elbogen, E. B., & the VA Mid-Atlantic MIRECC Workgroup. (2019). Anger, social support, and suicide risk in U.S. military veterans. *Journal of Psychiatric Research*, *109*, 139–144. https://doi.org/10.1016/j.jpsychires.2018.11.026

World Health Organization. (2001). *International classification of functioning, disability and health (ICF)*. http://www.WHO.int/classifications/icf/en/

Worthen, M., Rathod, S. D., Cohen, G., Sampson, L., Ursano, R., Gifford, R., Fullerton, C., Galea, S., & Ahern, J. (2014). Anger problems and posttraumatic stress disorder in male and female National Guard and Reserve Service members. *Journal of Psychiatric Research*, *55*, 52–58. https://doi.org/10.1016/j.jpsychires.2014.04.004

Worthen, M., Rathod, S. D., Cohen, G., Sampson, L., Ursano, R., Gifford, R., Fullerton, C., Galea, S., & Ahern, J. (2015). Anger and posttraumatic stress disorder symptom severity in a trauma-exposed military population: Differences by trauma context and gender. *Journal of Traumatic Stress*, *28*(6), 539–546. https://doi.org/10.1002/jts.22050

PART II ORGANIZATIONAL CONTEXT

3 MORAL INJURY AND ANGER IN THE WORKPLACE

ANDREA J. PHELPS, LISA DELL, AND KIM MURRAY

Of all the differences between man and the lower animals the moral sense or conscience is by far the most important.

—Charles Darwin (1871)

KEY POINTS

- Moral injury is a relatively new concept used to capture the psychosocial and spiritual impacts of events that involve betrayal or other deep transgressions of one's moral code and occur in high-stakes situations.
- The link between moral injury and anger is mediated by three key appraisals: betrayal (by leaders, the team, the organization), injustice (when others violate one's moral code), and shame (when one violates one's own moral code).

(*continues*)

https://doi.org/10.1037/0000244-004
Anger at Work: Prevention, Intervention, and Treatment in High-Risk Occupations, A. B. Adler and D. Forbes (Editors)

KEY POINTS (*Continued*)

- The relationship between moral injury and anger may be perpetuated by a vicious cycle of low detection threshold and high anger reactivity to further instances of betrayal, injustice, and/or shame.
- Moral injury at work can lead to the development of psychological disorders such as posttraumatic stress disorder and depression and can signal a psychological break with the organization.

Moral injury is an important new concept linked to high-stakes situations that can occur in high-risk organizations and has implications for clinical distress and occupational functioning. This chapter examines the link between moral injury and anger, mediated by three key appraisals of potentially morally injurious events (PMIEs):

- betrayal (by leaders, the team, the organization)
- injustice (when others violate one's moral code)
- shame (when one violates one's own moral code)

A conceptual model of the cycle of moral injury and anger is presented, with an emphasis on how this cyclical relationship may signal impending psychological disorder but also a psychological break with the organization. Finally, implications for workplace policies and procedures are discussed.

In the field of posttraumatic mental health, posttraumatic stress disorder (PTSD) has long been considered the signature disorder. Dominant models of PTSD (Brewin et al., 1996; Ehlers & Clark, 2000; Foa & Rothbaum, 1989) emphasize fear-based mechanisms in the development of the disorder. However, there is increasing recognition that the full range of reactions and impacts of exposure to war and other traumatic events involves emotions other than fear. In particular, traumatic events that involve transgression of one's moral code can lead to emotions such as shame and betrayal, which are mechanisms for the development of moral injury (Drescher et al., 2011; Litz et al., 2009). Most of the research into moral injury to date has been undertaken with military populations, but the concept also applies to the broader range of workers who are confronted with moral dilemmas in high-stakes situations during the course of their employment.

MORAL INJURY

Moral injury is a relatively new concept but growing rapidly in popularity. The term was first coined by American psychiatrist Jonathan Shay and stemmed from his extensive work with Vietnam veterans. In his seminal writing, *Achilles in Vietnam,* Shay (1994) drew parallels between the moral undoing of Achilles and the lived experience of the Vietnam veterans with whom he was working. His observation highlighted that since antiquity, military personnel have been confronted with moral insults and faced ethical dilemmas during the course of service. Importantly, these experiences can leave lasting impacts that go beyond periods of operational deployment (McCormack & Ell, 2017). Modern insurgencies, and post-9/11 conflicts in particular, have amplified these issues (Phelps et al., 2015). Such conflicts often require soldiers to act in multiple roles, including humanitarian aid, peacekeeping operations, and combat, in complex and dynamic environments where a soldier's values are constantly challenged (Evans, 2015). The ethical minefield associated with modern insurgencies increases the moral burden on modern service members.

Early definitions of moral injury emphasized the nature of morally injurious events themselves rather than their psychosocial and spiritual outcomes. Shay (2012) proposed that moral injury can be defined as a "(i) betrayal of what's right (ii) by someone who holds legitimate authority (in the military—a leader) (iii) in a high-stakes situation" (p. 59). His definition highlights the relational aspect of moral injury between soldiers, command, and the military culture as a whole. In times of high duress, a breakdown of trust is deeply harmful, and recent qualitative research with veterans of post-9/11 conflicts echo these sentiments, with "Military leadership perceived as incompetent and 'out of touch' with life on the ground" and "Military leadership perceived as self-serving and uncaring" among the most common cited organizational factors leading to moral injury (Currier, McCormick, & Drescher, 2015, p. 110).

Litz and colleagues (2009) popularized the term *moral injury* in the past decade, defining it as "the lasting psychological, biological, spiritual, behavioral and social impact of perpetrating, failing to prevent, or bearing witness to acts that transgress deeply held moral beliefs and expectations" (p. 697). In this definition, one's own personal value system takes center stage, as do one's own actions or inactions. A later definition focuses more on the impact of the event, characterizing the outcome of moral injury as "disruption in an individual's confidence and expectations about one's own or others' motivation or capacity to behave in a just and ethical manner" (Drescher et al., 2011, p. 9).

Although there is not yet a consensus definition of moral injury, there *is* consensus on the need to separate the morally injurious event itself from the impacts and on the importance of both components for the empirical study of this field to advance (Frankfurt & Frazier, 2016).

POTENTIALLY MORALLY INJURIOUS EVENTS

The use of the term *potentially morally injurious event* recognizes that such events do not inevitably lead to moral injury in the same way that potentially traumatic events do not inevitably lead to PTSD. Similarly, just as all stressful events do not satisfy the Criterion A stressor for PTSD, all morally challenging events would not be considered potentially morally injurious. Litz and Kerig (2019) presented moral stressors as lying on a continuum of potential for psychological, social, and spiritual harm and impairment. Moral challenges lie at the least severe end of the continuum. These events are highly prevalent but associated with minimal harm characterized by the authors as moral frustration. Moral stressors are located midway along the continuum. These events are less prevalent than moral challenges and have potential for moderate harm, termed *moral distress*. PMIEs lie at the most severe end of the continuum. These are low-prevalence events with potential for the most extreme harm or impairment, termed moral injury.

In general terms, Litz et al. (2009) described the scope of PMIEs as including acts of commission or omission, behaviors of others in the work group, and bearing witness to human suffering or horrific acts of violence perpetrated by oneself or by others. More specifically, events that may give rise to moral injury have been described as bearing witness to perceived immoral acts; failure to stop such actions; or perpetration of immoral acts, in particular, actions that are inhumane, cruel, depraved, or violent, bringing about pain, suffering, or death of others (Drescher et al., 2011); killing (Maguen et al., 2010); and combat losses (Currier & Holland, 2012).

Drescher and colleagues (2011) undertook a series of interviews with mental health providers, chaplains, researchers, and policymakers to identify subtypes of PMIEs. The four emergent themes related to betrayal by leaders, peers, trusted significant others, or oneself; disproportionate violence against the enemy; violence or property damage against civilians; and within-rank violence, including sexual trauma, friendly fire, and fragging.

The two most widely used scales that assess exposure to a PMIE are the Moral Injury Events Scale (Nash et al., 2013) and the Moral Injury

Questionnaire–Military Version (Currier, Holland, Drescher, & Foy, 2015). Key features of the two scales are presented in Table 3.1. Strengths of the Moral Injury Questionnaire–Military Version are that the questions are concrete and have been specifically tailored for those working with military samples that have been deployed. On the other hand, the Moral Injury Events Scale's broader questioning, which does not directly reference operational deployment experiences, makes it more generally applicable to military personnel overall. Both questionnaires, however, are limited by the inclusion of questions asking about experiencing a PMIE and the impacts simultaneously (Frankfurt & Frazier, 2016). Examples include "I am troubled by having acted in ways that violated my own morals or values" (Nash et al., 2013) and "I feel guilt over failing to save the life of someone in the war" (Currier, Holland, Drescher, & Foy, 2015).

Although most of the research to date has been with military personnel, the potential for exposure to similar events for workers in other high-risk organizations is clear. The most obvious among these are perhaps first responder organizations (police, fire, ambulance), but it could also apply to health, welfare, and aid workers and journalists deployed into high-stakes environments, domestically or overseas. A recent systematic review of mental health outcomes of PMIEs in occupational settings (Williamson et al., 2018), for example, identified four empirical studies of work-related moral injury for populations other than military: journalists who covered the 2011 Norway terror attack, teachers exposed to community violence in El Salvador, police officers who killed or seriously injured someone in the line of duty, and veterinarians who faced moral challenges in the course of their practice (e.g., euthanizing animals for reasons they did not agree with). Further, during the COVID-19 pandemic, the overburdening of health care systems

TABLE 3.1. Key Features of the MIES and MIQ-M

MIES	MIQ-M
• 9 items	• 20 items
• Developed using theoretical basis of PMIEs and expert consensus	• Assesses PMIEs that occur in war zone deployments, with items based on the empirical research of Drescher et al. (2011) as well as theoretical sources (Shay, 1994)
• Items loaded onto two factors: perceived transgression of moral codes by self or others and perceived betrayal of trust by others	• Items loaded onto a single factor and included betrayal, disproportionate violence, death/harm to civilians, within rank violence, inability to prevent death/suffering, and moral conflicts from decisions or actions

Note. MIES = Moral Injury Events Scale (Nash et al., 2013); MIQ-M = Moral Injury Questionnaire-Military Version (Currier, Holland, Drescher, & Foy, 2015); PMIE = potentially morally injurious event.

leading to a shortage of intensive care hospital beds, ventilators, and personal protective equipment has been identified as putting health care workers at risk of exposure to PMIEs (Williamson et al., 2020).

Of course, moral challenges can arise in many work roles outside of those operating in high-stakes situations or with exposure to potentially traumatic events. Lawyers, social workers, child protection officers, and refugee advocates, for example, deal with morally confronting circumstances as a matter of routine in the course of their work. They may well experience moral pain (a concept we elaborate later), but unless these events occur in the context of a high-stakes situation—which they may at times—their experience would not constitute exposure to a PMIE as currently understood.

IMPACTS OF MORALLY INJURIOUS EVENTS

The delineation of what constitutes a PMIE from the associated psychosocial-spiritual sequelae is a central issue in the field of moral injury research (Frankfurt & Frazier, 2016).

Litz et al.'s (2009) theoretical model posits the primary impacts of PMIEs by the self are intense feelings of shame, guilt, and anxiety that lead to social withdrawal and reinforced by self-criticism and forgiveness difficulties. This vicious cycle perpetuates through avoidance, haunting reminders of the event, and self-harming behaviors, with concealment on the part of the individual preventing the opportunity for corrective experience and thus further entrenching the individual's suffering. Central to Litz and colleagues' model is the argument that this constellation of impacts stems from cognitive dissonance between the PMIE and the individual's preexisting moral framework followed by "global" and "stable" interpretations regarding the PMIE—for example, concluding following an event that "I am a monster" (Held et al., 2018, p. 386).

Drescher et al. (2011) interviewed 23 professionals from a range of occupational backgrounds who had experience working with military personnel on the nature of the impacts of PMIEs. The participants agreed the concept of moral injury added utility to the field and that a range of psychosocial-spiritual consequences of PMIEs were not adequately explained by PTSD. In support of Litz's model, they identified social issues (including withdrawal) as the most common theme. Furthermore, self-criticism, which included shame, was a key indicator. Impacts on spirituality and existential meaning were also reported as common. Finally, anger and a sense of betrayal were identified by the interviewees and may be conceptually linked to other-based PMIEs (Jordan et al., 2017). It is important to add, however, that Drescher's research was conducted prior to the publication of the fifth edition of the

Diagnostic and Statistical Manual of Mental Disorders (*DSM-5*; American Psychiatric Association, 2013), which now incorporates a broader spectrum of persistent negative mood symptoms such as shame, and cognitions such as loss of trust, within the PTSD diagnosis.

More recent qualitative research with veterans (Held et al., 2019; Yeterian et al., 2019) echoes similar impacts and supports Drescher's earlier work. Held et al. (2019) identified significant negative emotional impacts such as shame, dwelling on the event, substance misuse, social withdrawal, and concealment as common outcomes of PMIEs. Furthermore, existential, spiritual, and occupational difficulties were identified as well as persistent negative beliefs about the self. Interestingly, a novel theme emerged, which the authors termed "attempts at repair." This theme consisted of examples such as generosity and compassionate behavior. At present it is difficult to conclude whether these prosocial acts are stemming from guilt or could be conceptualized more accurately within a posttraumatic growth framework (Tedeschi & Calhoun, 1996). Nonetheless, it is an interesting potential outcome for future exploration. The key themes arising from in-depth qualitative interviews of military personnel with moral injury, as well as chaplains and mental health practitioners who provide their care (Yeterian et al., 2019), were (a) *feelings* of guilt, shame, anger, sadness, anxiety, and disgust; (b) *changes in thoughts or beliefs related to self*, including poor self-esteem, high self-criticism, believing oneself to be bad, damaged, unworthy, or weak, self-handicapping behaviors; (c) *changes in thoughts or beliefs related to others*, including loss of faith in people, avoidance of intimacy, and lack of trust in authority figures; and (d) *existential or spiritual outcomes*, such as loss of previous religious beliefs and loss of belief in a just world.

To further the scientific understanding of the unique impacts of PMIEs, a small number of measures have been developed in the past few years (Currier et al., 2018; Koenig et al., 2018) or are underway (Yeterian et al., 2019). Of the measures currently available, the Expressions of Moral Injury Scale–Military version (Currier et al., 2018) demonstrated the more thorough process to identify relevant constructs through a review of the scientific literature and consultation with subject matter experts. Importantly, items that overlapped with PTSD and depression phenomenology were intentionally worded with a moral injury lens, linking back to the PMIE. Four anger items among the total of 17 items (constituting more than 20% of the scale items)—anger-related betrayal, revenge, resentment, and aggression—highlighted the importance of maladaptive anger as a key outcome in moral injury. Although the Expressions of Moral Injury Scale–Military showed strong and sound psychometric properties and was validated on a large sample, it is limited by the absence of participants with lived experience of moral injury contributing to item generation and being solely based on a U.S. sample. The International Moral Injury Outcome Scale Consortium, the group that is developing the Moral Injury Outcome Scale (Yeterian et al., 2019), seek to overcome these limitations. Key methodological considerations are to (a) ensure content validity by using a bottom-up approach in development; (b) gather phenomenological data from service members, veterans, clinicians, and chaplains; and (c) develop items from different countries to ensure international representation and applicability (Yeterian et al., 2019).

CURRENT CONTROVERSIES IN THE STUDY OF MORAL INJURY

As interest and research into the construct of moral injury continue to grow, two key controversies have emerged: (a) whether moral injury can be reliably distinguished from existing psychological disorders, notably PTSD and depression; and (b) whether moral injury pathologizes normal moral emotions. These controversies are both considered next.

Distinction Between Moral Injury and Other Psychological Disorders

With regard to the relationship between moral injury and existing psychological disorders, a recent review of the moral injury literature (Griffin et al., 2019) highlighted that increased endorsement of psychosocial-spiritual consequences of exposure to morally injurious events is associated with an increased rate of psychiatric symptoms, including symptoms of PTSD and depression (Currier et al., 2018; Koenig et al., 2018). However, these authors concluded that despite the range of measurement issues and the interrelated nature of moral injury, PTSD, and depression, discrete moral injury outcome profiles are evident.

Further, where the impacts of moral injury and the symptoms of PTSD appear to overlap, important phenomenological differences have been identified. With respect to reexperiencing symptoms, qualitative research has highlighted that although moral injury, like PTSD, is associated with haunting reexperiencing symptoms, the nature of the reexperiencing is more akin to rumination (Held et al., 2019) rather than being predominantly sensory in nature, that is, intrusions and flashback phenomenology of PTSD (American Psychiatric Association, 2013). Similarly, although avoidance is seen in both presentations, the function and meaning behind the avoidance are different. In PTSD, avoidance is more commonly driven by exaggerated concerns for safety, whereas in moral injury it is driven by shame, the fear of being judged, or the fear of being betrayed again (Farnsworth et al., 2017).

With respect to cognitions, Currier et al. (2018) argued that people with moral injury are more likely to have a hyperfocus on morality and how things "should" be and how people "should" behave, as compared with the exaggerated beliefs regarding safety observed in those with PTSD. Thus, there are important phenomenological and etiological differences between symptoms of PTSD and features of moral injury that on the surface may appear similar.

Although not a recognized psychological disorder, posttraumatic embitterment disorder is another relatively new and related construct worth considering in the context of moral injury and anger at work. Posttraumatic embitterment disorder has been proposed as an adjustment disorder in response to an exceptional negative life event that does not meet the *DSM-5* PTSD for a Criterion A event but is experienced as unjust, a personal insult, and involving a violation of basic beliefs and values (Linden, 2003). Core to the phenomenon are feelings of injustice, embitterment, and rage (Linden et al., 2007). More broadly, symptoms include intrusive thoughts and repetitive memories, low mood, social withdrawal, and aggression toward oneself and others. Although the proposed posttraumatic embitterment disorder is similar to moral injury in that the triggering event is related to perceived violations of deeply held beliefs, the *nature* of the triggering event is more narrowly conceptualized as relating to a personal affront, and the impacts are a narrower set of cognitive–affective states such as helplessness, self-blame, and the desire for vengeance. According to Linden et al. (2008), 20% of cases of posttraumatic embitterment disorder follow a trauma and 45% are related to adversity following a trauma, such as the compensation-seeking process. Thus, the concept of posttraumatic embitterment disorder could be another useful lens through which to view problems with anger at work. It is important, however, that practitioners are able to distinguish between posttraumatic embitterment disorder and moral injury, with the latter arising from a broader range of moral transgressions and associated with broader psychosocial-spiritual impacts that need to be addressed in treatment.

Risk of Pathologizing Normal Moral Emotions

A criticism of the field is the potential of moral injury to pathologize normal and appropriate moral emotions when culturally sanctioned norms and values have been transgressed. Just as one sees experiences of remorse as healthy in perpetrators of violence, Farnsworth et al. (2017) proposed that experiencing what they termed "moral pain" is both adaptive and a sign of an intact moral compass in response to perceived transgressions even in a socially sanctioned context such as war. Critical to this discussion is the difference between moral pain, which may be felt when one experiences a deep sense of betrayal or witnesses or acts in ways that violate one's value system (Farnsworth et al., 2017), and moral injury, when one suffers extreme mental, social, and spiritual harm and impairment (Litz & Kerig, 2019).

As described by Farnsworth and colleagues (2017), moral injury is the "expanded social, psychological, and spiritual suffering stemming from costly or unworkable attempts to manage, control, or cope with the experience of moral pain" (p. 392). It has been suggested that the interpretation and assimilation of PMIEs into one's sense of self, identity, and views about the world and other people is central to whether moral injury is likely to occur and, importantly, whether it is likely to persist (Currier, Holland, & Malott, 2015; Farnsworth et al., 2017; Litz et al., 2009).

Thus, in the same way that an individual's appraisal of the traumatic event is thought to be important in the development and maintenance of PTSD (Ehlers & Clark, 2000), appraisal of a PMIE influences the development and maintenance of moral injury (Hoffman et al., 2018). In this case, rather than a fear-based appraisal, moral injury is associated with moral transgression giving rise to appraisals related to betrayal, injustice, and shame. As detailed in the upcoming section on theoretical understanding of the relationship between moral injury and anger, we believe that the experience of anger is core to each of these appraisals: as a basic emotion in response to betrayal, as a moral emotion in response to injustice, and as a secondary reaction to shame.

THE LINK BETWEEN MORAL INJURY AND ANGER

Anger is widely recognized as a core, troubling, and enduring feature of moral injury. For example, in a large sample of U.S. military personnel, Bryan et al. (2018) used exploratory structural equation modeling to examine the relationship between symptoms of PTSD and moral injury. A two-factor model emerged, with anger loading onto what the authors termed the moral injury factor (low enjoyment, low cohesion, anger, shame, guilt, and inward hostility) and not the PTSD factor (flashbacks, memory loss, nightmares, insomnia, and startle reflex). Further, in a small qualitative study of veterans returning to civilian life, Worthen and Ahern (2014) found that veterans' experience of anger associated with moral injury persists for years and cements their feeling different from and apart from others.

Empirical Evidence for the Link Between Anger and Moral Injury

The mechanisms linking anger and moral injury have been explored empirically by a number of researchers. The experience of betrayal has been identified as the mechanism linking moral injury and anger in certain studies. For example, in Vietnam veterans, Shay (1994) observed that the cumulative effects of betrayal that led to loss of life in combat was associated with frenzied and uncontrollable rage, which he described as a "berserker" state. Perceived betrayal has also been found to lead to persistent anger in military members postdeployment, affecting trust in the intentions of command and impacting social relationships with loved ones in the community (McCormack & Ell, 2017). Worthen and Ahern (2014) identified betrayal by the chain of command as one of the key sources of anger associated with moral injury among veterans returning to civilian life. Similarly, in their research investigating the relationship between (a) perpetration and betrayal-based PMIEs and (b) PTSD, guilt/shame, and anger 8 months later, Jordan et al. (2017) found that the relationship between betrayal-based PMIEs and PTSD was mediated by anger. Consistent with this, Bryan et al. (2016) found elevated anger associated with betrayal in a military sample.

Similar to betrayal, the experience of a moral transgression perpetrated by others has also been identified as a mechanism linking moral injury and anger. In military populations, the psychological consequences of anger and desire for retribution for moral transgression perpetrated by others have been observed in veterans of recent conflicts and described as a key contextual factor that precipitates moral injury (Currier, McCormick, & Drescher, 2015). Similar findings have been reported in refugee populations, where moral transgressions perpetrated by other people have been found to predict anger among refugees (Hoffman et al., 2018; Nickerson et al., 2015). The link between anger and moral transgressions perpetrated by the self has also been observed in both military populations (Bryan et al., 2016) and refugees (Hoffman et al., 2018). Further, Hoffman and colleagues' (2018) study of refugees settled in Australia found that moral injury arising from a transgression perpetrated by oneself predicted anger more than it predicted PTSD.

Theoretical Understanding of the Link Between Anger and Moral Injury

In addition to understanding the empirical evidence for the mechanisms linking anger and moral injury, a theoretical understanding is also important in informing efforts to address moral injury in the workplace. As previously noted, we contend that betrayal, injustice, and shame-related appraisals of morally injurious events can lead to an anger response: as a basic emotion in response to betrayal or other transgression against the self, as a moral emotion in response to transgression against others, and as a secondary emotion in response to shame for actions perpetrated by the self, respectively. The theoretical links between anger and different types of moral injury are elaborated next and illustrated with case studies.

Anger as a Basic Emotion in Response to Betrayal or Other Transgression Against the Self

Basic emotions such as fear, anger, surprise, disgust, joy, and sadness are understood to help us to deal with fundamental life tasks such as facing an immediate danger, experiencing an irrevocable loss, and progressing toward the realization of a goal (Ekman, 1999). Accordingly, in the context of PMIEs, emotions that lead to danger or a perceived injustice against oneself—for example, feeling betrayed by leaders who have unnecessarily put you into harm's way—may elicit anger as a basic emotion. The following case study of a police member who developed moral injury following an event in which he felt betrayed by his line of command illustrates moral injury–related anger as a basic emotion. The case study is fictional.

CASE STUDY 1

ANGER AS A BASIC EMOTION

Phil, a police sergeant, with a junior officer alongside him, was in pursuit of an armed offender. They located the offender in a parked vehicle in a multistory car park. It was unclear whether the offender still had a weapon. Phil was in communication with his commanding officer back at the station. Phil advised the senior sergeant that the offender was not posing any immediate threat and he proposed to wait until a backup vehicle arrived to confront the offender. The senior sergeant was concerned that a delay would increase the risk of the offender escaping and ordered Phil to go in immediately. Phil and his junior partner left the car and proceeded to the vehicle, under cover of other parked cars. The offender got out of the car and saw them. The offender immediately put his hands up in the air. Phil called "Hold fire" to his partner, but in fear his partner fired three shots in quick succession and killed the offender. The partner was subsequently charged for his action and left the police force. Phil felt betrayed by the senior sergeant, who did not accept his recommended course of action, and harbors intense anger that has pervaded his career since. Phil has refused promotion, having a complete mistrust of anyone in a senior leadership position. He is constantly cynical about the actions of police hierarchy and interprets any error of judgment as a deliberate betrayal. He has been called before disciplinary hearings on multiple occasions for insubordinate and aggressive behavior.

Anger as a Moral Emotion in Response to Transgression Against Others

In the context of PMIEs that involve moral transgression on the part of the self or another, the anger response may be better understood as a moral emotion.

As opposed to basic emotions, moral emotions are considered social in nature and higher order, being based on self-awareness, self-consciousness, and the ability to empathize with others (Heerey et al., 2003). Haidt (2003) defined moral emotions as those that are linked to the interests of society or other people. According to Ayala (2010), human beings are moral beings by nature, having moral values or standards against which our own and others' actions are judged. Moral emotions arise when our sense of morality is challenged (Ayala, 2010) and, as such, are described as the guardians of the moral order (Tangney et al., 2007).

According to Haidt (2003), moral emotions have certain defining features: They are felt in disinterested situations (situations where there is no personal investment or consequences), and they are associated with highly prosocial action tendencies. In this context, he argued that anger, although usually considered a basic emotion, can also be a moral emotion. Specifically, anger is a basic emotion when triggered by perceived injustices against the self but a moral emotion when triggered by injustice against others. Consideration of the function of anger as a moral emotion may be important in addressing moral injury–related anger in the work context. According to Haidt, anger as a moral emotion puts the person into a motivational and cognitive state that motivates goal-related action—for instance, revenge that benefits others or upholds moral order. Similarly, Schweder et al. (1997) identified anger as an emotion that acts as a guardian of the moral order. These authors argued that rights and fairness are a core moral code that when violated, leads to anger. Anger motivates direct action to repair the moral order and make violators mend their ways. In a workplace context, consideration needs to be given to how anger can be resolved when revenge or reparation is not possible.

The following case study is of a journalist who developed moral injury following an event in which she witnessed an atrocity that she and police were unable to prevent. It serves to illustrate moral injury–related anger as a moral emotion arising from witnessing a moral transgression on the part of another person. Again, the case study is fictional.

CASE STUDY 2

ANGER AS A MORAL EMOTION

Sharon, a newspaper journalist covering the police round, received a tip-off that a number of police and ambulance vehicles were assembled near a beachside cliff top. She arrived at the scene and moved closer. Police had

(*continues*)

CASE STUDY 2

ANGER AS A MORAL EMOTION (*Continued*)

cordoned off the area, but Sharon managed to find a vantage point where she could see and hear what was happening. She first saw a young woman with ripped clothes and bleeding cuts on her arms and legs. The woman was screaming hysterically, "He's got my baby girl!" A man then came into Sharon's view. He appeared to be drug affected and was yelling unintelligibly. The man was holding a large kitchen knife in one hand and a baby girl in the other hand. The baby was crying. As Sharon watched, the man started swinging the baby around by the feet and threatened to throw her over the cliff. Sharon heard the order from the sergeant in command to the police not to shoot, as he was concerned that they would shoot the baby. Three times, the man dropped the baby on her head and picked her up again. Eventually the baby stopped crying, and Sharon knew that she was dead. The police moved in and apprehended the offender. Sharon was enraged by the event and the inability of the police to prevent the death of the baby. She struggled to continue covering the police round, aware that every crime scene she attended provoked a rage reaction in her. Sharon started to fantasize about enacting her own revenge on perpetrators, feeling that the punishment meted out by the criminal justice system was inadequate to fit the crime. Over time, Sharon started to feel this same rage around the office, whenever she felt that one of her coworkers was not doing their job properly or was "going soft" on reporting the details of crimes. Her relationships with colleagues deteriorated. She stopped socializing with them and became quite reclusive. She spent her spare time trawling the internet investigating judicial decisions and sending angry emails to judges who she felt had not imposed sufficiently severe penalties.

Anger as a Secondary Emotion in Response to Shame for Actions Perpetrated by the Self

The most extensively researched negatively valenced moral emotions are guilt and shame (Tangney et al., 2007). These two emotions are often distinguished by whether the object of disapproval is one's behavior (guilt) or the self (shame; Lewis, 1971). This distinction has been supported by research findings that stable, uncontrollable attributions for failure are associated with shame, whereas unstable, controllable attributions are associated with guilt (Tracy & Robins, 2006). Tangney and colleagues (2007) argued that guilt is an adaptive moral emotion, whereas shame is not. This argument is based on certain empirical differences between the two. First, they have opposite "action tendencies," with guilt often leading to attempts at reparation, whereas shame promotes defensiveness, interpersonal separation, and distance. Second, they are differentially related to empathy, with guilt associated with empathy for the other, whereas shame derails the empathic process through an egocentric focus on the "bad self." Third, guilt is more likely to be associated with constructive reactions to anger, such as taking direct corrective action, and less likely to be associated with acts of aggression. Shame, on the other hand, is associated with externalization of blame, intense anger, and destructive expressions of anger. Fourth, shame is associated with negative psychological impacts, including low self-esteem, depression, anxiety, eating disorders, PTSD, and suicidal ideation. Tangney and colleagues argued that unless it is associated with an exaggerated or distorted sense of responsibility for events beyond one's control or for which one has no personal involvement (e.g., survivor guilt; Kubany et al., 1995) or leads to shame, guilt is less likely to have a broader psychological impact. Finally, these authors noted that guilt and shame are differentially associated with problematic behavior. Guilt has been found to have an inhibitory influence on antisocial and risky behavior, whereas shame is correlated with externalizing symptoms of illegal, risky, or otherwise problematic behaviors. Furthermore, guilt but not shame is effective in motivating people to choose moral behavior. Thus, in the relationship between anger and moral injury arising from events in which the individual has transgressed their own moral code, the experience of shame is conceptually more likely than guilt to be the linking mechanism.

The following case study of an infantry soldier in Iraq, who developed moral injury following an incident in which he intentionally harmed a child whom he held responsible for the death of a friend, serves to illustrate moral injury–related anger as a secondary emotion to shame. Again, the case study is fictional.

CASE STUDY 3

ANGER AS SECONDARY EMOTION IN RESPONSE TO SHAME

Todd was deployed as an infantry soldier to Iraq in 2005. His combat unit was located in a dangerous area where insurgents were known to be operating. The local residents appeared to be supportive of the soldiers'

(*continues*)

CASE STUDY 3

ANGER AS SECONDARY EMOTION IN RESPONSE TO SHAME (*Continued*)

being there, and local children would often approach to say hello, looking for the small gifts that the soldiers would give them. On a particular patrol, the unit was unnerved by the absence of local people in the vicinity. Todd caught a glimpse of one of the men whom he knew by sight watching the unit from a safe distance behind the ruin of a building. The next thing Todd knew, a roadside bomb detonated and two of his fellow soldiers went flying through the air. He ran toward them and saw that both had been killed. One soldier was Scott, a close childhood friend. Todd was devastated. He withdrew into himself and became obsessed with plans to avenge Scott's death. A few days later, out on patrol, he saw the same man cutting a piece of rope with a knife. Todd quickly broke away from the rest of the unit and walked toward the man, grabbed the knife, and stabbed him in the abdomen. No one saw what had happened. Todd initially felt that his action was justified, but when he got home from deployment and started to reintegrate into his previous life, he became plagued with feelings of guilt and shame for what he had done. He was unable to reconcile his behavior with the person he thought that he was. Todd was filled with shame and hatred for himself. He was consumed with anger and started drinking heavily and getting into fights around his hometown. Any time his family or friends tried to reach out to him, he would be engulfed with feelings of shame and unworthiness, and he would respond with uncontrolled rage and aggression.

Just as we argue that betrayal, injustice, and shame-related appraisals of morally injurious events can lead to problematic anger, we propose that anger problems are maintained by a persistent and heightened sensitivity to situations that trigger these same appraisals.

A Conceptual Model of the Maintenance of Moral Injury–Related Anger

Chemtob et al.'s (1988) cognitive action theory of PTSD explains the self-perpetuating relationship between anger and PTSD with reference to the individual continuing to function in "survivor mode." In survivor mode, the individual is hyperalert to any sign of threat (see also Lawrence-Wood et al., Chapter 6, this volume). This hyperalertness leads to even mild or ambiguous evidence of threat activating a threat response. This threat response biases the individual to interpret ambiguous evidence as threatening, which further raises threat arousal and further activates threat response structures in a vicious cycle. In a similar vein, we propose that there is a self-perpetuating relationship between anger and moral injury, when the individual harbors fundamental, pervasive, and enduring beliefs that the self, other people, or the world are immoral. For these individuals, rather than the heightened sensitivity to threat seen in fear-based PTSD, there is a heightened sensitivity to betrayal, injustice, or shame. This sensitivity leads to a low threshold for detecting evidence of betrayal, injustice, or shame, with ambiguous or even neutral stimuli being interpreted through this lens. As a result of this bias, feelings of betrayal, injustice, or shame are readily triggered, leading to an anger response and reinforcement of the individual's beliefs about the immorality of the self, other people, or the world in a self-perpetuating vicious cycle. This cycle is illustrated in Figure 3.1.

FIGURE 3.1. Proposed Vicious Cycle of Betrayal, Injustice, and/or Shame Mediating the Course of Anger-Based Moral Injury

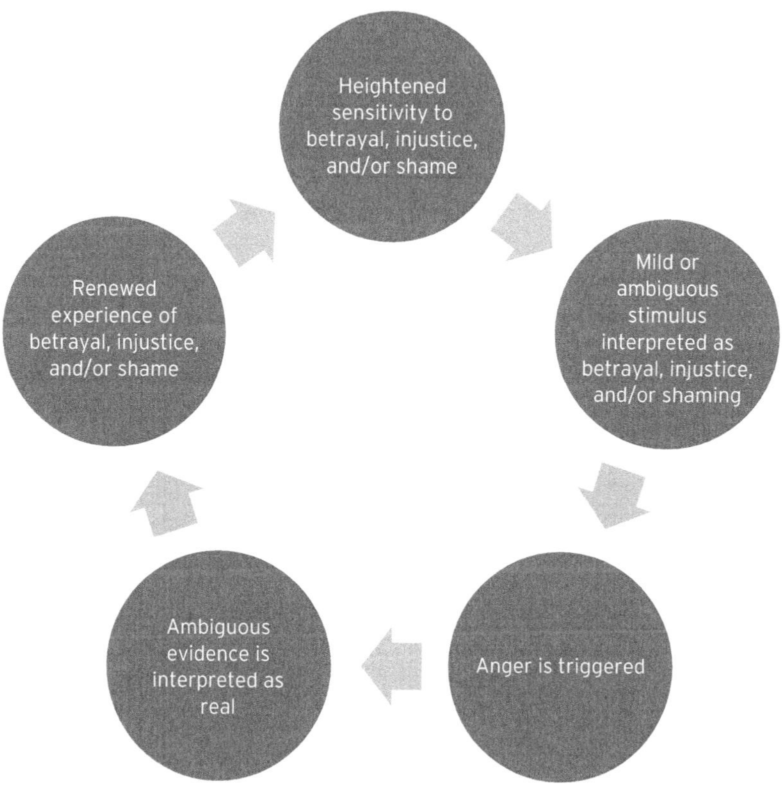

IMPLICATIONS FOR THE WORKPLACE

The case examples just presented are used to illustrate how this cycle may manifest within the workplace. In Case Study 1, following his experience of feeling betrayed by leadership, Phil has developed a deep-seated mistrust of anyone in authority or any leadership position. He now carries an expectation of further betrayal and has a heightened sensitivity to this occurring. When a change in policy on interactions with the media is introduced, Phil immediately concludes that the new policy is designed to protect the reputation of senior management rather than assist members on the ground, triggering a cynical anger response fueled by the thought that the rank and file are again being blamed for mistakes of the past. This anger in turn serves to reinforce his belief that those in leadership cannot be trusted.

In Case Study 2, Sharon has become preoccupied with perceived injustices in the world and actively seeks out examples of injustice that reinforce her worldview. Within the workplace, Sharon is enraged by what she perceives as a fellow journalist's dispassionate reporting on a court case in which she felt that a serious injustice had been done. She demanded to know why the journalist had not highlighted this injustice in his story; a heated argument ensued in the newsroom, in which she accused him of siding with the perceived wrongdoer and hence "being part of the problem." The news editor stepped in to challenge Sharon's interpretation of the facts, and it quickly became clear that she had selectively attended to elements of the story and ignored others. Sharon conceded that she "may have got it wrong this time" but argued that it was just one in a long list of examples of journalists ignoring injustices.

Finally, in Case Study 3, Todd's shame-based moral injury has led to him to live in constant fear that if he lets people get close, they will recognize him for the evil person that he believes himself to be. He is acutely sensitive and vigilant to any indication from other people that they are viewing him in a negative light or judging his actions. He is constantly watching his fellow soldiers, looking for any sign of dislike, criticism, or rejection. One particular day, Todd is having lunch in the mess on the base. Another soldier from his training group comes in and says hello to him but then walks across the room to sit with someone else. The two soldiers start talking and joking together. Todd interprets this as a sign of rejection, and this reinforces his self-loathing and belief that he is not worthy of others' friendship. He deliberately takes his mind back to his attack on the child and dwells on the feelings of deep shame, telling himself that he deserves nothing better. Suddenly overwhelmed with anger, Todd storms out of the room, gets in his car, and drives aggressively down the road, tailing other drivers closely and sounding his horn as he overtakes them. Afterward, the aggressive outburst adds to Todd's sense of shame, knowing that he has again put others' lives at risk.

It is easy to see how these vulnerabilities, if left unaddressed, could lead to ongoing and potentially worsening issues with moral injury–related anger. Not only does this risk the development of psychological disorder such as PTSD or depression (Williamson et al., 2018) but it also could lead to a psychological break with the organization in which the individual disengages from colleagues, or is actively ostracized, and loses a sense of collective belonging, purpose or mission. This psychological break is a particular problem in high-risk organizations, where the safety-critical mission depends on strong and cohesive teams and high morale. Thus, where the potential exists for moral injury to occur within the workplace, priority consideration should be given to measures to minimize the risk, detect early signs of moral distress, and intervene effectively. The following sections highlight recommendations at the levels of prevention, early intervention, and treatment, but it is important to acknowledge that the effectiveness of these interventions in preventing the development of moral injury has not been tested.

Prevention

In workplaces with a predictable risk of exposure to PMIEs, there is a role for pre-incident preparedness. This approach would involve preparing workers psychologically, socially, and spiritually for the moral risks they will face, through the integration of moral issues into skills training. In a military context, Zust and Krauss (2019) emphasized the importance of good military leadership that incorporates moral reasoning within all phases of training and mission command. These authors argued that leaders can mitigate the risk for moral injury by establishing realistic training that prepares members for the moral dilemmas they will encounter in combat and embed moral reasoning processes within mission command to establish clear boundaries for how combatants will operate. Research in the military (Wilk et al., 2013) has also established that cohesive units with high morale have lower behavioral health problems regardless of combat exposure. This result suggests that high cohesion and morale may protect against moral injury. Pre-incident preparedness should therefore focus not just on the psychological preparation of the individual but also on the cohesiveness and morale among the workgroup. The potential for preventative interventions should also be considered in nonmilitary workplaces in which staff have a predictable risk of exposure to PMIEs.

Early Intervention

When a PMIE occurs in the workplace, it is important to acknowledge the moral dilemma and help the individuals affected to actively work through and resolve any resulting moral conflict (Zust & Krauss, 2019). This attempt at resolution may involve encouraging people to acknowledge their values, accept responsibility for past actions or inaction, and be guided in their future actions by their values. Further, based on the finding that the inability to make meaning out of PMIEs is associated with greater PTSD, depression, and suicidality, it may be important to help the individual to make meaning of the experience (Currier, Holland, & Malott, 2015). This meaning making may involve, for example, engaging in discussion with individuals involved in a particular event, reinforcing the mission, promoting a sense of purpose in the activity, acknowledging the moral dilemmas, and reinforcing the principles that guide decision making in this context. Given the link between anger and moral injury, attention should be paid to interpretations of, or meaning given to, events that involve betrayal, injustice, or shame, as these may give rise to anger-related moral injury. Interventions that promote trust in leadership are also critical following exposure to a PMIE. For example, an open dialogue, in which reasons for actions or decisions are explained, may mitigate against a sense of betrayal or injustice through consideration of the potential outcomes of alternative courses of action. Similarly, creating an environment that facilitates the acknowledgment of and working through moral dilemmas, such as actions or inactions that have led to guilt or shame, may mitigate against shame-based anger and moral injury.

It may be possible to intervene with people who have experienced a PMIE before they develop a moral injury, with betrayal, injustice, or shame-based anger potential early warning signs. Drawing upon the work of Schweder et al. (1997), which highlights the motivating function of anger in repairing the moral order, actions that lead to reparation should be considered. The exact nature of this activity would need to be determined by the circumstances of the PMIE and the values of the individual concerned, but it may involve, for example, helping the family members of someone who has been harmed (following a moral transgression on the part of the individual) or seeking justice for a perceived moral transgression on the part of another. A sense of justice has been identified as a precondition for the individual to move toward forgiveness (Muldoon, 2008). Interventions to address betrayal, injustice, or shame-based anger and moral injury are discussed in more detail in the following section on treatment of moral injury.

Beyond early interventions that can be implemented in the workplace, it is important to encourage and facilitate help-seeking, whether that be psychological or spiritual, if there are early indicators of anger or other distress following exposure to a PMIE.

Treatment

For those who have developed moral injury–related anger problems, intervention is likely required. As highlighted throughout this chapter, understanding the mechanism of the link between moral injury and anger is important, and this understanding should guide the treatment approach. The most important distinction is possibly between betrayal or moral transgression perpetrated by another person, on one hand, and moral transgression perpetrated by oneself, on the other.

Addressing Moral Injury and Anger Arising From Betrayal and Moral Transgressions Perpetrated by Others

Muldoon (2008) argued that it is important to recognize the moral legitimacy of anger when it arises in response to willful harm or injustice. With respect to the types of PMIE just elucidated, this recognition would include betrayal and moral transgressions perpetrated by others. This notion goes back to Aristotle, who linked anger with honor. Aristotle defined anger as a response to unjustified insults to oneself or others that motivates revenge (*Rhetoric*, Book 2, Chapter 2, as cited in Haidt, 2003). More recent studies confirm that anger generally involves a motivation to attack, humiliate, or otherwise get back at the person who is perceived as acting unfairly or immorally (Izard, 1977; Shaver et al., 1987). The fact that anger often involves a motivation for revenge has been noted in a great many cultures (Nisbett & Cohen, 1996); the need for revenge is generally satisfied by societal sanctions against people who transgress right and wrong (Tangney et al., 2007). In the case of serious legal transgressions, revenge occurs through the retributive justice system. When an injustice has been perpetrated against us or another, the responsibility for retributive justice or punishment is passed on to a third party through the legal system. If a proportionate harm has been seen to be imposed on the perpetrator, this punishment can satisfy the demands of moral accountability without perpetuating cycles of violence (Muldoon, 2008).

This need for justice also applies when perceived wrongs or injustices are perpetrated in a work context. Retributive justice is achieved when the person who has transgressed is appropriately punished or held to account for their actions. However, retributive justice will not always occur, and the individual may be left with ongoing anger as a result of the unmet need for justice. In the absence of retributive justice for the perpetrator(s), restorative justice may serve as an alternative (Muldoon, 2008). Muldoon (2008) described restorative justice processes such as truth commissions as making an alternative model of justice possible. He argued that restorative justice processes in which victims have the opportunity to have their story heard restore dignity by recognizing that the suffering of victims is significant and ought not to be forgotten. They also allow the focus to shift to forgiveness, which is necessary for the anger to resolve (Muldoon, 2008).

Thus, when moral injury occurs in a work setting where people can be held to account for their actions, retribution may be possible, and this should contribute to healing. When this is not possible, the focus should be on restorative justice and forgiveness. In line with this reasoning, Litz et al. (2009) emphasized the importance of self and other forgiveness in recovering from moral injury. According to Litz, there are two routes to moral repair and renewal. The first is achieved through emotional processing of the moral transgression whereby aspects of the experience need to be uncovered and fully acknowledged and shared—for example, through exposure therapy. The second route to moral repair and renewal is through exposure to corrective life experience—that is, increasing positive judgments about the self by doing good deeds and positive judgments about the world by seeing others do good deeds. These routes are relevant to both self- and other-PMIEs.

Addressing Moral Injury and Anger Arising From One's Own Moral Transgression

Much of the existing work investigating interventions for moral injury is focused on moral injury arising from one's own moral transgressions. Thus, this focus is particularly relevant to individuals who are experiencing anger as a secondary reaction to shame. In reference to the high rate of suicide among U.S. veterans returning from Iraq and Afghanistan, Sherman (2014) highlighted that self-empathy, an attitude that promotes a fairer self-assessment, is required for healing of moral injury in war. She developed a psychotherapeutic approach built on this premise. Similarly, Worthington and Langberg (2012) emphasized the importance of self-condemnation arising from moral injury and describe a self-forgiveness intervention with six components:

- appealing to God or higher power for forgiveness
- making amends for wrongs that one perpetrated or failed to prevent
- examining and dealing with expectations that might have been too ambitious, perfectionistic, or unrealistic
- adjusting one's self-perception to accept oneself as a valuable though fallen human being
- practicing a life in which virtue is habitual
- giving oneself room to fail

The authors contended that the intervention can be presented in a religious or secular way.

Keenan et al. (2014) reported on the development of a treatment program developed to deal with the distress associated with grief, guilt about killing, or shame for letting buddies down. The approach draws on the previous work of Shay (1994) and Dewey (2004), which emphasizes the importance of veterans sharing their story with someone who can be trusted to listen, and is delivered in a group setting to foster connection and trust. The program addresses grief and loss, as well as guilt and shame arising from action or inaction that had a negative result—witnessing or perpetrating atrocities and killing. Unfortunately, none of these approaches has yet been evaluated for efficacy.

Two emerging interventions for individuals suffering moral injury are adaptive disclosure (Gray et al., 2012) and impact of killing (Maguen et al., 2017). Adaptive disclosure is a brief manualized cognitive behavior therapy protocol that draws on a range of existing empirically supported strategies including imaginal exposure, emotional processing, cognitive-behavioral techniques, and Gestalt therapy to address moral injury–based traumas. The empty chair exercise involves a moral authority figure to whom the individual is encouraged to disclose any transgressions and talk about the impact of guilt and shame on their life. Individuals are then invited to consider what the moral authority figure would say to them, with the therapist guiding the exercise to ensure that forgiveness-related content is evoked. This exercise is followed by cognitive restructuring and meaning-making strategies. As adaptive disclosure is intended to facilitate emotional processing of the event and promote self-forgiveness, it directly addresses the feelings of shame that contribute to problems with anger for some individuals.

The association between killing in war and suicidality in veterans (Maguen et al., 2012) together with the observation that veterans continued to report moral, interpersonal, spiritual, and existential impacts of killing after completing evidence-based treatment for PTSD (Purcell et al., 2016) has led to a dedicated psychological treatment for veterans who have killed in war (Maguen et al., 2017). Although not yet fully explored in the literature, it seems likely that the impact of killing will differ depending upon the particular circumstances and the individuals concerned. In considering individual factors, many veterans are able to reconcile killing in war as an inevitable and justifiable part of their job. For these individuals, killing may present a moral challenge but is perhaps less likely to lead to a moral injury. Others, for whom killing in any circumstances transgresses a fundamental belief that one should not kill, may not be able to reconcile killing in war and are more likely to experience it as a morally injurious event. In considering the influence of the particular circumstances of killing, the risk of moral injury is likely to increase for veterans involved in the killing of noncombatants or in accidental killing. Although low incidence, a final category of killing in war to be considered is intentional killing outside of the rules of engagement. This category of killing in war poses the greatest risk of shame-based moral injury. It may also signal a preexisting moral injury that has led to disruption in the individual's sense of personal morality and capacity to behave in a just and ethical manner (Drescher et al., 2011).

Impact of killing is a cognitive behavioral treatment designed specifically to address the maladaptive cognitions associated with killing-related guilt, shame, and self-condemnation. Self-forgiveness is at the core of the intervention and is addressed through acknowledging the wrong or harm done, feeling and processing negative feelings such as guilt and remorse, and recognizing that the act does not define who a person is, or will be, moving forward. Through therapy, barriers to self-forgiveness are identified and articulated, and the impact on the individual's life of their stance against self-forgiveness is explored. Therapy also involves identifying ways to make amends that will assist veterans to forgive themselves. For veterans who experience anger as a secondary emotion to shame, the impact of killing intervention can be expected to reduce anger as a function of addressing the shame.

Although the development of these interventions is a very positive step in the right direction, there is unfortunately little evidence to date of their effectiveness. A pilot study of adaptive disclosure (Gray et al., 2012) found improvement in PTSD from pre- to posttreatment in active duty marines and navy personnel; however, in the absence of a control condition, conclusions about effectiveness cannot be reached. A pilot study of impact of killing (Maguen et al., 2017) versus waitlist control found improvement in PTSD symptoms, general psychiatric symptoms, and quality of life. Although pilot studies are an appropriate and important first step in the evaluation of new treatments, further high-quality research is needed before these treatments can be recommended. Additionally, future research should move beyond PTSD as an outcome of these interventions and measure change in moral injury. This broadening of outcomes has been difficult in the absence of a gold standard measure of moral injury, but as noted earlier, the development of such a measure is underway (Yeterian et al., 2019). It will also be important to assess the impact of these interventions on moral injury–related anger specifically. The focus in adaptive disclosure on forgiveness is likely to be key in addressing betrayal and injustice mediated anger, and the focus of both interventions on shame and self-forgiveness is well targeted for anger that is mediated by shame. It should also be noted that although both interventions have been developed for military populations specifically, adaptive disclosure could be adapted to any other work contexts in which morally injurious events occur, and impact of killing would be applicable to those in law enforcement as well as military occupations.

CONCLUSION

The rapid uptake of the concept of moral injury among researchers, clinicians, and high-risk workplaces would seem to indicate that it fills a gap in our existing understanding of posttraumatic mental health. The notion that betrayal and other moral transgressions in high-stakes situations can lead to lasting psychosocial/spiritual injury that goes beyond psychological disorders such as PTSD or depression clearly resonates with those who have experienced such events, as well as those charged with their care. Anger appears to be a central component of moral injury, whether the event involves betrayal or other moral transgression on the part of the self or other. In understanding the perpetuation of the relationship between moral injury and anger, an extension to Chemtob et al.'s (1988) cognitive action theory of anger in PTSD is a useful model. This model proposes a mechanism of perpetuation through heightened sensitivity to betrayal, injustice, or shame; selective attention to potential triggers; and biased interpretation of ambiguous stimuli that ensures that new information is assimilated into existing schemas.

There is no doubt that the impact of moral injury on the individual can be devastating, with wide-ranging psychosocial-spiritual outcomes. However, we believe that it is also critical to consider the impact of moral injury within the workplace more broadly. Left unaddressed, the anger associated with moral injury is likely to compound over time as negative schemas about the self, others, and the world become entrenched. This anger may signal a psychological break from the organization with respect to shared mission and goals and fracturing of relationships with others within the work environment. A psychological break of this nature represents a risk for safety-critical functions that rely on teamwork, high morale, and shared mission. As such, organizations in which there is a predictable risk of exposure to PMIEs cannot ignore the possibility of moral injury within the workplace.

However, a key challenge for organizations is the absence of evidence to inform a best practice approach to prevention, early intervention, and treatment. Further research into the understanding of moral injury and its impact within the workplace is urgently needed, along with high-quality research to test effective interventions at the level of prevention, early intervention, and treatment. The scope of this research should include opportunities to minimize the occurrence of PMIEs, processes for monitoring the well-being of staff who are exposed to these events, the early identification of unresolved moral conflicts, and interventions that acknowledge and help the individual to work through these conflicts. Research into the link between moral injury and anger, exploring betrayal, injustice, and shame as mediating factors, is also needed to further our understanding of the development and maintenance of moral injury–related anger problems and guide therapeutic approaches to addressing them.

IMPLICATIONS

- In workplaces where there is a foreseeable risk of exposure to potentially morally injurious events, attention should be paid to prevention, early intervention, and treatment opportunities.
- Leaders have a critical role in preparing workers for moral dilemmas they will face in their role and in preventing the development of moral injury by acknowledging and helping individuals to resolve any moral conflicts arising.
- Acknowledgment of wrongdoing and retribution or restorative justice may help to address anger arising from betrayal or moral transgressions on the part of others; self-forgiveness may be important to recover from the shame-based moral injury associated with moral transgressions on one's own part.
- More research into prevention, early intervention, and treatment of moral injury is needed.

REFERENCES

American Psychiatric Association. (2013). *Diagnostic and statistical manual of mental disorders* (5th ed.). https://doi.org/10.1176/appi.books.9780890425596

Ayala, F. J. (2010). The difference of being human: Morality. *Proceedings of the National Academy of Sciences of the United States of America, 107*(Suppl. 2), 9015–9022. https://doi.org/10.1073/pnas.0914616107

Brewin, C. R., Dalgleish, T., & Joseph, S. (1996). A dual representation theory of posttraumatic stress disorder. *Psychological Review, 103*(4), 670–686. https://doi.org/10.1037/0033-295X.103.4.670

Bryan, C. J., Bryan, A. O., Anestis, M. D., Anestis, J. C., Green, B. A., Etienne, N., Morrow, C. E., & Ray-Sannerud, B. (2016). Measuring moral injury: Psychometric properties of the moral injury events scale in two military samples. *Assessment, 23*(5), 557–570. https://doi.org/10.1177/1073191115590855

Bryan, C. J., Bryan, A. O., Roberge, E., Leifker, F. R., & Rozek, D. C. (2018). Moral injury, posttraumatic stress disorder, and suicidal behavior among National Guard personnel. *Psychological Trauma: Theory, Research, Practice, and Policy*, *10*(1), 36–45. https://doi.org/10.1037/tra0000290

Chemtob, C., Roitblat, H. L., Hamada, R. S., Carlson, J. G., & Twentyman, C. T. (1988). A cognitive action theory of post-traumatic stress disorder. *Journal of Anxiety Disorders*, *2*(3), 253–275. https://doi.org/10.1016/0887-6185(88)90006-0

Currier, J. M., Farnsworth, J. K., Drescher, K. D., McDermott, R. C., Sims, B. M., & Albright, D. L. (2018). Development and evaluation of the Expressions of Moral Injury Scale–Military version. *Clinical Psychology & Psychotherapy*, *25*(3), 474–488. https://doi.org/10.1002/cpp.2170

Currier, J. M., & Holland, J. M. (2012). Examining the role of combat loss among Vietnam War veterans. *Journal of Traumatic Stress*, *25*(1), 102–105. https://doi.org/10.1002/jts.21655

Currier, J. M., Holland, J. M., Drescher, K., & Foy, D. (2015). Initial psychometric evaluation of the Moral Injury Questionnaire—Military version. *Clinical Psychology & Psychotherapy*, *22*(1), 54–63. https://doi.org/10.1002/cpp.1866

Currier, J. M., Holland, J. M., & Malott, J. (2015). Moral injury, meaning making, and mental health in returning veterans. *Journal of Clinical Psychology*, *71*(3), 229–240. https://doi.org/10.1002/jclp.22134

Currier, J. M., McCormick, W., & Drescher, K. D. (2015). How do morally injurious events occur? A qualitative analysis of perspectives of veterans with PTSD. *Traumatology*, *21*(2), 106–116. https://doi.org/10.1037/trm0000027

Darwin, C. R. (1871). *The descent of man, and selection in relation to sex*. Appleton and Company.

Dewey, L. (2004). *War and redemption*. Ashgate.

Drescher, K. D., Foy, D. W., Kelly, C., Leshner, A., Schutz, K., & Litz, B. (2011). An exploration of the viability and usefulness of the construct of moral injury in war veterans. *Traumatology*, *17*(1), 8–13. https://doi.org/10.1177/1534765610395615

Ehlers, A., & Clark, D. M. (2000). A cognitive model of posttraumatic stress disorder. *Behaviour Research and Therapy*, *38*(4), 319–345. https://doi.org/10.1016/S0005-7967(99)00123-0

Ekman, P. (1999). Basic emotions. In T. Dalgleish & M. J. Power (Eds.), *Handbook of cognition and emotion* (pp. 45–60). John Wiley and Sons. https://doi.org/10.1002/0470013494.ch3

Evans, M. (2015). A commander's perspective. In T. Frame (Ed.), *Moral injury: Unseen wounds in an age of barbarism* (pp. 63–78). UNSW Press.

Farnsworth, J. K., Drescher, K. D., Evans, W., & Walser, R. D. (2017). A functional approach to understanding and treating military-related moral injury. *Journal of Contextual Behavioral Science*, *6*(4), 391–397. https://doi.org/10.1016/j.jcbs.2017.07.003

Foa, E. B., & Rothbaum, B. O. (1989). Behavioural psychotherapy for post-traumatic stress disorder. *International Review of Psychiatry*, *1*(3), 219–226. https://doi.org/10.3109/09540268909110412

Frankfurt, S., & Frazier, P. (2016). A review of research on moral injury in combat veterans. *Military Psychology*, *28*(5), 318–330. https://doi.org/10.1037/mil0000132

Gray, M. J., Schorr, Y., Nash, W., Lebowitz, L., Amidon, A., Lansing, A., Maglione, M., Lang, A. J., & Litz, B. T. (2012). Adaptive disclosure: An open trial of a novel exposure-based intervention for service members with combat-related psychological stress injuries. *Behavior Therapy*, *43*(2), 407–415. https://doi.org/10.1016/j.beth.2011.09.001

Griffin, B. J., Purcell, N., Burkman, K., Litz, B. T., Bryan, C. J., Schmitz, M., Villierme, C., Walsh, J., & Maguen, S. (2019). Moral injury: An integrative review. *Journal of Traumatic Stress*, *32*(3), 350–362. https://doi.org/10.1002/jts.22362

Haidt, J. (2003). The moral emotions. In R. J. Davidson, K. R. Scherer, & H. H. Goldsmith (Eds.), *Handbook of affective sciences* (pp. 852–870). Oxford University Press.

Heerey, E. A., Keltner, D., & Capps, L. M. (2003). Making sense of self-conscious emotion: Linking theory of mind and emotion in children with autism. *Emotion*, *3*(4), 394–400. https://doi.org/10.1037/1528-3542.3.4.394

Held, P., Klassen, B. J., Brennan, M. B., & Zalta, A. K. (2018). Using prolonged exposure and cognitive processing therapy to treat veterans with moral injury-based PTSD: Two case examples. *Cognitive and Behavioral Practice*, *25*(3), 377–390. https://doi.org/10.1016/j.cbpra.2017.09.003

Held, P., Klassen, B. J., Hall, J. M., Friese, T. R., Bertsch-Gout, M. M., Zalta, A. K., & Pollack, M. H. (2019). "I knew it was wrong the moment I got the order": A narrative thematic analysis of moral injury in combat veterans. *Psychological Trauma: Theory, Research, Practice, and Policy*, *11*(4), 396–405. https://doi.org/10.1037/tra0000364

Hoffman, J., Liddell, B., Bryant, R. A., & Nickerson, A. (2018). The relationship between moral injury appraisals, trauma exposure, and mental health in refugees. *Depression and Anxiety*, *35*(11), 1030–1039. https://doi.org/10.1002/da.22787

Izard, C. E. (1977). *Human emotions*. Plenum Press.

Jordan, A. H., Eisen, E., Bolton, E., Nash, W. P., & Litz, B. T. (2017). Distinguishing war-related PTSD resulting from perpetration- and betrayal-based morally injurious events. *Psychological Trauma: Theory, Research, Practice, and Policy*, *9*(6), 627–634. https://doi.org/10.1037/tra0000249

Keenan, M. J., Lumley, V. A., & Schneider, R. B. (2014). A group therapy approach to treating combat posttraumatic stress disorder: Interpersonal reconnection through letter writing. *Psychotherapy*, *51*(4), 546–554. https://doi.org/10.1037/a0036025

Koenig, H. G., Ames, D., Youssef, N. A., Oliver, J. P., Volk, F., Teng, E. J., Haynes, K., Erickson, Z. D., Arnold, I., O'Garo, K., & Pearce, M. (2018). The Moral Injury Symptom Scale–Military version. *Journal of Religion and Health*, *57*(1), 249–265. https://doi.org/10.1007/s10943-017-0531-9

Kubany, E. S., Abueg, F. R., Owens, J. A., Brennan, J. M., Kaplan, A. S., & Watson, S. B. (1995). Initial examination of a multidimensional model of trauma-related guilt: Applications to combat veterans and battered women. *Journal of Psychopathology and Behavioral Assessment*, *17*(4), 353–376. https://doi.org/10.1007/BF02229056

Lewis, H. B. (1971). *Shame and guilt in neurosis*. International Universities Press.

Linden, M. (2003). Posttraumatic embitterment disorder. *Psychotherapy and Psychosomatics*, *72*(4), 195–202. https://doi.org/10.1159/000070783

Linden, M., Baumann, K., Rotter, M., & Schippan, B. (2007). The psychopathology of posttraumatic embitterment disorders. *Psychopathology*, *40*(3), 159–165. https://doi.org/10.1159/000100005

Linden, M., Baumann, K., Rotter, M., & Schippan, B. (2008). Posttraumatic embitterment disorder in comparison to other mental disorders. *Psychotherapy and Psychosomatics*, *77*(1), 50–56. https://doi.org/10.1159/000110060

Litz, B. T., & Kerig, P. K. (2019). Introduction to the special issue on moral injury: Conceptual challenges, methodological issues, and clinical applications. *Journal of Traumatic Stress, 32*(3), 341–349. https://doi.org/10.1002/jts.22405

Litz, B. T., Stein, N., Delaney, E., Lebowitz, L., Nash, W. P., Silva, C., & Maguen, S. (2009). Moral injury and moral repair in war veterans: A preliminary model and intervention strategy. *Clinical Psychology Review, 29*(8), 695–706. https://doi.org/10.1016/j.cpr.2009.07.003

Maguen, S., Burkman, K., Madden, E., Dinh, J., Bosch, J., Keyser, J., Schmitz, M., & Neylan, T. C. (2017). Impact of killing in war: A randomized, controlled pilot trial. *Journal of Clinical Psychology, 73*(9), 997–1012. https://doi.org/10.1002/jclp.22471

Maguen, S., Lucenko, B. A., Reger, M. A., Gahm, G. A., Litz, B. T., Seal, K. H., Knight, S. J., & Marmar, C. R. (2010). The impact of reported direct and indirect killing on mental health symptoms in Iraq war veterans. *Journal of Traumatic Stress, 23*(1), 86–90. https://doi.org/10.1002/jts.20434

Maguen, S., Metzler, T. J., Bosch, J., Marmar, C. R., Knight, S. J., & Neylan, T. C. (2012). Killing in combat may be independently associated with suicidal ideation. *Depression and Anxiety, 29*(11), 918–923. https://doi.org/10.1002/da.21954

McCormack, L., & Ell, L. (2017). Complex psychosocial distress postdeployment in veterans: Reintegration identity disruption and challenged moral integrity. *Traumatology, 23*(3), 240–249. https://doi.org/10.1037/trm0000107

Muldoon, P. (2008). The moral legitimacy of anger. *European Journal of Social Theory, 11*(3), 299–314. https://doi.org/10.1177/1368431008092564

Nash, W. P., Marino Carper, T. L., Mills, M. A., Au, T., Goldsmith, A., & Litz, B. T. (2013). Psychometric evaluation of the Moral Injury Events Scale. *Military Medicine, 178*(6), 646–652. https://doi.org/10.7205/MILMED-D-13-00017

Nickerson, A., Schnyder, U., Bryant, R. A., Schick, M., Mueller, J., & Morina, N. (2015). Moral injury in traumatized refugees. *Psychotherapy and Psychosomatics, 84*(2), 122–123. https://doi.org/10.1159/000369353

Nisbett, R. E., & Cohen, D. (1996). *Culture of honor: The psychology of violence in the south. New directions in social psychology*. Westview Press.

Phelps, A. J., Kartal, D., Lau, W., & Forbes, D. (2015). The utility of moral injury. In T. Frame (Ed.), *Moral injury: Unseen wounds in an age of barbarism* (pp. 150–166). UNSW Press.

Purcell, N., Koenig, C. J., Bosch, J., & Maguen, S. (2016). Veterans' perspectives on the psychosocial impact of killing in war. *The Counseling Psychologist, 44*(7), 1062–1099. https://doi.org/10.1177/0011000016666156

Schweder, R. A., Much, N. C., Mahapatra, M., & Park, L. (1997). The "Big Three" of morality (autonomy, community divinity) and the "Big Three" explanation of suffering. In A. Brandt & P. Rozin (Eds.), *Morality and health* (pp. 119–169). Routledge.

Shaver, P., Schwartz, J., Kirson, D., & O'Connor, C. (1987). Emotion knowledge: Further exploration of a prototype approach. *Journal of Personality and Social Psychology, 52*(6), 1061–1086. https://doi.org/10.1037/0022-3514.52.6.1061

Shay, J. (1994). *Achilles in Vietnam: Combat trauma and the undoing of character*. Scribner.

Shay, J. (2012). Moral injury. *Intertexts, 16*(1), 57–66. https://doi.org/10.1353/itx.2012.0000

Sherman, N. (2014). Recovering lost goodness: Shame, guilt, and self-empathy. *Psychoanalytic Psychology, 31*(2), 217–235. https://doi.org/10.1037/a0036435

Tangney, J. P., Stuewig, J., & Mashek, D. J. (2007). Moral emotions and moral behavior. *Annual Review of Psychology, 58*(1), 345–372. https://doi.org/10.1146/annurev.psych.56.091103.070145

Tedeschi, R. G., & Calhoun, L. G. (1996). The Posttraumatic Growth Inventory: Measuring the positive legacy of trauma. *Journal of Traumatic Stress, 9*(3), 455–471. https://doi.org/10.1002/jts.2490090305

Tracy, J. L., & Robins, R. W. (2006). Appraisal antecedents of shame and guilt: Support for a theoretical model. *Personality and Social Psychology Bulletin, 32*(10), 1339–1351. https://doi.org/10.1177/0146167206290212

Wilk, J. E., Bliese, P. D., Thomas, J. L., Wood, M. D., McGurk, D., Castro, C. A., & Hoge, C. W. (2013). Unethical battlefield conduct reported by soldiers serving in the Iraq war. *The Journal of Nervous and Mental Disease, 201*(4), 259–265. https://doi.org/10.1097/NMD.0b013e318288d302

Williamson, V., Murphy, D., & Greenberg, N. (2020). COVID-19 and experiences of moral injury in front-line key workers. *Occupational Medicine, 70*(5), 317–319. https://doi.org/10.1093/occmed/kqaa052

Williamson, V., Stevelink, S. A. M., & Greenberg, N. (2018). Occupational moral injury and mental health: Systematic review and meta-analysis. *The British Journal of Psychiatry, 212*(6), 339–346. https://doi.org/10.1192/bjp.2018.55

Worthen, M., & Ahern, J. (2014). The causes, course, and consequences of anger problems in veterans returning to civilian life. *Journal of Loss and Trauma, 19*(4), 355–363. https://doi.org/10.1080/15325024.2013.788945

Worthington, E. L., Jr., & Langberg, D. (2012). Religious considerations and self-forgiveness in treating complex trauma and moral injury in present and former soldiers. *Journal of Psychology and Theology, 40*(4), 274–288. https://doi.org/10.1177/009164711204000403

Yeterian, J. D., Berke, D. S., Carney, J. R., McIntyre-Smith, A., St Cyr, K., King, L., Kline, N. K., Phelps, A., Litz, B. T., & the Members of the Moral Injury Outcomes Project Consortium. (2019). Defining and measuring moral injury: Rationale, design, and preliminary findings from the moral injury outcome scale consortium. *Journal of Traumatic Stress, 32*(3), 363–372. https://doi.org/10.1002/jts.22380

Zust, J., & Krauss, S. (2019). Force protection from moral injury: Three objectives from military leaders. *Joint Force Quarterly, 92*(1), 44–49.

4 EMOTIONAL CULTURE AND THE ANGRY TEAM

OLIVIA (MANDY) O'NEILL

KEY POINTS

- A culture of anger
  - can have both functional and dysfunctional consequences;
  - includes assumptions, norms, and artifacts transmitted through both actual feelings and strategic, intentional enactments; and
  - can be created through top-down processes and bottom-up processes.
- Successful strategies for managing may include increasing presence of positive emotions, team training, customized human resources systems, and large-scale system change.

https://doi.org/10.1037/0000244-005
Anger at Work: Prevention, Intervention, and Treatment in High-Risk Occupations, A. B. Adler and D. Forbes (Editors)

Of all the emotions known to humankind, anger is one of the most universally recognized and easily understood (Ekman, 1973). Despite its pervasiveness, it is rare to find a balanced account of anger. This chapter builds on advances in research on anger and the emotional culture of organizations by explaining how anger can become a team characteristic, manifested across levels, shared across individuals, and managed by team leaders. Given the essential role of teams in high-risk occupations, anger at the team and leader level is critically important to consider. Anger is important to consider for every type of team, but it is particularly relevant to high-risk teams. In many high-risk occupations (e.g., firefighting, the military), the team is the focal unit of analysis, whether it be shifts, crews, squads, installations, or platoons. In addition, the implications of anger in high-risk occupations are highly consequential. High-risk occupations involve missions and situations that require close coordination and trust among team members and in which the consequences of a poorly managed emotional culture of anger can be lethal.

The chapter is organized into five sections. In the first section, I review the theoretical foundations of anger, placing it within a typology of discrete emotions and differentiating between its socially dysfunctional and socially functional forms. The chapter then turns to team emotional culture of anger and the mechanisms underlying its formation and transmission. Building on research on levels of analysis, the third section examines the processes through which anger becomes a team characteristic, distinguishing between top-down and bottom-up processes. In the fourth section, I present two case studies that examine the implications of anger in teams, distinguishing between its causes and consequences in high-risk occupations varying in frontline orientation and gender composition. In the final section of the chapter, I identify solutions for addressing the dysfunctional consequences of an emotional culture of anger in teams at the individual, team, and organizational system levels.

CONCEPTUALIZATIONS OF ANGER

One of the earliest conceptualizations of anger from organizational psychologists comes from Ilfeld (1978), who defined anger as a strong emotion of displeasure or antagonism, stimulated by injury or insult to one's self or others, or by the perceived intent to do such harm. Geddes et al. (2020) offered a similar definition of anger as "an emotion that involves an appraisal of responsibility for wrongdoing by another person or entity and often includes the goal of correcting the perceived wrong" (p. 29). Although similar in its appraisal of anger as unpleasantness, this latter definition points to others as the cause of wrongdoing and to anger's functional side, namely, its purpose of "righting a wrong." From an appraisal perspective, anger differs from other emotions through its *valence* (i.e., unpleasantness), *certainty* (in contrast to anxiety, e.g., which is characterized by uncertainty), and as resulting from a situation *not of one's own doing* (Smith & Ellsworth, 1985). Central to understanding the consequences of anger is the reality that people feeling anger are more likely to blame someone else for negative events instead of the situation or themselves.

Although anger is generally viewed as resulting in negative consequences for oneself and toward the source of anger (e.g., Deffenbacher et al., 1996), some have argued that this view oversimplifies the nature of anger. To begin this chapter, I contrast the dominant approach focused on the negative implications of anger for individuals and teams with an alternative approach grounded in social psychological and functional perspectives, which offer a more nuanced portrait of anger.

Two lines of research shed light on these alternative approaches to anger. The first is the social functional perspective on emotions. The concept of "functional" anger comes from Keltner and Haidt (1999), who identified the purpose of emotions at multiple levels of analysis. At the team level, emotions help individuals who share identities and goals to meet their shared goals or the superordinate goals of the group. One way in which this occurs is by helping individuals to define group boundaries and identify group members. This approach is relevant to anger, as its collective expression may help sharpen group boundaries between teams or, for example, between teams and management. Another function of emotions such as anger in teams is to help individuals define and negotiate group roles and status. Anger from this perspective can be seen as a way of establishing the perception of strong leadership, competence, and dominance (Tiedens, 2001). Finally, team-level emotions including anger help group members to negotiate group-related problems, such as displeasure with the organization's leaders or with management policies or practices. A second line of research focuses specifically on anger in the organizational context. Consistent with a social-functional perspective, this perspective highlights how anger serves to promote dialogue, to facilitate the airing of differences that can lead to improved working relationship and movement toward organizational goals and beneficial change (e.g., Callister et al., 2017).

How, then, do researchers reconcile approaches to anger that focus on how it can be beneficial with the dominant approach, which views anger as largely negative? One way to reconcile these approaches is to consider the variety of emotions contained within the anger prototype. According to Shaver et al.'s (1987) prototype approach, discrete emotions within a broad prototype vary in intensity and social function, with different implications for behavior. Consider, for example, the difference between feeling *frustration* or *annoyance* at someone and feeling *rage* or *fury*. All of these emotions are contained within the larger prototype of anger, but they differ in intensity. Other pertinent examples are *bitterness* and *contempt*, the latter of which has been shown to be uniformly negative for individuals (Melwani & Barsade, 2011) and dyads (Gottman, 1993), and presumably to teams as well.

A second way to think about the functional versus dysfunctional consequences of anger is to consider norms, or *thresholds for acceptability*. Although anger is generally seen as having a negative influence on team culture, a threshold perspective points to both favorable and unfavorable outcomes, depending on the situation (Geddes et al., 2020). According to the dual threshold perspective (Geddes & Callister, 2007), it is sometimes better to express anger so that it might help resolve problems rather than suppress anger and leave the problem unaddressed. Lindebaum et al. (2016), for example, described how soldiers who perceived their supervisor's anger as justified and fair responded to the anger by changing their behavior in an attempt to rectify the problem. This interaction pattern was helpful in combat training situations, where there was a perceived need to simulate possible combat responses. At the same time, individuals also need to pay attention to norms around how much anger is acceptable to express and where it is appropriate to be expressed, lest the anger be perceived as deviant and have negative consequences for individuals and teams. In addition to team and organizational norms, norms around the acceptability of expressing anger can vary by culture, as Adam and Shirako (2013) showed in a study of East Asian versus European negotiators. Nuances of the specific occupational context matter too. In firefighting teams, for example, anger expression is often acceptable (and sometimes encouraged) among firefighting teams at the station, but great importance is placed on being able to handle undesirable, "out of control" emotions such as anger while on calls. As Reid et al. (2018) reported, "keeping your cool" was seen as important for responding to frustrating noncritical emergency calls ("social service calls") or when there was a need to remain calm in a chaotic scene. Any firefighter who failed at this was seen as "thin-skinned," "emotional," and someone who "wear[s] your heart on your sleeve." Underlying these display rules (Ekman, 1973) were implicit assumptions about the consequences of mishandling feelings of anger. Failure to appropriately regulate negative emotions was seen as a problem not only for maintaining their mental health ("If you took it all to heart, we'd be wrecks") but also to on-scene performance during emergency calls ("We wouldn't be any better than bystanders").

As this introduction suggests, anger is a complex emotion whose myriad functions in teams are worth considering, depending on the specific form of anger and the norms around its expression. Anger can be adaptive, but there are many instances in which it is dysfunctional or inconsistent with the goals of the team or organization. This is particularly the case when anger is central to a team's emotional culture, the focus of the next section.

CREATION AND MAINTENANCE OF EMOTIONAL CULTURE

The theoretical foundations of the emotional culture construct lie in more than 35 years' worth of research on organizational culture, often described as an understanding of the patterns of meanings and behavior in an organization (Ostroff et al., 2003) and manifested through both "deep" instantiations (e.g., fundamental assumptions, values, beliefs) and visible artifacts (Schein, 2010), including symbols (e.g., logos and physical space), organizational language (e.g., jargon, slogans), narratives (e.g., stories, sagas), and practices (e.g., rituals, ceremonies; Denison, 1996; O'Reilly et al., 1991; Pettigrew, 1979; Trice & Beyer, 1993). Nascent research on emotional culture—which encompasses the behavioral norms, artifacts, and underlying values and assumptions reflecting the actual expression or suppression of discrete emotions and the degree of perceived appropriateness of discrete emotions (Barsade & O'Neill, 2014)—expands on Schein's (2010) conceptualization of culture, shifting the focus away from a legacy of research focused more on cognitive manifestations of culture (e.g., strategic values held in the minds and manifested in the behavior of organizational members through norms) to the discrete emotions experienced and expressed across employees and manifested across levels of the organization. Whereas earlier conceptualizations of culture had fleeting references to emotions and feelings, a comprehensive treatment of emotions at every level of culture was lacking before the construct of emotional culture appeared on scene.

The construct of emotional culture was first introduced in the context of a positively valenced emotion: companionate love, comprising affection, caring, compassion, and tenderness (Barsade & O'Neill, 2014). The construct can be applied to other emotions, however, including negative emotions. To begin to theorize about the nature and consequences of a team culture of anger, I first illustrate what anger looks like when it is diffused throughout a team, department, or organization. In such a culture, anger is experienced frequently, intensely, and pervasively, and it is expressed facially through furrowed brows, wide eyes, and tight-pressed lips (Keltner et al., 2019). In a strong culture of anger, there is both consensus and consistency among members, as well as intensity in terms of how tightly the values or norms (Gelfand et al., 2006; Jackson, 1966) around experiencing and expressing anger are held.

Interpersonally, expressions of a strong culture of anger are reinforced by shared angry faces, frequent disclosures of work-related irritations, and commonplace discussions about aspects of the work environment that make employees angry. Imagine a culture of anger among a team of National Guard officers, for example, where a routine "How are you?" is expected to be greeted with "Well, I'm pissed off about . . ." followed by a litany of irritations, including being overworked, abused by community members, and irritated by management practices. For a colleague to not engage in this would lead his or her peers to question their status as a trusted member or to think that they do not belong as part of the group. However, it is not just the normative expressions at play in an emotional culture of anger, as demonstrated in the previous example. Through emotional contagion (e.g., Barsade, 2002), these interpersonal norms can exacerbate high levels of felt anger, as employees feed off one another's frustrations and negative energy transferred outside of our conscious awareness. Anger contagion can also prompt reciprocal feedback loops, or "emotion cycles," in which one person's anger influences the anger of others, whose reactions then influence the anger present in future interactions with the person (Hareli & Rafaeli, 2008). In such a culture, expressions of anger become part of the normative environment; that is, expressing anger is not only acceptable but also expected. In such organizational contexts, social norms prescribe the expression of anger because it signals that employees are a part of the group.

Building on this brief portrait of what a strong culture of anger looks and feels like, I now expand on the underlying characteristics of an emotional culture of anger that are shared across emotions. Two aspects of the definition of emotional culture in particular are worth noting. First, the emotion or emotions that compose emotional culture (in this case, anger) are manifested across people and across levels of culture (i.e., artifacts, norms, values, assumptions; Schein, 2010). Second, the emotions are transmitted through the two sets of underlying mechanisms just described: feeling mechanisms (i.e., actually feeling the emotions) and normative mechanisms.

Barsade and O'Neill (2014) identified three types of feeling mechanisms, mechanisms through which employees come to actually feel the emotions central to the culture: internally felt emotions, emotional contagion, and "deep acting." When the first mechanism is activated—described in the preceding National Guard example—employees feel the same emotions that coincide with the emotions prescribed by the culture (Ashforth & Humphrey, 1993). A second way in which feelings of anger are generated among employees is through emotional contagion (Barsade, 2002; Hatfield et al., 1993), whereby employees "catch" the anger of other coworkers. As this process occurs outside of conscious awareness, employees are often unaware that the anger they catch from others is not their own. Nonverbal behavior is central to this mechanism, including facial expressions, tone, and body language that elicit mimicry and corresponding feelings (Strack et al., 1988). Although typically examined in face-to-face contexts, emotional contagion can also occur in virtual teams and in text-based communication (Cheshin et al., 2011). This point is particularly noteworthy as today's world becomes increasingly digital.

A third mechanism through which employees come to genuinely feel anger is through deep acting, whereby employees consciously try to genuinely feel anger because it is required by coworkers to be displayed at work (Grandey, 2003). An example might be a unionized police officer on strike with his coworkers at a reduced pay level. Although he and his coworkers might be less upset than their leaders about the situation (and instead are feeling anxiety about the looming bills they have to pay), in a strong culture of anger, union members would engage in deep acting, whereby anger is enacted in verbal statements, facial expressions, vocal tone, and body language, ultimately leading to the union members genuinely feeling the emotion.

In addition to the mechanisms just described, a team emotional culture of anger is cultivated and has influence over team outcomes through a secondary pathway involving normative enactments. This mechanism is distinct in that employees express emotions strategically and intentionally, largely to conform to group expectations around expressing anger, regardless (and in some cases, independent) of how they actually feel. The first mechanism is surface acting (Ashforth & Humphrey, 1993; Hochschild, 1983), which is related to a concept known as *display rules* (Ekman, 1973; Rafaeli & Sutton, 1987). *Surface acting* occurs when employees display emotions they do not feel but are required to express as part of their job (Ashforth & Humphrey, 1993; Hochschild, 1983). An example of this mechanism is Sutton's (1991) study of bill collectors, a role that required employees to express anger at customers in order to secure payments. In this research study, Sutton noted that the bill collectors are not actually feeling anger; rather, they are expressing anger strategically with the anticipation of having an impact on delinquent customers who haven't paid their bills. A second normative mechanism—*affective social exchange*—on the other hand, involves another normative enactment involving emotional reciprocity (Clark, 1997), such as when a coworker's moral outrage on behalf of another colleague's problem engenders a sense of obligation or pressure from the colleague to return the coworker's favor by acting angry about their issue at some point in the future. A third normative enactment is social influence (Asch, 1955; Sherif, 1936), whereby individuals conform to group norms of anger expression because of a desire to be liked and accepted by the group. This type of normative enactment is particularly pervasive among newcomers, who have a strong motivation to fit in with the group.

Figure 4.1 visualizes each of the mechanisms described here and their relationship to the definition of emotional culture, as well as to the antecedents and outcomes associated with anger, described in the following section.

Next, I explore how emotional culture applies specifically to teams, noting the antecedents of a team culture of anger from the perspective of levels of analysis.[1]

ANTECEDENTS OF ANGER IN TEAMS

In thinking about how anger comes to define the culture of teams, specifically about anger in high-performance teams, research on group emotion (Barsade & Gibson, 1998) and levels of analysis (Kozlowski & Klein, 2000) is helpful. From a teams and groups perspective, team anger can develop through what are sometimes called "top-down processes" or through "bottom-up processes." Top-down processes include characteristics of the team resulting from leadership characteristics and leadership style (e.g., Bass & Avolio, 1994). In the case of emotions specifically, one way in which

[1]The research outlines the mechanisms through which emotional culture is maintained in a culture. It is intentionally flexible with respect to what some refer to as the "level of analysis"—in other words, whether culture is conceptualized and measured at the organizational level (i.e., an entire base), the regional or divisional level (e.g., Southeast vs. Midwest), the department or team level, and so on. Although some organizational culture researchers restrict the use of culture to entire organizations (e.g., O'Reilly et al., 1991), the concept of culture has been shown to be more usefully applied to groups, departments, and divisions within organizations rather than the organization as a whole (Barsade & O'Neill, 2014; Martin, 1992; O'Neill & Rothbard, 2017; Van Maanen & Barley, 1985). This distinction is helpful for extrapolating the emotional culture research to the team level.

FIGURE 4.1. The Emotional Culture of Anger: Construct, Mechanisms, and Outcomes

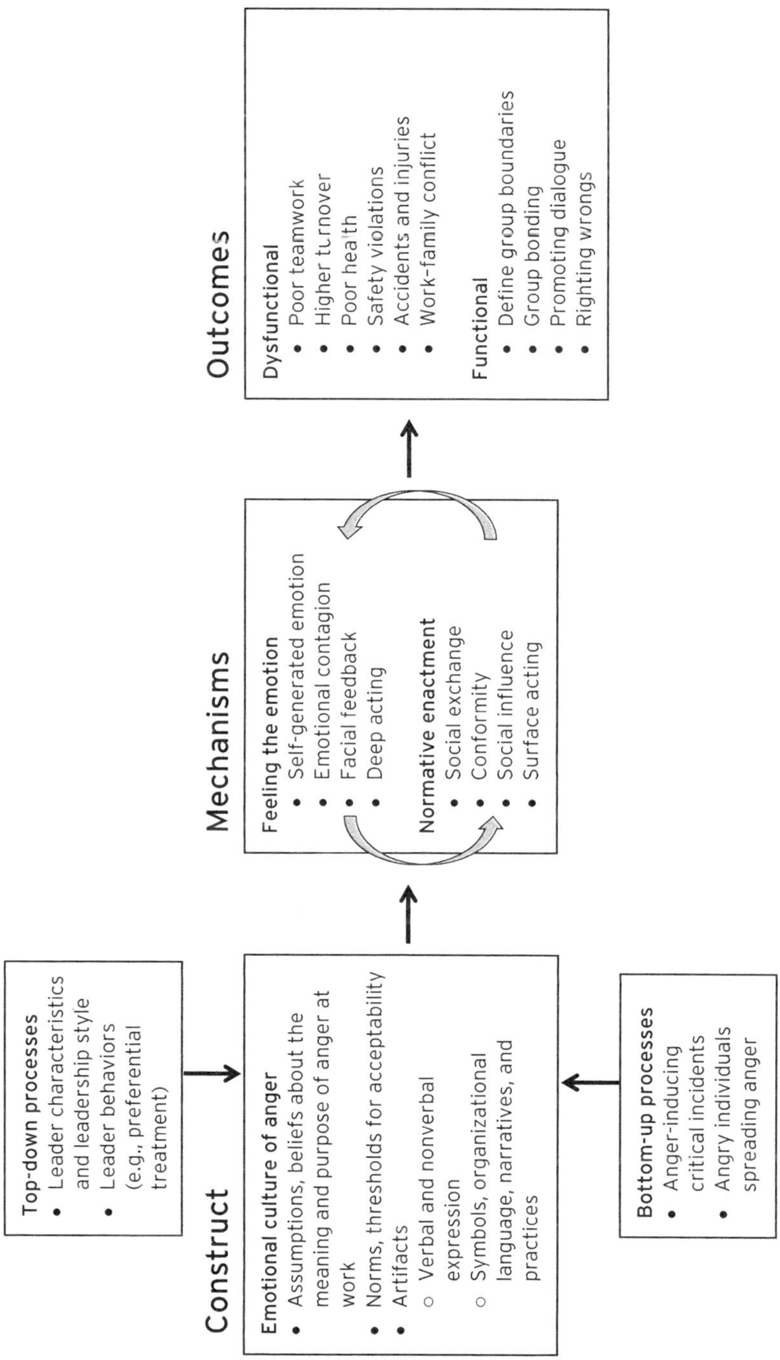

Note. From "What's Love Got to Do With It? A Longitudinal Study of the Culture of Companionate Love and Employee and Client Outcomes in a Long-Term Care Setting," by S. G. Barsade and O. A. O'Neill, 2014, *Administrative Science Quarterly*, *59*(4), pp. 551–598 (https://doi.org/10.1177/0001839214538636). Copyright 2014 by Sage. Adapted with permission.

this occurs is through emotion contagion from leaders and managers (Côté & Morgan, 2002). According to this process, anger expressed by leaders or managers is "caught" by subordinates, who feel more anger themselves or are compelled to express anger in adherence to norms. This top-down process also occurs through the behavior of leaders that elicits anger among team members, such as a leader who extends privileges or favors to certain departments or teams, resulting in anger from other departments or teams.

Anger can also spread through bottom-up processes, such as when dispositionally angry employees spread anger laterally to their colleagues. This can occur as a result of a negative incident that elicits widespread anger or negative perceptions of the organization. An example was reported by O'Neill et al. (2009) in their study of anger in store branches of a large retail organization. In this study, the researchers demonstrated that individual-level anger resulting from employees' perceptions of poor organizational support resulted in store-level anger, which spread across the employees in different store locations to form what some would refer to as an "affective climate" (Parke & Seo, 2017) defined by anger. Note here the deliberate use of term "climate" to describe the aggregate feeling of anger. Although the difference between climate and culture is sometimes vague (Denison, 1996), employees' perceptions of an organization's policies, practices, and procedures are core to the concept of climate and—in the O'Neill et al. (2009) study—were a direct cause of anger. This distinction suggests that, in the absence of assumptions, norms, and artifacts of anger (i.e., core manifestations of culture), the term "climate of anger" may be more appropriate when referring to anger that is primarily the result of shared employee anger resulting from management policies.

THE CULTURE OF ANGER IN HIGH-RISK OCCUPATIONS

Having established the groundwork for what anger is and how it comes to constitute the culture of teams, I now shift the focus to team culture of anger in high-risk occupations. Next, I present two case studies of how anger stems from and is expressed differently across two types of high-risk occupational teams: firefighting teams and hospital intensive care unit (ICU) teams.

The Culture of Anger in Firefighters

Unpublished data from a case study of firefighters based on the work of O'Neill and Rothbard (2017) provide a glimpse of the emotional culture of angry emergency response teams. O'Neill and Rothbard interviewed emergency responders at 27 fire stations within a large county surrounding a major metropolitan city in the eastern United States. Participants were 100 firefighters (97 men, three women). The data collection method consisted of 1- to 2-hour semistructured group interviews and observation within stations. All interviews were attended by two or three people who independently recorded quotations and observations in their field notes. To capture both highly salient and "hidden" aspects of emotions and culture, the researchers attempted to create a situation in which crew members interacted with one another naturally as a group, thereby allowing the researchers to observe spontaneous nonverbal manifestations of the emotional culture that emerged.

Rather than focusing on anger per se, the design of the study allowed researchers to capture the breadth of emotional cultures manifested in the emergency response teams as well as a base rate of teams' emotional culture of anger. This county, which spanned 16 separate municipalities, contained significant variation in geographic location (urban, suburban, and rural), station size (as reflected by the number of firefighters on duty, often a reflection of station busyness and population density), characteristics of the local population (e.g., age, socioeconomic status, ethnicity), and building construction type (e.g., modern with private sleeping quarters vs. traditional open style). Variation on these dimensions provided valuable contrasts in the emotional culture of the emergency response teams within. As reported in O'Neill and Rothbard (2017), anger was not the most prominent emotion explaining variation in the emotional culture of teams. On the contrary, two positive emotions—joviality (i.e., amusement) and companionate love (e.g., affection, caring, compassion, tenderness)—emerged as most prominent. Anger was present, however, in the emotional culture of some teams, which I describe next.

Although there were elements of anger in many teams, of the 27 teams interviewed, only one could clearly be described as having a strong emotional culture of anger. In this team, anger expressions were a common occurrence. For example, when described what he liked least about the job (an introductory question), one firefighter angrily stated, "We're treated like a public slave from both the public and from within, and you can tell management that!" A paramedic with more than 15 years' experience freely expressed extreme anger and bitterness toward patients. "They call every day to get a ride to avoid waiting in the waiting room of the hospital. Or, they're sick and would rather throw up or take a dump in your truck than their car." The group's irritation, anger, and bitterness were clear from the overt comments to researchers. "There are frequent flyer and 'seekers,' people looking for medicine and hopping from one hospital to the next." Although it is not possible to determine with certainty what it was about this team that caused it to become such a strong culture of anger, contagion of anger among the firefighters was clearly at play here, as evidenced by the way in which the other firefighters unconsciously "caught" their colleagues' anger after the initial outburst and began expressing anger themselves.

An underlying characteristic of the team's emotional culture of anger—consistent with the underlying appraisal dimensions of anger—was the perception of unreasonable obstacles and blocked goals caused by others. For example, the relationship between first responders and the emergency room staff at local hospitals[2] presented an obstacle in the form of admissions procedures preventing from achieving their goal, the transfer of patients. A firefighter in one team expressed annoyance at the local hospitals "not wanting to take anything" (i.e., to admit any patients). Another firefighter, attempting to take the perspective of the emergency room staff, noted that "hospitals are overwhelmed" and can be "bad to deal with," with hospital staff "taking out their frustrations on us." This example points to the contagion of anger across teams (indeed, across occupations) but also to the ways in which a team's specific job tasks and goals as emergency responders contribute to intergroup conflict, thereby exacerbating the anger experienced by everyone. As one firefighter noted, "Sometimes we're looked at as the enemy," leading to "an adversarial relationship with the hospital." This latter comment illustrates how the antecedents of emotional culture and mechanisms such as emotional contagion form a reinforcing cycle, with firefighters "catching" the anger and frustration of their emergency room colleagues or responding to their anger with anger, creating a feedback loop or cycle of anger.

Findings also reveal how norms around the appropriateness or inappropriateness of expressing anger among teams contributed to the culture of anger in teams. For instance, some teams detailed the frustration of not being able to express their anger freely, to bad-mouth "social service" calls or "frequent flyers." When asked how he handles "repeat callers" and the patients who call for help with minor problems, one firefighter said that it annoys him to have to wake up that early and go out for something that he wasn't needed for, but he can't make his frustrations apparent to his

[2]As in many regions in the United States, firefighters in this county were trained to respond to medical emergencies. Indeed, the majority of emergencies handled by firefighters in this county were medical in nature. Large-scale fires were increasingly rare occurrences.

patients, because "this whole job is customer service." Indeed, one firefighter explained that he and his colleagues get punished for expressing such negatively ("Headquarters doesn't like when they express that kind of attitude"). Years of suppression, a common firefighter emotion regulation strategy which involved "putting a lid" on emotions after the emotional experience has begun (Gross, 1998), led to second-order effects with more negative consequence than might be expected if the anger were expressed in the first place. For example, firefighters linked years of containing their emotions to debilitated health and poor performance on the job. Several firefighters speculated that their lifespans were shorter as a result of the stress and negativity of their jobs. One firefighter close to retirement detailed, "You get burned out and become too complacent around the patients." He explained that "being complacent" means "mouthing off to patients you are sick of"—presumably much more negatively after years of suppressing the emotions. In this way, management expectations that anger be suppressed may have paradoxically contributed to stronger feelings of anger and more negative long-term consequences such as burnout and worse health.

Patients were not the only source of anger, however. Hassle factors such as paperwork and bureaucracy also contributed to the culture of anger among firefighters. One firefighter reported,

> My problem is making them run call after call without a moment to calm down. You are expected to get the paperwork perfect even after 10 calls at 3 am. It's almost impossible when you do back-to-back calls before you can deal with the paperwork.

Consistent with O'Neill et al.'s (2009) findings in a retail setting, lack of appreciation from management contributed to a culture of anger and, in extreme cases, bitterness. One veteran firefighter close to retirement expressed his ire over management's inability to recognize firefighter contributions, particularly in situations in which colleagues took individual credit for achievements, a major violation of the core value placed on teamwork in firefighting teams. The group expressed similar exasperation about people who nominate themselves for honor awards, a violation of the team-oriented, collectivistic norms in most firefighting teams. Blame for the situation was directed at management: "Headquarters doesn't know anything [about who performs well on the job]. . . . It's a different mentality." The frustration with management builds up over time, leading one firefighter to observe, "You're just counting down the days until retirement."

The unpublished firefighter data indicate only one team that would be characterized by a strong culture of anger based on the defining characteristics of emotional culture (i.e., frequency of anger expressions), but focusing only on outward expressions of anger from one-time interviews and observational data is not a reliable way to assess the pervasiveness of cultures of anger. In addition, this method belies the existence and consequences of suppressed anger. In some instances, anger was not manifested outwardly, as observed among one team in which the anger lay slightly beneath the surface. At first blush, the emotional culture appeared to be one of contentedness and serenity. The researchers soon learned, however, that this emotional culture was masking more negative emotions that were unacceptable to express outside of the social group. After the group interview, one firefighter followed the researchers out of the building to share his negativity about his colleagues. As this example suggests, the absence of anger expressions might suggest a weak culture of anger, but the anger lay just belowground, suppressed or masked in everyday interactions or expressed in other ways (e.g., counterproductive work behavior).

The Culture of Anger in Hospital Intensive Care Units

One issue that arises when examining the culture of anger in firefighting teams is the role of emotional labor (Hochschild, 1983) relating to the "customer service" (Grandey, 2003) aspects of the profession. In other high-risk occupations, interactions with the public contribute less to anger felt and expressed at work than it did for firefighters. Additionally, the gender composition of the firefighting sample was predominantly male (97%), thus obscuring the extent to which the team emotional culture of anger—an emotion more acceptable for men to express (Brescoll & Uhlmann, 2008)—was driven by the gender composition of the organization and profession. In this regard, unpublished data from another professional context in which the emergencies involve fewer "frontline" interactions with the public and with a different gender composition are revealing.

Data for this second case study come from a longitudinal study of ICU providers and nursing staff across five ICUs of a large university teaching hospital in the United States. As part of this study, I conducted 79 semi-structured interviews with a sample of 67 health care workers over a 4-year period before, during, and after a major physical and organizational restructuring of the units. At two points in time, participants completed a survey of the units' emotional expression norms. In a recorded interview with leadership of the units reviewing the results of the study, the most surprising finding to leadership were data indicating that staff felt more comfortable expressing negative emotions such as anger than positive emotions such as joy or compassion (compassion was a core stated value of the organization and caregiving professions such as medicine). The strength of this finding was surprising to leaders, who were generally quite proud of the nationally ranked, high-performing specialized units they managed. In a debrief of the data, one nurse manager offered an explanation: "Well, naturally, humans tend to bond better over anger and negativity and venting than they do over positive things so maybe that's a reflection on our having a new unit with new people trying to bond with each other." Although the finding stood in stark contrast to the managers' perceptions of the pervasive emotions expressed on units, the explanation is consistent with a social functional approach to anger described earlier. According to this perspective, shared emotions such as anger serve to differentiate between groups and to bond members of a group.

Although this quotation points to the potentially functional side of anger (i.e., group bonding), other findings from the data collection point to the negative consequences of anger for teamwork. One unit in particular stands out for its emotional culture of anger. When asked to describe the culture of that unit in an interview with the researcher, a physician who works on the unit replied, "Angry. . . . I think there's just a culture of negativity: I think a lot of that trickles from the top down." The physician described how physicians, including some surgeons who commanded a great deal of status and respect in this hospital for their highly specialized training, contributed to the culture, which trickled down to other staff on the unit:

> When I hear that people are being interrupted during rounds, or angry with each other on rounds, or yelling at each other on rounds, those kinds of things are—that's not okay in any job. And I think the fact that that's been allowed to go on that way, and it's now that's just kind of how that service runs. I know there's a lot of turnover from their practice providers.

This quote points to the frequency of anger expressions and the norms around acceptability of expressing anger. It also points to one implication of strong cultures of anger: high turnover. In a strong culture of anger, even minor incidents become blown out of proportion. The fact that the culture still had a culture of anger even after some of the angry people left points to a central tenet of culture, namely, its stability over time. Even when angry people leave, in a strong culture of anger the underlying assumptions, norms, and values remain. One way in which this occurs is through stories told by current remember about incidents or times of the past. Stories are carriers of culture, serving the purpose of spreading anger among the cultural members who remain and those who leave the organization at a later time.

The culture of anger on the unit was so strong and toxic that visitors to the unit surmised the culture, even in the absence of overt anger expressions. One nurse described the difficulties working on the unit as a visitor:

> And I almost was scared to walk through [this unit] for a couple of weeks because they literally—no one would say a word to me—but there would be like, very snarky email responses back to people about, "this can't possibly work" and "no one's supporting us because you took away all our supplies at the bedside" and "how could we possibly manage a patient," or "thank you for leaving me only two blood tubes in my cart."

This quote greatly illuminates what a culture of anger in a team looks like from the perspective of coworkers from other teams interacting with the angry team. First, it describes how a culture of anger manifests itself not only directly (i.e., blowing up at someone) but also indirectly (i.e., sarcasm). Second, it points to some of the consequences of a team culture of anger, including negative employee attitudes, poor teamwork, and incivility, a finding reported in other studies (Riskin et al., 2015, 2017).

With respect to the mechanisms underlying a culture of anger, quotes from the ICU unit with the strong culture of anger reveal how contagion from one person's felt anger appears to contribute to team cultures of anger. One nurse explained, "We have—you know there's always somebody who is disgruntled and that's going to feed the fire and cause stress." Another nurse described how the culture of anger created negative feelings in coworkers: "To experience in the morning a bunch of nurses getting kind of angry every morning, that's not great." Even intense anger from one team member had the potential for negative contagion. One supervisor described an incident in which a nurse was angry about the way that patient care went. For several months, the nurse was angry, blaming, pointing fingers in the incident report. The supervised told her, ". . . there's so much emotion and blame and finger pointing, it's tearing us apart as a team."

Although the nature of the tasks and the workflow of ICUs differ from other emergency response teams, the high-intensity nature of emergency response work contributes to cultures of anger in similar ways. For example, one nurse described a colleague whose anger became a problem for the team.

She'll . . . think that nobody's paying attention . . . to the patient with her. . . . She gets very mad at other providers. . . . Calls them directly, yells at them, things like this. I mean, she just has a hard time managing that kind of stress sometimes.

Incidents such as this one highlight several properties of a team culture of anger. First, there was certainty regarding the nature of the situation, which was experienced as unpleasant and a block to the nurse's goals. Second, the blame lay with someone other than oneself, a key appraisal dimension of anger.

In addition to the day-to-day work involved in emergency response teams, critical incidents unrelated to the work itself can also spark collective anger, such as an incident that took place 3 years prior to data collection in which a popular nurse was fired, sparking collective anger among his former coworkers. The anger was not just isolated to one or two individuals; rather, it was distributed equally among the team. The fact that the team was still talking about the incident years later indicates that team emotional culture is not a fleeting experience of affect; rather, it is an enduring characteristic of the group.

> People left over that and we're still recovering from it actually. We had to do a lot of damage control and I don't think our management handled it [well]. . . . There was a lot of mistrust and I think we're still recovering from it.

The team's anger had significant consequences for the unit. Not only did the collective anger experienced by the team cause some individual team members to quit, the blowback was so strong that it caused some leaders to consider quitting.

Anger felt by the ICU teams often bled over into family life. Work–family conflict resulting from negative events at work was a common theme among firefighters (O'Neill & Rothbard, 2017), although more as a result of the trauma they experienced as first responders. Although staff in ICU units are further down the emergency response chain, anger shared among the team at work bled over into their home lives, too. One nurse described, "In the beginning, I would come home upset and I would come home—or angry or whatever feeling I was feeling from work that day, I would bring it home. It was a real struggle."

Although many of the incidents described thus far illustrate team anger directed at management or other colleagues in response to a specific discrete incident involving strong team bonds being tested, anger was also present as a result of absence of relational bonds in the team. In one unit, the lack of caring and concern was a cause for anger among some team members. One nurse described it in the following way:

> Some days I'm just like, I leave work angry because I don't feel that I have—I don't feel that people have checked in on me, that I've been running around like an idiot or been unreasonably busy, maybe, but I feel like I've been having to ask all day for help from people who are not busy themselves and been very frustrated about it. I get so frustrated when people don't—when I'm in charge, and I find that I can see it, but no one else seems to care. Like they're watching this—their fellow nurse drown, and they're chatting or they're on the internet or something like that, you know? And it just really pisses me off.

This quote is revealing for describing not only a novel cause for a culture of anger—one unrelated to an inaction rather than action—but also a violation of an implicit assumption held by many emergency response teams: Teamwork is paramount.

SOLUTIONS FOR MANAGING THE NEGATIVE IMPLICATIONS OF TEAM ANGER

Having established what an angry team looks like and described some of the implications of an angry team, I now turn to potential solutions for managing the negative implications of angry teams. In the following section, I describe interventions at the individual, team, and system levels (see Table 4.1 for an overview). Although these suggested interventions are borne out of existing research, it is important to acknowledge that the effectiveness of these interventions has not been validated specifically for mitigating team culture of anger.

Individual Interventions

As some of the case study data suggest, a team culture of anger is sometimes created by an angry team member whose oversized emotions shape the emotional culture of the team through feeling mechanisms such as contagion as well as normative enactments from those who feel obliged to express outrage on behalf of an offended peer. This culture is exacerbated when the angry team member is a leader, as research shows the emotion contagion is stronger (Côté & Morgan, 2002). As such, interventions targeting the angry team member are potentially beneficial.

Professional coaching is one intervention for individuals who contribute to a team culture of anger. Although many forms of coaching exist, most have in common a short-term relationship between an employee and a consultant with the purpose of improving the employee's work effectiveness. Coaching is relevant for team members who are aware of their anger and its negative implications, as well as those unaware of their anger problems. Indeed, research suggests that many individuals may be unaware of how their behavior impacts others, a situation exacerbated by the infrequency with which many people receive critical feedback about their personal and professional development. Although it is possible for managers to coach subordinates (i.e., in the event of an angry team member who is not the leader), most coaching is conducted by consultants who have no formal authority

TABLE 4.1. Anger Interventions Across Organizational Levels

Organizational level	Examples
Individual interventions	Coaching: a short-term relationship between an employee and a consultant with the purpose of improving the employee's work effectiveness • Many approaches focused on reducing the negative emotion • New approaches focus on acceptance of anger or buffering through positive emotions such as compassion Other interventions • Compassion-based therapy • Loving-kindness meditation, breathing, and compassion training interventions
Team interventions	Improve team competencies • Conflict resolution • Collaborative problem-solving • Communication • Goal setting and performance management • Planning and task coordination Increase team leaders' ability to understand a situation and to regulate their own and the team's emotions
System level interventions	Human resources systems • Hiring • Performance appraisals • Employee engagement surveys Leader selection and training • Transformational vs. transactional leadership System change • Organizational culture assessment and change

over clients, a factor linked to greater effectiveness. In a summary of the literature, Feldman and Lankau (2005) identified four approaches to coaching: (a) a *psychodynamic* approach, focusing on the client's unconscious thoughts and internal states to increase self-awareness; (b) a *behaviorist* approach, which uses behavioral principles such as positive and negative reinforcement to increase understanding of the consequences of angry behavior and how to change the behavior; (c) a *cognitive therapy* approach, focused on modifying patterns of distorted and irrational thinking leading to anger; and (d) a *systems* approach involving data gathering and analysis of the client's interactions with other individuals in the team or organization, organizational roles, and intergroup relations within the organization.

Some approaches to coaching, especially early in coaching history as an individual intervention, focused on deficiencies in employees' task performance. From this perspective, individuals or teams whose anger interferes with their effectiveness at work would be coached to reduce their felt and expressed anger. Unfortunately, as some of the earlier firefighter examples suggest, a common strategy for reducing the expression of anger is to engage in *emotion suppression,* that is, blocking the outward expression of emotion after the emotional experience has begun (Gross & John, 2003). A robust body of evidence shows that not only is suppression ineffective for reducing the experience of emotional states, it is also associated with negative second-order consequences such as reduced cognitive ability, impaired memory, and negative interpersonal interactions (Butler et al., 2003; Richards & Gross, 1999). The impetus for stopping the expression of emotion can be self-imposed (i.e., one's own emotion regulation strategies) or imposed to comply with organizational norms. In both instances, the act of suppression has negative effects. An alternative approach could be explored in coaching: One could identify the causes of the anger and see if those causes can be rectified (Geddes et al., 2020).

A different approach to managing anger lies with a relatively new therapeutic approach in counseling psychology known as *acceptance therapy* (Hofmann & Asmundson, 2008). This treatment is focused on counteracting people's tendencies to regulate undesired emotions through suppression by becoming more open to unpleasant feelings, learning not to overreact to them, and not avoiding situations where they are invoked. Although acceptance therapy has some advantages in terms of circumventing the tendency to suppress, this approach also focuses on the presence of anger as a deficiency to be managed (see also Morland et al., Chapter 8, this volume).

An alternative approach to the deficiency-focused approaches that have been gaining traction in the past 10 years is to focus on coaching that potentially reduces the influence of anger not by eliminating or containing anger but instead by increasing the presence of emotions that buffer or offset the negative impacts of the anger. Compassion-based therapy (Gilbert, 2010), for example, focuses on training people in compassion, such that the motives and emotions for affiliative, caring, and altruistic behavior offset the destructive potential of emotions such as anger. O'Neill and Rothbard (2017) observed that firefighting teams with a strong culture of companionate love (i.e., affection, caring, fondness, and tenderness) showed improved health and well-being relative to teams lower in companionate love. Other specific techniques that have been shown to be effective include loving-kindness meditation, breathing, and compassion training interventions (e.g., Hutcherson et al., 2008; Jazaieri et al., 2013; Seppälä et al., 2014). Evidence for the beneficial effects of these interventions is amassing, including in veteran populations (Seppälä et al., 2014). This evidence bodes well for the intervention potential among first responders, many of whom experience trauma similar to that of military veterans (O'Neill & Rothbard, 2017). More detail on clinical interventions for anger can be seen in Chapter 8, this volume, by Morland et al.

Team Interventions

Although many of the interventions for individuals discussed earlier could be generalized to the team level, other interventions specifically focus on improving team skills and team emotional culture. Past research identified five categories of task- and team-generic competencies: (a) conflict resolution, (b) collaborative problem-solving, (c) communication, (d) goal setting and performance management, and (e) planning and task coordination. In an experimental study of trained and untrained teams engaged in a military simulation, Ellis et al. (2005) found that trained teams showed increases in task knowledge and significantly greater proficiency than untrained teams in planning and task coordination, collaborative problem-solving, and communication in a novel team and task environment. Although this study did not measure emotions, previous research has shown that relationship conflict in teams is related to negative emotions such as anger (Meier et al., 2013) and that group-level anger and performance are reciprocally related (Glomb & Liao, 2003). Thus, it is reasonable to speculate that interventions targeting team skills would impact the team emotional culture of anger in a positive way.

In much of the extant literature, the assumption is that anger has a negative impact on team interactions and performance. As the introduction suggests, this assumption may be oversimplified. Team research on leader emotional displays adds important nuance to this perspective. Drawing on Geddes and Callister's (2007) dual threshold model of anger, a recent study of sports teams by Staw et al. (2019) revealed that the positive association between leaders' unpleasant affect and team performance turns negative only at high levels of intensity. Another study by van Kleef et al. (2009) found that the extent to which leader anger had a negative effect on team performance depended on the extent to which followers were motivated to interpret the meaning of the anger. When team members were motivated to develop a rich and accurate understanding of situations, leader anger had a positive impact on team members, as it prompted team members to address issues around insufficient task progress. When the motivation to understand situations was low, anger had opposite effects. This distinction suggests the importance of raising team leaders' ability to regulate emotions depending on the situation and of increasing followers' motivation to understand situations so the functional benefits of leader anger are realized.

System-Level Interventions

A third level of analysis for addressing team emotional cultures of anger is the system level. Lepak and Snell (2002) suggested that rather than assuming that all employers should be managed with the same standardized human resources (HR) system, HR systems should be customized to match the needs and requirements of particular employee groups. Although the employment modes that these authors examined focus on skill development and incentive systems, the idea that HR systems should be developed to address the specific needs of specific occupational populations is helpful for thinking about the policies, practices, and procedures that could help alleviate emotional cultures of anger in high-risk occupations. For those hiring organizations responsible for staffing emergency response teams, modifications to these HR levers could influence the composition of teams. For example, to the extent that team anger is caused by dispositionally angry employees, hiring interviews could focus on surveying applicant trait levels of anger and focus their selection procedures on individuals low in trait anger. Performance appraisal systems that incorporate 360-degree feedback could also be used to target employees who are disproportionately contributing to the anger levels in a team by spreading anger or causing anger in others through other types of behavior, as in the case of "brilliant jerks" (Groysberg, 2010). To reduce levels of situational anger, HR business partners could increase the use of employee engagement surveys and focus groups to capture employees' perceptions of management and organizational systems early on and modify organizational practices or procedures that are causing anger before the anger becomes a problem for team performance and morale.

Leader selection and training are also potentially helpful for attenuating the team emotional culture of anger. At the highest level, top management change can influence the cultures of teams within the organization. One pathway through which this occurs is through a change in leadership style. A shift from a transactional leader to a transformational leader is one example. Whereas transactional leaders focus only on satisfactory performance and attend more to followers' mistakes and failures, transformational leaders motivate respect and pride, communicate the organization's purpose and importance of organization's mission, and attend to followers' individual needs. Schaubroeck et al. (2007) identified the influence of transformational leadership on team performance, particularly for teams higher in power distance and collectivism—two common attributes of teams in high-risk occupations. To the extent that some high-risk professions tend to be male dominated, promoting greater gender diversity may also promote a shift from transactional to transformational leadership, as meta-analytic results indicate that women are higher in transformational leadership styles (Eagly et al., 2003). If a change in leadership is not likely, leader training is also relevant. Marks et al. (2000), for example, found that leader briefings and team interaction training positively influenced team communication processes and team performance, two key issues associated with angry teams.

The most comprehensive form of change is an intervention designed to target changes in an entire organization. Such interventions are warranted when team anger is widespread (i.e., not isolated to one or two teams with an angry emotional culture); team anger is linked to widespread organizational performance problems such as high costs, reduced productivity, low morale, poor employee health, or increased withdrawal; and there is top management support for organizational change. Sometimes the change initiative is intentional, such as when an organization develops a strategic plan to implement over 3 to 5 years. Other times, organizations may be forced to change because of circumstances that are imperative to address, such as updated economic or regulatory requirements, an organizational crisis, or an unexpected leader departure (Cummings & Feyerherm, 1995).

An example of one type of large-scale intervention is an organizational culture assessment and culture change intervention aimed at changing the organization's emotional culture. Such an intervention requires widespread participation and multiple activities spread over a long period (e.g., 3–5 years). For such interventions to be effective, the following recommendations are worth considering:

- Establish the business case in moral and monetary terms, supplemented by a strong rationale and "hard" evidence (e.g., decreased cost, improved safety record).
- Cultivate or seize a sense of urgency.
- Partner with change agents outside HR to establish greater credibility.
- Select midlevel leaders and supervisors carefully, and partner closely with them and other "influencers" (i.e., change agents) across the organization.

- Encourage face-to-face interactions whenever possible.
- Cultivate a meaningful and authentic culture that can be understood and embodied by the majority of organizational members.

Given the scope of large-scale interventions, a major commitment is necessary to institute this kind of change. Although it isn't easy, it is possible. One example is the story of retired U.S. Navy Captain L. David Marquet, who described in his 2013 book, *Turn the Ship Around!*, how he transformed the negative emotional culture of the *USS Santa Fe*, a nuclear submarine that suffered under extreme command-and-control leadership before he took over.

CONCLUSION

Given the essential role of teams in high-risk occupations, addressing anger at the team and leader levels is critically important to creating solutions to the issue of anger in organizations. This chapter builds on advances in the emotional culture of teams by explaining how anger comes to define a team's emotional culture, shared across individuals and influenced by top-down and bottom-up processes. I illustrated the nature of an emotional culture of anger and its consequences through two case studies of specific emergency response teams, firefighters and ICU staff members. These case studies show the influence of leadership, organizational practices and policies, and interaction with the public while exploring how a team culture of anger manifests itself in male-dominant emergency service occupations versus female-dominant emergency service professions. Finally, I explored individual, team, and organizational interventions for addressing team emotional cultures of anger, contrasting deficiency-based approaches aimed at reducing anger with approaches grounded in positive emotions that buffer or offset the impact anger.

Looking ahead, future research would do well to consider conceptualizing anger from the emotional culture perspective presented here. For example, there is little research on the effectiveness of interventions designed specifically to modify the emotional culture of teams and organizations. This research is a necessary next step for academics and practitioners interested in not only diagnosing but also changing the emotional culture of teams. In addition, far more attention has been paid to the negative, dysfunctional perspectives on anger, with far less attention to the potentially positive, functional consequences of anger, such as group bonding or as a collective response to injustice. It would be important to examine the positive consequences of expressing anger not only to harness its potential to do good but also to discourage unhealthy suppression and deviant forms of expression (Geddes et al., 2020). Finally, it would be beneficial to distinguish among the various manifestations of anger within the larger emotion prototype, including between emotions differing in intensity (e.g., rage and fury vs. irritation and annoyance) or in functionality (e.g., anger directed toward organizational change vs. contempt toward others). By developing a clearer understanding of how anger functions at the group level, and how this problematic anger can be mitigated, high-risk occupational teams can be guided to function effectively under dangerous conditions.

IMPLICATIONS

- Attempts to reduce the negative emotions (e.g., suppression) can often backfire.
- A more successful approach may be to focus on buffering negative or increasing presence of positive emotions (e.g., compassion, joviality).
- One must take into account nuances such as extant norms and level of intensity.
- Team training must take into account situational factors that increase the likelihood of successful intervention.
- Customized HR systems are helpful to match the needs and requirements of particular employee groups.
- System change is sometimes warranted, but it requires top management support and a great investment of time and resources.

REFERENCES

Adam, H., & Shirako, A. (2013). Not all anger is created equal: The impact of the expresser's culture on the social effects of anger in negotiations. *The Journal of Applied Psychology*, *98*(5), 785–798. https://doi.org/10.1037/a0032387

Asch, S. E. (1955). Opinions and social pressure. *Scientific American*, *193*(5), 31–35. https://doi.org/10.1038/scientificamerican1155-31

Ashforth, B. E., & Humphrey, R. H. (1993). Emotional labor in service roles: The influence of identity. *Academy of Management Review*, *18*(1), 88–115. https://doi.org/10.5465/amr.1993.3997508

Barsade, S. G. (2002). The ripple effect: Emotional contagion and its influence on group behavior. *Administrative Science Quarterly, 47*(4), 644–675. https://doi.org/10.2307/3094912

Barsade, S. G., & Gibson, D. E. (1998). Group emotion: A view from top and bottom. In D. H. Gruenfeld (Ed.), *Research on managing groups and teams: Vol. 1. Composition* (pp. 81–102). Elsevier Science/JAI Press.

Barsade, S. G., & O'Neill, O. A. (2014). What's love got to do with it? A longitudinal study of the culture of companionate love and employee and client outcomes in a long-term care setting. *Administrative Science Quarterly, 59*(4), 551–598. https://doi.org/10.1177/0001839214538636

Bass, B. M., & Avolio, B. J. (Eds.). (1994). *Improving organizational effectiveness through transformational leadership*. Sage Publications.

Brescoll, V. L., & Uhlmann, E. L. (2008). Can an angry woman get ahead? Status conferral, gender, and expression of emotion in the workplace. *Psychological Science, 19*(3), 268–275. https://doi.org/10.1111/j.1467-9280.2008.02079.x

Butler, E. A., Egloff, B., Wilhelm, F. H., Smith, N. C., Erickson, E. A., & Gross, J. J. (2003). The social consequences of expressive suppression. *Emotion, 3*(1), 48–67. https://doi.org/10.1037/1528-3542.3.1.48

Callister, R. R., Geddes, D., & Gibson, D. F. (2017). When is anger helpful or hurtful? Status and role impact on anger expression and outcomes. *Negotiation and Conflict Management Research, 10*(2), 69–87. https://doi.org/10.1111/ncmr.12090

Cheshin, A., Rafaeli, A., & Bos, N. (2011). Anger and happiness in virtual teams: Emotional influences of text and behavior on others' affect in the absence of non-verbal cues. *Organizational Behavior and Human Decision Processes, 116*(1), 2–16. https://doi.org/10.1016/j.obhdp.2011.06.002

Clark, C. (1997). *Misery and company: Sympathy in everyday life*. University of Chicago Press. https://doi.org/10.7208/chicago/9780226107585.001.0001

Côté, S., & Morgan, L. M. (2002). A longitudinal analysis of the association between emotion regulation, job satisfaction, and intentions to quit. *Journal of Organizational Behavior, 23*(8), 947–962. https://doi.org/10.1002/job.174

Cummings, T. G., & Feyerherm, A. E. (1995). Interventions in large systems. In W. Rothwell, R. Sullivan, & G. N. McLean (Eds.), *Practicing organizational development: A guide for consultants* (pp. 203–234). Pfieffer.

Deffenbacher, J. L., Oetting, E. R., Lynch, R. S., & Morris, C. D. (1996). The expression of anger and its consequences. *Behaviour Research and Therapy, 34*(7), 575–590. https://doi.org/10.1016/0005-7967(96)00018-6

Denison, D. R. (1996). What is the difference between organizational culture and organizational climate? A native's point of view on a decade of paradigm wars. *Academy of Management Review, 21*(3), 619–654. https://doi.org/10.5465/amr.1996.9702100310

Eagly, A. H., Johannesen-Schmidt, M. C., & van Engen, M. L. (2003). Transformational, transactional, and laissez-faire leadership styles: A meta-analysis comparing women and men. *Psychological Bulletin, 129*(4), 569–591. https://doi.org/10.1037/0033-2909.129.4.569

Ekman, P. (1973). *Darwin and facial expression: A century of research in review*. Academic Press.

Ellis, A. P., Bell, B. S., Ployhart, R. E., Hollenbeck, J. R., & Ilgen, D. R. (2005). An evaluation of generic teamwork skills training with action teams: Effects on cognitive and skill-based outcomes. *Personnel Psychology*, *58*(3), 641–672. https://doi.org/10.1111/j.1744-6570.2005.00617.x

Feldman, D. C., & Lankau, M. J. (2005). Executive coaching: A review and agenda for future research. *Journal of Management*, *31*(6), 829–848. https://doi.org/10.1177/0149206305279599

Geddes, D., & Callister, R. R. (2007). Crossing the line(s): A dual threshold model of anger in organizations. *Academy of Management Review*, *32*(3), 721–746. https://doi.org/10.5465/amr.2007.25275495

Geddes, D., Callister, R. R., & Gibson, D. E. (2020). A message in the madness: Functions of workplace anger in organizational life. *The Academy of Management Perspectives*, *34*(1), 28–47. https://doi.org/10.5465/amp.2016.0158

Gelfand, M. J., Nishii, L. H., & Raver, J. L. (2006). On the nature and importance of cultural tightness-looseness. *The Journal of Applied Psychology*, *91*(6), 1225–1244. https://doi.org/10.1037/0021-9010.91.6.1225

Gilbert, P. (2010). An introduction to compassion focused therapy in cognitive behavior therapy. *International Journal of Cognitive Therapy*, *3*(2), 97–112. https://doi.org/10.1521/ijct.2010.3.2.97

Glomb, T. M., & Liao, H. (2003). Interpersonal aggression in work groups: Social influence, reciprocal, and individual effects. *Academy of Management Journal*, *46*(4), 486–496. https://doi.org/10.2307/30040640

Gottman, J. M. (1993). The roles of conflict engagement, escalation, and avoidance in marital interaction: A longitudinal view of five types of couples. *Journal of Consulting and Clinical Psychology*, *61*(1), 6–15. https://doi.org/10.1037/0022-006X.61.1.6

Grandey, A. A. (2003). When "the show must go on": Surface acting and deep acting as determinants of emotional exhaustion and peer-rated service delivery. *Academy of Management Journal*, *46*(1), 86–96.

Gross, J. J. (1998). Antecedent- and response-focused emotion regulation: Divergent consequences for experience, expression, and physiology. *Journal of Personality and Social Psychology*, *74*(1), 224–237. https://doi.org/10.1037/0022-3514.74.1.224

Gross, J. J., & John, O. P. (2003). Individual differences in two emotion regulation processes: Implications for affect, relationships, and well-being. *Journal of Personality and Social Psychology*, *85*(2), 348–362. https://doi.org/10.1037/0022-3514.85.2.348

Groysberg, B. (2010). *Chasing stars: The myth of talent and the portability of performance*. Princeton University Press. https://doi.org/10.1515/9781400834389

Hareli, S., & Rafaeli, A. (2008). Emotion cycles: On the social influence of emotion in organizations. *Research in Organizational Behavior*, *28*, 35–59. https://doi.org/10.1016/j.riob.2008.04.007

Hatfield, E., Cacioppo, J. T., & Rapson, R. L. (1993). *Emotional contagion*. Cambridge University Press.

Hochschild, A. R. (1983). *The managed heart: Commercialization of human feeling*. University of California Press.

Hofmann, S. G., & Asmundson, G. J. G. (2008). Acceptance and mindfulness-based therapy: New wave or old hat? *Clinical Psychology Review*, *28*(1), 1–16. https://doi.org/10.1016/j.cpr.2007.09.003

Hutcherson, C. A., Seppala, E. M., & Gross, J. J. (2008). Loving-kindness meditation increases social connectedness. *Emotion*, *8*(5), 720–724. https://doi.org/10.1037/a0013237

Ilfeld, F. W., Jr. (1978). Psychologic status of community residents along major demographic dimensions. *Archives of General Psychiatry*, *35*(6), 716–724. https://doi.org/10.1001/archpsyc.1978.01770300058006

Jackson, J. (1966). A conceptual and measurement model for norms and roles. *Pacific Sociological Review*, *9*(1), 35–47. https://doi.org/10.2307/1388305

Jazaieri, H., Jinpa, G. T., McGonigal, K., Rosenberg, E. L., Finkelstein, J., Simon-Thomas, E., Cullen, M., Doty, J. R., Gross, J. J., & Goldin, P. R. (2013). Enhancing compassion: A randomized controlled trial of a compassion cultivation training program. *Journal of Happiness Studies*, *14*(4), 1113–1126. https://doi.org/10.1007/s10902-012-9373-z

Keltner, D., & Haidt, J. (1999). Social functions of emotions at four levels of analysis. *Cognition and Emotion*, *13*(5), 505–521. https://doi.org/10.1080/026999399379168

Keltner, D., Sauter, D., Tracy, J., & Cowen, A. (2019). Emotional expression: Advances in basic emotion theory. *Journal of Nonverbal Behavior*, *43*(2), 133–160. https://doi.org/10.1007/s10919-019-00293-3

Kozlowski, S. W., & Klein, K. J. (2000). A multilevel approach to theory and research in organizations: Contextual, temporal, and emergent processes. In K. J. Klein & S. W. Kozlowski (Eds.), *Multilevel theory, research, and methods in organizations: Foundations, extensions, and new directions* (pp. 3–85). Jossey-Bass.

Lepak, D. P., & Snell, S. A. (2002). Examining the human resource architecture: The relationships among human capital, employment, and human resource configurations. *Journal of Management*, *28*(4), 517–543. https://doi.org/10.1177/014920630202800403

Lindebaum, D., Jordan, P. J., & Morris, L. (2016). Symmetrical and asymmetrical outcomes of leader anger expression: A qualitative study of army personnel. *Human Relations*, *69*(2), 277–300. https://doi.org/10.1177/0018726715593350

Marks, M. A., Zaccaro, S. J., & Mathieu, J. E. (2000). Performance implications of leader briefings and team-interaction training for team adaptation to novel environments. *The Journal of Applied Psychology*, *85*(6), 971–986. https://doi.org/10.1037/0021-9010.85.6.971

Marquet, L. D. (2013). *Turn the ship around! A true story of turning followers into leaders*. Penguin.

Martin, J. (1992). *Cultures in organizations: Three perspectives*. Oxford University Press.

Meier, L. L., Gross, S., Spector, P. E., & Semmer, N. K. (2013). Relationship and task conflict at work: Interactive short-term effects on angry mood and somatic complaints. *Journal of Occupational Health Psychology*, *18*(2), 144–156. https://doi.org/10.1037/a0032090

Melwani, S., & Barsade, S. G. (2011). Held in contempt: The psychological, interpersonal, and performance consequences of contempt in a work context. *Journal of Personality and Social Psychology*, *101*(3), 503–520. https://doi.org/10.1037/a0023492

O'Neill, O. A., & Rothbard, N. P. (2017). Is love all you need? The effects of emotional culture, suppression, and work–family conflict on firefighter risk-taking and health. *Academy of Management Journal, 60*(1), 78–108. https://doi.org/10.5465/amj.2014.0952

O'Neill, O. A., Vandenberg, R. J., Dejoy, D. M., & Wilson, M. G. (2009). Exploring relationships among anger, perceived organizational support, and workplace outcomes. *Journal of Occupational Health Psychology, 14*(3), 318–333. https://doi.org/10.1037/a0015852

O'Reilly, C. A., Chatman, J., & Caldwell, D. F. (1991). People and organizational culture: A profile comparison approach to assessing person-organization fit. *Academy of Management Journal, 34*(3), 487–516. https://doi.org/10.2307/256404

Ostroff, C., Kinicki, A. J., & Tamkins, M. M. (2003). Organizational culture and climate. In W. C. Borman, D. R. Ilgen, & R. J. Klimoski (Eds.), *Handbook of psychology: Vol. 12. Industrial and organizational psychology* (pp. 565–593). John Wiley & Sons.

Parke, M. R., & Seo, M. G. (2017). The role of affect climate in organizational effectiveness. *Academy of Management Review, 42*(2), 334–360. https://doi.org/10.5465/amr.2014.0424

Pettigrew, A. M. (1979). On studying organizational cultures. *Administrative Science Quarterly, 24*(4), 570–581. https://doi.org/10.2307/2392363

Rafaeli, A., & Sutton, R. I. (1987). Expression of emotion as part of the work role. *Academy of Management Review, 12*(1), 23–37. https://doi.org/10.5465/amr.1987.4306444

Reid, E. M., O'Neill, O. A., & Blair-Loy, M. (2018). Masculinity in male-dominated occupations: How teams, time, and tasks shape masculinity contests. *Journal of Social Issues, 74*(3), 579–606. https://doi.org/10.1111/josi.12285

Richards, J. M., & Gross, J. J. (1999). Composure at any cost? The cognitive consequences of emotion suppression. *Personality and Social Psychology Bulletin, 25*(8), 1033–1044. https://doi.org/10.1177/01461672992511010

Riskin, A., Erez, A., Foulk, T. A., Kugelman, A., Gover, A., Shoris, I., Riskin, K. S., & Bamberger, P. A. (2015). The impact of rudeness on medical team performance: A randomized trial. *Pediatrics, 136*(3), 487–495. https://doi.org/10.1542/peds.2015-1385

Riskin, A., Erez, A., Foulk, T. A., Riskin-Geuz, K. S., Ziv, A., Sela, R., Pessach-Gelblum, L., & Bamberger, P. A. (2017). Rudeness and medical team performance. *Pediatrics, 139*(2), e20162305. https://doi.org/10.1542/peds.2016-2305

Schaubroeck, J., Lam, S. S., & Cha, S. E. (2007). Embracing transformational leadership: Team values and the impact of leader behavior on team performance. *The Journal of Applied Psychology, 92*(4), 1020–1030. https://doi.org/10.1037/0021-9010.92.4.1020

Schein, E. H. (2010). *Organizational culture and leadership* (4th ed.). Jossey-Bass.

Seppälä, E. M., Nitschke, J. B., Tudorascu, D. L., Hayes, A., Goldstein, M. R., Nguyen, D. T., Perlman, D., & Davidson, R. J. (2014). Breathing-based meditation decreases posttraumatic stress disorder symptoms in U.S. military veterans: A randomized controlled longitudinal study. *Journal of Traumatic Stress, 27*(4), 397–405. https://doi.org/10.1002/jts.21936

Shaver, P., Schwartz, J., Kirson, D., & O'Connor, C. (1987). Emotion knowledge: Further exploration of a prototype approach. *Journal of Personality and Social Psychology, 52*(6), 1061–1086. https://doi.org/10.1037/0022-3514.52.6.1061

Sherif, M. (1936). *The psychology of social norms*. Harper.

Smith, C. A., & Ellsworth, P. C. (1985). Patterns of cognitive appraisal in emotion. *Journal of Personality and Social Psychology*, *48*(4), 813–838. https://doi.org/10.1037/0022-3514.48.4.813

Staw, B. M., DeCelles, K. A., & de Goey, P. (2019). Leadership in the locker room: How the intensity of leaders' unpleasant affective displays shapes team performance. *The Journal of Applied Psychology*, *104*(12), 1547–1557. https://doi.org/10.1037/apl0000418

Strack, F., Martin, L. L., & Stepper, S. (1988). Inhibiting and facilitating conditions of the human smile: A nonobtrusive test of the facial feedback hypothesis. *Journal of Personality and Social Psychology*, *54*(5), 768–777. https://doi.org/10.1037/0022-3514.54.5.768

Sutton, R. I. (1991). Maintaining norms about expressed emotions: The case of bill collectors. *Administrative Science Quarterly*, *36*(2), 245–268. https://doi.org/10.2307/2393355

Tiedens, L. Z. (2001). Anger and advancement versus sadness and subjugation: The effect of negative emotion expressions on social status conferral. *Journal of Personality and Social Psychology*, *80*(1), 86–94. https://doi.org/10.1037/0022-3514.80.1.86

Trice, H. M., & Beyer, J. M. (1993). *The cultures of work organizations*. Prentice-Hall.

van Kleef, G. A., Homan, A. C., Beersma, B., Van Knippenberg, D., Van Knippenberg, B., & Damen, F. (2009). Searing sentiment or cold calculation? The effects of leader emotional displays on team performance depend on follower epistemic motivation. *Academy of Management Journal*, *52*(3), 562–580. https://doi.org/10.5465/amj.2009.41331253

Van Maanen, J., & Barley, S. R. (1985). Cultural organization: Fragments of a theory. In P. J. Frost, L. F. Moore, M. Louis, C. Lundberg, & J. Martin (Eds.), *Organizational culture* (pp. 31–54). Sage.

5 ANGER AND THE ROLE OF SUPERVISORS AT WORK

LESLIE B. HAMMER, JAMES D. LEE, CYNTHIA D. MOHR, AND SHALENE J. ALLEN

KEY POINTS

- Organizational stressors are the primary contributors to supervisor anger.
- Supervisor anger is more likely to occur in high-risk occupations.
- Supervisor anger is related to negative employee outcomes.
- The effects of supervisor anger on employees can spill over to family functioning.

The experience of anger in the workplace is ubiquitous—some estimates report that half of all employees feel "a little angry" at work, with approximately one fourth of workers experiencing chronic anger in the workplace (Gibson & Barsade, 1999). Anger can take on multiple forms, according to Spielberger et al.'s (1983) state–trait theory of anger, which defines *state anger* as an acute "emotional state that consists of feelings that vary in

https://doi.org/10.1037/0000244-006
Anger at Work: Prevention, Intervention, and Treatment in High-Risk Occupations,
A. B. Adler and D. Forbes (Editors)

intensity, from mild irritation or annoyance to intense fury and rage" (p. 160). In contrast, *trait anger* describes an individual's propensity to experience state anger with greater intensity, duration, and frequency.

Although many factors explain what influences anger in the workplace, one of the most critical is the role of supervisors. Supervisors tend to set the tone for team-based climate in the workplace, and they have significant influence on their employees. The role of supervisors is critically important in facilitating their employees' anger at work, given their positions as gatekeepers and linchpins between organizational leadership and frontline employees. The chronic experience of anger, whether suppressed (concealed) or expressed, has short- and long-term consequences for the workplace and may lead to negative health outcomes for both supervisors and their employees, such as increased systolic blood pressure or the development of coronary heart disease (Booth-Kewley & Friedman, 1987; Spicer & Chamberlain, 1996). Furthermore, left unmitigated, the effects of supervisor anger can lead to deleterious workplace outcomes for employees, ranging from sabotage and withdrawal behaviors to aggression and violence (Deffenbacher et al., 1996; Fitness, 2000; Glomb, 2002). In this chapter, we discuss the antecedents and outcomes of supervisor anger at work while calling out effects in high-risk occupations where anger is especially salient. We also review the antecedents of supervisor anger, employee outcomes of supervisor anger, and organizational strategies for mitigating supervisor anger.

EXPRESSION OF SUPERVISOR ANGER

Anger is classified as an affect, and it has been discussed by some as possibly serving a positive function within organizations (i.e., Geddes et al., 2020); here we focus primarily on the behavioral component that has generally been classified as aggression and is defined as "any behavior directed toward another individual that is carried out with the immediate intent to cause harm" (Anderson & Bushman, 2002, p. 28). Thus, anger at work, often manifested as workplace aggression, can exist in various forms ranging from ambiguous, low-intensity behavior (incivility) to low base-rate physical violence. Specifically, the experience of anger at work and the corresponding mistreatment that may result from being the recipient of that anger have led to much overlap and multiple classifications of aggression (i.e., the behavioral manifestation of anger), including bullying, incivility, emotional abuse, and abusive supervision. In an attempt to parse apart the effects of competing constructs, Hershcovis (2011) conducted a meta-analysis and found no significant differences among incivility, abusive supervision, bullying, and interpersonal conflict in terms of their impact on employee job satisfaction, turnover intent, psychological and physical well-being, and affective commitment. The most common construct related to the role of anger among supervisors is abusive supervision, the behavioral manifestation of supervisor anger toward employees. According to Tepper (2000), abusive supervision is based on subordinates' perceptions of supervisors displaying "hostile verbal and nonverbal behaviors, excluding physical contact" (p. 178).

It should also be noted that specific personality characteristics of supervisors have been linked to abusive supervision and displays of hostile and aggressive behaviors at work. For example, Inness et al. (2008) found a main effect for trait anger when measuring subordinate-targeted aggression. Kiazad et al. (2010) found that supervisor Machiavellianism—individuals solely focused on their own interests and how to obtain them—was significantly related to employees perceiving their direct supervisors as abusive. These findings suggest that supervisors who exhibit traits relating to Machiavellianism are predisposed to showing aggression at work and outright anger outbursts. Similarly, Tepper (2007) pointed toward narcissism and a family history of violence to be key indicators of predicting abusive supervisors. This literature explains some of the personal and individual characteristics that might predispose supervisors to exhibit anger or lead to the perception of abusive supervision in the workplace.

IMPORTANCE OF THE ORGANIZATIONAL CONTEXT

We contend that anger at work should be examined from an ecological systems perspective by understanding the potential ways that the organizational context (e.g., poor communication, situational constraints, high-risk/high-stress occupations) impact supervisor anger. Taking an organizational systems view of anger is critical, as it offers a more complete analysis of anger at work generally, and supervisor anger at work specifically. For example, using an organizational frustration-aggression model, Fox and Spector (1999) found that organizational situational constraints were associated with counterproductive organizational behaviors through affective responses to frustration; the strongest predictors of aggression were trait anger and believing that one could harm their organization without negative ramifications. An earlier meta-analysis by Hershcovis et al. (2007) found that organizational factors such as poor leadership and workplace injustice (unfairness) were both predictors and outcomes of workplace aggression. This organizational-systems perspective is also elucidated in Neuman and Baron's (1998) theoretical model of workplace aggression, suggesting that the occurrence of workplace aggression is predicated on the interplay between social (i.e., unfair treatment, frustrating events), situational (i.e., downsizing, restructuring), and personal (i.e., Type A and self-monitoring behaviors) determinants of workplace stressors. It is crucial that organizations address workplace anger and the corresponding aggression, as it may lead to reductions in work effort and job turnover (Pearson & Porath, 2005), sexual harassment (Lim & Cortina, 2005), and spillover effects whereby employees take their frustrations out on clients or customers (Gonthier & Morrissey, 2002). One aspect of the organizational context that contributes to anger at work is the risk level of the job, as anger and aggression are particularly high in occupations involving perilous tasks such as the military, first responders, and others in which physical danger is a prevalent part of the job. High-risk occupations are also associated with higher levels of job stress (Sauter & Murphy, 1995), and job stressors have been shown to be predictors of anger and aggression (e.g., L. A. Smith et al., 2005). Thus, the role of anger and aggression in high-risk, high-stress occupations is of particular interest in this volume.

ANGER IN HIGH-RISK OCCUPATIONS

Anger is a common occurrence in high-risk occupations (e.g., military, law enforcement/first responders, emergency medicine/health care, and construction; American Psychological Association, 2011) for a number of reasons. Employees in high-risk occupations tend to experience psychological, organizational, and physical impairments more frequently than those in lower risk occupations (Benedek et al., 2007; Johnson et al., 2005; Milczarek, 2011). Keeping the well-being of employees in high-risk occupations in mind, the review of supervisor anger, aggression, and incivility is vital to understanding and exploring the complex nature of anger in the workplace. This has been particularly evident in the recent COVID-19 pandemic, during which high-risk occupations in fields such as health care have experienced enormous stress, and increasing knowledge on how to mitigate the stress may result in not only improved psychological health but also reductions in anger and aggression. The psychological health challenges of health care workers during the COVID-19 pandemic have been linked to anger (N. Greenberg et al., 2020), and evidence is growing regarding similar reactions in essential workers who fear for their safety yet cannot afford to lose their jobs.

For those in high-risk occupations, there can be deleterious consequences of anger for organizations, supervisors, and employees. For example, Aytac (2015) found that the responsibilities and stress levels associated with police officers often resulted in anger expression. Employees in high-risk occupations such as the military, specifically, are at an increased risk for a higher prevalence of anger (Reyes & Hicklin, 2005). This is partially due to the male-dominated nature of these occupations, where men have been found to accept risks and endure physical and psychological pain without seeking treatment relative to women—a propensity that may influence their occupational health and safety as well as their greater tendency for aggression (Hennessy, 2008; Stergiou-Kita et al., 2015). Yet the experience of anger is not restricted to male employees. For example, Cortina et al. (2001) found that women had a higher rate of incivility than men; however, this finding was not specific to type of occupation.

Although viewed as low intensity for harm, workplace incivility—an expression of anger at work—can have significant consequences for organizations, supervisors, and employees in high-risk occupations if left unaddressed. For example, nurses in high-stress/high-risk environments typically have less burnout and better retention rates when their environments are free of uncivil behaviors (Laschinger et al., 2009). Acts of incivility also have the potential to spiral into aggression and negative workplace behaviors (e.g., supervisors pounding their fists or swearing, and employees shouting at each other; L. M. Andersson & Pearson, 1999).

Thus, it is important to understand the antecedents of anger and abusive supervision, especially in high-risk occupations. Focusing specifically on the antecedents that will directly affect the role of supervisor anger, we review organizational and individual antecedents of supervisor anger. Concentrating on supervisors is critical because of their central position in the organization between leadership and frontline employees, as they are also the most likely to set the tone for the culture of the work team or unit. Supervisors have the power to deliver rewards and/or dole out punitive actions and are therefore in strong positions to influence their employees. Supervisors are also impacted by top leadership, the organizational context, and play a central role in delivering support or attenuating anger via interactions with their employees.

ANTECEDENTS OF SUPERVISOR ANGER

Consistent with the previously mentioned meta-analysis of workplace aggression (Hershcovis et al., 2007), we have identified organizational and individual antecedents of supervisor anger, as shown in Figure 5.1. This model provides an illustration of the potential effects of supervisor anger in the workplace and suggested strategies for reducing the negative effects of such anger at work. We take a primary prevention approach rooted in ecological systems theory by focusing on the organizational antecedents, as they are considered the best targets for strategies that can be implemented to reduce or mitigate the effects of supervisor anger.

As anger and workplace aggression have been studied for several decades, numerous organizational, psychosocial, and physical hazards have been identified as antecedents (e.g., Barling, 1996; Glomb, 2002; Hershcovis et al., 2007; Neuman & Baron, 1998). More specifically, in assessing the various antecedents engendering workplace anger, research has found organizational factors such as goal interference, unjust treatment, and the experience of rejection or humiliation to be contributing factors (Canary et al., 1998; Fitness, 2000), as well as a lack of adequate support and poor communication (Booth & Mann, 2005).

In an effort to explicate how anger is manifested in the workplace, Gibson and Callister's (2010) episodic model of anger in organizations proposes a feedback loop in which work events (i.e., injustice, goal interference, and interpersonal conflict) lead to subjective, physiological, and cognitive experiences of anger. These experiences then lead an individual to express or regulate their anger, which ultimately influences anger outcomes. For example, Eissa and Lester (2017) discussed similar ideas surrounding perceptions of injustice, or perceived fairness; in essence, the authors contended that organizations should make clear, identifiable roles, as well as allocate job roles and assignments in ways that make everyone feel as though they are being treated as fairly as possible. Otherwise, there could be potential for resentment, opening the possibility of anger building over time and presenting itself as abusive supervision directed at subordinate employees. Many of the antecedents identified represent general stressors at work that can be categorized as extraorganizational stressors and intraorganizational stressors.

Extraorganizational Stressors

According to Bhatti et al. (2010), 33% of overall stress comes from outside the organization compared with 67% of the stress that occurs within the

FIGURE 5.1. Model of Supervisor Anger at Work

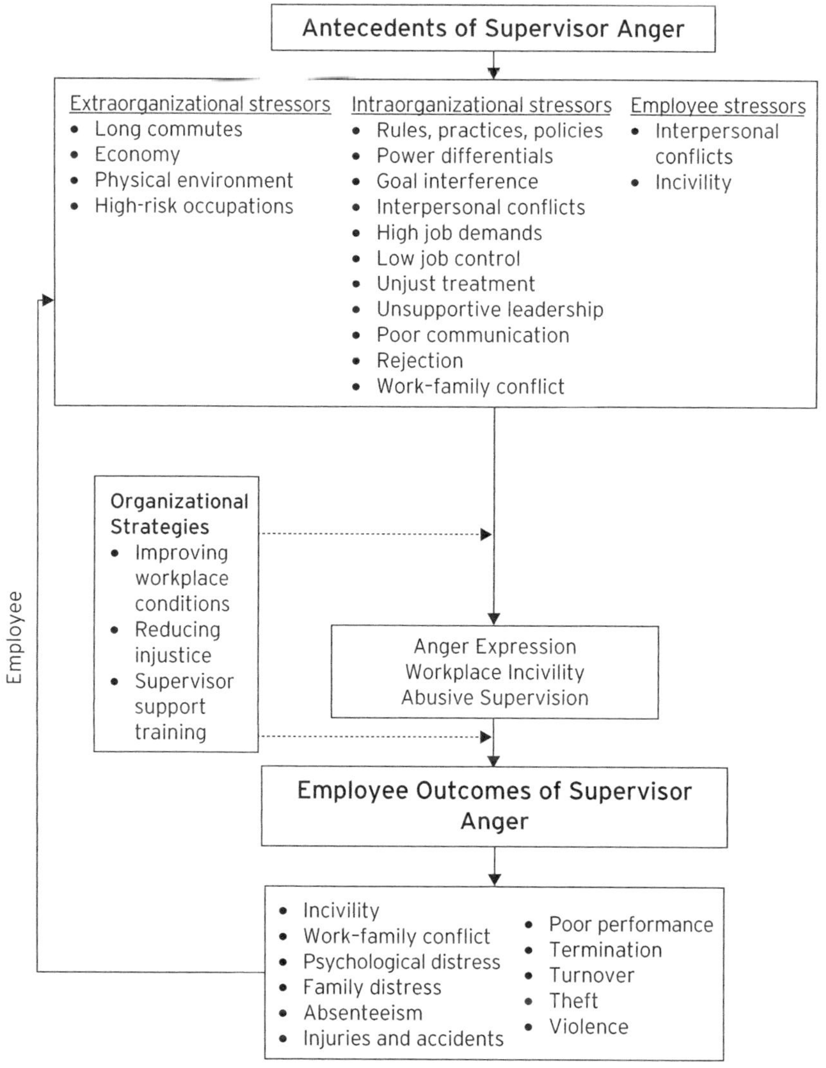

workplace, making the evaluation of both types of organizational stressors important to the overall health and well-being, and potential anger, of supervisors. Extraorganizational stressors include macrolevel stressors that are outside of the workplace but have an impact on organizational functioning, such as the economy, competition, geographical location, and the general nature of the risk level of the occupation.

Extraorganizational stressors also include daily hassles that can add unwanted stress and anxiety to an already taxing workday. For example, supervisors who have lengthy, grueling commutes could have potential spillover of anger, negative behaviors, attitudes, and feelings from what they experienced while driving to work (Hennessy, 2008). Similarly, Wurhofer et al. (2015) found that time of day predicted anger among those who experienced commuter stress; higher levels of anger were also found when traffic was unexpected rather than expected.

The physical environment can also play a role in the type of stress and anger that managers display. For example, individuals who were surrounded by landscape and nature paintings at their offices actually experienced less stress and decreased state anger (Kweon et al., 2008). Although these seem to be simple fixes, these kinds of small changes aimed at reducing anger and stress may also be applicable to high-risk occupations even when supervisors are not in an office setting for the majority of their workdays, as is the case for warfighters or police officers on patrol. As previously mentioned, supervisor anger is of particular interest in high-risk occupations because of the high-stress nature of the jobs and consequently are more likely to elicit anger responses.

Intraorganizational Stressors

Intraorganizational stressors include organizational rules, practices, and policies that can have negative effects on supervisors, and broader organizational outcomes such as productivity. An organization's practices and policies have the potential to adversely affect supervisors. For example, having overreaching or difficult goals, unsupportive organizational climates, or unfair practices, set the stage for increased supervisor anger. In addition, psychosocial stressors such as interpersonal conflicts, constant pressures, unjust treatment, and low control have been related to supervisor anger and ultimately abusive supervision (e.g., Gibson & Callister, 2010).

Power differentials are also considered a type of intraorganizational stressor and may prohibit or engender expressions of anger at work. For example, Averill (1982, 1997) described the expression of anger as an emotional privilege among supervisors in which they can freely express anger with reduced fear of organizational consequences. This perspective has been supported by other studies, which have found that individuals who occupy higher levels of an organizational hierarchy or a higher prestige occupation are more likely to be direct in their expression of anger (Sloan, 2004). Similarly, Fitness (2000) found that 45% of subordinate employees who were angered by their superiors confronted them, whereas 71% of respondents who were angered by their subordinates confronted them. In considering the effects of workplace anger from the employee–supervisor dichotomy, it becomes clear that supervisors may be less affected by their subordinates' anger than the antithesis, as supervisors have more power and autonomy within the organization because of their position and may regulate their subordinates' behavior through reward and punishment (Chi & Ho, 2014; Conway et al., 1999). There have also been display differences in terms of frequency and intensity found within anger episodes among employees based on power. Specifically, lower status employees experience higher intensity of anger and longer anger episodes when compared with higher status employees yet are likely to suppress their anger because of their position in the organizational hierarchy (Sloan, 2004; Stets & Tsushima, 2001).

High-risk occupations have traditional intraorganizational workplace stressors and hazards unique to the job, which in turn are associated with anger. For example, Collins and Gibbs (2003) found that workplace stressors in a sample of police officers were frequently the result of psychosocial stressors that have been related to anger (i.e., work–family conflict, poor communication, lack of control over workload, lack of support, and overload of work demands). Robinson and Mitchell (1993) identified anger in response to unjust treatment in individuals who are employed as emergency service personnel (i.e., ambulance personnel, firefighters, and police officers) and hospital personnel who carry with them high stress levels. With the unique stress and additional challenges for those employed in high-risk occupations, there should be thoughtful consideration of how to manage and employ these groups of individuals to better serve their specific needs, as well as the specific needs of the organizations, without compromising employee health, well-being, and quality of life. These studies provide helpful insight into organizational precursors that spill over into supervisor anger.

The organizational context, especially intraorganizational stressors, have a grave impact on the stress and burden felt by supervisors, leading to potential anger, negative supervisory behaviors, and abusive supervision.

Organizational strategies for reducing anger are discussed later in this chapter. Although organizational factors play a large role in supervisory anger, individual antecedents also contribute to the experience of anger at work.

Employee Antecedents of Supervisor Anger

Another group of antecedents of supervisor anger includes interpersonal conflicts and acts of incivility in the workplace carried out by their employees. Scholars have explored anger episodes in the workplace and the interactions that take place between supervisors, subordinates, and coworkers. Fitness (2000) found that supervisors are easily angered by morally reprehensible behaviors of their employees, especially in the case of high-risk occupations in which the consequences for such behaviors can be life or death. Schyns and Hansbrough (2010) explained how difficult employees can provoke the abusive or destructive side of leaders through deviant behaviors (e.g., insubordination, theft, and high absenteeism) to a point where they show outbursts of anger and aggression. These findings shed light on the cyclical nature of supervisor anger at work in addition to how such anger expression leads to negative employee behaviors, which in turn feed back to elicit further supervisor anger.

In contrast, supervisors who are supportive, are helpful, and treat their employees fairly usually have subordinates who are less likely to experience anger outbursts, who exhibit fewer counterproductive work behaviors, and who display higher levels of gratitude toward their supervisor (Ford et al., 2018), suggesting that the feedback loop from supervisor anger to employees and back can be positive. This pattern also suggests that supervisor-support training may be offered as a strategy for mitigating the negative effects of supervisor anger on employees. We suggest here that although supervisor anger has direct and indirect effects on the respective outcomes of supervisors and their subordinates, such outcomes can also feed back to the experience of supervisor anger.

Throughout this section, we shed light on antecedents of supervisor anger and abusive supervision at work. Namely, we identified organizational and employee stressors that need to be considered when focusing on the causes and triggers of supervisor anger. These antecedents of supervisor anger and abusive supervision provide avenues for prevention of supervisor anger at work, as is discussed later in the chapter. As described earlier, the expression of anger can take emotional, behavioral, and cognitive forms and frequently manifests in workplace incivility and abusive supervision. This manifestation ultimately has consequences for the supervisor and for the subordinate.

Although the adverse effects of workplace anger have also been shown to affect one's own health and well-being through stress and coronary heart disease (T. W. Smith et al., 2004), those effects are beyond the focus of this chapter (see Lawrence-Wood et al., Chapter 6 in this volume).

EMPLOYEE OUTCOMES OF SUPERVISOR ANGER

The occurrence of anger in the workplace is common, leading to a myriad of outcomes, mostly related to one's subordinates but also related to supervisors themselves. Organizational factors such as norms and workplace culture add a layer of complexity when examining the relationship between anger and positive/negative outcomes. This complexity was evidenced by Linkh and Sonnek (2003), who described the paradoxical nature of anger and aggression within the armed forces. On one hand, military culture prides itself on fostering good order, discipline, and self-control; on the other hand, military culture acknowledges the utility of anger expression and aggression in combat applications, which is often crucial for national defense.

Although extant research has found that supervisors may use anger expression in the form of aggression to boost the performance and productivity of their subordinates (Lovaglia & Houser, 1996), these expressions may run the risk of being perceived as bullying (Hershcovis, 2011; Tepper & Henle, 2011) or lead to negative outcomes. Other research has examined how anger may be displaced or displayed toward employees differentially. For example, Tepper et al. (2006) demonstrated that supervisors displace their aggression toward "safe" employees, or employees who are thought to be weaker and unable to defend themselves. The effects of supervisor anger on employees at work vary based on a number of factors.

Positive Versus Negative Employee Outcomes

Anger is not always associated with negative outcomes, as research has found that 40% to 61% of anger expressions in the workplace are associated with positive outcomes (Geddes et al., 2020; Gibson et al., 2009; Kassinove et al., 1997), such as declaring one's social status (Sloan, 2004), redressing perceived injustices (Averill, 1982; Tavris, 1989), and increasing work motivation (Glomb & Hulin, 1997). Although the study of beneficial outcomes of supervisor anger is in its infancy (e.g., Geddes et al., 2020), many more studies have reported on the negative outcomes of supervisor anger. In their qualitative assessment of status and anger outcomes, Callister et al. (2017)

found that when employees were targets of their supervisor's anger, they reported twice as many negative outcomes as positive outcomes.

The issue of anger being associated with positive or negative outcomes is also impacted by perceptions of emotional displays that can be regarded as inappropriate because of norms of emotional display, characteristics of the displayer (e.g., gender), characteristics of the display (e.g., video conferencing vs. in person), and characteristics of the context (e.g., topic of interaction), regardless of the emotional intent of the displayer (Cheshin, 2020). Thus, the effects of a supervisor's display of emotions may be perceived as positive or negative based on many interacting factors impacting the employee's perceptions of that display as appropriate or not appropriate. Furthermore, display rules are likely to differ by occupation, especially in high-risk occupations where such display rules may include a much wider tolerance level.

Considering that anger expressions among high-powered individuals is more permissible, some leaders may use and direct anger toward their subordinates with the belief that their methods are effective (e.g., coaches or drill sergeants) at enhancing the work performance of their employees. Sometimes, anger becomes a normalized part of the job in certain professions. The findings of anger expression among leaders, however, have yielded mixed results. Although much of the literature has examined symmetrical outcomes of leader anger (i.e., leaders' anger adversely affecting their followers), few studies have examined positive outcomes associated with leader anger expression (asymmetrical/beneficial outcomes). The effects of supervisor anger may depend on the occupation. Within the military and other high-risk occupations, anger may have a facilitative effect.

Of the limited studies examining asymmetrical/beneficial outcomes of supervisor anger, Lindebaum et al. (2016) found that military personnel were motivated to make sense of the events that set off their leader's anger in order to improve their subsequent performance; similar findings were also noted by Van Kleef et al. (2009) among graduate students. Within the construction sector, Lindebaum and Fielden (2011) found that anger expression was linked to perceived leader effectiveness.

In an attempt to parse apart conflicting findings of whether anger is associated with positive or negative outcomes, Wang et al. (2018) elucidated expressions of leader anger and argued that the effects of anger should be examined while considering the type of leader and the type of anger being expressed. The authors found that outcomes were dependent on whether the leader's anger expression was due to competence or integrity-related violations, as well as whether the leader in question was perceived to be an abusive supervisor. When leaders expressed anger because of integrity-based infractions (e.g., an employee taking credit for someone else's work), followers perceived them to be effective. In contrast, leader anger expressions related to subordinate competency (e.g., an employee not performing well because of a lack of education or experience) were associated with followers perceiving them as less effective. The findings varied as a function of which leaders were perceived to be abusive; when "abusive" leaders reacted with anger because of a competency-related event, the negative effects were more damaging. The positive effects of integrity-based anger expression were also weakened among leaders who were perceived to be abusive. Considering the contradictory evidence in regard to whether expressed anger leads to positive or negative outcomes, it becomes clear that findings are predicated on the social and cultural norms of each organization and should be interpreted accordingly.

Negative Employee Outcomes of Supervisor Anger

Outcomes of workplace anger expressed by supervisors can adversely affect the organization through effects on subordinates. Negative employee outcomes of anger include endangering the status of relationships and communication accuracy (Rothman & Magee, 2016; Wubben et al., 2009), reducing productivity (Fitness, 2000; Jehn, 1995), and increasing theft and violence (Chen & Spector, 1992; L. Greenberg & Barling, 1999). Leadership studies have found that the expression of anger among leaders has been linked to perceptions of decreased leader effectiveness (Lewis, 2000) and may place employees at risk for problem drinking (Bamberger & Bacharach, 2006). Furthermore, recent research has indicated that leader anger may give impetus to increased supervisor-directed deviance and work effort among followers (Schwarzmüller et al., 2018). Specifically, it was determined that leader anger led to increased work effort through an employee's anxiety, which if left unmanaged may take a toll on employee well-being and work performance (Haslam et al., 2005).

It is also possible that the expression of anger in the workplace elicits increased incivility (Andersson & Pearson, 1999; Aryee et al., 2007) and a propensity for revenge (Bies & Tripp, 2000) within an organization. Justice theory has been used to explain the relationship between supervisor anger and these counterproductive work behaviors (Zhang et al., 2019). Finally, Yang et al. (2020) found a relationship between abusive supervision and reduced safety behaviors and performance, further illustrating the importance of recognizing and mitigating abusive supervision, precipitated by anger, at work.

Whereas research on the outcomes of workplace anger have been limited, many more studies have focused on outcomes of specific forms of aggression. O'Neill et al. (2009) explored the relationship between perceived organizational support (POS), anger, and workplace outcomes and found that POS had an indirect negative association through anger on turnover intentions, workplace accidents, and absences at work. They also found that anger had positive direct associations with turnover intentions, workplace accidents, and absences at work, as well as an increase in high-risk health behaviors.

Anger in the form of abusive supervision, especially in high-risk occupations, can have detrimental effects on employees and their families, and in turn may result in further negative outcomes for supervisors themselves. Tepper (2000) identified several consequences associated with abusive supervision. Not only are employees more likely to quit their jobs, but employees who stay in their positions with abusive supervisors tend to experience a decrease in work and life satisfaction and increases in work and family conflict and psychological distress. Employees subject to abusive supervisors are also more likely to displace their anger or aggression for fear of being fired, causing negative effects on family members in the home (Hoobler & Brass, 2006).

In their investigation of suicide rates among U.S. military personnel, Erickson et al. (2015) found that employees who had a destructive leader were more likely to have committed suicide in the previous year, based on a sample of 30 U.S. soldiers in Iraq. Some of the contributing factors, as indicated by Erickson et al., included supervisors who become frustrated when their goals are not being achieved because of difficult subordinates who retaliate, play politics, or are incompetent. Thus, leaders might find it increasingly difficult to deal with these types of employees and may exhibit signs of aggression and frustration over time. Erickson and colleagues also found that destructive leadership and abusive supervision are positively associated with anger, bitterness, and irritation outcomes. This study, in particular, demonstrates the importance of identifying precursors of anger and abusive supervision as well as understanding their outcomes in order to help managers and organizations gain insight and develop tools to better mitigate destructive leadership behaviors before tragedies such as suicide take place.

Another approach in considering the effects of leader anger on subordinates centers on interpersonal mechanisms. Using his framework of emotions as social information model, Van Kleef (2009) highlighted the interpersonal nature of emotional expression and demonstrates how an individual's behavior is influenced by the emotional display of others. In essence, Van Kleef posits that an observer's behavior can be influenced through inferential processes as well as affective reactions. By viewing workplace exchanges of anger through the lens of the emotions as social information model, we can recognize that when a supervisor displays anger, it may enable a subordinate to draw inferences in regard to their leaders' feelings, which in turn may influence the subordinate's behavior in future interactions. In terms of affective reactions, angry supervisors may also influence their followers to be angry through emotional-contagion processes, as evidenced by Van Kleef and colleagues (2009), who found that work-groups with angry leaders led to subordinate anger.

Evidence also suggests that workplace anger can have adverse effects on an employee's family. Although the majority of studies examining family outcomes have done so using aggression constructs (i.e., incivility, bullying, abusive supervision), it is probable that these relationships were precipitated by anger. Similarly, in observing the path between anger and aggression, some research has also suggested that anger can lead to aggression by attenuating self-regulatory inhibitions (Spector et al., 2006). Once anger leads to various forms of aggression, it may then afflict an employee's family through spillover and crossover effects. For instance, Haines et al. (2006) found that job stress as the result of workplace aggression was demonstrated to have a crossover effect from an employee to their partner. Similarly, Ferguson (2012) reported that workplace incivility had negative main effects on the marital satisfaction of the employee and their partner while leading to family-to-work conflict of the employee's partner.

Organizational Strategies for Reducing Anger at Work

We have identified antecedents and outcomes of anger in the scholarly literature, but very little attention has been given to organizational strategies for reducing such anger and aggression, and even less has been given to high-risk occupations in which problematic anger may be particularly disruptive. Given the impact that organizational contextual factors such as policies, situational constraints, and poor leadership have on supervisor anger and abusive supervision (Tepper, 2007), we suggest that this complex process be understood from an ecological systems perspective. This perspective is further illustrated by Hoobler and Brass's (2006) findings that abusive supervision not only affects subordinates but also adversely affects employee' family members. Thus, focusing interventions and strategies at the organizational level may have far-reaching effects on decreasing anger and aggression in supervisors and also lead to beneficial effects on subordinates and their family members. Such organizational strategies can moderate the effects of antecedents of supervisor anger on actual anger expression. These strategies can also help to ameliorate the effects of actual anger expression such as workplace incivility and abusive supervision on employee outcomes of anger. We suggest that the organizational level is a more impactful target for anger reduction at work because so many sources of the anger are under the control of the organization. We have grouped the organizational approaches into three primary areas: improving workplace conditions and constraints, reducing injustice, and improving supervisor support via training.

Improving Workplace Conditions

Poor workplace conditions such as low control, high demands, long work hours, unsafe environments, and shiftwork are psychosocial stressors that have been related to numerous poor health and safety outcomes, suggesting their negative impact on workers. Research has revealed that such poor working conditions are also related to supervisor aggression through perceptions of injustice (Dupré & Barling, 2006). Karasek's (1979) job demands–job control model depicts that the increased stress and strain that result from work environments that are high on job demands and low on job control contribute to aggressive behavior. In particular, high-risk occupations with personnel such as first responders, military personnel, construction workers, and health care workers are more susceptible to anger and aggression because of their characteristically high-demand and low-control jobs. Addressing organizational structural issues, such as decreasing job demands, work hours, and shiftwork and improving perceived control via autonomy and increased decision making, is likely to have a positive impact on supervisor and employee anger reduction. A specific psychosocial stressor that is a special case of poor working conditions is injustice at work.

Reducing Injustice

Justice theory, psychological contract theory, and social exchange theories have all been used to help explain why anger and aggression occur at work and are particularly useful in understanding abusive supervision (e.g., Tepper, 2007). Thus, strategies that address reducing injustices are beneficial in addressing supervisor and subordinate anger at work. For example, Brockner (2002) and others have focused on improving procedural justice—

the process or procedures for making a fair decision—as a strategy for improving fairness perceptions that can originate at the time of hiring (e.g., Truxillo et al., 2004). Others have found that improvements in distributive justice—fairness in the distribution of resources—also help improve fairness and justice perceptions overall. Furthermore, reducing organizational barriers to organizational advancement can also help to reduce unjust perceptions. Finally, clear and honest communication by organizational leaders can help to improve procedural justice and reduce the possibility of psychological contract violations.

Psychological contract violations are the result of feeling betrayed by the organization (Morrison & Robinson, 1997) and are particularly critical for high-risk occupations in which individuals are willing to jeopardize their own lives with the understanding that the organization will look out for them, train them, equip them, and provide them the best leadership possible (Adler & Castro, 2013). Psychological contracts can be improved through POS (Aselage & Eisenberger, 2003). Using social exchange theory (Blau, 1964)—the idea that behavior is the result of social exchanges between people based on an evaluation of costs and benefits—we suggest that organizations that encourage positive social interactions and exchanges between leaders and subordinates will have lower levels of perceived unfairness and improved POS, resulting in reductions of supervisor and subordinate anger and aggression. Additionally, Patterson (2003) argued that positive social interactions that come in the form of social support aid to buffer the effects of psychological distress, specifically in the high-risk occupation of police officers, suggesting that improving social support via supervisor training is a strategy that shows promise in reducing anger.

Supervisor Support Training

Supervisors are critical in contributing to a culture of support for employees, as supervisor support leads to improvements in employee health, well-being, and work outcomes (e.g., Hammer et al., 2011). Supervisors have power over workers because they provide direction on how to do the job, provide rewards for performance, and are the gatekeepers to top organizational leaders and to accessing key organizational programs and policies. Thus, training supervisors on how to support workers offers an organizational strategy to reduce the effects of supervisor anger on their employees, as support and anger tend to involve conflicting emotions and behaviors. Changing the workplace culture through supervisor supportive training has been shown to lead to improved employee outcomes such as performance and retention, health, and well-being of employees and their families (e.g., Hammer et al., 2011, 2015; Odle-Dusseau et al., 2016), and thus this may be used as a strategy to mitigate the impact of supervisor anger. Research on family supportive supervisor behaviors (Hammer et al., 2009) is based on four types of supervisor support: instrumental, emotional, role modeling, and creative work–life management support. *Emotional support* involves supervisors demonstrating that an employee is being cared for and that his or her feelings are being considered. This support can be achieved through increasing face-to-face contact with employees and asking how employees are doing, or communicating genuine concern about employees' work/life challenges. *Instrumental support* involves helping workers manage schedules and working with employees to solve schedule conflicts. Role modeling occurs when supervisors demonstrate they are taking care of their own work/life challenges. Finally, *creative work–family management/win–win management* is aimed at redesigning work to support the conflicting employee work–life demands in a manner that is a positive for both employees and employers. An example of this type of support is promoting cross-training and the ability for shift trades to jointly enable employee scheduling flexibility needs and work coverage.

This supervisor supportive training has been evaluated and modified in several randomized controlled trials, demonstrating its effectiveness using rigorous research designs (e.g., Hammer et al., 2011, 2020). The idea of training supervisors how to be more supportive of workers in different domains of work beyond work–family support has extended to training supervisors on how to provide support for veterans transitioning into the civilian workforce, training supervisors on how to provide support for workplace violence prevention, training supervisors on how to provide sleep support, training supervisors on how to provide support for safety communications at work, and training supervisors on more general culture of health issues.

Based on social support theory (Cohen & Wills, 1985), supervisor supportive training is the only known approach in teaching supervisors about how they can exercise their critical role and behave in ways that better support workers, leading to improvements in work and well-being outcomes. Social support theory suggests that social support has direct effects on stress reduction, psychological health, and physical health. In addition, extensive evidence demonstrates the benefits of supervisor social support for a number of workplace outcomes (e.g., Hammer et al., 2007; Kossek et al., 2011).

As an example, recent research has extended the effects of family supportive supervisor behavior training to the high-risk occupational context of the military (Hammer et al., 2019). Specifically Hammer et al. (2019) trained supervisors to be more supportive of post-9/11 veterans who were transitioning into the workplace. Given that posttraumatic stress disorder, head injury, and alcohol abuse have all been associated with increased anger among veterans, coupled with the fact that anger might disrupt the workplace and derail the employee's career progression following military service, developing evidence-based interventions to address postdeployment adjustment is critical (Elbogen et al., 2010). Thus, it is advantageous to apply this evidence-based approach to supervisors of veterans with the aim of providing better support to our returning service members (Hammer et al., 2019). Evaluations of Hammer et al.'s (2019) training efficacy are ongoing, but recent analyses have suggested that the intervention improved supervisors' self-reported views of veteran employees, as well as the health and work outcomes of veterans, but only when their supervisor support was high at baseline. This finding suggests there may need to be a certain level of engagement and support from supervisors before they engage in the supportive training for attitude change to occur. Finally, veteran baseline job demands significantly moderated the effect of the training on veteran self-reported anger at 3- and 9-months posttraining. More specifically, veterans with higher job demands at baseline reported reduced anger following the supervisor training intervention (Allen et al., 2019). This result suggests that this supervisor training may be most beneficial for those employees who stand to gain the most/need it most.

Supervisors are critical to organizational functioning, so it should not be surprising that they are critical for impacting most employees' work lives. Thus, ensuring that supervisors receive the correct training on how to best support workers can be a key solution to mitigating anger of employees in the workplace. Unfortunately, supervisors tend to receive little training on how to do their jobs, and what training they do receive is primarily related to technical skills rather than social skills. Very little attention has been given to teaching managers and supervisors how to treat people with respect and support. Sometimes this is as simple as raising supervisors' awareness of the importance of engaging in active listening while taking an interest in the lives of their employees. When supervisors are taught to be more supportive of employees, it is likely that employees will feel more gratitude toward the organization and will want to contribute more toward organizational goals, as suggested by social exchange theory (Blau, 1964). Anger, on the other hand, can result from being in unsupportive workplaces (Ford et al., 2018), especially high-risk occupations that have extreme demands on workers. Likewise, when employees feel more supported they are, in turn, more likely to engage in positive organizational citizenship behaviors, and when they are treated poorly, they tend to behave more negatively in workplaces (e.g., Mitchell & Ambrose, 2007) and engage in counterproductive work behaviors (Aryee et al., 2007). For example, Koning and van Kleef (2015) found that leader displays of negative emotions such as anger lead to a decrease in positive organizational citizenship behaviors at work. In essence, we suggest that training supervisors to be more supportive may result in reducing supervisor anger and in turn improve employee behaviors such as organizational citizenship while reducing counterproductive behaviors.

Similarly, Gonzalez-Morales et al. (2018) found that training supervisors to increase support for employees resulted in reduced instances of abusive supervision. Two training groups were trained offsite, one with 13 supervisors and one with 10 supervisors in a series of in-person lectures, group discussions, and role-play activities. Supervisors were trained on four supportive behaviors—benevolence, sincerity, fairness, and mindfulness—for a total of 8 hours of training. This is important research, as it demonstrated a direct link between training supervisors on general supportive behaviors and reduced abusive supervision.

While supervisor training has been identified as one way to mitigate anger in the workplace, organizational scholars have identified other types of strategies for reducing anger at work. Using an ecological systems approach, we advocate for organizational strategies over individual strategies for reducing anger and aggression at work. These strategies involve reducing injustice, improving the workplace conditions, and improving supervisor support via training. These strategies can be enacted by organizational leadership in terms of culture changes or training supervisors and have the potential of leading to positive outcomes for employees and their family members.

DIVERSITY PERSPECTIVE ON SUPERVISOR ANGER AT WORK

Throughout this chapter, we have explored various consequences of expressed anger in the workplace, which are largely negative, though outcomes can include the conferral of higher status on a supervisor who engages in such an expression. Certain individuals, however, may not experience similar outcomes from anger expressions, including women and underrepresented minority group members. Indeed, people from these groups may experience a unique set of consequences associated with their expression of anger and may be less likely to engage in expressions of anger. In particular, societal expectations surrounding anger and aggression are closely tied to sex roles, especially masculine roles typifying agency or dominance/assertiveness (Eagly, 1987; Eagly & Karau, 2002). Norms for leaders in the workplace have been largely modeled after masculine roles—this is particularly true given the male-dominated nature of high-risk occupations. Women, on the other hand, are expected to display more communal behaviors or the antithesis of aggression (Eagly, 1987; Eagly & Karau, 2002), which can create a role conflict between feminine gender role and leadership role and lead to discrimination against women who behave agentically (e.g., in an assertive, dominating way; Eagly & Karau, 2002).

Consistent with this theorizing, researchers have documented that male professionals are not penalized and indeed may be rewarded when acting in ways consistent with the masculine norm and displaying anger (Brescoll & Uhlmann, 2008), whereas women are penalized for displaying anger in terms of lower wages, lower conferred status, and lower perceived competence, whether they occupy low-status or high-status roles (i.e., trainee vs. CEO). Men's anger is attributed to external causes, whereas women's anger is considered reflective of their stable traits. Livingston et al. (2012) elaborated on these results by documenting that the race of men and women corporate leaders represented an important moderating factor, such that White women and Black men were penalized (with lower status ratings) for displaying assertive (agency) behaviors, whereas Black women and White men were not. Alternately, when women (or racially diverse) leaders' express anger because of injustice experienced by subordinates, they are viewed more positively (possessing more agentic and communal traits) than male leaders, or displaying more empathic anger (Keck, 2019).

FUTURE RESEARCH

Interestingly, anger has not received much attention in the organizational sciences beyond the research on abusive supervision, and thus little is known about the varying effects of anger in the workplace or the extent to which it is a function of psychosocial factors across organizational domains. Anger has also not received much attention in high-risk occupations, where the need for addressing issues and concerns is even more necessary given the high stress and increased concerns about psychological distress associated with these jobs. These shortcomings may be due to the complexity of the emotion of anger as it exists in various forms, including state and trait anger, and how it is processed in a variety of different ways (e.g., suppressed, expressed, deviant), which may lead to divergent outcomes. Although many organizational studies have investigated the various types of aggression (e.g., incivility, aggression, abusive supervision) and their respective outcomes, more research is needed on the organizational strategies that can be employed to reduce anger at work.

The research area of organizational anger could particularly be improved by examining the interplay between an individual's anger profile and an organization's norms for displayed anger to determine how their interactions influence anger outcomes in the workplace. These findings could shed light on the anger outcomes of individuals who transition from high-risk occupations (e.g., law enforcement, military), where anger expression may be more tolerated, to occupations that are considered low risk (e.g., administrative, office jobs), where anger expression may be more frequently met with organizational sanctions.

The extant literature has also yielded few organizational or supervisor strategies for reducing anger among employees, and thus the field could be enhanced by implementing longitudinal dyadic studies between supervisors and their employees to assess the efficacy of various anger mitigation techniques. Such findings could also clarify the accuracy between displayed and perceived supervisor anger while demonstrating which forms of leadership (e.g., transactional, transformational) interact with anger expressions to produce positive work outcomes. Finally, efforts should be made to understand how work–family conflict and family–work conflict manifest as anger and whether these outcomes penetrate home and workplace domains. Such approaches may delineate the extent to which intraorganizational stressors and extraorganizational stressors interact and lead to anger while adversely affecting the employee and their family, coworkers, supervisors, and the organization altogether.

IMPLICATIONS

- Organizations should put forth time and resources in educating supervisors and employees about the antecedents and outcomes of anger at work, specifically highlighting the spillover repercussions into family and personal domains. Organizations should promote transparency between themselves, supervisors, and the employees in the workplace.

Improving workplace conditions and constraints

- Organizations should make efforts to improve workplace conditions while attenuating constraints. Whenever possible, implementing a flexible workplace structure in terms of job demands, work hours, and shiftwork. These policies may improve perceived control through autonomy and thus decrease overall stress and strain on employees.

Reducing injustice

- Many adverse organizational outcomes could be prevented by reducing injustice in the workplace. Organizations can reduce injustice and simultaneously reduce perceptions of injustice by enhancing communication at the time of hiring, improving distributive justice, and reducing organizational barriers to advancement.

Improving supervisor support via training

- Supervisors play a critical role in the lives of those they oversee, and organizations would fare well in adopting supervisor supportive training tools. Such approaches could benefit supervisors by shedding light on the impacts they can have on their employees while offering useful social and behavioral approaches of support to implement in their respective workplaces. These strategies also lead to improved health and well-being of employees.

REFERENCES

Adler, A. B., & Castro, C. A. (2013). An occupational mental health model for the military. *Military Behavioral Health*, *1*(1), 41–45. https://doi.org/10.1080/21635781.2012.721063

Allen, S. J., Brady, J. M., Hammer, L. B., & Perry, M. L. (2019, April). *Effects of a veteran-supportive supervisor training on veteran anger* [Paper presentation]. Society for Industrial and Organizational Psychology 34th Annual Conference, National Harbor, MD.

American Psychological Association. (2011). *High-risk jobs and high-risk populations*. https://www.apa.org/wsh/past/2011/high-risk-jobs

Anderson, C. A., & Bushman, B. J. (2002). Human aggression. *Annual Review of Psychology*, *53*(1), 27–51. https://doi.org/10.1146/annurev.psych.53.100901.135231

Andersson, L. M., & Pearson, C. M. (1999). Tit for tat? The spiraling effect of incivility in the workplace. *Academy of Management Review*, *24*(3), 452–471. https://doi.org/10.5465/amr.1999.2202131

Aryee, S., Chen, Z. X., Sun, L. Y., & Debrah, Y. A. (2007). Antecedents and outcomes of abusive supervision: Test of a trickle-down model. *The Journal of Applied Psychology, 92*(1), 191–201. https://doi.org/10.1037/0021-9010.92.1.191

Aselage, J., & Eisenberger, R. (2003). Perceived organizational support and psychological contracts: A theoretical integration. *Journal of Organizational Behavior, 24*(5), 491–509. https://doi.org/10.1002/job.211

Averill, J. A. (1982). *Anger and aggression: An essay on emotion*. Springer-Verlag. https://doi.org/10.1007/978-1-4612-5743-1

Averill, J. A. (1997). The emotions: An integrative approach. In R. Hogan, J. Johnson, & S. Briggs (Eds.), *Handbook of personality psychology* (pp. 513–541). Academic Press.

Aytac, S. (2015). The sources of stress, the symptoms of stress and anger styles as a psychosocial risk at occupational health and safety: A case study on Turkish police officers. *Procedia Manufacturing, 3*, 6421–6428. https://doi.org/10.1016/j.promfg.2015.07.915

Bamberger, P. A., & Bacharach, S. B. (2006). Abusive supervision and subordinate problem drinking: Taking resistance, stress and subordinate personality into account. *Human Relations, 59*(6), 723–752. https://doi.org/10.1177/0018726706066852

Barling, J. (1996). The prediction, experience, and consequences of workplace violence. In G. R. VandenBos & E. Q. Bulatao (Eds.), *Violence on the job: Identifying risks and developing solutions* (pp. 29–49). American Psychological Association. https://doi.org/10.1037/10215-001

Benedek, D. M., Fullerton, C., & Ursano, R. J. (2007). First responders: Mental health consequences of natural and human-made disasters for public health and public safety workers. *Annual Review of Public Health, 28*, 55–68. https://doi.org/10.1146/annurev.publhealth.28.021406.144037

Bhatti, N., Shar, A. H., Shaikh, F. M., & Nazar, M. S. (2010). Causes of stress in organization, a case study of Sukkur. *International Journal of Business and Management, 5*(11), 3–14. https://doi.org/10.5539/ijbm.v5n11p3

Bies, R. J., & Tripp, T. M. (2000). A passion for justice: The rationality and morality of revenge. In R. Cropanzano (Ed.), *Justice in the workplace* (pp. 197–208). JAI Press.

Blau, P. (1964). *Power and exchange in social life*. John Wiley & Sons.

Booth, J., & Mann, S. (2005). The experience of workplace anger. *Leadership and Organization Development Journal, 26*(4), 250–262. https://doi.org/10.1108/01437730510600634

Booth-Kewley, S., & Friedman, H. S. (1987). Psychological predictors of heart disease: A quantitative review. *Psychological Bulletin, 101*(3), 343–362. https://doi.org/10.1037/0033-2909.101.3.343

Brescoll, V. L., & Uhlmann, E. L. (2008). Can an angry woman get ahead? Status conferral, gender, and expression of emotion in the workplace. *Psychological Science, 19*(3), 268–275. https://doi.org/10.1111/j.1467-9280.2008.02079.x

Brockner, J. (2002). Making sense of procedural fairness: How high procedural fairness can reduce or heighten the influence of outcome favorability. *Academy of Management Review, 27*(1), 58–76. https://doi.org/10.5465/amr.2002.5922363

Callister, R. R., Geddes, D., & Gibson, D. F. (2017). When is anger helpful or hurtful? Status and role impact on anger expression and outcomes. *Negotiation and Conflict Management Research, 10*(2), 69–87. https://doi.org/10.1111/ncmr.12090

Canary, D. J., Spitzberg, B. H., & Semic, B. A. (1998). The experience and expression of anger in interpersonal settings. In P. A. Anderson & L. K. Guerrero (Eds.), *Handbook of communication and emotion: Research, theory, applications and contexts* (pp. 189–213). Academic Press.

Chen, P. Y., & Spector, P. E. (1992). Relationships of work stressors with aggression, withdrawal, theft and substance use: An exploratory study. *Journal of Occupational and Organizational Psychology, 65*(3), 177–184. https://doi.org/10.1111/j.2044-8325.1992.tb00495.x

Cheshin, A. (2020). The impact of non-normative displays of emotion in the workplace: How inappropriateness shapes the interpersonal outcomes of emotional displays. *Frontiers in Psychology, 11*, Article 6. https://doi.org/10.3389/fpsyg.2020.00006

Chi, N. W., & Ho, T. R. (2014). Understanding when leader negative emotional expression enhances follower performance: The moderating roles of follower personality traits and perceived leader power. *Human Relations, 67*(9), 1051–1072. https://doi.org/10.1177/0018726714526626

Cohen, S., & Wills, T. A. (1985). Stress, social support, and the buffering hypothesis. *Psychological Bulletin, 98*(2), 310–357. https://doi.org/10.1037/0033-2909.98.2.310

Collins, P. A., & Gibbs, A. C. C. (2003). Stress in police officers: A study of the origins, prevalence and severity of stress-related symptoms within a county police force. *Occupational Medicine, 53*(4), 256–264. https://doi.org/10.1093/occmed/kqg061

Conway, M., Di Fazio, R., & Mayman, S. (1999). Judging others' emotions as a function of the others' status. *Social Psychology Quarterly, 62*(3), 291–305. https://doi.org/10.2307/2695865

Cortina, L. M., Magley, V. J., Williams, J. H., & Langhout, R. D. (2001). Incivility in the workplace: Incidence and impact. *Journal of Occupational Health Psychology, 6*(1), 64–80. https://doi.org/10.1037/1076-8998.6.1.64

Deffenbacher, J. L., Oetting, E. R., Lynch, R. S., & Morris, C. D. (1996). The expression of anger and its consequences. *Behaviour Research and Therapy, 34*(7), 575–590. https://doi.org/10.1016/0005-7967(96)00018-6

Dupré, K. E., & Barling, J. (2006). Predicting and preventing supervisory workplace aggression. *Journal of Occupational Health Psychology, 11*(1), 13–26. https://doi.org/10.1037/1076-8998.11.1.13

Eagly, A. H. (1987). *Sex differences in social behavior: A social-role analysis*. Lawrence Erlbaum Associates.

Eagly, A. H., & Karau, S. J. (2002). Role congruity theory of prejudice toward female leaders. *Psychological Review, 109*(3), 573–598. https://doi.org/10.1037/0033-295X.109.3.573

Eissa, G., & Lester, S. W. (2017). Supervisor role overload and frustration as antecedents of abusive supervision: The moderating role of supervisor personality. *Journal of Organizational Behavior, 38*(3), 307–326. https://doi.org/10.1002/job.2123

Elbogen, E. B., Fuller, S., Johnson, S. C., Brooks, S., Kinneer, P., Calhoun, P. S., & Beckham, J. C. (2010). Improving risk assessment of violence among military veterans: An evidence-based approach for clinical decision-making. *Clinical Psychology Review, 30*(6), 595–607. https://doi.org/10.1016/j.cpr.2010.03.009

Erickson, A., Shaw, B., Murray, J., & Branch, S. (2015). Destructive leadership: Causes, consequences and countermeasures. *Organizational Dynamics*, *44*(4), 266–272. https://doi.org/10.1016/j.orgdyn.2015.09.003

Ferguson, M. (2012). You cannot leave it at the office: Spillover and crossover of coworker incivility. *Journal of Organizational Behavior*, *33*(4), 571–588. https://doi.org/10.1002/job.774

Fitness, J. (2000). Anger in the workplace: An emotion script approach to anger episodes between workers and their superiors, co-workers and subordinates. *Journal of Organizational Behavior*, *21*(2), 147–162. https://doi.org/10.1002/(SICI)1099-1379(200003)21:2<147::AID-JOB35>3.0.CO;2-T

Ford, M. T., Wang, Y., Jin, J., & Eisenberger, R. (2018). Chronic and episodic anger and gratitude toward the organization: Relationships with organizational and supervisor supportiveness and extrarole behavior. *Journal of Occupational Health Psychology*, *23*(2), 175–187. https://doi.org/10.1037/ocp0000075

Fox, S., & Spector, P. E. (1999). A model of work frustration–aggression. *Journal of Organizational Behavior*, *20*(6), 915–931. https://doi.org/10.1002/(SICI)1099-1379(199911)20:6<915::AID-JOB918>3.0.CO;2-6

Geddes, D., Callister, R. R., & Gibson, D. E. (2020). A message in the madness: Functions of workplace anger in organizational life. *The Academy of Management Perspectives*, *34*(1), 28–47. https://doi.org/10.5465/amp.2016.0158

Gibson, D. E., & Barsade, S. G. (1999, August). The experience of anger at work: Lessons from the chronically angry. In R. R. Callister (Chair), *Anger in organizations: Its causes and consequences* [Symposium]. Academy of Management Annual Conference, Chicago, IL, United States.

Gibson, D. E., & Callister, R. R. (2010). Anger in organizations: Review and integration. *Journal of Management*, *36*(1), 66–93. https://doi.org/10.1177/0149206309348060

Gibson, D. E., Schweitzer, M. E., Callister, R. R., & Gray, B. (2009). The influence of anger expressions on outcomes in organizations. *Negotiation and Conflict Management Research*, *2*(3), 236–262. https://doi.org/10.1111/j.1750-4716.2009.00039.x

Glomb, T. M. (2002). Workplace anger and aggression: Informing conceptual models with data from specific encounters. *Journal of Occupational Health Psychology*, *7*(1), 20–36. https://doi.org/10.1037/1076-8998.7.1.20

Glomb, T. M., & Hulin, C. L. (1997). Anger and gender effects in observed supervisor-subordinate dyadic interactions. *Organizational Behavior and Human Decision Processes*, *72*(3), 281–307. https://doi.org/10.1006/obhd.1997.2741

Gonthier, G., & Morrissey, K. (2002). *Rude awakenings: Overcoming civility crisis in the workplace*. Dearborn Trade Publishing.

Gonzalez-Morales, M. G., Kernan, M. C., Becker, T. E., & Eisenberger, R. (2018). Defeating abusive supervision: Training supervisors to support subordinates. *Journal of Occupational Health Psychology*, *23*(2), 151–162. https://doi.org/10.1037/ocp0000061

Greenberg, L., & Barling, J. (1999). Predicting employee aggression against coworkers, subordinates and supervisors: The roles of person behaviors and perceived workplace factors. *Journal of Organizational Behavior*, *20*(6), 897–913. https://doi.org/10.1002/(SICI)1099-1379(199911)20:6<897::AID-JOB975>3.0.CO;2-Z

Greenberg, N., Docherty, M., Gnanapragasam, S., & Wessely, S. (2020). Managing mental health challenges faced by healthcare workers during covid-19 pandemic. *BMJ*, *368*, m1211. https://doi.org/10.1136/bmj.m1211

Haines, V. Y., III, Marchand, A., & Harvey, S. (2006). Crossover of workplace aggression experiences in dual-earner couples. *Journal of Occupational Health Psychology*, *11*(4), 305–314. https://doi.org/10.1037/1076-8998.11.4.305

Hammer, L. B., Brady, J., & Perry, M. (2020). Training supervisors to support veterans at work: Effects on supervisor attitudes and employee sleep and stress. *Journal of Occupational and Organizational Psychology*, *93*(2), 273–301. https://doi.org/10.1111/joop.12299

Hammer, L. B., Kossek, E. E., Anger, W. K., Bodner, T., & Zimmerman, K. L. (2011). Clarifying work-family intervention processes: The roles of work–family conflict and family-supportive supervisor behaviors. *The Journal of Applied Psychology*, *96*(1), 134–150. https://doi.org/10.1037/a0020927

Hammer, L. B., Kossek, E. E., Yragui, N. L., Bodner, T. E., & Hanson, G. C. (2009). Development and validation of a multidimensional measure of family supportive supervisor behaviors (FSSB). *Journal of Management*, *35*(4), 837–856. https://doi.org/10.1177/0149206308328510

Hammer, L. B., Kossek, E. E., Zimmerman, K., & Daniels, R. (2007). Clarifying the construct of family supportive supervisory behaviors (FSSB): A multilevel perspective. In P. L. Perrewe & D. C. Ganster (Eds.), *Research in occupational stress and well-being: Exploring the work and non-work interface* (Vol. 6, pp. 171–211). Elsevier.

Hammer, L., Truxillo, D., Bodner, T., Rineer, J., Pytlovany, A., & Richman, A. (2015). Effects of a workplace intervention targeting psychosocial risk factors on safety and health outcomes: Psychosocial factors and workers health and safety. *BioMed Research International*, *2015*, Article 836967. https://doi.org/10.1155/2015/836967

Hammer, L. B., Wan, W. H., Brockwood, K. J., Bodner, T., & Mohr, C. D. (2019). Supervisor support training effects on veteran health and work outcomes in the civilian workplace. *The Journal of Applied Psychology*, *104*(1), 52–69. https://doi.org/10.1037/apl0000354

Haslam, C., Atkinson, S., Brown, S., & Haslam, R. A. (2005). Perceptions of the impact of depression and anxiety and the medication for these conditions on safety in the workplace. *Occupational and Environmental Medicine*, *62*(8), 538–545. https://doi.org/10.1136/oem.2004.016196

Hennessy, D. A. (2008). The impact of commuter stress on workplace aggression. *Journal of Applied Social Psychology*, *38*(9), 2315–2335. https://doi.org/10.1111/j.1559-1816.2008.00393.x

Hershcovis, M. S. (2011). “Incivility, social undermining, bullying . . . oh my!”: A call to reconcile constructs within workplace aggression research. *Journal of Organizational Behavior*, *32*(3), 499–519. https://doi.org/10.1002/job.689

Hershcovis, M. S., Turner, N., Barling, J., Arnold, K. A., Dupré, K. E., Inness, M., LeBlanc, M. M., & Sivanathan, N. (2007). Predicting workplace aggression: A meta-analysis. *The Journal of Applied Psychology*, *92*(1), 228–238. https://doi.org/10.1037/0021-9010.92.1.228

Hoobler, J. M., & Brass, D. J. (2006). Abusive supervision and family undermining as displaced aggression. *The Journal of Applied Psychology*, *91*(5), 1125–1133. https://doi.org/10.1037/0021-9010.91.5.1125

Inness, M., Leblanc, M. M., & Barling, J. (2008). Psychosocial predictors of supervisor-, peer-, subordinate-, and service-provider-targeted aggression. *The Journal of Applied Psychology*, *93*(6), 1401–1411. https://doi.org/10.1037/a0012810

Jehn, K. A. (1995). A multimethod examination of the benefits and detriments of intragroup conflict. *Administrative Science Quarterly*, *40*(2), 256–282. https://doi.org/10.2307/2393638

Johnson, S., Cooper, C., Cartwright, S., Donald, I., Taylor, P., & Millet, C. (2005). The experience of work-related stress across occupations. *Journal of Managerial Psychology*, *20*(2), 178–187. https://doi.org/10.1108/02683940510579803

Karasek, R. A. (1979). Job demands, job decision latitude and mental strain: Implications for job redesign. *Administrative Science Quarterly*, *24*(2), 285–308. https://doi.org/10.2307/2392498

Kassinove, H., Sukhodolsky, D. G., Tsytsarev, S. V., & Solovyova, S. (1997). Self-reported anger episodes in Russia and America. *Journal of Social Behavior and Personality*, *12*(2), 301–324.

Keck, S. (2019). Gender, leadership, and the display of empathic anger. *Journal of Occupational and Organizational Psychology*, *92*(4), 953–977. https://doi.org/10.1111/joop.12264

Kiazad, K., Restubog, S. L. D., Zagenczyk, T. J., Kiewitz, C., & Tang, R. L. (2010). In pursuit of power: The role of authoritarian leadership in the relationship between supervisors' Machiavellianism and subordinates' perceptions of abusive supervisory behavior. *Journal of Research in Personality*, *44*(4), 512–519. https://doi.org/10.1016/j.jrp.2010.06.004

Koning, L. F., & van Kleef, G. A. (2015). How leaders' emotional displays shape followers' organizational citizenship behavior. *The Leadership Quarterly*, *26*(4), 489–501. https://doi.org/10.1016/j.leaqua.2015.03.001

Kossek, E. E., Pichler, S., Bodner, T., & Hammer, L. B. (2011). Workplace social support and work–family conflict: A meta-analysis clarifying the influence of general and work–family specific supervisor and organizational support. *Personnel Psychology*, *64*(2), 289–313. https://doi.org/10.1111/j.1744-6570.2011.01211.x

Kweon, B. S., Ulrich, R. S., Walker, V. D., & Tassinary, L. G. (2008). Anger and stress: The role of landscape posters in an office setting. *Environment and Behavior*, *40*(3), 355–381. https://doi.org/10.1177/0013916506298797

Laschinger, H. K. S., Leiter, M., Day, A., & Gilin, D. (2009). Workplace empowerment, incivility, and burnout: Impact on staff nurse recruitment and retention outcomes. *Journal of Nursing Management*, *17*(3), 302–311. https://doi.org/10.1111/j.1365-2834.2009.00999.x

Lewis, K. M. (2000). When leaders display emotion: How followers respond to negative emotional expression of male and female leaders. *Journal of Organizational Behavior*, *21*(2), 221–234. https://doi.org/10.1002/(SICI)1099-1379(200003)21:2<221::AID-JOB36>3.0.CO;2-0

Lim, S., & Cortina, L. M. (2005). Interpersonal mistreatment in the workplace: The interface and impact of general incivility and sexual harassment. *The Journal of Applied Psychology*, *90*(3), 483–496. https://doi.org/10.1037/0021-9010.90.3.483

Lindebaum, D., & Fielden, S. (2011). 'It's good to be angry': Enacting anger in construction project management to achieve perceived leader effectiveness. *Human Relations*, *64*(3), 437–458. https://doi.org/10.1177/0018726710381149

Lindebaum, D., Jordan, P. J., & Morris, L. (2016). Symmetrical and asymmetrical outcomes of leader anger expression: A qualitative study of army personnel. *Human Relations*, *69*(2), 277–300. https://doi.org/10.1177/0018726715593350

Linkh, D. J., & Sonnek, S. M. (2003). An application of cognitive-behavioral anger management training in a military/occupational setting: Efficacy and demographic factors. *Military Medicine*, *168*(6), 475–478. https://doi.org/10.1093/milmed/168.6.475

Livingston, R. W., Rosette, A. S., & Washington, E. F. (2012). Can an agentic Black woman get ahead? The impact of race and interpersonal dominance on perceptions of female leaders. *Psychological Science*, *23*(4), 354–358. https://doi.org/10.1177/0956797611428079

Lovaglia, M. J., & Houser, J. A. (1996). Emotional reactions and status in groups. *American Sociological Review*, *61*(5), 867–883. https://doi.org/10.2307/2096458

Milczarek, M. (Ed.). (2011). *Emergency services: A literature review on occupational safety and health risks*. Publications Office of the European Union.

Mitchell, M. S., & Ambrose, M. L. (2007). Abusive supervision and workplace deviance and the moderating effects of negative reciprocity beliefs. *The Journal of Applied Psychology*, *92*(4), 1159–1168. https://doi.org/10.1037/0021-9010.92.4.1159

Morrison, E. W., & Robinson, S. L. (1997). When employees feel betrayed: A model of how psychological contract violation develops. *Academy of Management Review*, *22*(1), 226–256. https://doi.org/10.5465/amr.1997.9707180265

Neuman, J., & Baron, R. A. (1998). Workplace violence and workplace aggression: Evidence concerning specific forms, potential causes, and preferred targets. *Journal of Management*, *24*(3), 391–419. https://doi.org/10.1177/014920639802400305

Odle-Dusseau, H. N., Hammer, L. B., Crain, T. L., & Bodner, T. E. (2016). The influence of family-supportive supervisor training on employee job performance and attitudes: An organizational work–family initiative. *Journal of Occupational Health Psychology*, *21*, 296–308. https://doi.org/10.1037/a0039961

O'Neill, O. A., Vandenberg, R. J., Dejoy, D. M., & Wilson, M. G. (2009). Exploring relationships among anger, perceived organizational support, and workplace outcomes. *Journal of Occupational Health Psychology*, *14*(3), 318–333. https://doi.org/10.1037/a0015852

Patterson, G. T. (2003). Examining the effects of coping and social support on work and life stress among police officers. *Journal of Criminal Justice*, *31*(3), 215–226. https://doi.org/10.1016/S0047-2352(03)00003-5

Pearson, C. M., & Porath, C. L. (2005). On the nature, consequences and remedies of workplace incivility: No time for "nice"? Think again. *The Academy of Management Perspectives*, *19*(1), 7–18. https://doi.org/10.5465/ame.2005.15841946

Reyes, V. A., & Hicklin, T. A. (2005). Anger in the combat zone. *Military Medicine*, *170*(6), 483–487. https://doi.org/10.7205/MILMED.170.6.483

Robinson, R. C., & Mitchell, J. T. (1993). Evaluation of psychological debriefings. *Journal of Traumatic Stress*, *6*(3), 367–382. https://doi.org/10.1002/jts.2490060307

Rothman, N. B., & Magee, J. C. (2016). Affective expressions in groups and inferences about members' relational well-being: The effects of socially engaging and disengaging emotions. *Cognition and Emotion*, *30*(1), 150–166. https://doi.org/10.1080/02699931.2015.1020050

Sauter, S. L., & Murphy, L. R. (Eds.). (1995). *Organizational risk factors for job stress*. American Psychological Association. https://doi.org/10.1037/10173-000

Schwarzmüller, T., Brosi, P., & Welpe, I. M. (2018). Sparking anger and anxiety: Why intense leader anger displays trigger both more deviance and higher work effort in followers. *Journal of Business and Psychology*, *33*(6), 761–777. https://doi.org/10.1007/s10869-017-9523-8

Schyns, B., & Hansbrough, T. (Eds.). (2010). *When leadership goes wrong: Destructive leadership, mistakes, and ethical failures*. Information Age Publishing.

Sloan, M. M. (2004). The effects of occupational characteristics on the experience and expression of anger in the workplace. *Work and Occupations*, *31*(1), 38–72. https://doi.org/10.1177/0730888403260734

Smith, L. A., Roman, A., Dollard, M. F., Winefield, A. H., & Siegrist, J. (2005). Effort–reward imbalance at work: The effects of work stress on anger and cardiovascular disease symptoms in a community sample. *Stress and Health*, *21*(2), 113–128. https://doi.org/10.1002/smi.1045

Smith, T. W., Glazer, K., Ruiz, J. M., & Gallo, L. C. (2004). Hostility, anger, aggressiveness, and coronary heart disease: An interpersonal perspective on personality, emotion, and health. *Journal of Personality*, *72*(6), 1217–1270. https://doi.org/10.1111/j.1467-6494.2004.00296.x

Spector, P. E., Fox, S., & Domagalski, T. (2006). Emotions, violence and counterproductive work behavior. In E. K. Kelloway, J. Barling, & J. J. Hurrell, Jr. (Eds.), *Handbook of workplace violence* (pp. 29–46). Sage Publications.

Spicer, J., & Chamberlain, K. (1996). Cynical hostility, anger, and resting blood pressure. *Journal of Psychosomatic Research*, *40*(4), 359–368. https://doi.org/10.1016/0022-3999(95)00546-3

Spielberger, C. D., Jacobs, G., Russell, S., & Crane, R. S. (1983). Assessment of anger: The state–trait anger scale. In J. N. Butcher & C. D. Spielberger (Eds.), *Advances in personality assessment* (Vol. 2, pp. 159–187). Routledge.

Stergiou-Kita, M., Mansfield, E., Bezo, R., Colantonio, A., Garritano, E., Lafrance, M., Lewko, J., Mantis, S., Moody, J., Power, N., Theberge, N., Westwood, E., & Travers, K. (2015). Danger zone: Men, masculinity and occupational health and safety in high risk occupations. *Safety Science*, *80*, 213–220. https://doi.org/10.1016/j.ssci.2015.07.029

Stets, J. E., & Tsushima, T. M. (2001). Negative emotion and coping responses within identity control theory. *Social Psychology Quarterly*, *64*(3), 283–295. https://doi.org/10.2307/3090117

Tavris, C. (1989). *Anger: The misunderstood emotion*. Simon and Schuster.

Tepper, B. J. (2000). Consequences of abusive supervision. *Academy of Management Journal*, *43*(2), 178–190. https://doi.org/10.2307/1556375

Tepper, B. J. (2007). Abusive supervision in work organizations: Review, synthesis, and research agenda. *Journal of Management*, *33*(3), 261–289. https://doi.org/10.1177/0149206307300812

Tepper, B. J., Duffy, M. K., Henle, C. A., & Lambert, L. S. (2006). Procedural injustice, victim precipitation, and abusive supervision. *Personnel Psychology*, *59*(1), 101–123. https://doi.org/10.1111/j.1744-6570.2006.00725.x

Tepper, B. J., & Henle, C. A. (2011). A case for recognizing distinctions among constructs that capture interpersonal mistreatment in work organizations. *Journal of Organizational Behavior, 32*(3), 487–498. https://doi.org/10.1002/job.688

Truxillo, D. M., Steiner, D. D., & Gilliland, S. W. (2004). The importance of organizational justice in personnel selection: Defining when selection fairness really matters. *International Journal of Selection and Assessment, 12*(1–2), 39–53. https://doi.org/10.1111/j.0965-075X.2004.00262.x

Van Kleef, G. A. (2009). How emotions regulate social life. *Current Directions in Psychological Science, 18*(3), 184–188. https://doi.org/10.1111/j.1467-8721.2009.01633.x

Van Kleef, G. A., Homan, A. C., Beersma, B., Van Knippenberg, D., Van Knippenberg, B., & Damen, F. (2009). Searing sentiment or cold calculation? The effects of leader emotional displays on team performance depend on follower epistemic motivation. *Academy of Management Journal, 52*(3), 562–580. https://doi.org/10.5465/amj.2009.41331253

Wang, L., Restubog, S., Shao, B., Lu, V., & Van Kleef, G. A. (2018). Does anger expression help or harm leader effectiveness? The role of competence-based versus integrity-based violations and abusive supervision. *Academy of Management Journal, 61*(3), 1050–1072. https://doi.org/10.5465/amj.2015.0460

Wubben, M. J., De Cremer, D., & Van Dijk, E. (2009). When and how communicated guilt affects contributions in public good dilemmas. *Journal of Experimental Social Psychology, 45*(1), 15–23. https://doi.org/10.1016/j.jesp.2008.07.015

Wurhofer, D., Krischkowsky, A., Obrist, M., Karapanos, E., Niforatos, E., & Tscheligi, M. (2015, September). Everyday commuting: Prediction, actual experience and recall of anger and frustration in the car. In *Proceedings of the 7th International Conference on Automotive User Interfaces and Interactive Vehicular Applications* (pp. 233–240). ACM Press.

Yang, L.-Q., Zheng, X., Liu, X., Lu, C.-q., & Schaubroeck, J. M. (2020). Abusive supervision, thwarted belongingness, and workplace safety: A group engagement perspective. *The Journal of Applied Psychology, 105*(3), 230–244. https://doi.org/10.1037/apl0000436

Zhang, Y., Liu, X., Xu, S., Yang, L. Q., & Bednall, T. C. (2019). Why abusive supervision impacts employee OCB and CWB: A meta-analytic review of competing mediating mechanisms. *Journal of Management, 45*(6), 2474–2497. https://doi.org/10.1177/0149206318823935

PART III CLINICAL CONTEXT

6 ANGER IN OCCUPATIONS CHARACTERIZED BY REPEATED THREAT AND STRESS EXPOSURE

The Longitudinal View in the Military Context

ELLIE LAWRENCE-WOOD, MIRANDA VAN HOOFF, AND ALEXANDER McFARLANE

KEY POINTS

- In military populations, there is evidence that levels of anger and aggression increase over time. They increase further during the process of leaving the full-time service environment in the period of transition to civilian life.
- Expression and escalation of problematic anger and aggression over time may be compounded by aspects of military life, including
  - a culture of authority and requirement to contain and respond to threat with action, and
  - repeated and prolonged exposure to threatening environments.
- Problematic anger and aggression are, in part, a symptomatic/behavioral reflection of underlying priming and sensitization of neural networks associated with threat detection and activation of the sympathetic nervous system response. These processes are shared with the neurobiological underpinnings of posttraumatic stress disorder.

https://doi.org/10.1037/0000244-007
Anger at Work: Prevention, Intervention, and Treatment in High-Risk Occupations, A. B. Adler and D. Forbes (Editors)

Occupations including police, emergency responders, and the military are considered high risk and involve high stress. Not only are members of these occupations regularly exposed to events that are inherently traumatic and intrinsically dangerous, they are often required to perform their duties in environments of extreme uncertainty, involving direct risk of injury or death. These environmental challenges can result in long-lasting impacts on their ability to moderate ongoing feelings of vulnerability and threat, beyond situations requiring them to be watchful or on guard.

A common response to feelings of vulnerability and threat in these populations over time is anger. Anger is an adaptive emotion primed for survival goals, occurs as a defensive reaction to threat perception (Novaco, 2016), and is marked by increased activation of the sympathetic nervous system (Lang et al., 1998). In particular, in the military context, anger may also be primed as a response to threat in order to facilitate and mobilize engagement with, rather than avoidance of, the source of threat. However, anger also has the potential to be maladaptive because of its problematic consequences if inappropriately directed.

Militaries and other first responders, such as police, are required to project an image of authority, the ability to contain potentially hazardous situations, and an intent to act against those who transgress rules with a degree of intimidation. Thus, the assertive posturing of dominance is culturally appropriate within such occupational contexts and serves to support the functional use of anger and aggression, and to make the recognition of maladaptive anger in this setting difficult. Furthermore, inherent within these occupations are certain organizational factors and stressors that are known to mediate or moderate the relationship between incident exposure and poor mental health outcomes such as problematic anger. These factors include leadership style, management practices, group morale and cohesion, workload, shift duties, and interpersonal conflict (Adler et al., 2017; Dyches et al., 2017; Lindebaum et al., 2016; E. A. Stanley & Larsen, 2019).

Anger is often considered a "negative" emotion; however, it also has positive utility at the intrapersonal, interpersonal, and sociocultural levels. At an intrapersonal level, the feeling of anger provides important information to the self about the environmental context. Further, the physiological changes that accompany the experience of anger (such as increased adrenaline and blood pressure) are motivating and preparatory, and they place the individual in a state of readiness for action (Geddes et al., 2020).

At an interpersonal level, anger represents a useful communication strategy to increase the likelihood of concessions from adversaries during conflict. Anger can be both intimidating and persuasive, and in a negotiation or a conflict, the display of anger signals toughness (Van Kleef & Côté, 2007) as well as serving as a warning to others, and in this way may in fact act to de-escalate a conflict situation. The expression of anger can also generate action on the part of others, whereby the anger expressed by a leader positively influences the behaviors of those they lead (Geddes et al., 2020).

However, the utility of anger is also dependent on the sociocultural content in which it occurs and is dependent on the intensity and appropriateness of its expression (Adam & Brett, 2018). The dual threshold model of anger proposes that anger in an occupational context can be suppressed (felt anger that is not expressed), or it can be expressed in an "acceptable" or "deviant" manner. The cultural norms of the occupational context determine the thresholds of acceptable and deviant anger expressions, as well as conditions under which anger may be suppressed. Where an occupation has a high tolerance for expressed anger, there is likely to be a lower tendency for anger to be suppressed or inappropriately expressed. Thus in high-risk occupations such as the military, where the tolerance for anger is high, inappropriate or deviant anger expressions may in fact be less likely.

Unfortunately, when occupational stressors and exposure to threatening events accumulate, the potential for anger to become dysregulated arises. This dysregulation may be indicative of emerging psychological distress such as subsyndromal posttraumatic stress disorder (PTSD) and can be manifested as an increased reactivity to threat. Problematic dysregulation of anger responses, particularly in occupational settings where anger has the potential to be accepted, and in some instances encouraged as an adaptive response to threat, has the potential to create a culture of acceptance around anger being an appropriate response, even when it may be problematic on a number of levels (see O'Neill, Chapter 4 in this volume, and Hammer et al., Chapter 5 in this volume, for an in-depth discussion of anger in teams and the role of supervisors/leaders, respectively). Although it is acknowledged that anger can be adaptive (Adler et al., 2017), over the longer term, escalations in anger may serve to undermine social, interpersonal, and occupational functioning. Elevated anger may also increase one's propensity for engaging in risk-taking behaviors such violence toward others and self, and it may play a more mechanistic role in the emergence, maintenance, and severity of mental health symptoms and conditions. Escalations in anger and associated sequelae also have the potential to compound any mental health problems (Adler et al., 2011; MacManus et al., 2013, 2015).

This chapter documents anger as a risk factor for employee adjustment in high-risk, high-stress occupations where anger is sometimes accepted as a culturally fitting response. As an example, we focus on anger in the military environment, presenting recent findings regarding the experience of anger in relation to deployment and other military-specific occupational stressors and regarding its association with the emergence and progression of other mental health symptoms and disorders, as well as care-seeking and recovery trajectories. The issue of traumatic brain injury (TBI) in relation to anger, mental disorders such as PTSD, and the findings are discussed in relation to the specific cultural and operational requirements of the military and other high-risk, high-stress occupations and highlight the importance of anger as a risk factor for the development and progression of mental disorders. The chapter concludes by highlighting important clinical implications in regard to prevention and early intervention.

THE PREVALENCE OF ANGER IN THE MILITARY

Symptoms of anger and aggression are commonly reported by military populations around the world. In U.S. veterans, for example, 11.2% of those returning from Afghanistan and Iraq reported perceived problems controlling violent behavior, which was significantly associated with both aggressive impulses and difficulty managing anger (Elbogen et al., 2010). Similar rates have been reported in U.K. veterans returning from deployment to Iraq and Afghanistan, with 12% reporting violent behavior and 10% reporting physical assault (MacManus et al., 2012, 2015; Turgoose & Murphy, 2018). These rates of anger and aggression are significantly greater in treatment-seeking veterans (74% and 28%, respectively), highlighting the considerable overlap between anger and other mental health conditions such as posttraumatic stress disorder (PTSD; Turgoose & Murphy, 2018). Furthermore, anger and aggression have been observed to be a common response to a range of lifetime and deployment-related traumas, including being in a combat role (particularly those involving violent combat exposures; Killgore et al., 2008), as well as predeployment violence (Newby et al., 2005) and childhood trauma and adversity (Begić & Jokić-Begić, 2001; Elbogen et al., 2010), all of which are more common in military populations compared with the general community and are strongly associated with PTSD. Although anger can be present with all anxiety disorders and depression, it has a particularly strong association with PTSD (Olatunji et al., 2010), with anger and anxiety linked as defensive reactions to threat, both marked by activation of the sympathetic nervous system (Lang et al., 1998). Anger, therefore, is of particular relevance when considering occupations in which regular and repeated trauma and stress exposure are the norm and PTSD rates are known to be high.

In Australia, the rate of PTSD (8.3%) is higher among currently serving Australian Defence Force (ADF) members than among those observed in the general population (5.2%; McFarlane et al., 2011). These rates dramatically increase when members transition out of regular service (Van Hooff et al., 2018), with 17.1% of ADF members meeting criteria for PTSD in the first 5 years following transition. One explanation for the elevated rates of PTSD following transition is that the emotional and structural supports inherent to military life may mask functional impairments of PTSD symptoms during service (Adler & Castro, 2013). When these supports are removed, distress and dysfunction emerge. Emerging symptoms of PTSD may also contribute to one's decision to leave military service. Given the known association between PTSD and anger from international research, anger may be a prominent feature in the lives of ADF members currently making the transition from military to civilian life.

The Transition and Wellbeing Research Programme examined the mental, physical, and social health and well-being of an entire population of recently transitioned (specifically those who transitioned from regular service between 2010 and 2014) and current regular serving ADF members (Van Hooff et al., 2018). This program included two longitudinal cohorts who were assessed both during an earlier time point and in 2015: a cohort of ADF members who were regular serving in 2010 (Bryant et al., 2019) and a combat-deployed cohort assessed prior to and following deployment to the Middle East Area of Operations between 2010 and 2012 (Lawrence-Wood et al., 2019). Self-reported anger frequency, intensity, and duration and the perceived negative impact of anger on social relationships (examined using the five-item Dimensions of Anger Reactions Scale [DAR-5]; Forbes et al., 2004) were measured in this study. In addition to establishing the prevalence of anger in the population as a whole, the study was able to map the role of anger over time, in relation to the emergence and progression of mental disorder as well as in relation to deployment and combat exposure specifically.

Results of the Transition and Wellbeing Research Programme support much of the previous international research, indicating anger to be a common symptom in current and recently transitioned ADF members. Significantly greater levels of anger were reported by ADF members who had recently transitioned from military to civilian life (M DAR-5 = 9.8, SE = 0.1), 95% confidence interval (CI) [9.6, 10.0], compared with currently serving regular ADF members (M DAR-5 = 8.2, SE = 0.5), 95% CI [7.9, 8.5], adjusted regression coefficient = 1.3 (0.2), $p < .001$. An estimated 30.2% ($n = 7{,}533$), 95% CI [28.6, 31.9], of the transitioned ADF and 16.2% ($n = 8{,}410$), 95% CI [13.27, 19.21], of the 2015 regular ADF scored equal to or above the DAR-5 cutoff of 12, indicating levels of problematic anger (Van Hooff et al., 2018). These findings are consistent with elevated problematic anger observed in 38% of treatment-seeking veterans in the United States (Sayer et al., 2010; Sippel et al., 2016).

Furthermore, anger frequency, intensity and duration, and antagonism toward others, as well as the impacts of anger on social relationships, were significantly higher among the currently serving regular ADF in 2015 when compared with the currently serving ADF population in 2010. Together with findings from the two longitudinal cohorts discussed next, this pattern of results indicates an increase in anger over time in all ADF members independent of the role of transition. This increase also followed the same pattern as other mental health symptoms. One explanation for the observed increase in symptoms across multiple domains over time is the corresponding accumulation of occupational stress exposure over the course of a military career. Considering the relationship between anger and posttraumatic stress symptoms in this context is important. Anger is one feature of PTSD, and as such it is included within the fifth edition of the *Diagnostic and Statistical Manual of Mental Disorders* (*DSM-5*; American Psychiatric Association, 2013) diagnostic criteria. It has also been shown to co-occur with the disorder independent of its role as a diagnostic component (Barrett et al., 2013; Jakupcak et al., 2007; Novaco, 2007); in fact, PTSD and anger may have a number of similar drivers and underlying mechanisms, including attentional dysregulation and emotional disinhibition, discussed later in this chapter.

THE LONGITUDINAL COURSE OF ANGER IN THE MILITARY

A key strength of the Transition and Wellbeing Research Programme was the inclusion of two longitudinal cohorts: one a general sample of ADF members, and the other a deployed cohort. This allowed for the course of anger in relation to other mental health outcomes to be examined over the 5-year period between 2010 and 2015. Similar to what was observed at a population level, levels of self-reported anger in the general sample of ADF members ($N = 8{,}497$) were significantly higher among those who had transitioned from regular service compared with those who remained in regular service (Bryant et al., 2019). Additionally, the more disconnected the member was from their regular military service (i.e., an ex-serving member who has little to do with Defence from an occupational perspective compared with an active reservist who may still be largely active within the workforce), the greater the anger, with the highest levels observed among those who were ex serving. Of interest, as just discussed, the *rate of increase* in anger problems over time was similar for both those who had transitioned and those who remained in regular service, with the reported anger level doubling in this cohort between 2010 and 2014 (Bryant et al., 2019). This finding suggests a general propensity for anger to increase with the passage of time among ADF members more generally.

One possible explanation for the general increase in anger over time is that anger represents an early manifestation of distress and reactivity associated with development of anxiety disorders and PTSD, and may indicate risk for the worsening of symptoms over time (Barrett et al., 2013; Novaco, 2016; Rona et al., 2015; Vasterling & Proctor, 2011). In line with this, self-reported anger in 2010 was found to predict the development of subthreshold psychological distress and posttraumatic stress symptoms in 2015, as well as predicting further accrual of symptoms over time (Bryant et al., 2019).

In relation to the elevated anger among those who were ex-serving, elevated rates of anxiety disorders and PTSD were observed among this group in 2015, and higher rates of problematic anger existed 5 years prior among ADF members who went on to transition by 2015 (Bryant et al., 2019). Thus, the greater levels of anger observed among those who were ex-serving are likely to partly reflect their greater level of psychological morbidity (and associated accrual of symptoms) but also suggest that factors relating to the transition to civilian life may play a role.

Anger itself is a significant risk to interpersonal, social, and occupational functioning, which in turn impacts psychological health (Meffert et al., 2014). In general, one of the maladaptive consequences of anger is its role in inhibiting fear responses, in turn inhibiting self-protective withdrawal from risk and threat, which then may lead to increased exposure to risk and trauma and subsequently to worsening of PTSD symptoms (Foa et al., 1995). It is also possible that anger may be indicative of underlying neurobiological dysregulation that underpins the emergence of symptoms in trauma-exposed populations. Importantly, this dysregulation may have differential impacts inside compared with outside the occupational context.

DEPLOYMENT, COMBAT EXPOSURE, AND ANGER

A major body of evidence highlights the association between combat and deployment specifically, and anger, both directly and in the context of posttraumatic stress symptoms and disorder. Although inhibition of fear may be maladaptive more generally, in the occupational context of combat deployment, controlled anger has utility, both at the individual level by ameliorating fear and at an interpersonal level by signifying strength and power. Equally, however, the increasing evidence of the deleterious physical, psychological, and social consequences of elevated anger requires consideration. One potential risk is that the emotions experienced and the emotional responses exhibited while on deployment and during combat exposure persist beyond the context in which they have adaptive value. This persistence of symptoms has the potential to be highly disruptive and maladaptive, particularly when emotional responses such as anger are perceived to be helpful by the individual. Adler et al. (2017), for example, found that the more anger was generally perceived as helpful and facilitated productivity and action in a sample of combat soldiers, the more likely that these soldiers had other comorbid mental health symptoms (Adler et al., 2017). In fact, as symptoms of anger (and other mental health conditions) increased over time, so too did perceptions of anger as an adaptive response mode.

The Impact of Combat Study (Lawrence-Wood et al., 2019), part of the Australian Transition and Wellbeing Research Programme, provided further specific insights into understanding how combat and trauma exposure may be related to anger in a healthy military population, prior to the emergence of any overt indicators of ill health. This study followed up with a cohort of combat-deployed ADF members prior to deployment to the Middle East Area of Operations (2010–2012), after this index deployment, and then 3 to 5 years later. The cohort was surveyed regarding trauma exposure both preceding deployment and during deployment. Rates of problematic anger using the DAR-5 (Forbes et al., 2004) in this cohort tended to be particularly low at baseline and showed modest increases following deployment. However, like other mental health symptoms, a large jump in the rate of problematic anger was observed at 3 to 5 years postdeployment, suggesting increased psychological reactivity over time. In general, across numerous mental and physical health indicators, trauma and combat exposures on deployment play a significant role in the indicators' emergence. In considering the impacts of combat over the longer term, anger continues to be implicated in adjustment even many years later, particularly in the context of PTSD (Germain et al., 2016).

In relation to the pattern of anger over time in combat-exposed populations, Cabrera et al. (2016) identified four trajectories of aggression in combat troops in the 12 months following deployment: low stable, delayed, recovered, and chronic. They found that those in the low stable groups had lower combat exposure and posttraumatic stress symptoms compared with the delayed and chronic trajectories, with very few predictors of the difference between the symptomatic trajectories. The impacts of combat exposure were cumulative, with a greater breadth of exposure associated with greater risk for being in an aggressive trajectory; however, it is interesting that subjective combat "stressfulness" did not have an effect. This finding lends support to the idea that combat exposures may be driving anger symptoms via underlying neurobiological mechanisms rather than through cognitive appraisal processes. When considering the possible neurobiological impacts of combat exposures, the issue of TBI is of relevance. TBI can be associated with structural, physiological, and/or functional changes in the brain that can lead to immediate and longer term neurological, cognitive, and behavioral symptoms, including problematic anger and aggression (Jeter et al., 2013; Oehr & Anderson, 2017; Pietrzak et al., 2014; Vasterling et al., 2020). As deployment-related TBI is often comorbid with psychological disorders, including PTSD, and may share precipitating exposures, and symptoms, disentangling them is a complex issue. For this reason, a detailed account of the relationship between TBI and anger is beyond the scope of this chapter.

Consequences of Anger for Deployment

Given this evidence, effective regulation of emotions such as anger in the deployed environment may be one driver of optimal long-term adaptation. In any threatening or potentially threatening situation, as referred to previously, the ability to assess and respond in an effective and adaptive manner is crucial, and this ability may include the suppression of instincts to flee from a situation. In the combat environment, this process involves activation of the fight response and engagement with threat. Anger may have a particular adaptive utility in this scenario, driving action and performance.

Over time, however, ongoing or repeated engagement in the fight response can lead to increased threat sensitivity and reactivity, which can drive hypervigilance (Heesink et al., 2017). Elevated anger in this context may reflect underlying affect dysregulation, which has consequences, including loss of appropriate appraisal and impaired information processing and less discerning reactivity to threat (Chemtob et al., 1997; Clausen et al., 2016; Gilam et al., 2017; Lebel, 2017; McFarlane et al., 2002; Novaco, 2007; E. A. Stanley & Larsen, 2019). In the deployed environment, cognitive control, fear suppression, and effective high-stakes decision making are critical. Emerging difficulties in anger regulation can pose a significant risk to these higher level cognitive tasks, resulting in poor decision making and behavioral disinhibition. Practically, this risk can result in excessive reactivity to threat and represent a risk that an individual might not adhere to the rules of engagement. Findings from Wilk et al. (2013) among a sample of combat-deployed U.S. military personnel lend support to this contention. Specifically, Wilk et al. (2013) found an association between combat exposures, aggression, and unethical battlefield behaviors (including aggression and insults toward noncombatants and unnecessarily damaging private property). Although this study found that specific types of combat exposure, such as witnessing atrocities, were associated with unethical behaviors, the authors also suggested that aggression may be a contributory factor. As argued earlier in this chapter, it is possible that impaired decision making and behavioral disinhibition resulting from exposures in the combat environment could explain both inappropriate aggression and unethical battlefield behaviors.

Correlates of Anger and Aggression and the Impacts of the Outward Versus the Inward Direction of Anger

Outside the context of deployment, anger may become a default mode of response despite the potentially detrimental ramifications (Adler et al., 2017). The less discerning decision-making and behavioral disinhibition associated with anger contribute to increased risk-taking behaviors and aggression (Adler et al., 2011; Begić & Jokić-Begić, 2001; Bensley et al., 2018; Blakey et al., 2018; Contractor et al., 2015, 2017; Killgore et al., 2008; Kim-Spoon et al., 2015; MacManus et al., 2015; Maniaci et al., 2017).

A study by Killgore and colleagues (2008), for example, followed up with service members 12 months after deployment and found an association between deployment combat exposures, and aggression and risk-taking behaviors. In particular, extensively violent and traumatic experiences during deployment were found to predict future aggression and risky behaviors. The authors proposed that these types of exposures may have led to a perception of invincibility, which in turn explained a propensity for that individual to underestimate future risk. The nature of the trauma may also have had some enduring impact beyond just driving a perception of invincibility, via traumatic memories, and processes of kindling and sensitization (McFarlane et al., 2002). Specifically, traumatic memories can drive an increased biased reactivity to environmental cues, via sensitization of neural pathways, leading to hyper- and less discriminant threat detection both inside and out of the occupational environment. This sensitization can result in a response bias of anger/aggression, primed through experience and as a result of behavioral disinhibition. This process may be associated with impaired risk detection (and possibly retraumatization), as well as uncontrolled aggression.

The experience and expression of anger can be directed externally or internally, with varying consequences when the anger is dysregulated and maladaptive. In the specific example just discussed, externally directed anger may emerge as aggressive, hostile, or risk-taking behavior, whereas internally directed anger may manifest in suicidality and self-harm.

The issue of internally directed anger and hostility is one of importance in considering the possible impacts of anger on postdeployment adjustment. Whereas outwardly directed anger, hostility, and aggression are somewhat observable, the deleterious effects of internally directed anger may be less visible, manifesting as self-harm or suicidality. In the case of internally directed anger, McKinney et al. (2017) found that the association between posttraumatic stress symptoms and suicidality in a combat-exposed veteran population was partly mediated by internal hostility. They proposed that one mechanism underlying the link between PTSD and internal hostility is impaired emotional regulation. As an example, an inability to distance the self from a traumatic experience may lead to an overidentification and subsequent integration of these experiences with self-identity and to associated rumination about the self and negative events. This overidentification and rumination can be associated with deficits in emotional regulatory ability, resulting in uncontrolled internalized anger (Germain et al., 2016). Thus, dysregulated anger is one possible pathway by which military service may increase risk for suicidality (see also Naifeh et al., Chapter 7 in this volume).

Mechanisms Underlying the Development of Anger in Deployed Populations

In understanding how combat and trauma are related to anger, two interlinked processes that drive behavioral response (and were mentioned earlier) are central: threat detection and emotion regulation. Two theoretical frameworks in particular address these two issues: fear avoidance theory and survival mode theory.

Fear avoidance theory proposes that anger and aggression are threat management techniques, serving as a mode of avoidance of or distraction from fear (Foa et al., 1995; Lin et al., 2017). In high-risk, high-stress workforces such as the military or police, which require the service member to confront threat, anger may be particularly adaptive. However, in the case of fear avoidance, anger can also serve to perpetuate the development and maintenance of posttraumatic stress symptoms via inhibition of withdrawal from risk or threat (and subsequent reexposure) and avoidance of fear-related processing of threatening events (Foa et al., 1995; Lin et al., 2017).

Survival mode theory provides a related alternative explanation: Exposure to a threatening environment is associated with increased vigilance and loss of self-regulation, which in turn promote rapid aggressive impulses (Chemtob et al., 1997; Lin et al., 2017). This explanation is particularly relevant to the combat context, which often involves extended exposure to threatening environments and where actual threat is imminent. In this case, automatic threat detection and rapid aggressive impulses can be an adaptive mode of response (hence, "survival" mode). However, this mode of response becomes maladaptive outside a realistically threatening environment, where biased assessment of, and inappropriate responses to, neutral events can occur.

Chemtob et al. (1997) found that PTSD in particular is associated with a propensity to enter survival mode rapidly because of underlying hypervigilance to threat, which in turn triggers anger and aggression. This disposition occurs in a feedback loop, where survival mode prompts both action without deep appraisal of the situation and a bias to interpret stimuli as threatening. An inability to suppress the automatic anger response leads to aggressive/anger behavior, and this experience of anger acts to prime the system to be hypervigilant to threat. Although Chemtob et al. explained this process in people who have PTSD, it is also relevant to the potential effects of repeated stress and combat exposure, as well as the emergence or early stages of posttraumatic stress symptoms. Analysis of the first two waves of data collection from our Australian combat-deployed sample (Blunt, 2016) identified a dose–response relationship between level of combat exposure and the accrual of hyperarousal symptoms specifically, despite the generally very low levels of PTSD symptoms in this cohort. The accrual of PTSD symptoms such as hypervigilance with repeated combat exposure would also serve to reinforce the likelihood of survival mode responding and the corresponding automatic anger response.

As already highlighted, the role of anger in postcombat psychological health is likely to be multidimensional. Both within and outside the threatening combat environment, anger reactivity can influence behavior and likelihood of repeated traumatic exposure via inhibition of withdrawal from risk/threat and increasingly disinhibited responses to risk/threat. Interpretations of and responses to the environment are also likely to be influenced by preexisting anger reactivity and trait anger.

In relation to preexisting anger reactivity, a study of 50 newly enlisted Israeli soldiers following intensive advanced combat training is relevant (Lin et al., 2017). Lin et al. (2017) found that state anger could predict subsequent PTSD symptomology following combat operations. In particular, preexisting state anger led to an attentional bias to angry cues, resulting in a greater likelihood of an aggressive or hostile behavioral response (see Arad & Bar-Haim, Chapter 9 in this volume, for an in-depth discussion of cognitive bias). In the Lin et al. study, amygdala modulation was implicated in anger reactivity; thus, amygdala hyperactivity may be associated with not only an exaggerated fear response but also aggressive impulses. The finding that attentional bias toward angry faces was associated with an anger response characterized by neural activation of the limbic system, and that this bias was associated with later posttraumatic stress symptoms, suggests that anger could be implicated in the etiology of PTSD. However, limitations of the study included the healthy cohort, which had very low posttraumatic stress symptoms, and the lack of a baseline measurement. Of interest, this sample is very similar to our Impact of Combat Study sample, which likewise found a robust relationship between anger problems and posttraumatic stress symptoms. Future analysis of our data set, focusing on the neurocognitive data collected as part of the study—in particular, measures of attention and response inhibition—may shed further light on the relationship between anger dysregulation and the emergence of posttraumatic stress symptoms over time.

The findings just discussed raise the question of the possible role of trait anger in contributing to these processes. The role of trait anger in relation to reactivity to stressors has been explored in a number of studies. Lievaart et al. (2016) examined the association between trait anger and inhibitory control measured by event-related potentials. The authors found no differences between those with high trait versus low trait anger in inhibitory control or automatic error detection; however, they did find a between-groups difference in more conscious error processing. Those high in trait anger showed reduced amplitudes compared with the low-anger group. The authors propose that this reduction indicates that those high in anger show less discernment of the motivational relevance of their errors—in practical terms, this reduction may be associated with continuance of behaviors/actions, even in the face of negative consequences. In relation to the anger feedback loop implied by Lin et al.'s (2017) findings, if hypervigilance to threat is present, coupled with reduced regulatory control of anger responses, this impairment to conscious error processing could increase the likelihood of dysfunctional anger, reinforcing this feedback loop. Furthermore, impairments to decision making could make additional exposure to stressors more likely. These findings are also relevant to the issue of elevated risk-taking behavior in the veteran populations discussed earlier in this chapter (e.g., Killgore et al., 2008). Although an increased propensity for risky and aggressive behaviors may partly reflect a perception of invincibility, it may also be underpinned by behavioral disinhibition, possibly in relation to acquired emotion regulation deficits (e.g., Kim-Spoon et al., 2015). This area requires further research.

Wilk et al. (2015) also examined trait anger, finding that it moderated the association between posttraumatic stress symptoms and aggression among a sample of combat troops. Specifically, the pathway between combat exposure and aggression (well documented in a number of studies) via PTSD symptoms was particularly pronounced under conditions of high trait anger. This marries with the neural findings suggesting that emotional reactivity may be a predisposing factor to the emergence of posttraumatic stress symptoms following stress exposure, whereas emotional regulation difficulties may emerge as a consequence of the exposure and posttraumatic stress symptoms. Thus, understanding how existing state or trait anger may interact with or modify the experience of combat stress is important to consider.

When considering how anger reactivity might influence threat detection and appraisal, a number of studies are of relevance. Gilam et al. (2017) found a correlation between (a) neural activation of brain areas associated with anger regulation and aggression and (b) posttraumatic stress symptoms. They proposed that emotional regulation difficulties may represent a vulnerability factor for future emergence of posttraumatic stress symptoms following a stressor (e.g., combat exposure). In fact, they proposed that stress symptoms (including posttraumatic stress) are underpinned by a dysfunctionality of the emotional regulation system. Heesink et al. (2017) also focused on neural activation associated with anger and aggression, specifically among veterans, finding evidence of increased attentional vigilance to all stimuli (not just negative). This attentional hypervigilance, coupled with difficulties in emotional regulation (e.g., Gilam et al., 2017; Lin et al., 2017), in turn may be associated with uncontrolled anger or aggression. However, the association between these processes is bidirectional. Emotion regulation deficits may drive hostile attribution biases (Heesink et al., 2017), and appraisal of ambiguous stimuli as threatening, also leading to potentially inappropriate anger responses.

Analysis of our Impact of Combat Study sample (Zuj et al., 2017) identified an attentional bias toward threat that emerged postdeployment, specifically among those with elevated posttraumatic stress symptoms. This bias is in line with a hyperreactive early threat detection system. Preliminary further analyses of anger data in this combat-deployed cohort show that the trajectory of anger symptoms mirrors the trajectories of PTSD symptoms and is likely predicted by the same factors that drive posttraumatic stress symptom recruitment over time, namely, lifetime trauma history and combat exposures on deployment. A number of studies have found that this association between combat exposure and anger (Adler et al., 2011; Cabrera et al., 2016; Chemtob et al., 1997; Dyches et al., 2017; Gilam et al., 2017; Hoge et al., 2004; Killgore et al., 2008; MacManus et al., 2015; Rona et al., 2015) and lifetime trauma, particularly occurring in childhood, has been reliably associated with impairment to emotional regulation and threat detection systems (Marusak et al., 2015), both implicated in problematic anger and aggression. Importantly, it appears that the same or similar mechanisms may underpin these relationships, providing some explanation for the link between anger and PTSD. It may in fact be that anger and PTSD have a shared mechanistic pathway, which serves to contribute to the emergence and maintenance of symptoms of both. This proposed pathway has important implications for transdiagnostic screening and intervention at the level of mechanisms.

Taken together, there is increasing evidence that combat and stress exposures play a role in the emergence and persistence over time of problematic anger, aggression, and risk-taking behavior, as well as suicidality, among deployed military populations. As outlined in Figure 6.1, in addition to the different manifestations of anger, the time at which anger emerges and impacts health, well-being, and symptom accrual is also variable. Existing trait or state anger present prior to stress exposure may serve as a vulnerability factor. As anger emerges, it may perpetuate itself as well as be implicated in the emergence and maintenance of other symptoms and disorders—in particular, PTSD—and it may be a continued comorbidity over the longer term, carrying its own significant functional and social impairments.

THE RELATIONSHIP BETWEEN ANGER AND CARE-SEEKING AND RECOVERY TRAJECTORIES

Given the clear association between combat and stress exposure, and anger as well as other mental health symptoms and disorder, the issue of how anger is managed in relation to care-seeking and recovery in deployed veteran populations is of great importance.

From a service provision perspective, it is important to consider whether current treatment programs for combat-exposed populations are adequately addressing the issue of aggression. It is likely, for example, that if anger reactivity and aggression reflect hypervigilance and emotional reactivity, individuals with this type of symptom presentation will be less sensitive to

FIGURE 6.1. Model of Neurobiological Process Contributing to Emergence, Maintenance, and Escalation of Problematic Anger and Aggression

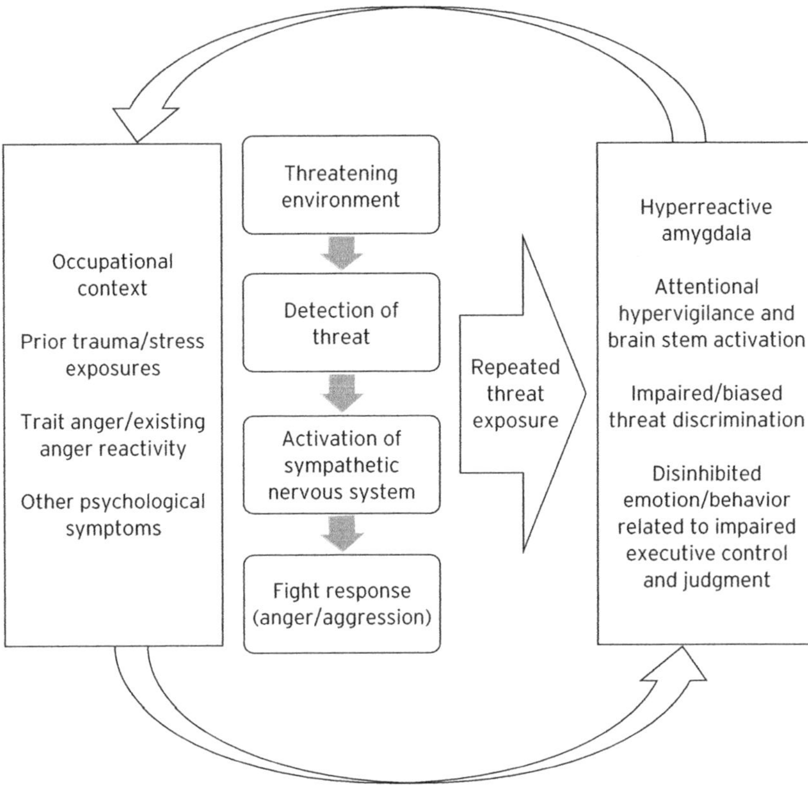

therapies designed to deal with perceptions and cognitions and may require, at least in the early stages, more targeted work to manage emotional dysregulation specifically. As anger inhibits fear, presentations of this type may also undermine the effectiveness of exposure-based therapies of PTSD specifically (Foa et al., 1995; Forbes et al., 2008). Finally, there may also be an increased risk of retraumatization as a result of affect dysregulation and impairments to threat and risk appraisal. This risk is particularly important for those showing an increase in symptomatology because of the known association between anger and reactivity and impaired social functioning and intimate relationships (Meffert et al., 2014). Such explanations as to why individuals exhibiting both PTSD and anger/aggression may not respond to more targeted interventions for PTSD (Rodenburg et al., 2016) may at least partly explain the corresponding increased anger with increased PTSD severity.

Specific programs have been developed to treat anger (Cash et al., 2018; Mackintosh et al., 2017; Morland et al., 2010), and early interventions that target anger during military service may reduce the likelihood of maladaptive anger worsening in the years following discharge, as well as contribute to improved treatment efficacy for other conditions. If anger is implicated in the development of disorder, early intervention also has the potential to halt the progression of symptoms into full disorder. Importantly, if there is in fact a shared neurobiological pathway underpinning problematic anger and PTSD symptoms, this has important implications for the use of trans-diagnostic interventions at the level of these mechanisms rather than specific to the symptomatic outcomes.

Although anger may interfere with recovery and treatment efficacy, there is also evidence that it can be a *driver* of care seeking. In the Transition and Wellbeing Research Programme, anger was one of the most commonly reported reasons for seeking assistance among those who reported having a concern about their mental health (transitioned ADF = 12.43%, 2015 regular ADF = 12.96%). Others included depression (transitioned ADF = 27.22%, 2015 regular ADF = 21.01%), anxiety (transitioned ADF = 17.80%, 2015 regular ADF = 19.64%), and relationship problems (transitioned ADF = 11.05%, 2015 regular ADF = 18.72%), with these four issues also driving help-seeking among those with a probable 30-day mental disorder (Forbes et al., 2018). This primacy of depression, anxiety, and anger problems driving engagement with treatment is consistent with studies of U.S. veterans, even those specifically diagnosed with PTSD (Rosen et al., 2011). Findings from our research, and internationally, highlight the role of family members and friends in motivating and facilitating access to treatment among veterans with mental health problems (Forbes et al., 2018). Presumably, the negative relationship consequences of uncontrolled anger, hostility, and aggression may be behind this association.

CONCLUSION

Problematic levels of anger and aggression are commonly reported by military populations around the world, effecting approximately 11% to 16% of currently serving members and up to 30% of those who have recently transitioned back into civilian life. Australian and international evidence show that problematic anger and aggression appear to increase over time in these populations, and compelling evidence suggests that neurobiological mechanisms may play a role in this. The mechanistic pathways underlying the emergence of problematic anger and aggression outlined in this chapter also have relevance for other occupations such as police and emergency responders, all of which are characterized by repeated and at times prolonged exposure to stress and threatening environments. The accompanying evidence of the cumulative effects of workplace exposures on emerging psychological symptoms, disorder, and risky behaviors among police (Violanti et al., 2017), firefighters (Cowlishaw et al., 2020; Jahnke et al., 2016), and other emergency responders (I. H. Stanley et al., 2016; Walker et al., 2016) provides further support for the applicability of this model beyond the military context.

The greater levels of anger and aggression observed among ex-serving veterans in particular suggest that factors relating to the transition back to civilian life, such as change in environmental, cultural, and social context, are also likely to be important. Collectively, military, police, and emergency responders generally have highly authoritative, masculine cultures with a majority male workforce (Hale, 2012; Silvestri, 2017; Tracy & Scott, 2006). These factors were not the focus of this chapter but are likely to contribute to the issue of anger, aggression, and risky behaviors in these populations. Understanding the way in which these factors might interact with occupational exposures, underlying neurobiology, and symptoms, and how these play out in the transition to civilian life, is an important focus for future research.

High levels of and increasing anger over time, together with the potential role of anger in the emergence, treatment, and prognosis of other mental disorders such as PTSD, strongly support the need to consider anger in the treatment of high-risk, high-stress occupations moving forward. Current trauma-based interventions for PTSD may not be optimal for treating anger because of underlying functional changes in threat detection and emotion regulation systems, which can inhibit treatment efficacy. Targeting early intervention toward these processes, therefore, is one promising avenue for addressing not only anger itself but also risk for emergence of other mental health conditions over time.

Anger is formally acknowledged in the *DSM-5* PTSD criteria (Friedman et al., 2011) and is recognized as a common feature of PTSD (Barrett et al., 2013), The link between anger and the elevated arousal and exaggerated vigilance that are frequent in PTSD may contribute to more disinhibited aggression in response to perceived threats (Jakupcak et al., 2007). Anger may also impede treatment effectiveness where a disorder exists and can contribute to impaired functioning through disruption of social functioning and close interpersonal relationships (Meffert et al., 2014). For all these reasons, consideration of anger in its own right is critical when considering the health of individuals employed in high-risk occupations characterized by stress and trauma exposure.

Together, these findings highlight the complexity in understanding the role of anger in the context of high-risk, high-stress occupations such as the military and poststress adjustment. However, they also provide promising insights for understanding and managing anger and, in turn, reducing overall mental and social health morbidity.

IMPLICATIONS

- Impairments to attention and inhibitory control may also be associated with impaired risk detection; thus, assessment of the behavioral and social sequelae, including risky behaviors and interpersonal, relationship, and family violence, is important.
- From a service provision perspective, current treatment programs for combat and complex trauma-exposed populations should assess and provide interventions addressing anger and the mechanisms underlying symptomatic presentations.
- The relationship between anger and PTSD, in part reflecting shared neurobiological pathways, has important implications for the use of transdiagnostic interventions at the level of these mechanisms rather than specific to the symptomatic outcomes.
- Although anger can be a significant problem in its own right, and interfere with recovery and treatment efficacy, there is also evidence that it can be a *driver* of care-seeking. This presentation provides an important opportunity for screening and early intervention for a broad range of clinical disorders and their social consequences.
- These findings have general relevance beyond the military context, in particular for other occupations such as police and emergency responders, all of which are characterized by repeated and at times prolonged exposure to stress and threatening environments.

REFERENCES

Adam, H., & Brett, J. M. (2018, May). Everything in moderation: The social effects of anger depend on its perceived intensity. *Journal of Experimental Social Psychology*, *76*, 12–18. https://doi.org/10.1016/j.jesp.2017.11.014

Adler, A. B., Britt, T. W., Castro, C. A., McGurk, D., & Bliese, P. D. (2011). Effect of transition home from combat on risk-taking and health-related behaviors. *Journal of Traumatic Stress, 24*(4), 381–389. https://doi.org/10.1002/jts.20665

Adler, A. B., Brossart, D. F., & Toblin, R. L. (2017). Can anger be helpful? Soldier perceptions of the utility of anger. *The Journal of Nervous and Mental Disease, 205*(9), 692–698. https://doi.org/10.1097/NMD.0000000000000712

Adler, A. B., & Castro, C. A. (2013). An occupational mental health model for the military. *Military Behavioral Health, 1*(1), 41–45. https://doi.org/10.1080/21635781.2012.721063

American Psychiatric Association. (2013). *Diagnostic and statistical manual of mental disorders* (5th ed.). https://doi.org/10.1176/appi.books.9780890425596

Barrett, E. L., Mills, K. L., & Teesson, M. (2013). Mental health correlates of anger in the general population: Findings from the 2007 National Survey of Mental Health and Wellbeing. *The Australian and New Zealand Journal of Psychiatry, 47*(5), 470–476. https://doi.org/10.1177/0004867413476752

Begić, D., & Jokić-Begić, N. (2001). Aggressive behavior in combat veterans with post-traumatic stress disorder. *Military Medicine, 166*(8), 671–676. https://doi.org/10.1093/milmed/166.8.671

Bensley, K. M., Seelig, A. D., Armenta, R. F., Rivera, A. C., Peterson, A. V., Jacobson, I. G., Littman, A. J., Maynard, C., Bricker, J. B., Boyko, E. J., Rull, R. P., & Williams, E. C. (2018). Posttraumatic Stress Disorder Symptom Association With Subsequent Risky And Problem Drinking Initiation. *Journal of Addiction Medicine, 12*(5), 353–362. https://doi.org/10.1097/ADM.0000000000000420

Blakey, S. M., Love, H., Lindquist, L., Beckham, J. C., & Elbogen, E. B. (2018). Disentangling the link between posttraumatic stress disorder and violent behavior: Findings from a nationally representative sample. *Journal of Consulting and Clinical Psychology, 86*(2), 169–178. https://doi.org/10.1037/ccp0000253

Blunt, J. D. (2016, March). *Hyperarousal: The critical determinant of post-trauma sequelae* [Doctoral dissertation, The University of Adelaide]. https://digital.library.adelaide.edu.au/dspace/bitstream/2440/103576/1/01front.pdf

Bryant, R., Lawrence-Wood, E., Baur, J., McFarlane, A., Hodson, S., Sadler, N., Benassi, H., Howell, S., Abraham, M., Iannos, M., Hansen, C., Searle, A., & Van Hooff, M. (2019). *Mental health changes over time: A longitudinal perspective: Mental health and wellbeing transition study*. Department of Defence and Department of Veterans' Affairs. https://researchmgt.monash.edu/ws/portalfiles/portal/290359995/290359889_oa.pdf

Cabrera, O. A., Adler, A. B., & Bliese, P. D. (2016). Growth mixture modeling of post-combat aggression: application to soldiers deployed to Iraq. *Psychiatry Research, 246*, 539–544. https://doi.org/10.1016/j.psychres.2016.10.035

Cash, R., Varker, T., McHugh, T., Metcalf, O., Howard, A., Lloyd, D., Costello, J., Said, D., & Forbes, D. (2018). Effectiveness of an anger intervention for military members with PTSD: A clinical case series. *Military Medicine, 183*(9–10), e286–e290. https://doi.org/10.1093/milmed/usx115

Chemtob, C. M., Novaco, R. W., Hamada, R. S., Gross, D. M., & Smith, G. (1997). Anger regulation deficits in combat-related posttraumatic stress disorder. *Journal of Traumatic Stress, 10*(1), 17–36. https://doi.org/10.1002/jts.2490100104

Clausen, A. N., Youngren, W., Sisante, J.-F. V., Billinger, S. A., Taylor, C., & Aupperle, R. L. (2016). Combat PTSD and implicit behavioral tendencies for positive affective stimuli: A brief report. *Frontiers in Psychology*, *7*, 758. https://doi.org/10.3389/fpsyg.2016.00758

Contractor, A. A., Armour, C., Wang, X., Forbes, D., & Elhai, J. D. (2015). The mediating role of anger in the relationship between PTSD symptoms and impulsivity. *Psychological Trauma: Theory, Research, Practice, Policy*, *7*(2), 138–145. https://doi.org/10.1037/a0037112

Contractor, A. A., Weiss, N. H., Dranger, P., Ruggero, C., & Armour, C. (2017). PTSD's risky behavior criterion: Relation with *DSM-5* PTSD symptom clusters and psychopathology. *Psychiatry Research*, *252*, 215–222. https://doi.org/10.1016/j.psychres.2017.03.008

Cowlishaw, S., Little, J., Sbisa, A., McFarlane, A. C., Van Hooff, M., Lawrence-Wood, E., O'Donnell, M., Hinton, M., Sadler, N., Savic, A., Forbes, D., & Metcalf, O. (2020). Prevalence and implications of gambling problems among firefighters. *Addictive Behaviors*, *105*, 106326. https://doi.org/10.1016/j.addbeh.2020.106326

Dyches, K. D., Saboe, K. N., Anderson, J. A., Wilk, J. E., Hinman, S. J., Sipos, M. L., & Quartana, P. J. (2017). Modeling the indirect association of combat exposure with anger and aggression during combat deployment: The moderating role of perceived unit morale. *Military Psychology*, *29*(4), 260–270. https://doi.org/10.1037/mil0000165

Elbogen, E. B., Wagner, H. R., Fuller, S. R., Calhoun, P. S., Kinneer, P. M., Mid-Atlantic Mental Illness Research, Education, and Clinical Center Workgroup, & Beckham, J. C. (2010). Correlates of anger and hostility in Iraq and Afghanistan war veterans. *The American Journal of Psychiatry*, *167*(9), 1051–1058. https://doi.org/10.1176/appi.ajp.2010.09050739

Foa, E. B., Riggs, D. S., Massie, E. D., & Yarczower, M. (1995). The impact of fear activation and anger on the efficacy of exposure treatment for posttraumatic stress disorder. *Behavior Therapy*, *26*(3), 487–499. https://doi.org/10.1016/S0005-7894(05)80096-6

Forbes, D., Hawthorne, G., Elliott, P., McHugh, T., Biddle, D., Creamer, M., & Novaco, R. W. (2004). A concise measure of anger in combat-related posttraumatic stress disorder. *Journal of Traumatic Stress*, *17*(3), 249–256. https://doi.org/10.1023/B:JOTS.0000029268.22161.bd

Forbes, D., Parslow, R., Creamer, M., Allen, N., McHugh, T., & Hopwood, M. (2008). Mechanisms of anger and treatment outcome in combat veterans with posttraumatic stress disorder. *Journal of Traumatic Stress*, *21*(2), 142–149. https://doi.org/10.1002/jts.20315

Forbes, D., Van Hooff, M., Lawrence-Wood, E., Sadler, N., Hodson, S., Benassi, H., Hansen, C., Avery, J., Varker, T., O'Donnell, M., Phelps, A., Frederickson, J., Sharp, M., Searle, A., & McFarlane, A. (2018). *Pathways to Care, Mental Health and Wellbeing Study*. Department of Defence and Department of Veterans' Affairs, Canberra.

Friedman, M. J., Resick, P. A., Bryant, R. A., & Brewin, C. R. (2011). Considering PTSD for *DSM-5*. *Depression and Anxiety*, *28*(9), 750–769. https://doi.org/10.1002/da.20767

Geddes, D., Callister, R. R., & Gibson, D. E. (2020). A message in the madness: Functions of workplace anger in organizational life. *The Academy of Management Perspectives*, *34*(1), 28–47. https://doi.org/10.5465/amp.2016.0158

Germain, C. L., Kangas, M., Taylor, A., & Forbes, D. (2016). The role of trauma-related cognitive processes in the relationship between combat-PTSD symptom severity and anger expression and control. *Australian Journal of Psychology, 68*(2), 73–81. https://doi.org/10.1111/ajpy.12097

Gilam, G., Lin, T., Fruchter, E., & Hendler, T. (2017). Neural indicators of interpersonal anger as cause and consequence of combat training stress symptoms. *Psychological Medicine, 47*(9), 1561–1572. https://doi.org/10.1017/S0033291716003354

Hale, H. C. (2012). The role of practice in the development of military masculinities. *Gender, Work and Organization, 19*(6), 699–722. https://doi.org/10.1111/j.1468-0432.2010.00542.x

Heesink, L., Kleber, R., Häfner, M., van Bedaf, L., Eekhout, I., & Geuze, E. (2017). Anger and aggression problems in veterans are associated with an increased acoustic startle reflex. *Biological Psychology, 123*, 119–125. https://doi.org/10.1016/j.biopsycho.2016.12.004

Hoge, C. W., Castro, C. A., Messer, S. C., McGurk, D., Cotting, D. I., & Koffman, R. L. (2004). Combat duty in Iraq and Afghanistan, mental health problems, and barriers to care. *The New England Journal of Medicine, 351*(1), 13–22. https://doi.org/10.1056/NEJMoa040603

Jahnke, S. A., Poston, W. S. C., Haddock, C. K., & Murphy, B. (2016). Firefighting and mental health: Experiences of repeated exposure to trauma. *Work, 53*(4), 737–744. https://doi.org/10.3233/WOR-162255

Jakupcak, M., Conybeare, D., Phelps, L., Hunt, S., Holmes, H. A., Felker, B., Klevens, M., & McFall, M. E. (2007). Anger, hostility, and aggression among Iraq and Afghanistan War veterans reporting PTSD and subthreshold PTSD. *Journal of Traumatic Stress, 20*(6), 945–954. https://doi.org/10.1002/jts.20258

Jeter, C. B., Hergenroeder, G. W., Hylin, M. J., Redell, J. B., Moore, A. N., & Dash, P. K. (2013). Biomarkers for the diagnosis and prognosis of mild traumatic brain injury/concussion. *Journal of Neurotrauma, 30*(8), 657–670. https://doi.org/10.1089/neu.2012.2439

Killgore, W. D., Cotting, D. I., Thomas, J. L., Cox, A. L., McGurk, D., Vo, A. H., Castro, C. A., & Hoge, C. W. (2008). Post-combat invincibility: Violent combat experiences are associated with increased risk-taking propensity following deployment. *Journal of Psychiatric Research, 42*(13), 1112–1121. https://doi.org/10.1016/j.jpsychires.2008.01.001

Kim-Spoon, J., Holmes, C., & Deater-Deckard, K. (2015). Attention regulates anger and fear to predict changes in adolescent risk-taking behaviors. *Journal of Child Psychology and Psychiatry, and Allied Disciplines, 56*(7), 756–765. https://doi.org/10.1111/jcpp.12338

Lang, P. J., Cuthbert, B. N., & Bradley, M. M. (1998). Measuring emotion in therapy: Imagery, activation, and feeling. *Behavior Therapy, 29*(4), 655–674. https://doi.org/10.1016/S0005-7894(98)80024-5

Lawrence-Wood, E., McFarlane, A., Lawrence, A., Sadler, N., Hodson, S., Benassi, H., Bryant, R., Korgaonkar, M., Rosenfeld, J., Sim, M., Kelsall, H., Abraham, M., Baur, J., Howell, S., Hansen, C., Iannos, M., Searle, A., & Van Hooff, M. (2019). *Impact of combat report, impact of combat study*. Department of Defence and Department of Veterans' Affairs. https://researchmgt.monash.edu/ws/portalfiles/portal/290362298/290362250_oa.pdf

Lebel, R. D. (2017). Moving beyond fight and flight: A contingent model of how the emotional regulation of anger and fear sparks proactivity. *Academy of Management Review, 42*(2), 190–206. https://doi.org/10.5465/amr.2014.0368

Lievaart, M., van der Veen, F. M., Huijding, J., Naeije, L., Hovens, J. E., & Franken, I. H. (2016). Trait anger in relation to neural and behavioral correlates of response inhibition and error-processing. *International Journal of Psychophysiology, 99,* 40–47. https://doi.org/10.1016/j.ijpsycho.2015.12.001

Lin, T., Gilam, G., Raz, G., Or-Borichev, A., Bar-Haim, Y., Fruchter, E., & Hendler, T. (2017). Accessible neurobehavioral anger-related markers for vulnerability to post-traumatic stress symptoms in a population of male soldiers. *Frontiers in Behavioral Neuroscience, 11,* 38. https://doi.org/10.3389/fnbeh.2017.00038

Lindebaum, D., Jordan, P. J., & Morris, L. (2016). Symmetrical and asymmetrical outcomes of leader anger expression: A qualitative study of army personnel. *Human Relations, 69*(2), 277–300.

Mackintosh, M.-A., Niehaus, J., Taft, C. T., Marx, B. P., Grubbs, K., & Morland, L. A. (2017). Using a mobile application in the treatment of dysregulated anger among veterans. *Military Medicine, 182*(11), e1941–e1949. https://doi.org/10.7205/MILMED-D-17-00063

MacManus, D., Dean, K., Al Bakir, M., Iversen, A. C., Hull, L., Fahy, T., Wessely, S., & Fear, N. T. (2012). Violent behaviour in U.K. military personnel returning home after deployment. *Psychological Medicine, 42*(8), 1663–1673. https://doi.org/10.1017/S0033291711002327

MacManus, D., Dean, K., Jones, M., Rona, R. J., Greenberg, N., Hull, L., Fahy, T., Wessely, S., & Fear, N. T. (2013). Violent offending by UK military personnel deployed to Iraq and Afghanistan: A data linkage cohort study. *Lancet, 381*(9870), 907–917. https://doi.org/10.1016/S0140-6736(13)60354-2

MacManus, D., Rona, R., Dickson, H., Somaini, G., Fear, N., & Wessely, S. (2015). Aggressive and violent behavior among military personnel deployed to Iraq and Afghanistan: Prevalence and link with deployment and combat exposure. *Epidemiologic Reviews, 37*(1), 196–212. https://doi.org/10.1093/epirev/mxu006

Maniaci, G., Picone, F., van Holst, R. J., Bolloni, C., Scardina, S., & Cannizzaro, C. (2017). Alterations in the emotional regulation process in gambling addiction: The role of anger and alexithymia. *Journal of Gambling Studies, 33*(2), 633–647. https://doi.org/10.1007/s10899-016-9636-4

Marusak, H. A., Martin, K. R., Etkin, A., & Thomason, M. E. (2015). Childhood trauma exposure disrupts the automatic regulation of emotional processing. *Neuropsychopharmacology, 40*(5), 1250–1258. https://doi.org/10.1038/npp.2014.311

McFarlane, A. C., Hodson, S., Van Hooff, M., Verhagen, A., & Davies, C. (2011). *Mental health in the Australian Defence Force: 2010 ADF Mental Health and Wellbeing Study: Full report.* Department of Defence.

McFarlane, A. C., Yehuda, R., & Clark, C. R. (2002). Biologic models of traumatic memories and post-traumatic stress disorder. The role of neural networks. *The Psychiatric Clinics of North America, 25*(2), 253–270. https://doi.org/10.1016/S0193-953X(01)00008-9

McKinney, J. M., Hirsch, J. K., & Britton, P. C. (2017). PTSD symptoms and suicide risk in veterans: Serial indirect effects via depression and anger. *Journal of Affective Disorders, 214,* 100–107. https://doi.org/10.1016/j.jad.2017.03.008

Meffert, S. M., Henn-Haase, C., Metzler, T. J., Qian, M., Best, S., Hirschfeld, A., McCaslin, S., Inslicht, S., Neylan, T. C., & Marmar, C. R. (2014). Prospective study of police officer spouse/partners: A new pathway to secondary trauma and relationship violence? *PLOS ONE, 9*(7), e100663. https://doi.org/10.1371/journal.pone.0100663

Morland, L. A., Greene, C. J., Rosen, C. S., Foy, D., Reilly, P., Shore, J., He, Q., & Frueh, B. C. (2010). Telemedicine for anger management therapy in a rural population of combat veterans with posttraumatic stress disorder: A randomized noninferiority trial. *The Journal of Clinical Psychiatry*, *71*(7), 855–863. https://doi.org/10.4088/JCP.09m05604blu

Newby, J. H., Ursano, R. J., McCarroll, J. E., Liu, X., Fullerton, C. S., & Norwood, A. E. (2005). Postdeployment domestic violence by U.S. Army soldiers. *Military Medicine*, *170*(8), 643–647. https://doi.org/10.7205/MILMED.170.8.643

Novaco, R. W. (2007). Anger dysregulation. In T. A. Cavell & K. T. Malcolm (Eds.), *Anger, aggression and interventions for interpersonal violence* (pp. 3–54). Lawrence Erlbaum Associates Publishers.

Novaco, R. W. (2016). *Anger stress: Concepts, cognition, emotion, and behavior*. Elsevier.

Oehr, L., & Anderson, J. (2017). Diffusion-tensor imaging findings and cognitive function following hospitalized mixed-mechanism mild traumatic brain injury: A systematic review and meta-analysis. *Archives of Physical Medicine and Rehabilitation*, *98*(11), 2308–2319. https://doi.org/10.1016/j.apmr.2017.03.019

Olatunji, B. O., Ciesielski, B. G., & Tolin, D. F. (2010). Fear and loathing: A meta-analytic review of the specificity of anger in PTSD. *Behavior Therapy*, *41*(1), 93–105. https://doi.org/10.1016/j.beth.2009.01.004

Pietrzak, R. H., Feder, A., Schechter, C. B., Singh, R., Cancelmo, L., Bromet, E. J., Katz, C. L., Reissman, D. B., Ozbay, F., Sharma, V., Crane, M., Harrison, D., Herbert, R., Levin, S. M., Luft, B. J., Moline, J. M., Stellman, J. M., Udasin, I. G., El-Gabalawy, R., Landrigan, P. J., & Southwick, S. M. (2014). Dimensional structure and course of post-traumatic stress symptomatology in World Trade Center responders. *Psychological Medicine*, *44*(10), 2085–2098. https://doi.org/10.1017/S0033291713002924

Rodenburg, J., Heesink, L., & Droûdek, B. (2016). PTSD, anger, and aggression: Epidemiology, etiology and clinical practice. *Comprehensive Guide to Post-Traumatic Stress Disorders*, pp. 739–758.

Rona, R. J., Jones, M., Hull, L., MacManus, D., Fear, N. T., & Wessely, S. (2015). Anger in the UK Armed Forces: Strong association with mental health, childhood antisocial behavior, and combat role. *The Journal of Nervous and Mental Disease*, *203*(1), 15–22. https://doi.org/10.1097/NMD.0000000000000228

Rosen, C. S., Greenbaum, M. A., Fitt, J. E., Laffaye, C., Norris, V. A., & Kimerling, R. (2011). Stigma, help-seeking attitudes, and use of psychotherapy in veterans with diagnoses of posttraumatic stress disorder. *The Journal of Nervous and Mental Disease*, *199*(11), 879–885. https://doi.org/10.1097/NMD.0b013e3182349ea5

Sayer, N. A., Noorbaloochi, S., Frazier, P., Carlson, K., Gravely, A., & Murdoch, M. (2010). Reintegration problems and treatment interests among Iraq and Afghanistan combat veterans receiving VA medical care. *Psychiatric Services*, *61*(6), 589–597. https://doi.org/10.1176/ps.2010.61.6.589

Silvestri, M. (2017). Police culture and gender: Revisiting the "cult of masculinity." *Policing. Journal of Policy Practice*, *11*(3), 289–300.

Sippel, L. M., Mota, N. P., Kachadourian, L. K., Krystal, J. H., Southwick, S. M., Harpaz-Rotem, I., & Pietrzak, R. H. (2016). The burden of hostility in U.S. veterans: Results from the National Health and Resilience in Veterans Study. *Psychiatry Research*, *243*, 421–430. https://doi.org/10.1016/j.psychres.2016.06.040

Stanley, E. A., & Larsen, K. L. (2019). Difficulties with emotion regulation in the contemporary U.S. Armed Forces: Structural contributors and potential solutions. *Armed Forces & Society, 47*(1), 77–105. https://doi.org/10.1177/0095327X19848018

Stanley, I. H., Hom, M. A., & Joiner, T. E. (2016). A systematic review of suicidal thoughts and behaviors among police officers, firefighters, EMTs, and paramedics. *Clinical Psychology Review, 44*, 25–44. https://doi.org/10.1016/j.cpr.2015.12.002

Tracy, S. J., & Scott, C. (2006). Sexuality, masculinity, and taint management among firefighters and correctional officers: Getting down and dirty with "America's heroes" and the "scum of law enforcement." *Management Communication Quarterly, 20*(1), 6–38. https://doi.org/10.1177/0893318906287898

Turgoose, D., & Murphy, D. (2018). Anger and aggression in UK treatment-seeking veterans with PTSD. *Healthcare, 6*(3), 86. https://doi.org/10.3390/healthcare6030086

Van Hooff, M., Lawrence-Wood, E., Hodson, S., Sadler, N., Benassi, H., Hansen, C., Grace, B., Avery, J., Searle, A., Iannos, M., Abraham, M., Baur, J., & McFarlane, A. (2018). *Mental health prevalence, mental health and wellbeing transition study*. Department of Defence and the Department of Veterans' Affairs, Canberra.

Van Kleef, G. A., & Côté, S. (2007). Expressing anger in conflict: When it helps and when it hurts. *The Journal of Applied Psychology, 92*(6), 1557–1569. https://doi.org/10.1037/0021-9010.92.6.1557

Vasterling, J. J., Aslan, M., Proctor, S. P., Ko, J., Leviyah, X., & Concato, J. (2020). Long-term negative emotional outcomes of warzone TBI. *The Clinical Neuropsychologist, 34*(6), 1088–1104. https://doi.org/10.1080/13854046.2020.1749935

Vasterling, J. J., & Proctor, S. P. (2011). Understanding the neuropsychological consequences of deployment stress: A public health framework. *Journal of the International Neuropsychological Society, 17*(1), 1–6. https://doi.org/10.1017/S1355617710001116

Violanti, J. M., Charles, L. E., McCanlies, E., Hartley, T. A., Baughman, P., Andrew, M. E., Fekedulegn, D., Ma, C. C., Mnatsakanova, A., & Burchfiel, C. M. (2017). Police stressors and health: A state-of-the-art review. *Policing, 40*(4), 642–656.

Walker, A., McKune, A., Ferguson, S., Pyne, D. B., & Rattray, B. (2016). Chronic occupational exposures can influence the rate of PTSD and depressive disorders in first responders and military personnel. *Extreme Physiology & Medicine, 5*(1), Article 8. https://doi.org/10.1186/s13728-016-0049-x

Wilk, J. E., Bliese, P. D., Thomas, J. L., Wood, M. D., McGurk, D., Castro, C. A., & Hoge, C. W. (2013). Unethical battlefield conduct reported by soldiers serving in the Iraq war. *The Journal of Nervous and Mental Disease, 201*(4), 259–265. https://doi.org/10.1097/NMD.0b013e318288d302

Wilk, J. E., Quartana, P. J., Clarke-Walper, K., Kok, B. C., & Riviere, L. A. (2015). Aggression in U.S. soldiers post-deployment: Associations with combat exposure and PTSD and the moderating role of trait anger. *Aggressive Behavior, 41*(6), 556–565. https://doi.org/10.1002/ab.21595

Zuj, D. V., Felmingham, K. L., Palmer, M. A., Lawrence-Wood, E., Van Hooff, M., Lawrence, A. J., Bryant, R. A., & McFarlane, A. C. (2017). Neural activity and emotional processing following military deployment: Effects of mild traumatic brain injury and posttraumatic stress disorder. *Brain and Cognition, 118*, 19–26. https://doi.org/10.1016/j.bandc.2017.07.001

7 THE COST OF ANGER

Suicide in the U.S. Army

JAMES A. NAIFEH, OSCAR I. GONZALEZ,
HOLLY B. HERBERMAN MASH, CAROL S. FULLERTON,
AND ROBERT J. URSANO

KEY POINTS

- Substantial increases in suicidal behavior were documented among U.S. Army soldiers during the wars in Iraq and Afghanistan.
- Anger and anger-relevant mental disorders are important for understanding suicide among military service members and other high-risk occupations.
- Anger is an important and adaptive component of military culture and training, but it becomes maladaptive when it is dysregulated and/or context inappropriate.

(*continues*)

The opinions and assertions expressed herein are those of the authors and do not necessarily reflect the official policy or position of the Uniformed Services University, the Department of Defense, or the Henry M. Jackson Foundation for the Advancement of Military Medicine, Inc.

https://doi.org/10.1037/0000244-008
Anger at Work: Prevention, Intervention, and Treatment in High-Risk Occupations, A. B. Adler and D. Forbes (Editors)

KEY POINTS (*Continued*)

- Anger problems, anger-relevant mental disorders, and suicidal thoughts and behaviors often begin prior to military service.
- Among deployed soldiers, mid-deployment is a particularly high-risk time for emotional distress and suicidal thoughts and behavior.
- Identification of those at risk for perpetration of family violence and crime (particularly violent crime) may allow for targeted interventions that reduce suicide risk among both victims and perpetrators.

Suicide, the 10th leading cause of death in the United States (Centers for Disease Control and Prevention, 2019), is a complex multidetermined phenomenon (Nock et al., 2013). Anger is one of many important factors to consider in understanding risk for suicidal thoughts and behaviors (Brezo et al., 2006; Giegling et al., 2009; Horesh et al., 1997; Kotler et al., 2001). Although there has been concern about suicide among workers in many high-risk occupations, such as first responders (e.g., police, paramedics; Stanley et al., 2016), it is likely that no group in recent history has received as much scrutiny as the U.S. military. Nearly 2 decades ago, Operation Enduring Freedom (OEF) commenced in Afghanistan (in 2001), followed less than 2 years later by Operation Iraqi Freedom (OIF). The U.S. military suicide rate, which for decades had been lower than that of the sex- and age-adjusted U.S. general population, began to increase sharply in 2004 (Department of Defense Task Force on the Prevention of Suicide by Members of the Armed Forces, 2010).

The U.S. Army had the largest increase in suicide deaths among U.S. military branches, from approximately nine per 100,000 in 2001 to 22 per 100,000 in 2011, surpassing the adjusted civilian rate for the first time in 2008 (Lineberry & O'Connor, 2012; Nock et al., 2013). During this time, there was a corresponding increase in medically documented suicide ideation and nonfatal suicide attempts among soldiers (Ursano, Kessler, Heeringa, et al., 2015; Ursano, Naifeh, et al., 2018). Despite a significant decline in the scope and intensity of combat operations in recent years, the suicide rate among soldiers remains elevated (Gibson et al., 2017; Pruitt et al., 2017; Reger et al., 2018).

In this chapter, we discuss the complex role of anger across phases of military service and examine the potential role of anger and its correlates (e.g., mental disorders, substance abuse, family violence, and crime perpetration) in military suicides. Although we give particular focus to U.S. Army soldiers, understanding the role of anger in suicide risk is relevant to the health and functioning of personnel in other militaries and high-risk occupations worldwide. We begin with a brief review of recent epidemiologic research on suicidal thoughts and behaviors among soldiers, followed by discussion of suicide risk in the context of anger before, during, and after military service; specific mental disorders that often co-occur with anger (posttraumatic stress disorder [PTSD], major depressive disorder [MDD], bipolar disorder [BP], substance use disorder [SUD], and intermittent explosive disorder [IED]); and violence inside and outside the family. Along the way, we highlight relevant research in other high-risk occupations. We conclude with a discussion of future directions and recommendations aimed at improving our ability to understand and prevent anger-related suicidal behaviors.

Among many efforts to address the emerging public health crisis of military suicide, the U.S. Army and National Institute of Mental Health awarded funding of the Army Study to Assess Risk and Resilience in Servicemembers (Army STARRS), the largest epidemiological and neurobiological study of suicide risk and resilience ever conducted in the U.S. Army (Ursano et al., 2014). Army STARRS examined the administrative records of all 1.66 million soldiers who served on active duty at some point from 2004 through 2009 and conducted representative population surveys in which more than 100,000 soldiers participated. In addition to weighting all data to be representative of the target population (Heeringa et al., 2013; Kessler, Heeringa, et al., 2013), a clinical reappraisal study was conducted to ensure diagnostic concordance between mental disorder screening instruments in Army STARRS surveys and clinical interviews (Kessler, Santiago, et al., 2013). Given its intent, scope, and representativeness, we highlight Army STARRS findings that are particularly relevant to understanding suicidal behavior among soldiers and the role that anger may play in influencing risk (these and other Army STARRS findings are reviewed in Naifeh, Mash, et al., 2019).

Before proceeding, it is important to distinguish between the various types of suicidal thoughts and behaviors that are mentioned in this chapter. *Suicide ideation* refers to thoughts about ending one's own life and must include content related to self-injury and/or a desire to die. This should generally be considered distinct from passive thoughts about death or dying (e.g., a soldier experiencing thoughts about their own mortality or death following a combat deployment). A *suicide plan* refers to the development of a strategy by which one intends to die (e.g., date, time, place, and method).

Suicide attempt refers to engagement in a potentially self-injurious behavior with intent to die. Although some people use this term broadly to refer to outcomes that are either fatal (e.g., "fatal suicide attempt") or nonfatal (e.g., "nonfatal suicide attempt"), our use of the term *suicide attempt* throughout this chapter refers specifically to nonfatal events. *Suicide* refers to a self-inflicted injury with intent to die, which results in death.

Army STARRS survey data demonstrate that risk for suicidal thoughts and behaviors is present through all stages of a soldier's life and military career. In a representative Army STARRS survey of active duty soldiers, lifetime prevalence estimates of suicide ideation, suicide plans, and suicide attempts were 13.9%, 5.3%, and 2.4%, respectively (Nock et al., 2014). More than 17% of active duty soldiers with lifetime suicide ideation report that they subsequently attempted suicide (Nock et al., 2014). Across Army STARRS survey populations, the majority of soldiers who transitioned from ideation to attempt did so within the first year after ideation onset (Millner et al., 2018; Nock et al., 2014; Ursano, Heeringa, et al., 2015). While a broad discussion of risk factors is beyond the scope of this chapter, it is important to note that risk for suicidal thoughts and behaviors consistently differs by gender. Unlike suicide death, which has a significantly higher rate among men (Gilman et al., 2014; Schoenbaum et al., 2014), both administratively documented and self-reported suicide ideation and attempts are more likely among women (Millner et al., 2018; Nock et al., 2014; Ursano, Kessler, Stein, et al., 2015; Ursano et al., 2016). It is also noteworthy that risk for all suicidal outcomes (ideation, attempts, and deaths) is typically highest among soldiers of non-Hispanic White race-ethnicity (Schoenbaum et al., 2014; Ursano, Kessler, Stein, et al., 2015, 2017), although American Indian/Alaska Native soldiers are an understudied population that may also be at increased risk (O'Keefe & Reger, 2017).

Research on suicidal thoughts and behaviors among first responders suggests that individuals in those high-risk occupations may have elevated risk, but findings are somewhat inconsistent, vary by occupation and geographic location, and often rely on convenience samples that may not be representative (for a review, see Stanley et al., 2016). A representative survey of diverse Australian emergency medical personnel (e.g., police, fire and rescue, ambulance) found self-reported rates of lifetime suicide ideation, plans, and attempts were 12.3%, 5.7%, and 1.9%, respectively, whereas rates of those outcomes in the past 12 months were 5.3%, 2.0%, and 0.3%, respectively (Kyron et al., 2021). In contrast, a convenience sample of 1,027 current and former U.S. firefighters found remarkably higher rates of self-reported lifetime ideation (46.8%), plans (19.2%), and attempts (15.5%; Stanley et al., 2015). Evidence suggests that risk of death by suicide may be increased among first responders relative to other occupations (e.g., Vigil et al., 2019), although considerable variation exists in the findings and methodological rigor of extant studies (Stanley et al., 2016). Although suicides that occur in the workplace are rare, one study found that protective service occupations—a U.S. Bureau of Labor Statistics occupational category that includes law enforcement and firefighters (among others)—is the major occupational category with the highest rate of workplace suicide at 5.3 per 1,000,000 (Tiesman et al., 2015).

The prevalence of suicidal behavior in high-risk occupations is important not only because of the significant consequences for the individual (e.g., injury or death) but also because of the potential impact on others. Military service members and veterans who report knowing someone who died by suicide have increased risk for PTSD, anxiety, depression, and suicidal thoughts and behaviors (Bryan et al., 2017; Cerel et al., 2015; Hom et al., 2017). While it is also common for first responders to know someone who died by suicide, many individuals in those occupations are also exposed directly to suicide as a function of their job. For example, a survey of law enforcement officers found that 95% had responded to the scene of a suicide, with exposure to an average of 30 suicide scenes over the course of their career (Cerel et al., 2019). Furthermore, officers who reported that a suicide scene had "stayed with them" (including having nightmares) were at increased risk for PTSD, depression, anxiety, and suicide ideation.

It is also important to recognize that the military and other high-risk occupations are not mutually exclusive populations. For example, some firefighters may also be certified as emergence medical technicians, and one epidemiologic study found that more than 37% of U.S. firefighters who died by suicide had previously served in the military (Pennington et al., 2021). Service in multiple high-risk occupations may confer additional risk for suicidal thoughts and behaviors (Stanley et al., 2015), perhaps because of greater cumulative exposure to occupational stressors.

THE COMPLEX ROLE OF ANGER IN MILITARY SERVICE

Anger and aggression are distinct but overlapping responses that can be both adaptive and maladaptive depending on level of control and environmental context. High-risk occupations, which often involve exposure to actual or perceived threats to life and physical integrity, may at times require aggressive action in which anger is an adaptive response. Not surprising, anger has been identified in the emotional climate of first responders, including police officers (Daus & Brown, 2012; Kale & Gedik, 2018; Leonard & Alison, 1999), ambulance workers (Halpern et al., 2009), and paramedics (Avraham et al., 2014; Jamner et al., 1991; Regehr, 2005). Although the association between anger and suicide is an important consideration in all high-risk occupations, the remainder of this chapter focuses primarily on service in the U.S. Army, which provides unique opportunities to examine anger in the context of culture, training, and a rapidly growing body of research on suicidal thoughts and behaviors.

Military training and culture echo Aristotle's notion that anger is needed and that "no battle can be won without it" (DiGiuseppe & Tafrate, 2007, p. 90). With more than 1 million soldiers on active duty and in the reserve components, the army is the U.S. military's largest force. Soldiers represent more than half of the 2 million U.S. military forces deployed to Afghanistan and Iraq in support of OEF/OIF (Bonds et al., 2010). Among soldiers who participated in the Millennium Cohort Study, a large prospective study of U.S. service members that began in 2001, more than one fifth reported problematic anger, and rates of problematic anger were significantly higher among army personnel than among members of the air force and navy/coast guard (but comparable to rates among marines; Adler et al., 2020). Another recent nationally representative survey found that nearly half of soldiers (48.9%) engaged in at least one serious anger-related behavior (e.g., get angry at someone and yell, get angry and punch something, make a violent threat, fight/hit someone) in the past 30 days, and 10.2% reported five or more such behaviors (Meadows et al., 2018). All soldiers, regardless of deployment experience, are inherently linked to anger and aggression via the army's mission, training, and culture (Adler et al., 2017; Meyer et al., 2017; Novaco, 1994). The role of anger and anger control in the psychosocial health and functioning of soldiers varies across the different stages of military service. Importantly, risk for suicidal thoughts and behavior is also present throughout these stages. Figure 7.1 provides simplified examples of how anger may fluctuate before, during, and after military service; the potential co-occurrence of anger with life events and stressors; and the emergence of suicidal thoughts and behaviors.

Premilitary

Anger and its regulation (e.g., control/management) are components of normal psychosocial development that play a significant role in an individual's health prior to military service. A number of preenlistment demographic

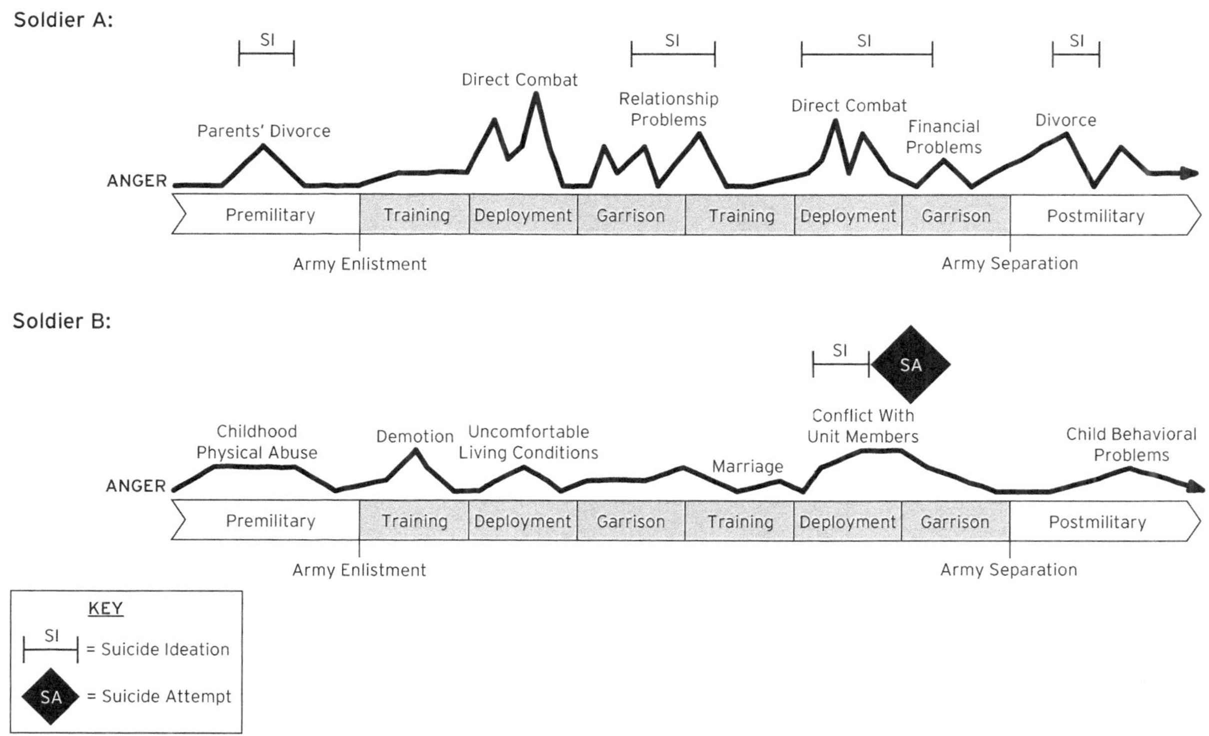

Note. Soldiers A and B represent two simplified examples of how anger may fluctuate over the life and career of soldiers who experience suicidal thoughts and behaviors. Major phases of army service are represented, including training, garrison (regular duties at a military post), and deployment. Also indicated are potential life events and stressors that may correspond with changes in anger and/or suicide risk. Soldier A experiences episodic suicide ideation throughout the life course but never acts on those thoughts, whereas Soldier B attempts suicide following first onset of ideation during army service. These simplified examples do not show other mental health symptoms that may co-occur with anger (e.g., depression, substance abuse) or the daily/hourly changes in anger that may correspond with increases or decreases in acute suicide risk.

and psychiatric factors have been associated with elevated anger responses (Banks & Albertson, 2018; Rosellini et al., 2016). U.S. Army accessions (individuals entering military service) are mostly young (17–20 years old; 65%) and male (86%; Office of the Under Secretary of Defense for Personnel and Readiness, 2017). Increased anger has been associated with younger age and male sex in both military (Novaco et al., 2012; Rona et al., 2015) and civilian populations. Compared with older adults, those who are younger are more likely to experience anger in response to interpersonal tension and less willing and able to adaptively manage anger (Birditt & Fingerman, 2003; Zimmermann & Iwanski, 2014).

Not only are the individuals entering military service at risk for problematic anger given their demographics, but they may join the military with certain expectations about how anger is regarded within the organization. With respect to sociocultural and environmental factors, popular media (e.g., Hollywood war movies) typically present anger as a normal part of military life and a highly valued means to enhance status, exhibit power, and assert masculinity (Chapin et al., 2017; Kiliçarslan, 2009), which may influence expectations prior to enlistment. Military culture is depicted in a milieu of emotional inflexibility, in which individuals are expected to adapt and complete the mission, relying on strength and aggression, with no place for other emotions such as fear and sadness. Arguably, the decision to voluntarily enlist in the army involves the appeal of military culture and, by extension, willingness to comply with norms.

For many soldiers, suicide risk also develops long before military service. Army STARRS survey data indicate that most active duty soldiers who have ever thought about or attempted suicide did so for the first time prior to army enlistment (Millner et al., 2019), with soldiers in their first week of basic training reporting substantial rates of preenlistment suicide ideation (14.1%), suicide plans (2.3%), and suicide attempts (1.9%; Ursano, Heeringa, et al., 2015). The same survey found that 38.7% of new soldiers reported a preenlistment history of mental disorders (Rosellini et al., 2015), and those preenlistment disorders were associated with increased risk of suicidal thoughts and behaviors (Nock et al., 2015). The early development of psychopathology appears to play an important role in soldier health and performance, as disorders with a preenlistment onset were found to be more consistent and powerful predictors of severe role impairment during service than disorders that began postenlistment (Kessler et al., 2014). Although meta-analyses have shown robust associations between anger and mental disorders among soldiers (Olatunji et al., 2010; Orth & Wieland, 2006), the degree to which preenlistment anger may be involved in the developmental trajectories of mental disorders and suicidal thoughts and behaviors among military personnel is not yet known. The importance of preservice suicide risk is not limited to military populations, with research finding that firefighters and emergency medical services (EMS) personnel reported higher rates of suicide ideation and attempts before joining their department than after joining (Martin et al., 2017).

It may be that childhood adversities are important contributors to suicidal behaviors, mental disorders, and dysregulated anger responses that emerge prior to enlistment. Army STARRS found that nearly 20% of new soldiers reported childhood maltreatment, including neglect and sexual, physical, and emotional abuse (Stein et al., 2018). Even after accounting for mental disorders and other types of trauma exposure, childhood maltreatment was associated with increased odds of lifetime suicide ideation, progression from ideation to a suicide plan, and progression from a plan to a suicide attempt (Stein et al., 2018). Childhood bullying victimization, reported by 33.2% of new soldiers, also increased the likelihood of preenlistment suicidal thoughts and behaviors, an association that persisted after adjusting for mental disorders and other childhood maltreatment (Campbell-Sills et al., 2017). Although the mechanisms involved in these associations are not yet known, childhood adversity may increase risk by sensitizing individuals to subsequent stressors (Bandoli et al., 2017). Adversities early in life are also associated with increases in trait anger during adulthood (Springer et al., 2007), possibly through biological alterations in executive control and processing of threat-related stimuli (Kim et al., 2018). Importantly, the negative consequences of childhood adversity are likely not limited to preenlistment outcomes, with survey research indicating that risk of problematic anger among current and former service members increases as the number of traumatic childhood experiences increases (Adler et al., 2020). Improved understanding of the developmental consequences of childhood adversity, particularly the ways in which it may alter sensitivity to perceived threats and the regulation of anger and other emotional responses, may illuminate the degree to which suicidal thoughts and behaviors during military service and other high-risk occupations are influenced by preemployment factors.

Military Training

Basic training, which defines the first phase of the civilian-to-soldier transition, represents a major socialization process featuring physical training and education on the army culture. Given its capacity to influence performance and enhance survival, basic training (and U.S. Army combat-related training in general) aims to override a fear-based "flight" response. During this initial phase, recruits engage in regimented behaviors that promote integration into military culture (i.e., "warrior culture") and conformity to military norms, including norms related to anger and its expression. Subsequent phases incorporate anger into a range of actions, from activating anger in order to push through adversity to practicing anger control in soldier–civilian conflict simulation training. Before proceeding, it is worth noting that warrior culture may not be entirely unique to the military. In particular, police officers may vary in approaching their job with a warrior versus guardian mindset, which may influence attitudes toward excessive use of force (McLean et al., 2020).

During initial army training, anger responses are modeled by training leaders (i.e., drill sergeants) and peers, with reflexive or automatic anger-enhanced, combat-appropriate responses developed through repetition and conditioning. These responses may range from yelling with anger in response to being summoned by superiors to pairing anger with physical training or combat maneuvers, and they are reinforced through rewards and punishments. Although fear is also a natural response to threat, because of its paralyzing nature, it is deemed dangerous and largely undesirable.

Importantly, it is during this initial training period, as new soldiers are working to adapt to military life, that rates of medically documented suicide ideation and attempts are highest. Army STARRS administrative data indicate that risk for both ideation and attempts peaks near the end of basic training and then declines as time in service increases (Ursano, Kessler, Stein, et al., 2015, 2017). Similarly, studies suggest that firefighters and police with fewer years of service are more likely to report suicide ideation, plans, and attempts (Stanley et al., 2015; Violanti, 2004).

Throughout a soldier's career, the ability to recognize and manage anger has important implications for success, both on and off the battlefield. Considering anger's association with approach motivational systems and survival value (Novaco, 2016), soldiers in combat may find anger useful in responding to threats and motivating behaviors in others. At garrison, anger may serve to communicate urgency and overcome daily obstacles. However, anger may also be problematic when dysregulated or inappropriate. Whether anger is problematic or not may be gauged by the context of occurrence and reaction parameters (e.g., intensity, duration, frequency, direction, and expression). Poorly managed anger may adversely impact soldiers' performance, team dynamics, and the organizational climate. Promoting anger control, stress management, and mental health in the context of the traditional warrior ethos is a significant but important challenge to address (Nash et al., 2011).

Anger Within Army Units

Although anger in the military can be adaptive, be appropriately directed, and optimize performance under many circumstances, it may also interfere with a service member's ability to function within social and occupational contexts if anger expression and intensity cannot be adequately regulated (Adler, 2018; Novaco et al., 2012). In the workplace, anger may be related to negative and antisocial interactions with coworkers (Struthers et al., 2001), as well as aggression toward peers, supervisors, and subordinates (Hershcovis et al., 2007; Inness et al., 2008), which can significantly interfere with unit cohesion and mission performance. This reduction in cohesion can have important implications for the well-being of unit members, as an Army STARRS survey of soldiers before and after combat deployment found that lower perceived unit cohesion was prospectively associated with increased risk of mental disorders and suicide ideation postdeployment (Anderson et al., 2019). When soldiers act on those suicidal thoughts, it may have effects that further disrupt unit functioning. Army STARRS administrative data indicate that risk of suicide attempt is higher among soldiers in units with a history of suicide attempts in the past year, and this risk increases as the number of previous unit suicide attempts increases (Ursano, Kessler, Naifeh, et al., 2017). Despite the potentially disruptive effects of anger on unit cohesion, which may in turn increase risk for suicidal thoughts and behaviors, many soldiers perceive anger as beneficial. This complex role of anger is highlighted by research indicating that nearly half (48%) of soldiers assessed after returning from deployment to Afghanistan indicated that anger was at least sometimes helpful in performing their duties, yet those soldiers were more likely to report mental and physical health symptoms and impaired functioning (Adler et al., 2017).

Work and Disciplinary Actions

Anger reactivity has a role in negative work-related behaviors, which can lead to disciplinary actions, termination, and in some cases legal consequences. Among civilians, anger is related to increased incidence of absenteeism, sabotage, theft, and plans to quit (P. Y. Chen & Spector, 1992; O'Neill et al., 2009). Among soldiers, anger is associated with unethical conduct during deployment (Wilk et al., 2013). Research on veterans has identified a number of factors, including combat exposure, PTSD, traumatic brain injury, and alcohol misuse, that increase risk for anger, aggression, and antisocial behavior, leading to disciplinary actions in the military as well as subsequent legal problems and incarceration (Backhaus et al., 2016).

Military Deployment

The recent conflicts in Afghanistan and Iraq have been marked by unconventional warfare and countless anger-eliciting circumstances. Soldiers are endangered by a virtually invisible enemy, often camouflaged within the civilian population, who employs improvised explosive devices and car bombs (Belmont et al., 2010). In contrast to other single-episode life events, such as motor vehicle accidents, natural disasters, or physical assault, deployment entails repeated and chronic exposure to potentially anger-provoking events (e.g., being shot at or wounded, witnessing human suffering or death, experiencing problems at home). Stressors that threaten physical and psychosocial well-being, such as being ambushed and/or captured, losing a friend, or killing, also often elicit anger (Henning & Frueh, 1997; Kam & Bond, 2008; Singer, 2004; Tangney, 1991). In a study of stressors among soldiers in Iraq, the events rated as most distressing were "Received hostile incoming fire" (32.9%) and "Received bad news from home" (28.6%; Lee et al., 2011). Combat stress reactions may also manifest as anger (Chemtob et al., 1997; McHugh et al., 2012; Novaco & Chemtob, 2002). Furthermore, soldiers are typically deployed more than once, and for relatively long periods (Bonds et al., 2010), potentially exposing soldiers to many anger-provoking circumstances.

Studies conducted on the battlefield further support the notion that anger is considerably prevalent during deployment. Field reports by behavioral health personnel in OEF/OIF found that anger was one of the most common mental health problems (Mental Health Advisory Team [MHAT] V, 2008). Many deployed soldiers reported high levels of concern over potentially anger-evoking conditions not directly linked to war-fighting, such as lack of privacy, boring or repetitive work, separation from family, and base camp rules and policies with no apparent linkage to maintaining combat readiness (MHAT IV, 2006). Reports also revealed both substantial frequency of anger episodes (e.g., getting angry at others) and problematic anger expression (e.g., get angry and kick something, slam the door, punch the wall) on the battlefield (Joint MHAT 8, 2013). However, not all soldiers expressed their anger outward toward others, with data showing that 40% reported keeping their anger "bottled up inside" (Joint MHAT 8, 2013).

Anger has also been linked to poor ethical behavior on the battlefield. Soldiers with high levels of anger in-theater were more than twice as likely as those with low anger to engage in unethical or inappropriate behavior (insulted/cursed noncombatants, damaged property unnecessarily, physically hit/kicked noncombatant; MHAT IV, 2006). Consequently, the MHAT advised that "leaders at all levels need to ensure that Soldiers who are having difficulty controlling their anger receive immediate corrective training" (MHAT IV, 2006, p. 81). Around mid-deployment, self-reported unethical behavior peaks (MHAT V, 2008). Importantly, mid-deployment is also the point at which self-reported individual and unit morale are lowest and rates of depression, anxiety, acute stress, and suicide ideation are highest (MHAT V, 2008). Based on Army STARRS administrative data, medically documented suicide attempts also peak around mid-deployment (Ursano et al., 2016). Assessment and treatment of anger in-theater (Reyes & Hicklin, 2005), particularly during the middle phase of deployment, may be an important component of improving soldier well-being and reducing suicide risk. The potential for uncontrolled anger to negatively affect decision making, including ethical decision making (Kligyte et al., 2013), is relevant to other high-risk occupations as well, particularly police officers (Brown & Daus, 2015). The influence of anger on decision making is important not only because of concerns about police misconduct, such as physical, sexual, or psychological victimization of citizens (DeVylder et al., 2017), but also because impaired decision making is associated with increased risk of attempting suicide, including increased risk of making the transition from ideation to attempt (Jollant et al., 2011; Saffer & Klonsky, 2018).

Postdeployment and Postmilitary

After deployment or military service, returning home is a complex process that may be both a relief and a stressor. Such transitions typically include significant alterations in physical (e.g., battlefield vs. home), cognitive (e.g., perceived threat vs. safety), social (e.g., combat buddies vs. family and new friends), and occupational (e.g., sniper vs. mail carrier) domains. Separation and relocation can erode social support, and new demands and roles can strain resources and threaten identities (Adler et al., 2017). Difficulty adapting after homecoming can trigger anger and negatively affect individuals and families (Riviere & Merrill, 2011; Sayer et al., 2010).

The potential mechanisms underlying the relationship of homecoming to anger remain unclear. Soldiers may face challenges associated with important transition-related factors, such as control over timing, resources, social support, and coping strategies (Schlossberg et al., 1995). Factors that elicit anger in soldiers during deployment, such as boredom, change of roles, and lack of preparedness, are likely to cause anger during homecoming as well. The homecoming–anger relationship is likely influenced by the interplay of factors arising before (e.g., combat stressors), during (e.g., difficulty managing PTSD), and after (e.g., unclear sense of identity) the transition.

Mental health seems particularly relevant to transition-related anger. Not only are PTSD and depression highly prevalent and independently associated with anger, the common co-occurrence of these disorders significantly intensifies anger (Gonzalez et al., 2016). The relationship between anger, mental health, and suicide risk after deployment may become more important over time. Self-reported mental health concerns are significantly greater 3 to 6 months postdeployment than immediately upon return (Milliken et al., 2007), and Army STARRS administrative data indicate that documented suicide attempts follow the same pattern, with risk peaking at 5 months postdeployment (Ursano et al., 2016). Furthermore, administrative records from the army's postdeployment mental health screening programs indicate that soldiers who screen positive for depression or PTSD after returning from deployment are more likely to attempt suicide than those who screen negative, and risk is particularly high for those who screen positive both immediately after returning home and again several months later (Ursano et al., 2016). Separation from the military and reintegration into civilian life is a life-course transition that may be associated with increased suicide risk (Bullman et al., 2018; Wang et al., 2020), and survey data indicate that rates of problematic anger are higher among veterans than those still serving (Adler et al., 2020). It is possible that postseparation suicide risk is not similarly elevated for those in other high-risk occupations, with one study finding that separated or retired police officers had substantially lower suicide risk than those still serving (Violanti et al., 2011).

Interpersonal Relationships and Anger After Deployment

Soldiers may experience a variety of interpersonal stressors upon returning from deployment, including role changes (e.g., a spouse becoming more independent and handling financial and family decisions while the soldier was gone), feeling misunderstood and/or unappreciated by civilians who have never experienced combat, and difficulty discussing deployment experiences with family and friends. Postdeployment research suggests that anger is an "unmistakable readjustment problem" (Novaco & Chemtob, 2015, p. 490) for soldiers as they transition home, significantly affecting interpersonal relationships. Soldiers' concerns about interpersonal conflict increase substantially over the initial months postdeployment (Milliken et al., 2007), reflecting the impact that anger may have on relationships during this period. Studies examining large samples of OEF/OIF soldiers after deployment found that aggressive behaviors, including getting angry with someone and kicking, smashing, or punching something; threatening someone with physical violence; and getting into a fight and pushing or hitting someone were reported by between 14% and 38% of soldiers (Gallaway et al., 2012; Thomas et al., 2010), with 67.3% of soldiers endorsing aggressive behavior in the past month (Wright et al., 2012). Experiences during deployment may be predictive of adverse outcomes in soldiers upon return home, with combat exposure specifically found to be associated with anger and relationship problems upon returning home (Killgore et al., 2008; Maguen et al., 2010). Interventions that help soldiers manage anger (Linkh & Sonnek, 2003) and early symptoms of psychological trauma (Forbes et al., 2011) may help prevent more severe distress, interpersonal violence, and suicide risk.

ANGER, MENTAL DISORDERS, AND SUICIDAL BEHAVIOR

While a range of internalizing (i.e., covert, difficult to observe) and externalizing (i.e., overt, highly observable) mental disorders may contribute to our understanding of suicide in the military and other high-risk occupations (Millner et al., 2019; Nock et al., 2015; Stanley et al., 2016), here we highlight several specific disorders because of their relevance to, and co-occurrence with, both anger and suicidal behavior among soldiers: PTSD, MDD, BP, SUD, and IED (see Table 7.1). We discuss associations of these disorders with suicide ideation and suicide attempts, as well as with attempts among ideators. The latter is crucial for understanding the transition from suicidal thoughts to suicidal behavior. This area of ongoing research is important, as studies to date have found that most apparent risk factors for suicide attempt in the population are really only risk factors for suicide ideation and do not predict attempts among ideators (Nock et al., 2016).

Although the majority of research findings are based on self-report survey data, evidence also highlights the importance of clinician diagnosis. For example, among U.S. suicide decedents, firefighters were less likely than others to have a depressive disorder diagnosis but more likely to have a PTSD diagnosis (Pennington et al., 2021). Army STARRS administrative data have shown that soldiers who receive a diagnosis of PTSD, depression, or SUD, particularly a recent diagnosis, are more likely to subsequently attempt suicide, and this remains true whether they have never deployed, are currently deployed (i.e., in-theater), or had previously deployed (Ursano et al., 2016).

Posttraumatic Stress Disorder

PTSD, anger, and aggression often co-occur in military and first responder populations (Heinrichs et al., 2005; Jakupcak et al., 2007; Meffert et al., 2008;

TABLE 7.1. Associations of Mental Disorders With Subsequent Suicidal Thoughts and Behaviors in an Army STARRS Survey of U.S. Soldiers Worldwide

	Lifetime suicidal thoughts and behaviors					
	Men			Women		
Mental disorder[a]	Suicide ideation	Suicide attempt	Attempt among ideators	Suicide ideation	Suicide attempt	Attempt among ideators
Posttraumatic stress disorder	+	+		+	+	
Major depressive disorder	+	+		+	+	
Bipolar disorder	+	+		+	+	
Substance use disorder	+	+	+	+	+	
Intermittent explosive disorder	+	+	+	+	+	

Note. A plus sign indicates that a mental disorder has a positive association with (increases risk for) the outcome indicated in the column. Data are from the Army Study to Assess Risk and Resilience in Servicemembers (Army STARRS) Consolidated All Army Survey, which is representative of all U.S. Army soldiers around the world, exclusive of those in basic training (Millner et al., 2019).
[a]Each disorder was examined separately in a multivariable logistic regression model that adjusted for sociodemographic and army career characteristics.

Taft et al., 2007; Wilk et al., 2015), which may increase risk of suicidal behavior (Hellmuth et al., 2012; Jakupcak et al., 2009). Research examining these interrelationships among Iraq and Afghanistan veterans found that the *Diagnostic and Statistical Manual of Mental Disorders* (4th ed.; American Psychiatric Association, 1994) PTSD reexperiencing cluster was directly related to aggression, and the PTSD emotional numbing and hyperarousal clusters were indirectly related to aggression, mediated by trait anger (Hellmuth et al., 2012). Interestingly, in addition to an overall association between PTSD symptom severity and lifetime suicide ideation and attempts among firefighters and EMS personnel (Martin et al., 2017), there is evidence that risk for suicide-related outcomes may be specifically associated with the reexperiencing and emotional numbing clusters (Boffa et al., 2017).

Army STARRS surveys found that the lifetime prevalence of PTSD among all soldiers who had completed in basic training was 31.7% for men and 41.6% for women, with 31.1% to 42.4% of men–women reporting preenlistment first onset (Millner et al., 2019). The 30-day prevalence of PTSD was 8.6% (Kessler et al., 2014). Soldiers entering basic training also report substantial rates of lifetime PTSD (12.6%; Rosellini et al., 2015). Among new soldiers with a preenlistment history of attempted suicide, 14% reported preattempt onset of PTSD (Nock et al., 2015). Controlling for other mental disorders and sociodemographic and army career characteristics, temporally prior PTSD predicted suicide ideation, suicide attempt, and attempts among ideators in the total army population (Millner et al., 2019; Nock et al., 2015). However, when the population was stratified by gender and attempts were disaggregated, preenlistment PTSD predicted the transition from ideation to postenlistment attempts only among men (Millner et al., 2019). The importance of PTSD was further supported by a separate army STARRS case-control study that found PTSD to be one of the few variables that differentiated soldiers hospitalized for attempted suicide from soldiers stationed at the same army installations who reported 30-day suicide ideation but did not make an attempt (Naifeh, Ursano, et al., 2019). In the context of military health, anger is far more than a symptom of PTSD—it can affect the severity, course, and treatment of PTSD, and it is associated with major adjustment problems for soldiers (Gonzalez et al., 2016; Novaco et al., 2012).

Major Depressive Disorder

Depressive symptom severity has been associated with increased risk for lifetime suicide ideation and suicide attempt in firefighters and EMS personnel (Martin et al., 2017). Anger is commonly reported among individuals diagnosed with MDD (Fava et al., 2010; Judd et al., 2013; Novaco, 2010). Among soldiers with self-reported MDD or PTSD, 50% reported alcohol misuse or fighting or hitting others at least once within the past month (Thomas et al., 2010). For individuals with depression, in addition to exhibiting anger and aggression directed at others, they may also direct anger toward themselves, expressed as suicidal thoughts and/or behavior (Novaco, 2010). Among men in particular, the externalizing symptoms that may be associated with depression (e.g., anger, risk-taking, substance use and abuse) increase risk of suicide attempt (Rice et al., 2018).

An Army STARRS survey representative of all soldiers worldwide (exclusive of those in basic training) found that the prevalence of lifetime MDD was 22.4% among men and 34.9% among women, with slightly more than half (50.3% of men, 54.1% of women) reporting first onset prior to enlistment (Millner et al., 2019). The 30-day prevalence of MDD was 4.8% (Kessler et al., 2014). Soldiers entering basic training also reported substantial rates of MDD (7.8%) prior to army enlistment (Rosellini et al., 2015), with 17% of preenlistment suicide attempters reporting temporally prior MDD

(Nock et al., 2015). Controlling for other mental disorders and sociodemographic and army career characteristics, soldiers with a history of MDD were more likely than those without to report lifetime suicide ideation and attempt (Millner et al., 2019; Nock et al., 2015). Although MDD predicted attempts among ideators in the total population (Nock et al., 2015, 2018), when the predictors and outcomes were disaggregated and soldiers were stratified by gender, the only significant association was that preenlistment MDD predicted postenlistment attempts among male ideators (Millner et al., 2019). Not only is the salience of MDD reflected in its association with anger, high prevalence, and frequent co-occurrence with PTSD, evidence further reveals that anger is significantly greater among veterans screening positive for both MDD and PTSD, compared with those meeting screening criteria for either disorder alone or neither (Gonzalez et al., 2016).

Bipolar Disorder

Anger can play a prominent role in BP, with irritability presenting as a feature particularly during hypomanic episodes (Novaco, 2010). Although anger has been associated with episodes of both MDD and BP, anger attacks are more likely to be observed in individuals with BP (Perlis et al., 2004). Risk of suicide among individuals with BP is high, with 29% of patients reporting at least one lifetime suicide attempt (Y.-W. Chen & Dilsaver, 1996). Patients with BP who attempted suicide are more likely to have a history of aggression, which increases the likelihood of acting on feelings of anger (Oquendo et al., 2000).

In Army STARRS surveys, assessment of BP included a combination of BP I and II, plus subthreshold BP (hypomania without history of major depression or subthreshold hypomania). The prevalence of lifetime BP among all soldiers worldwide (exclusive of those in basic training) was 3.7% among both men and women, with slightly more than half (39.7%–45.7% of women–men) reporting first onset prior to enlistment (Millner et al., 2019). The 30-day prevalence of BP was 3.3% (Kessler et al., 2014). A similar lifetime rate was reported among soldiers entering basic training (3.6%; Rosellini et al., 2015). Controlling for other mental disorders and sociodemographic and army career characteristics, soldiers with a history of BP were more likely to report lifetime suicide ideation and attempt (Millner et al., 2019; Nock et al., 2015). Although BP predicted the preenlistment transition from suicide ideation to unplanned attempt among soldiers entering basic training, it did not predict the ideation-to-attempt transition in more experienced soldiers (Millner et al., 2019; Nock et al., 2018). Specific features of BP, such as high affective lability that presents as a rapid switch from neutral affect to anger, can predict suicide ideation (Ducasse et al., 2017). Difficulties related to anger in individuals with BP continue to be observed outside of depressive and manic episodes (Ballester et al., 2014), often related to emotion-relevant impulsivity even during periods of remission (Johnson & Carver, 2016), making the risk of anger-related aggression and violence worthy of clinical attention in this population.

Substance Abuse

SUD constitutes a major health problem for military populations and their families, with service members reporting higher rates of alcohol misuse than civilians (Sirratt et al., 2012) and army rates being particularly elevated among U.S. military branches (Stahre et al., 2009). Elevated rates of alcohol abuse have been identified among first responders as well, although the extent of such problems may differ by country (Ballenger et al., 2011; Richmond et al., 1998; Sterud et al., 2007). A survey of male firefighters in the United States found that alcohol was consumed an average of 10 days in the past month, with 53% reporting that they consumed at least three drinks on the days they drank and 56% reporting past-month binge drinking (Haddock et al., 2012). Among soldiers, alcohol consumption and binge drinking are more common among those with high levels of combat exposure (Meadows et al., 2018). SUD and anger often co-occur in military populations (Novaco & Chemtob, 2015; Teten et al., 2009). One in 14 (7.4%) soldiers reported that drinking led to serious anger-related consequences in the past year (e.g., "I hit my spouse/significant other after having too much to drink"; Meadows et al., 2018). While anger may be a consequence of substance abuse (Giancola, 2000), anger also has been found to increase alcohol use among veterans (Lane et al., 2019; Simpson et al., 2012).

An Army STARRS survey of soldiers entering basic training found that the lifetime prevalence of preenlistment SUD was 12.6%, which did not differ from comparable civilians (Rosellini et al., 2015). Among all other male and female soldiers, lifetime prevalence estimates of SUD were 14.4% and 11.0%, respectively (Millner et al., 2019). Among men, 44.3% of those with lifetime SUD had a preenlistment onset. Similarly, 43.6% of women with lifetime SUD reported a preenlistment onset. The 30-day prevalence of SUD among nondeployed soldiers was 4.8% (Kessler et al., 2014). Army-wide, a history of SUD was associated with subsequent suicide ideation and attempt, even after controlling for other mental disorders and for sociodemographic and army career variables (Millner et al., 2019; Nock et al., 2015). Although SUD predicted suicide attempts among ideators overall

(Nock et al., 2015, 2018), disaggregation of the variables and stratification by gender found that preenlistment SUD predicted the transition to post-enlistment suicide attempts only among male ideators (Millner et al., 2019).

Focusing specifically on the lifetime use and abuse of alcohol among soldiers entering basic training, 27.2% of men and 18.9% of women reported a preenlistment history of binge drinking, and 13.9% and 9.4% reported a history of heavy drinking (consuming five or more alcoholic drinks at least 1 day a week; Stein et al., 2017). Binge drinking, heavy drinking, and alcohol use disorder (AUD) were all associated with increased odds of lifetime and past 30-day suicide ideation. Associations between AUD and suicide ideation were bidirectional, such that AUD was associated with subsequent onset of suicide ideation and suicide ideation was associated with subsequent onset of AUD (Stein et al., 2017). It is also important to consider the potential role of prescription drug misuse, which has been found to differentiate Australian emergency services personnel who reported a suicide attempt from those who reported only a history of suicide ideation (Kyron et al., 2021). Given the association of anger and substance misuse observed in wounded combat veterans who were prescribed sedatives for pain or mental health issues (Kelley et al., 2019), and the elevated levels of anger found to be associated with SUD persistence in both treatment samples and among the general population (Barrett et al., 2013; Reilly & Shopshire, 2000), strategies to manage anger should be an important target in SUD interventions. Previous research indicating that increased anger predicts poor SUD treatment outcomes (Witkiewitz & Villarroel, 2009) further highlights its potential role in clinical interventions.

Intermittent Explosive Disorder

Anger is central to the diagnosis of IED, an impulse control disorder characterized by frequent behavioral outbursts that may take the form of physical aggression and verbal arguments. Although the prevalence of IED is relatively low in the general population, with 12-month and lifetime rates of 3.9% and 7.3%, respectively (Kessler et al., 2005), the negative occupational, legal, financial, and relationship consequences for those with IED can be far-reaching. General population surveys have found that IED is associated with suicide ideation and attempt and, importantly, predicts attempts among ideators (Nock et al., 2008, 2009, 2010). Similarly, higher rates of suicide ideation were found among Australian emergency services personnel reporting intermittent explosive anger (Kyron et al., 2021). Individuals for whom IED is comorbid with PTSD exhibit particularly high levels of aggressive behavior and are at an elevated risk for suicide attempt (Fanning et al., 2016). Considering the high rates of trauma exposure and PTSD in military and first responder populations, attention to the co-occurrence of IED is important for mitigating suicide risk.

In a representative Army STARRS survey of all soldiers worldwide (exclusive of those in basic training), the lifetime prevalence of IED was 19.8% among men and 14.8% among women, with 71.6%–78.7% of women–men reporting first onset prior to enlistment (Millner et al., 2019; Nock et al., 2015). The 30-day prevalence of IED was 11.2% (Kessler et al., 2014). Among new soldiers entering basic training, the preenlistment prevalence of IED was 14.6%, which does not differ significantly from comparable civilians (Rosellini et al., 2015). Among both new and experienced soldiers, temporally prior IED was associated with lifetime suicide ideation and suicide attempt, even after controlling for other mental disorders and sociodemographic and army career characteristics (Millner et al., 2019; Nock et al., 2015). Twenty-five percent of new soldiers with a preenlistment suicide attempt reported temporally prior IED, making it one of the most prevalent disorders among attempters. Among those entering basic training with a history suicide ideation, IED did not predict the critical transition from thinking about suicide to acting on those thoughts (Nock et al., 2015). However, a survey of all other soldiers worldwide found that male ideators with a history of IED were twice as likely to have made a planned suicide attempt (Millner et al., 2019). Focusing on postenlistment suicide attempts, which are most relevant to understanding suicide in the context of army service, both pre- and postenlistment onsets of IED were associated with postenlistment suicide attempts among men, but only preenlistment IED predicted the transition from ideation to postenlistment attempt (Nock et al., 2015). IED was not associated with the transition from ideation to lifetime or postenlistment suicide attempt among women (Millner et al., 2019), suggesting that there may be important gender differences in the relationship between IED and suicidal behavior among active duty soldiers. Importantly, the diagnostic criteria for IED represent a particular manifestation of problematic anger limited to explosive outbursts of aggression. There is a need for representative survey research examining other forms of anger and aggression in relation to suicidal behaviors among soldiers, particularly the transition from ideation to attempt.

Anger in the Context of Co-Occurring Mental Disorders

While the Army STARRS survey results just summarized indicate that anger-relevant mental disorders are associated with suicide attempts in the army general population, even after controlling for the presence of other disorders, few of those findings speak directly to the independent contribution of anger. One exception to this is IED, which in addition to its association with suicide attempts above and beyond other comorbid disorders is one of the few disorders that predicted the transition from ideation to attempt (Millner et al., 2019; Nock et al., 2014). In fact, IED continued to predict attempts among ideators even after accounting for other important characteristics related to self-injury, including history of nonsuicidal self-injury (i.e., self-harm without intent to die) and the frequency, duration, and controllability of suicide ideation (Nock et al., 2018). It is not yet known whether the broader range of anger-related experiences, beyond the narrow confines of IED criteria, are similarly associated with suicidal behavior independent of comorbid disorders. There also is a paucity of research on the interactive effects of anger and co-occurring disorders on suicidal behavior, an important consideration given evidence that anger among combat veterans is intensified in the presence comorbid PTSD and depression (Gonzalez et al., 2016).

FAMILY VIOLENCE AND CRIME PERPETRATION

Exposure to interpersonal violence before or during military service is associated with increased risk of suicidal thoughts and behavior in service members (Afifi et al., 2016; Bryan et al., 2015; Cox et al., 2011; Gradus et al., 2013; Perales et al., 2012), and this association persists even after adjusting for mental health problems (Belik et al., 2009). The influence of interpersonal violence on suicidal behavior is particularly important within the context of a family, which is a source of social support that may protect against suicide ideation following combat deployment (Gradus et al., 2015). An Army STARRS analysis of administrative records found that soldiers with documented family violence during service (as either victims or perpetrators) were more likely than other soldiers to subsequently attempt suicide (Ursano, Stein, et al., 2018), an association that was present among males and females, deployed and nondeployed soldiers, and those with and without a history of mental health diagnosis (Ursano, Kessler, et al., 2018; Ursano, Stein, et al., 2018). Furthermore, risk of suicide attempt increased as the number and recency of family violence events increased (Ursano, Stein, et al., 2018).

Most research on family violence (e.g., physical or sexual abuse of spouses/partners or children) has focused on those victimized by such acts, with evidence suggesting that family violence victimization increases risk for suicidal thoughts and behaviors among active duty service members and veterans (Belik et al., 2009; Cerulli et al., 2014; Langhinrichsen-Rohling et al., 2011; Ursano, Stein, et al., 2018). Although perpetration of family violence has received less attention as a risk factor for suicidal behavior, it is particularly relevant in the context of a discussion about anger (Birkley & Eckhardt, 2015). Army STARRS found that family violence perpetration, as documented in legal, family services, and medical records, was associated with elevated risk of subsequent suicide attempt (Ursano, Kessler, et al., 2018). Although risk of suicide attempt was elevated for both victims and perpetrators overall, male perpetrators were more likely to attempt suicide than male victims, whereas female perpetrators and female victims did not differ in risk of a subsequent suicide attempt (Ursano, Stein, et al., 2018). Family violence may be a concern in other high-risk occupations as well, with one review finding that prevalence rates of self-reported domestic violence perpetration among law enforcement officers ranged widely, from 4.8% to 40% (Mennicke & Ropes, 2016).

Violent interpersonal behavior has been associated with anger, impulsivity, and PTSD in service members and veterans (Beckham et al., 1998; Worthen et al., 2014). These characteristics, in turn, have been predictive of suicidal behavior (Bender et al., 2011; Conner et al., 2006; Nock et al., 2014; Swogger et al., 2011; Zouk et al., 2006). For example, in a study of military recruits in basic training, those with histories of suicide ideation and attempt reported greater impulsivity than those without a history of suicidal thoughts and behaviors (Klonsky & May, 2010).

Beyond family violence, perpetration of crime is another behavior relevant to both anger and suicidal behavior. Crime perpetration is associated with elevated suicide risk in general population studies (Webb et al., 2011, 2012), and military research has found that service members who received an enlistment waiver for a history of violating the law were more likely to die by suicide (Shen et al., 2016). In an analysis of administrative records, Army STARRS found that documented crime perpetration was associated with suicide attempts among soldiers with and without a history of mental health diagnosis (Ursano, Kessler, et al., 2018). Specifically, soldiers who perpetrated any category of crime (major violent, minor violent, nonviolent) were more likely to subsequently attempt suicide than those with no crime perpetration, and this was true whether or not they had a previous mental health diagnosis. Perpetrators of major violent crime were more than 3 times as likely as nonperpetrators to attempt suicide (Ursano, Kessler, et al., 2018).

FUTURE DIRECTIONS AND RECOMMENDATIONS

To further understand and address the relationship between anger and suicide in high-risk occupations, particularly military service members, targeted intervention programs and research are recommended.

Anger Assessment

The military is required to administer annual mental health assessments that examine PTSD, depression, alcohol misuse, and risk of suicide and violence, from which service members may be referred for care based on these assessments (Office of the Under Secretary of Defense, 2018). It may be valuable to incorporate brief assessments of anger and aggression. Additionally, given the substantial proportion of new recruits entering army service with a history of suicidal behavior and mental disorders, early screening may help identify problems with co-occurring anger before they are exacerbated by the stressors associated with military acculturation, training, deployment, homecoming, and separation. In addition to considering positive endorsements of anger, suicidal thoughts and behaviors, and other mental health symptoms on screening instruments, it may be valuable to consider patterns of nonresponse as potential indicators of risk. For example, a study of diverse emergency services personnel (e.g., police, fire and rescue, ambulance) found that individuals who preferred not to answer suicide-related questions reported higher levels of depression and anxiety and lower levels of well-being and social support compared with both those who reported suicide ideation and those who reported no ideation (Kyron et al., 2020).

Anger Management

Because of the consistent relationship of anger to adverse mental and physical health outcomes and violent behavior, and its role as a risk factor for suicidal behavior, early identification and management of life/occupational stressors is an important component of preventive interventions. For example, soldiers returning home from combat deployment may misinterpret ambiguous stimuli as potentially dangerous or perceive minor events as carrying malicious intent, which can result in inappropriately aggressive responses (Morland et al., 2012). Interventions that include anger management strategies, such as guided practice techniques (e.g., focused relaxation and behavioral response training), and cognitive behavior therapy (CBT) have been found to be effective in managing anger (i.e., reducing anger affect and aggressive behaviors and increasing positive behaviors; DiGiuseppe & Tafrate, 2003; Morland et al., 2012; see also the chapter by Morland et al., Chapter 8, this volume). CBT, in particular, was identified in a meta-analysis as the most successful in treating problems with anger outbursts (Del Vecchio & O'Leary, 2004). Although research on the effects of anger management treatment with military populations is limited, CBT-based group anger management treatment was found to reduce self-reported state and trait anger in a military and Department of Defense civilian sample (Linkh & Sonnek, 2003). Treatment for anger symptoms may also be incorporated into interventions for co-occurring mental disorders, such as PTSD (Forbes et al., 2005). Efforts to improve anger management may be aided by advancements in mobile technology, such as smartphones and wearable sensors (Mackintosh et al., 2017). The U.S. Department of Veterans Affairs recently launched a web-based anger management course as a resource for current and former service members (https://www.veterantraining.va.gov/aims/). It is also important to consider steps that can be taken before significant problems develop following combat or other occupational trauma exposure. For example, psychological first aid is an early posttrauma intervention that aims to promote emotion regulation in order to reduce distress and assist recovery (Forbes et al., 2011). Additionally, there has been recent interest in mindfulness training to enhance service member resilience through improved cognitive, emotional, and behavioral regulation (Jha et al., 2010, 2020). Mindfulness-based interventions may benefit personnel in other high-risk occupations as well, with preliminary evidence suggesting that a mindfulness training improved resilience and reduced aggression in law enforcement officers (Chopko et al., 2018; Christopher et al., 2018). To be successful, programs that promote anger control and mental health must be designed and implemented in ways that recognize and respect the cultures of high-risk occupations (e.g., the army's warrior culture; e.g., Brintz et al., 2020).

Any efforts to change the cultural role of anger in these occupations should be undertaken in ways that value the organization's primary goals (e.g., to fight and win wars; aid those in need) and appreciate the adaptive role that anger plays in the context of high threat and urgency. Unlike the more static work environments of other occupations, the "workplace" in high-risk occupations can be chaotic, fast-paced, dynamic, and life-threatening, whether it is soldiers being ambushed, police officers attempting to arrest a fleeing suspect, paramedics engaged in crowd control during an emergency, or firefighters trying to evacuate residents from a building. The challenge is to communicate to personnel that anger can become problematic when it is context inappropriate, too frequent, too lasting, or too intense, or when it negatively influences health or functioning within biological, psychological, or social domains. In the army, leaders, chaplains, and mental health providers can help soldiers recognize that anger can be both an asset and a vulnerability depending on the context (e.g., the battlefield vs. at home with family), understand the difference between feeling anger and how one expresses that anger, and learn how to express alternatives to anger.

Social Support

Social support is a protective factor associated with lower risk of suicidal thoughts and behavior (Kleiman & Liu, 2013). Among firefighters, occupational stress was associated with suicide ideation in those with low social support, whereas high social support buffered the effects occupational stress (Carpenter et al., 2015). Dysregulated anger and aggression may erode important support networks, reducing the quality, quantity, and reliability of social support available to a soldier, veteran, or first responder. Developing programs to enhance social support from family, friends, leaders, and peers may help mitigate anger-related distress and aggressive/violent behavior directed toward oneself and others. More research is needed to determine the timing (e.g., during training, before/during/after deployment, while in garrison), source (e.g., family, friends, peers, leaders), and mode (e.g., in-person, online, mobile) of the most effective interventions. In addition to programs that aim to foster support from peers (e.g., battle buddies, support groups) and family members (e.g., couples therapy, family therapy), there is a need to explore universal interventions that can help individuals across the organization develop adaptive social and emotional skills. For example, a cognitive-behavioral program administered to entire divisions of U.S. Navy recruits during basic training was found to reduce anger expression and improve group cohesion, perceived social support, and use of problem-solving coping strategies, resulting in lower attrition from service (Williams et al., 2007). Early-career training programs such as this may provide service members and first responders with valuable skills that promote adaptive intra- and interpersonal functioning, helping them to establish and maintain social connections. Sustaining the positive effects of an early-career intervention may require booster trainings, as career transitions (e.g., joining a new unit, reintegrating after deployment) can introduce new stressors and disrupt established social networks. It is also important for programs to address the unique social challenges and needs of individuals who are leaving service and returning to civilian life, a major transition that often results in difficulty maintaining previous friendships, making new friends, and getting along with family members (Drebing et al., 2018; Sayer et al., 2010).

Research

Systematic research is needed to develop a deeper, more textured understanding of anger in high-risk occupations. Longitudinal studies can illuminate how anger symptoms evolve over time in the context of different career phases, stressors, and transitions. There is also a need to understand risk among individuals who have served in multiple high-risk occupations, such as law enforcement officers or firefighters with a with prior military service. The continuation of Army STARRS, now called STARRS-LS for "longitudinal study" (https://www.starrs-ls.org), includes repeated follow-up interviews with the original survey respondents as they move through their army career and back into civilian life. Its extensive databases provide opportunities to investigate the demographic, psychological, biological, neurocognitive, behavioral, and social correlates of anger and anger-related outcomes.

Areas of research needing further investigation include the role of anger in the etiology and maintenance of suicidal thoughts and behaviors, including the independent and interactive associations of anger in the presence of other psychological vulnerabilities and mental disorders (Start et al., 2019); the developmental impact of childhood adversities on anger regulation and the potential role of adversity-related biological alterations in subsequent risk for suicidal thoughts and behaviors; resilience factors that protect against the development and intensification of dysregulated anger responses; and a more nuanced understanding of anger as both an adaptive and maladaptive emotion in the context of military service and service in other high-risk occupations. It is also important to determine the extent to which research based on U.S. military service members and veterans, including the Army STARRS findings reviewed in this chapter, translate to other militaries and high-risk occupations around the world. In addition to differences in occupation-specific roles, cultural factors, and stressors, there may be important selection biases (e.g., career choice, voluntary vs. compulsory military service) that influence the psychosocial characteristics of those in various high-risk occupations. Research is needed to understand whether such factors modify the influence of anger on health, functioning, and suicide risk.

Risk Prediction

The negative outcomes associated with family violence and crime perpetration, including suicidal behavior, could be reduced through better identification of at-risk soldiers. Consistent with a precision medicine approach, Army STARRS has developed machine learning algorithms to improve prediction of sexual violence perpetration (Ursano, Kessler, et al., 2018), nonfamilial major physical violent crime perpetration (Rosellini et al., 2017), and minor violent crime perpetration (Rosellini et al., 2016), and even interpersonal violence during deployment (Rosellini et al., 2018). Such models may serve as decision-support tools for clinicians and leaders, assisting in more cost-effectively targeting interventions to soldiers with the highest level of need and, ultimately, matching individual soldiers to the right intervention.

CONCLUSION

Anger is an important consideration in both the adaptive and maladaptive behaviors of soldiers and first responders. Addressing the suicide risk associated with anger, anger-related mental disorders, family violence, and crime perpetration requires understanding of the important and complex role of anger within the culture of each high-risk occupation. It also requires awareness of when, where, and why maladaptive anger responses arise over the course of an individual's life and career. Many individuals enter service with a history of anger-related mental health problems and suicidal thoughts and behaviors, and anger-related outcomes are subsequently influenced by the stressors encountered in high-risk occupations (e.g., training, deployment, homecoming, separation). Prevention of these negative outcomes, including suicidal behavior, may be aided by screening for anger-related problems, implementing evidence-based therapies (e.g., CBT for anger management) and early posttrauma interventions (e.g., psychological first aid), enhancing social support from important people in an individual's life, targeted research to better understand anger in the context of specific high-risk occupations, and developing risk algorithms that can help direct resources to personnel with the greatest need.

IMPLICATIONS

- It is important to assess and treat co-occurring anger in the context of mental disorders that increase suicide risk, including PTSD, MDD, BP, and SUD.
- Assessment and treatment of IED may be particularly important for preventing the transition from suicide ideation to suicide attempt.

- Programs are needed to help personnel effectively regulate anger responses in order to preserve the adaptive role of anger in job performance while diminishing uncontrolled and context-inappropriate anger responses.
- Mid-deployment is a particularly important time for assessment and intervention focused on anger, mental health, and suicide risk among soldiers.
- It is important for future research to examine the role of anger in predicting the transition from thinking about suicide to acting on those thoughts.
- Machine learning algorithms may be useful in predicting which individuals are at greatest risk for family violence and crime perpetration.

REFERENCES

Adler, A. B. (2018). How helpful is anger when soldiers return from combat? *Public Health Post*. https://www.publichealthpost.org/research/helpful-anger-soldiers-return-combat/

Adler, A. B., Brossart, D. F., & Toblin, R. L. (2017). Can anger be helpful? Soldier perceptions of the utility of anger. *The Journal of Nervous and Mental Disease, 205*(9), 692–698. https://doi.org/10.1097/NMD.0000000000000712

Adler, A. B., LeardMann, C. A., Roenfeldt, K. A., Jacobson, I. G., & Forbes, D., for the Millennium Cohort Study Team. (2020). Magnitude of problematic anger and its predictors in the Millennium Cohort. *BMC Public Health, 20*(1), 1168. https://doi.org/10.1186/s12889-020-09206-2

Afifi, T. O., Taillieu, T., Zamorski, M. A., Turner, S., Cheung, K., & Sareen, J. (2016). Association of child abuse exposure with suicidal ideation, suicide plans, and suicide attempts in military personnel and the general population in Canada. *JAMA Psychiatry, 73*(3), 229–238. https://doi.org/10.1001/jamapsychiatry.2015.2732

American Psychiatric Association. (1994). *Diagnostic and statistical manual of mental disorders* (4th ed.).

Anderson, L., Campbell-Sills, L., Ursano, R. J., Kessler, R. C., Sun, X., Heeringa, S. G., Nock, M. K., Bliese, P. D., Gonzalez, O. I., Wynn, G. H., Jain, S., & Stein, M. B. (2019). Prospective associations of perceived unit cohesion with postdeployment mental health outcomes. *Depression and Anxiety, 36*(6), 511–521. https://doi.org/10.1002/da.22884

Avraham, N., Goldblatt, H., & Yafe, E. (2014). Paramedics' experiences and coping strategies when encountering critical incidents. *Qualitative Health Research, 24*(2), 194–208. https://doi.org/10.1177/1049732313519867

Backhaus, A., Gholizadeh, S., Godfrey, K. M., Pittman, J., & Afari, N. (2016). The many wounds of war: The association of service-related and clinical characteristics with problems with the law in Iraq and Afghanistan veterans. *International*

Journal of Law and Psychiatry, *49*(Pt. B), 205–213. https://doi.org/10.1016/j.ijlp.2016.10.007

Ballenger, J. F., Best, S. R., Metzler, T. J., Wasserman, D. A., Mohr, D. C., Liberman, A., Delucchi, K., Weiss, D. S., Fagan, J. A., Waldrop, A. E., & Marmar, C. R. (2011). Patterns and predictors of alcohol use in male and female urban police officers. *The American Journal on Addictions*, *20*(1), 21–29. https://doi.org/10.1111/j.1521-0391.2010.00092.x

Ballester, J., Goldstein, B., Goldstein, T. R., Yu, H., Axelson, D., Monk, K., Hickey, M. B., Diler, R. S., Sakolsky, D. J., Sparks, G., Iyengar, S., Kupfer, D. J., Brent, D. A., & Birmaher, B. (2014). Prospective longitudinal course of aggression among adults with bipolar disorder. *Bipolar Disorders*, *16*(3), 262–269. https://doi.org/10.1111/bdi.12168

Bandoli, G., Campbell-Sills, L., Kessler, R. C., Heeringa, S. G., Nock, M. K., Rosellini, A. J., Sampson, N. A., Schoenbaum, M., Ursano, R. J., & Stein, M. B. (2017). Childhood adversity, adult stress, and the risk of major depression or generalized anxiety disorder in US soldiers: A test of the stress sensitization hypothesis. *Psychological Medicine*, *47*(13), 2379–2392. https://doi.org/10.1017/S0033291717001064

Banks, J., & Albertson, K. (2018). Veterans and violence: An exploration of pre-enlistment, military and post-service life. *European Journal of Criminology*, *15*(6), 730–747. https://doi.org/10.1177/1477370818764825

Barrett, E. L., Mills, K. L., & Teesson, M. (2013). Mental health correlates of anger in the general population: Findings from the 2007 National Survey of Mental Health and Wellbeing. *The Australian and New Zealand Journal of Psychiatry*, *47*(5), 470–476. https://doi.org/10.1177/0004867413476752

Beckham, J. C., Feldman, M. E., & Kirby, A. C. (1998). Atrocities exposure in Vietnam combat veterans with chronic posttraumatic stress disorder: Relationship to combat exposure, symptom severity, guilt, and interpersonal violence. *Journal of Traumatic Stress*, *11*(4), 777–785. https://doi.org/10.1023/A:1024453618638

Belik, S. L., Stein, M. B., Asmundson, G. J. G., & Sareen, J. (2009). Relation between traumatic events and suicide attempts in Canadian military personnel. *Canadian Journal of Psychiatry*, *54*(2), 93–104. https://doi.org/10.1177/070674370905400207

Belmont, P. J., Schoenfeld, A. J., & Goodman, G. (2010). Epidemiology of combat wounds in Operation Iraqi Freedom and Operation Enduring Freedom: Orthopaedic burden of disease. *Journal of Surgical Orthopaedic Advances*, *19*(1), 2–7.

Bender, T. W., Gordon, K. H., Bresin, K., & Joiner, T. E., Jr. (2011). Impulsivity and suicidality: The mediating role of painful and provocative experiences. *Journal of Affective Disorders*, *129*(1–3), 301–307. https://doi.org/10.1016/j.jad.2010.07.023

Birditt, K. S., & Fingerman, K. L. (2003). Age and gender differences in adults' descriptions of emotional reactions to interpersonal problems. *The Journals of Gerontology: Series B, Psychological Sciences and Social Sciences*, *58*(4), 237–245. https://doi.org/10.1093/geronb/58.4.P237

Birkley, E. L., & Eckhardt, C. I. (2015). Anger, hostility, internalizing negative emotions, and intimate partner violence perpetration: A meta-analytic review. *Clinical Psychology Review*, *37*, 40–56. https://doi.org/10.1016/j.cpr.2015.01.002

Boffa, J. W., Stanley, I. H., Hom, M. A., Norr, A. M., Joiner, T. E., & Schmidt, N. B. (2017). PTSD symptoms and suicidal thoughts and behaviors among firefighters. *Journal of Psychiatric Research, 84,* 277–283. https://doi.org/10.1016/j.jpsychires.2016.10.014

Bonds, T. M., Baiocchi, D., & McDonald, L. L. (2010). *Army deployments to OIF and OEF*. RAND Corporation.

Brezo, J., Paris, J., & Turecki, G. (2006). Personality traits as correlates of suicidal ideation, suicide attempts, and suicide completions: A systematic review. *Acta Psychiatrica Scandinavica, 113*(3), 180–206. https://doi.org/10.1111/j.1600-0447.2005.00702.x

Brintz, C. E., Miller, S., Olmsted, K. R., Bartoszek, M., Cartwright, J., Kizakevich, P. N., Butler, M., Asefnia, N., Buben, A., & Gaylord, S. A. (2020). Adapting mindfulness training for military service members with chronic pain. *Military Medicine, 185*(3–4), 385–393. https://doi.org/10.1093/milmed/usz312

Brown, S. G., & Daus, C. S. (2015). The influence of police officers' decision-making style and anger control on responses to work scenarios. *Journal of Applied Research in Memory and Cognition, 4*(3), 294–302. https://doi.org/10.1016/j.jarmac.2015.04.001

Bryan, C. J., Bryan, A. O., & Clemans, T. A. (2015). The association of military and premilitary sexual trauma with risk for suicide ideation, plans, and attempts. *Psychiatry Research, 227*(2–3), 246–252. https://doi.org/10.1016/j.psychres.2015.01.030

Bryan, C. J., Cerel, J., & Bryan, A. O. (2017). Exposure to suicide is associated with increased risk for suicidal thoughts and behaviors among National Guard military personnel. *Comprehensive Psychiatry, 77,* 12–19. https://doi.org/10.1016/j.comppsych.2017.05.006

Bullman, T., Schneiderman, A., & Bossarte, R. (2018). Suicide risk by unit component among veterans who served in Iraq or Afghanistan. *Archives of Suicide Research, 22*(1), 1–10. https://doi.org/10.1080/13811118.2017.1304308

Campbell-Sills, L., Kessler, R. C., Ursano, R. J., Rosellini, A. J., Afifi, T. O., Colpe, L. J., Heeringa, S. G., Nock, M. K., Sampson, N. A., Sareen, J., Schoenbaum, M., Sun, X., Jain, S., Stein, M. B., & the Army STARRS Collaborators. (2017). Associations of childhood bullying victimization with lifetime suicidal behaviors among new U.S. Army soldiers. *Depression and Anxiety, 34*(8), 701–710. https://doi.org/10.1002/da.22621

Carpenter, G. S. J., Carpenter, T. P., Kimbrel, N. A., Flynn, E. J., Pennington, M. L., Cammarata, C., Zimering, R. T., Kamholz, B. W., & Gulliver, S. B. (2015). Social support, stress, and suicidal ideation in professional firefighters. *American Journal of Health Behavior, 39*(2), 191–196. https://doi.org/10.5993/AJHB.39.2.5

Centers for Disease Control and Prevention. (2019). *Web-based Injury Statistics Query and Reporting System (WISQARS)*. https://www.cdc.gov/injury/wisqars/

Cerel, J., Jones, B., Brown, M., Weisenhorn, D. A., & Patel, K. (2019). Suicide exposure in law enforcement officers. *Suicide & Life-Threatening Behavior, 49*(5), 1281–1289. https://doi.org/10.1111/sltb.12516

Cerel, J., van de Venne, J. G., Moore, M. M., Maple, M. J., Flaherty, C., & Brown, M. M. (2015). Veteran exposure to suicide: Prevalence and correlates. *Journal of Affective Disorders, 179,* 82–87. https://doi.org/10.1016/j.jad.2015.03.017

Cerulli, C., Stephens, B., & Bossarte, R. (2014). Examining the intersection between suicidal behaviors and intimate partner violence among a sample of males receiving services from the Veterans Health Administration. *American Journal of Men's Health*, *8*(5), 440–443. https://doi.org/10.1177/1557988314522828

Chapin, J., Mendoza-Burcham, M., & Pierce, M. (2017). Third-force influences: Hollywood's war films. *Parameters*, *47*(3), 79–88.

Chemtob, C. M., Novaco, R. W., Hamada, R. S., Gross, D. M., & Smith, G. (1997). Anger regulation deficits in combat-related posttraumatic stress disorder. *Journal of Traumatic Stress*, *10*(1), 17–36. https://doi.org/10.1002/jts.2490100104

Chen, P. Y., & Spector, P. E. (1992). Relationship of work stressors with aggression, withdrawal, theft and substance use: An exploratory study. *Journal of Occupational and Organizational Psychology*, *65*(3), 177–184. https://doi.org/10.1111/j.2044-8325.1992.tb00495.x

Chen, Y.-W., & Dilsaver, S. C. (1996). Lifetime rates of suicide attempts among subjects with bipolar and unipolar disorders relative to subjects with other Axis I disorders. *Biological Psychiatry*, *39*(10), 896–899. https://doi.org/10.1016/0006-3223(95)00295-2

Chopko, B. A., Papazoglou, K., & Schwartz, R. C. (2018). Mindfulness-based psychotherapy approaches for first responders: From research to clinical practice. *American Journal of Psychotherapy*, *71*(2), 55–64. https://doi.org/10.1176/appi.psychotherapy.20180015

Christopher, M. S., Hunsinger, M., Goerling, L. R. J., Bowen, S., Rogers, B. S., Gross, C. R., Dapolonia, E., & Pruessner, J. C. (2018). Mindfulness-based resilience training to reduce health risk, stress reactivity, and aggression among law enforcement officers: A feasibility and preliminary efficacy trial. *Psychiatry Research*, *264*, 104–115. https://doi.org/10.1016/j.psychres.2018.03.059

Conner, K. R., Hesselbrock, V. M., Schuckit, M. A., Hirsch, J. K., Knox, K. L., Meldrum, S., Bucholz, K. K., Kramer, J., Kuperman, S., Preuss, U., & Soyka, M. (2006). Precontemplated and impulsive suicide attempts among individuals with alcohol dependence. *Journal of Studies on Alcohol*, *67*(1), 95–101. https://doi.org/10.15288/jsa.2006.67.95

Cox, D. W., Ghahramanlou-Holloway, M., Szeto, E. H., Greene, F. N., Engel, C., Wynn, G. H., Bradley, J., & Grammer, G. (2011). Gender differences on documented trauma histories: Inpatients admitted to a military psychiatric unit for suicide-related thoughts or behaviors. *The Journal of Nervous and Mental Disease*, *199*(3), 183–190. https://doi.org/10.1097/NMD.0b013e31820c71c9

Daus, C. S., & Brown, S. (2012). The emotion work of police. In N. Ashkanasy, C. Härtel, & W. Zerbe (Eds.), *Experiencing and managing emotions in the workplace* (pp. 305–328). Emerald Group Publishing.

Del Vecchio, T., & O'Leary, K. D. (2004). Effectiveness of anger treatments for specific anger problems: A meta-analytic review. *Clinical Psychology Review*, *24*(1), 15–34. https://doi.org/10.1016/j.cpr.2003.09.006

Department of Defense Task Force on the Prevention of Suicide by Members of the Armed Forces. (2010). *The challenge and the promise: Strengthening the force, preventing suicide and saving lives*. https://urldefense.com/v3/__https://www.health.mil/Reference-Center/Reports/2010/12/01/Task-Force-of-the-Prevention-of-Suicide-by-Member-of-the-Armed-Forces__;!!HgxT5Xd5qx1T!B4o1NfzvHS3VbBef6Sm4MYDQ3hnco2ut2CIt3Pi-jE4FBfetim3ix2QXu2ippA$

DeVylder, J. E., Oh, H. Y., Nam, B., Sharpe, T. L., Lehmann, M., & Link, B. G. (2017). Prevalence, demographic variation and psychological correlates of exposure to police victimisation in four US cities. *Epidemiology and Psychiatric Sciences*, *26*(5), 466–477. https://doi.org/10.1017/S2045796016000810

DiGiuseppe, R., & Tafrate, R. C. (2003). Anger treatment for adults: A meta-analytic review. *Clinical Psychology: Science and Practice*, *10*(1), 70–84. https://doi.org/10.1093/clipsy.10.1.70

DiGiuseppe, R., & Tafrate, R. C. (2007). *Understanding anger disorders*. Oxford University Press.

Drebing, C. E., Reilly, E., Henze, K. T., Kelly, M., Russo, A., Smolinsky, J., Gorman, J., & Penk, W. E. (2018). Using peer support groups to enhance community integration of veterans in transition. *Psychological Services*, *15*(2), 135–145. https://doi.org/10.1037/ser0000178

Ducasse, D., Jaussent, I., Guillaume, S., Azorin, J. M., Bellivier, F., Belzeaux, R., Bougerol, T., Etain, B., Gard, S., Henry, C., Kahn, J. P., Leboyer, M., Loftus, J., Passerieux, C., Olié, E., Courtet, P., & the FondaMental Advanced Centers of Expertise in Bipolar Disorders (FACE-BD) Collaborators. (2017). Affect lability predicts occurrence of suicidal ideation in bipolar patients: A two-year prospective study. *Acta Psychiatrica Scandinavica*, *135*(5), 460–469. https://doi.org/10.1111/acps.12710

Fanning, J. R., Lee, R., & Coccaro, E. F. (2016). Comorbid intermittent explosive disorder and posttraumatic stress disorder: Clinical correlates and relationship to suicidal behavior. *Comprehensive Psychiatry*, *70*, 125–133. https://doi.org/10.1016/j.comppsych.2016.05.018

Fava, M., Hwang, I., Rush, A. J., Sampson, N., Walters, E. E., & Kessler, R. C. (2010). The importance of irritability as a symptom of major depressive disorder: Results from the National Comorbidity Survey Replication. *Molecular Psychiatry*, *15*(8), 856–867. https://doi.org/10.1038/mp.2009.20

Forbes, D., Bennett, N., Biddle, D., Crompton, D., McHugh, T., Elliott, P., & Creamer, M. (2005). Clinical presentations and treatment outcomes of peacekeeper veterans with PTSD: Preliminary findings. *The American Journal of Psychiatry*, *162*(11), 2188–2190. https://doi.org/10.1176/appi.ajp.162.11.2188

Forbes, D., Lewis, V., Varker, T., Phelps, A., O'Donnell, M., Wade, D. J., Ruzek, J. I., Watson, P., Bryant, R. A., & Creamer, M. (2011). Psychological first aid following trauma: Implementation and evaluation framework for high-risk organizations. *Psychiatry*, *74*(3), 224–239. https://doi.org/10.1521/psyc.2011.74.3.224

Gallaway, M. S., Fink, D. S., Millikan, A. M., & Bell, M. R. (2012). Factors associated with physical aggression among US Army soldiers. *Aggressive Behavior*, *38*(5), 357–367. https://doi.org/10.1002/ab.21436

Giancola, P. R. (2000). Executive functioning: A conceptual framework for alcohol-related aggression. *Experimental and Clinical Psychopharmacology*, *8*(4), 576–597. https://doi.org/10.1037/1064-1297.8.4.576

Gibson, N., Corrigan, E., Kateley, K., Youmans Watkins, E., & Pecko, J. A. (2017, December). *Surveillance of Suicidal Behavior: January through December 2016* (PHR No. S.0008057-16). Army Public Health Center.

Giegling, I., Olgiati, P., Hartmann, A. M., Calati, R., Möller, H.-J., Rujescu, D., & Serretti, A. (2009). Personality and attempted suicide. Analysis of anger, aggression and impulsivity. *Journal of Psychiatric Research*, *43*(16), 1262–1271. https://doi.org/10.1016/j.jpsychires.2009.04.013

Gilman, S. E., Bromet, E. J., Cox, K. L., Colpe, L. J., Fullerton, C. S., Gruber, M. J., Heeringa, S. G., Lewandowski-Romps, L., Millikan-Bell, A. M., Naifeh, J. A., Nock, M. K., Petukhova, M. V., Sampson, N. A., Schoenbaum, M., Stein, M. B., Ursano, R. J., Wessely, S., Zaslavsky, A. M., Kessler, R. C., & the Army STARRS Collaborators. (2014). Sociodemographic and career history predictors of suicide mortality in the United States Army 2004–2009. *Psychological Medicine*, *44*(12), 2579–2592. https://doi.org/10.1017/S003329171400018X

Gonzalez, O. I., Novaco, R. W., Reger, M. A., & Gahm, G. A. (2016). Anger intensification with combat-related PTSD and depression comorbidity. *Psychological Trauma: Theory, Research, Practice and Policy*, *8*(1), 9–16. https://doi.org/10.1037/tra0000042

Gradus, J. L., Shipherd, J. C., Suvak, M. K., Giasson, H. L., & Miller, M. (2013). Suicide attempts and suicide among Marines: A decade of follow-up. *Suicide & Life-Threatening Behavior*, *43*(1), 39–49. https://doi.org/10.1111/j.1943-278X.2012.00126.x

Gradus, J. L., Smith, B. N., & Vogt, D. (2015). Family support, family stress, and suicidal ideation in a combat-exposed sample of Operation Enduring Freedom/Operation Iraqi Freedom veterans. *Anxiety, Stress, and Coping*, *28*(6), 706–715. https://doi.org/10.1080/10615806.2015.1006205

Haddock, C. K., Jahnke, S. A., Poston, W. S. C., Jitnarin, N., Kaipust, C. M., Tuley, B., & Hyder, M. L. (2012). Alcohol use among firefighters in the Central United States. *Occupational Medicine*, *62*(8), 661–664. https://doi.org/10.1093/occmed/kqs162

Halpern, J., Gurevich, M., Schwartz, B., & Brazeau, P. (2009). What makes an incident critical for ambulance workers? Emotional outcomes and implications for intervention. *Work and Stress*, *23*(2), 173–189. https://doi.org/10.1080/02678370903057317

Heeringa, S. G., Gebler, N., Colpe, L. J., Fullerton, C. S., Hwang, I., Kessler, R. C., Naifeh, J. A., Nock, M. K., Sampson, N. A., Schoenbaum, M., Zaslavsky, A. M., Stein, M. B., & Ursano, R. J. (2013). Field procedures in the Army Study to Assess Risk and Resilience in Servicemembers (Army STARRS). *International Journal of Methods in Psychiatric Research*, *22*(4), 276–287. https://doi.org/10.1002/mpr.1400

Heinrichs, M., Wagner, D., Schoch, W., Soravia, L. M., Hellhammer, D. H., & Ehlert, U. (2005). Predicting posttraumatic stress symptoms from pretraumatic risk factors: A 2-year prospective follow-up study in firefighters. *The American Journal of Psychiatry*, *162*(12), 2276–2286. https://doi.org/10.1176/appi.ajp.162.12.2276

Hellmuth, J. C., Stappenbeck, C. A., Hoerster, K. D., & Jakupcak, M. (2012). Modeling PTSD symptom clusters, alcohol misuse, anger, and depression as they relate to aggression and suicidality in returning U.S. veterans. *Journal of Traumatic Stress*, *25*(5), 527–534. https://doi.org/10.1002/jts.21732

Henning, K. R., & Frueh, B. C. (1997). Combat guilt and its relationship to PTSD symptoms. *Journal of Clinical Psychology*, *53*(8), 801–808. https://doi.org/10.1002/(SICI)1097-4679(199712)53:8<801::AID-JCLP3>3.0.CO;2-I

Hershcovis, M. S., Turner, N., Barling, J., Arnold, K. A., Dupré, K. E., Inness, M., LeBlanc, M. M., & Sivanathan, N. (2007). Predicting workplace aggression: A meta-analysis. *The Journal of Applied Psychology*, *92*(1), 228–238. https://doi.org/10.1037/0021-9010.92.1.228

Hom, M. A., Stanley, I. H., Gutierrez, P. M., & Joiner, T. E., Jr. (2017). Exploring the association between exposure to suicide and suicide risk among military service members and veterans. *Journal of Affective Disorders*, *207*, 327–335. https://doi.org/10.1016/j.jad.2016.09.043

Horesh, N., Rolnick, T., Iancu, I., Dannon, P., Lepkifker, E., Apter, A., & Kotler, M. (1997). Anger, impulsivity and suicide risk. *Psychotherapy and Psychosomatics*, *66*(2), 92–96. https://doi.org/10.1159/000289115

Inness, M., Leblanc, M. M., & Barling, J. (2008). Psychosocial predictors of supervisor-, peer-, subordinate-, and service-provider-targeted aggression. *The Journal of Applied Psychology*, *93*(6), 1401–1411. https://doi.org/10.1037/a0012810

Jakupcak, M., Conybeare, D., Phelps, L., Hunt, S., Holmes, H. A., Felker, B., Klevens, M., & McFall, M. E. (2007). Anger, hostility, and aggression among Iraq and Afghanistan War veterans reporting PTSD and subthreshold PTSD. *Journal of Traumatic Stress*, *20*(6), 945–954. https://doi.org/10.1002/jts.20258

Jakupcak, M., Cook, J., Imel, Z., Fontana, A., Rosenheck, R., & McFall, M. (2009). Posttraumatic stress disorder as a risk factor for suicidal ideation in Iraq and Afghanistan War veterans. *Journal of Traumatic Stress*, *22*(4), 303–306. https://doi.org/10.1002/jts.20423

Jamner, L. D., Shapiro, D., Goldstein, I. B., & Hug, R. (1991). Ambulatory blood pressure and heart rate in paramedics: Effects of cynical hostility and defensiveness. *Psychosomatic Medicine*, *53*(4), 393–406. https://doi.org/10.1097/00006842-199107000-00005

Jha, A. P., Stanley, E. A., Kiyonaga, A., Wong, L., & Gelfand, L. (2010). Examining the protective effects of mindfulness training on working memory capacity and affective experience. *Emotion*, *10*(1), 54–64. https://doi.org/10.1037/a0018438

Jha, A. P., Zanesco, A. P., Denkova, E., Morrison, A. B., Ramos, N., Chichester, K., Gaddy, J. W., & Rogers, S. L. (2020). Bolstering cognitive resilience via train-the-trainer delivery of mindfulness training in applied high-demand settings. *Mindfulness*, *11*(3), 683–697. https://doi.org/10.1007/s12671-019-01284-7

Johnson, S. L., & Carver, C. S. (2016). Emotion-relevant impulsivity predicts sustained anger and aggression after remission in bipolar I disorder. *Journal of Affective Disorders*, *189*, 169–175. https://doi.org/10.1016/j.jad.2015.07.050

Joint Mental Health Advisory Team 8. (2013). *Joint Mental Health Advisory Team 8 (J-MHAT 8): Operation Enduring Freedom 2012: Afghanistan*. Army Medicine. https://armymedicine.health.mil/Reports

Jollant, F., Lawrence, N. L., Olié, E., Guillaume, S., & Courtet, P. (2011). The suicidal mind and brain: A review of neuropsychological and neuroimaging studies. *The World Journal of Biological Psychiatry*, *12*(5), 319–339. https://doi.org/10.3109/15622975.2011.556200

Judd, L. L., Schettler, P. J., Coryell, W., Akiskal, H. S., & Fiedorowicz, J. G. (2013). Overt irritability/anger in unipolar major depressive episodes: Past and current characteristics and implications for long-term course. *JAMA Psychiatry*, *70*(11), 1171–1180. https://doi.org/10.1001/jamapsychiatry.2013.1957

Kale, A., & Gedik, Z. (2018). Quality of life in riot police: Links to anger, emotion regulation, depression, and anxiety. *Applied Research in Quality of Life*, *15*(1), 107–125.

Kam, C. C.-S., & Bond, M. H. (2008). Role of emotions and behavioural responses in mediating the impact of face loss on relationship deterioration: Are Chinese more face-sensitive than Americans? *Asian Journal of Social Psychology, 11*(2), 175–184. https://doi.org/10.1111/j.1467-839X.2008.00254.x

Kelley, M. L., Bravo, A. J., Votaw, V. R., Stein, E., Redman, J. C., & Witkiewitz, K. (2019). Opioid and sedative misuse among veterans wounded in combat. *Addictive Behaviors, 92,* 168–172. https://doi.org/10.1016/j.addbeh.2018.12.007

Kessler, R. C., Chiu, W. T., Demler, O., Merikangas, K. R., & Walters, E. E. (2005). Prevalence, severity, and comorbidity of 12-month *DSM-IV* disorders in the National Comorbidity Survey Replication. *Archives of General Psychiatry, 62*(6), 617–627. https://doi.org/10.1001/archpsyc.62.6.617

Kessler, R. C., Heeringa, S. G., Colpe, L. J., Fullerton, C. S., Gebler, N., Hwang, I., Naifeh, J. A., Nock, M. K., Sampson, N. A., Schoenbaum, M., Zaslavsky, A. M., Stein, M. B., & Ursano, R. J. (2013). Response bias, weighting adjustments, and design effects in the Army Study to Assess Risk and Resilience in Servicemembers (Army STARRS). *International Journal of Methods in Psychiatric Research, 22*(4), 288–302. https://doi.org/10.1002/mpr.1399

Kessler, R. C., Heeringa, S. G., Stein, M. B., Colpe, L. J., Fullerton, C. S., Hwang, I., Naifeh, J. A., Nock, M. K., Petukhova, M., Sampson, N. A., Schoenbaum, M., Zaslavsky, A. M., Ursano, R. J., & the Army STARRS Collaborators. (2014). Thirty-day prevalence of *DSM-IV* mental disorders among nondeployed soldiers in the US Army: Results from the Army Study to Assess Risk and Resilience in Servicemembers (Army STARRS). *JAMA Psychiatry, 71*(5), 504–513. https://doi.org/10.1001/jamapsychiatry.2014.28

Kessler, R. C., Santiago, P. N., Colpe, L. J., Dempsey, C. L., First, M. B., Heeringa, S. G., Stein, M. B., Fullerton, C. S., Gruber, M. J., Naifeh, J. A., Nock, M. K., Sampson, N. A., Schoenbaum, M., Zaslavsky, A. M., & Ursano, R. J. (2013). Clinical reappraisal of the Composite International Diagnostic Interview Screening Scales (CIDI-SC) in the Army Study to Assess Risk and Resilience in Servicemembers (Army STARRS). *International Journal of Methods in Psychiatric Research, 22*(4), 303–321. https://doi.org/10.1002/mpr.1398

Kiliçarslan, C. (2009). The masculinist ideology and war-combat films: Reassertion of masculinity in Hollywood. *Journal of Faculty of Letters, 26,* 101–120.

Killgore, W. D. S., Cotting, D. I., Thomas, J. L., Cox, A. L., McGurk, D., Vo, A. H., Castro, C. A., & Hoge, C. W. (2008). Post-combat invincibility: Violent combat experiences are associated with increased risk-taking propensity following deployment. *Journal of Psychiatric Research, 42*(13), 1112–1121. https://doi.org/10.1016/j.jpsychires.2008.01.001

Kim, M. J., Scult, M. A., Knodt, A. R., Radtke, S. R., d'Arbeloff, T. C., Brigidi, B. D., & Hariri, A. R. (2018). A link between childhood adversity and trait anger reflects relative activity of the amygdala and dorsolateral prefrontal cortex. *Biological Psychiatry: Cognitive Neuroscience and Neuroimaging, 3*(7), 644–649.

Kleiman, E. M., & Liu, R. T. (2013). Social support as a protective factor in suicide: Findings from two nationally representative samples. *Journal of Affective Disorders, 150*(2), 540–545. https://doi.org/10.1016/j.jad.2013.01.033

Kligyte, V., Connelly, S., Thiel, C., & Devenport, L. (2013). The influence of anger, fear, and emotion regulation on ethical decision making. *Human Performance, 26*(4), 297–326. https://doi.org/10.1080/08959285.2013.814655

Klonsky, E. D., & May, A. (2010). Rethinking impulsivity in suicide. *Suicide & Life-Threatening Behavior, 40*(6), 612–619. https://doi.org/10.1521/suli.2010.40.6.612

Kotler, M., Iancu, I., Efroni, R., & Amir, M. (2001). Anger, impulsivity, social support, and suicide risk in patients with posttraumatic stress disorder. *The Journal of Nervous and Mental Disease, 189*(3), 162–167. https://doi.org/10.1097/00005053-200103000-00004

Kyron, M. J., Podlogar, M. C., Joiner, T. E., McEvoy, P. M., Page, A. C., & Lawrence, D. (2020). Allowing nondisclosure in surveys with suicide content: Characteristics of nondisclosure in a national survey of emergency services personnel. *Psychological Assessment, 32*(12), 1106–1117. https://doi.org/10.1037/pas0000949

Kyron, M. J., Rikkers, W., Page, A. C., O'Brien, P., Bartlett, J., LaMontagne, A., & Lawrence, D. (2021). Prevalence and predictors of suicidal thoughts and behaviours among Australian police and emergency services employees. *Australian & New Zealand Journal of Psychiatry, 55*(2), 180–195. https://doi.org/10.1177/0004867420937774

Lane, A. R., Waters, A. J., & Black, A. C. (2019). Ecological momentary assessment studies of comorbid PTSD and alcohol use: A narrative review. *Addictive Behaviors Reports, 10*, 100205. https://doi.org/10.1016/j.abrep.2019.100205

Langhinrichsen-Rohling, J., Snarr, J. D., Slep, A. M., Heyman, R. E., Foran, H. M., & the United States Air Force Family Advocacy Program. (2011). Risk for suicidal ideation in the U.S. Air Force: An ecological perspective. *Journal of Consulting and Clinical Psychology, 79*(5), 600–612. https://doi.org/10.1037/a0024631

Lee, H.-J., Goudarzi, K., Baldwin, B., Rosenfield, D., & Telch, M. J. (2011). The Combat Experience Log: A web-based system for the in theater assessment of war zone stress. *Journal of Anxiety Disorders, 25*(6), 794–800. https://doi.org/10.1016/j.janxdis.2011.03.018

Leonard, R., & Alison, L. (1999). Critical incident stress debriefing and its effects on coping strategies and anger in a sample of Australian police officers involved in shooting incidents. *Work and Stress, 13*(2), 144–161. https://doi.org/10.1080/026783799296110

Lineberry, T. W., & O'Connor, S. S. (2012). Suicide in the US Army. *Mayo Clinic Proceedings, 87*(9), 871–878. https://doi.org/10.1016/j.mayocp.2012.07.002

Linkh, D. J., & Sonnek, S. M. (2003). An application of cognitive-behavioral anger management training in a military/occupational setting: Efficacy and demographic factors. *Military Medicine, 168*(6), 475–478. https://doi.org/10.1093/milmed/168.6.475

Mackintosh, M.-A., Niehaus, J., Taft, C. T., Marx, B. P., Grubbs, K., & Morland, L. A. (2017). Using a mobile application in the treatment of dysregulated anger among veterans. *Military Medicine, 182*(11), e1941–e1949. https://doi.org/10.7205/MILMED-D-17-00063

Maguen, S., Lucenko, B. A., Reger, M. A., Gahm, G. A., Litz, B. T., Seal, K. H., Knight, S. J., & Marmar, C. R. (2010). The impact of reported direct and indirect killing on mental health symptoms in Iraq war veterans. *Journal of Traumatic Stress, 23*(1), 86–90. https://doi.org/10.1002/jts.20434

Martin, C. E., Tran, J. K., & Buser, S. J. (2017). Correlates of suicidality in firefighter/EMS personnel. *Journal of Affective Disorders, 208*, 177–183. https://doi.org/10.1016/j.jad.2016.08.078

McHugh, T., Forbes, D., Bates, G., Hopwood, M., & Creamer, M. (2012). Anger in PTSD: Is there a need for a concept of PTSD-related posttraumatic anger? *Clinical Psychology Review, 32*(2), 93–104. https://doi.org/10.1016/j.cpr.2011.07.013

McLean, K., Wolfe, S. E., Rojek, J., Alpert, G. P., & Smith, M. R. (2020). Police officers as warriors or guardians: Empirical reality or intriguing rhetoric? *Justice Quarterly, 37*(6), 1096–1118. https://doi.org/10.1080/07418825.2018.1533031

Meadows, S. O., Engel, C. C., Collins, R. L., Beckman, R. L., Cefalu, M., Hawes-Dawson, J., Doyle, M., Kress, A. M., Sontag-Padilla, L., Ramchand, R., & Williams, K. M. (2018). *2015 Department of Defense Health Related Behaviors Survey (HRBS)*. RAND. https://www.rand.org/pubs/periodicals/health-quarterly/issues/v8/n2/05.html

Meffert, S. M., Metzler, T. J., Henn-Haase, C., McCaslin, S., Inslicht, S., Chemtob, C., Neylan, T., & Marmar, C. R. (2008). A prospective study of trait anger and PTSD symptoms in police. *Journal of Traumatic Stress, 21*(4), 410–416. https://doi.org/10.1002/jts.20350

Mennicke, A. M., & Ropes, K. (2016). Estimating the rate of domestic violence perpetrated by law enforcement officers: A review of methods and estimates. *Aggression and Violent Behavior, 31*, 157–164. https://doi.org/10.1016/j.avb.2016.09.003

Mental Health Advisory Team IV. (2006). *Mental Health Advisory Team (MHAT) IV: Operation Iraqi Freedom 05-07: Final report* (Tech. Rep. 201005). Office of the Surgeon General. https://ntrl.ntis.gov/NTRL/dashboard/searchResults/titleDetail/PB2010103335.xhtml

Mental Health Advisory Team V. (2008, February 14). *Operation Iraqi Freedom 06-08: Iraq; Operation Enduring Freedom 8: Afghanistan*. Army Medicine. https://armymedicine.health.mil/Reports

Meyer, E. G., McCarroll, J. E., & Ursano, R. J. (Eds.). (2017). *U.S. Army culture: An introduction for behavioral health researchers*. Center for the Study of Traumatic Stress. https://www.cstsonline.org/assets/media/documents/US%20Army%20Culture%20for%20Researchers%20(2017).pdf

Milliken, C. S., Auchterlonie, J. L., & Hoge, C. W. (2007). Longitudinal assessment of mental health problems among active and reserve component soldiers returning from the Iraq war. *Journal of the American Medical Association, 298*(18), 2141–2148. https://doi.org/10.1001/jama.298.18.2141

Millner, A. J., Ursano, R. J., Hwang, I., King, A. J., Naifeh, J. A., Sampson, N. A., Zaslavsky, A. M., Stein, M. B., Kessler, R. C., Nock, M. K., & the STARRS-LS Collaborators. (2018). Lifetime suicidal behaviors and career characteristics among U.S. Army soldiers: Results from the Army Study to Assess Risk and Resilience in Servicemembers (Army STARRS). *Suicide & Life-Threatening Behavior, 48*(2), 230–250. https://doi.org/10.1111/sltb.12363

Millner, A. J., Ursano, R. J., Hwang, I., King, A. J., Naifeh, J. A., Sampson, N. A., Zaslavsky, A. M., Stein, M. B., Kessler, R. C., Nock, M. K., & the STARRS-LS Collaborators. (2019). Prior mental disorders and lifetime suicidal behaviors among U.S. Army soldiers in the Army Study to assess risk and resilience in servicemembers (Army STARRS). *Suicide & Life-Threatening Behavior, 49*(1), 3–22. https://doi.org/10.1111/sltb.12394

Morland, L. A., Love, A. R., Mackintosh, M.-A., Greene, C. J., & Rosen, C. S. (2012). Treating anger and aggression in military populations: Research updates and clinical implications. *Clinical Psychology: Science and Practice, 19*(3), 305–322. https://doi.org/10.1111/cpsp.12007

Naifeh, J. A., Mash, H. B. H., Stein, M. B., Fullerton, C. S., Kessler, R. C., & Ursano, R. J. (2019). The Army Study to Assess Risk and Resilience in Servicemembers

(Army STARRS): Progress toward understanding suicide among soldiers. *Molecular Psychiatry, 24*(1), 34–48. https://doi.org/10.1038/s41380-018-0197-z

Naifeh, J. A., Ursano, R. J., Kessler, R. C., Zaslavsky, A. M., Nock, M. K., Dempsey, C. L., Bartolanzo, D., Ng, T. H. H., Aliaga, P. A., Zuromski, K. L., Dinh, H. M., Fullerton, C. S., Kao, T.-C., Mash, H. B. H., Sampson, N. A., Wynn, G. H., & Stein, M. B. (2019). Transition to suicide attempt from recent suicide ideation in U.S. Army soldiers: Results from the Army Study to Assess Risk and Resilience in Servicemembers (Army STARRS). *Depression and Anxiety, 36*(5), 412–422. https://doi.org/10.1002/da.22870

Nash, W. P., Krantz, L., Stein, N., Westphal, R. J., & Litz, B. (2011). Comprehensive soldier fitness, battlemind, and the stress continuum model: Military organizational approaches to prevention. In J. I. Ruzek, P. P. Schnurr, J. J. Vasterling, & M. J. Friedman (Eds.), *Caring for veterans with deployment-related stress disorders* (pp. 193–214). American Psychological Association. https://doi.org/10.1037/12323-009

Nock, M. K., Borges, G., Bromet, E. J., Alonso, J., Angermeyer, M., Beautrais, A., Bruffaerts, R., Chiu, W. T., de Girolamo, G., Gluzman, S., de Graaf, R., Gureje, O., Haro, J. M., Huang, Y., Karam, E., Kessler, R. C., Lepine, J. P., Levinson, D., Medina-Mora, M. E., . . . Williams, D. (2008). Cross-national prevalence and risk factors for suicidal ideation, plans and attempts. *The British Journal of Psychiatry, 192*(2), 98–105. https://doi.org/10.1192/bjp.bp.107.040113

Nock, M. K., Deming, C. A., Fullerton, C. S., Gilman, S. E., Goldenberg, M., Kessler, R. C., McCarroll, J. E., McLaughlin, K. A., Peterson, C., Schoenbaum, M., Stanley, B., & Ursano, R. J. (2013). Suicide among soldiers: A review of psychosocial risk and protective factors. *Psychiatry, 76*(2), 97–125. https://doi.org/10.1521/psyc.2013.76.2.97

Nock, M. K., Hwang, I., Sampson, N. A., & Kessler, R. C. (2010). Mental disorders, comorbidity and suicidal behavior: Results from the National Comorbidity Survey Replication. *Molecular Psychiatry, 15*(8), 868–876. https://doi.org/10.1038/mp.2009.29

Nock, M. K., Hwang, I., Sampson, N., Kessler, R. C., Angermeyer, M., Beautrais, A., Borges, G., Bromet, E., Bruffaerts, R., de Girolamo, G., de Graaf, R., Florescu, S., Gureje, O., Haro, J. M., Hu, C., Huang, Y., Karam, E. G., Kawakami, N., Kovess, V., . . . Williams, D. R. (2009). Cross-national analysis of the associations among mental disorders and suicidal behavior: Findings from the WHO World Mental Health Surveys. *PLOS Medicine, 6*(8), Article e1000123. https://doi.org/10.1371/journal.pmed.1000123

Nock, M. K., Kessler, R. C., & Franklin, J. C. (2016). Risk factors for suicide ideation differ from those for the transition to suicide attempt: The importance of creativity, rigor, and urgency in suicide research. *Clinical Psychology: Science and Practice, 23*(1), 31–34. https://doi.org/10.1111/cpsp.12133

Nock, M. K., Millner, A. J., Joiner, T. E., Gutierrez, P. M., Han, G., Hwang, I., King, A., Naifeh, J. A., Sampson, N. A., Zaslavsky, A. M., Stein, M. B., Ursano, R. J., & Kessler, R. C. (2018). Risk factors for the transition from suicide ideation to suicide attempt: Results from the Army Study to Assess Risk and Resilience in Servicemembers (Army STARRS). *Journal of Abnormal Psychology, 127*(2), 139–149. https://doi.org/10.1037/abn0000317

Nock, M. K., Stein, M. B., Heeringa, S. G., Ursano, R. J., Colpe, L. J., Fullerton, C. S., Hwang, I., Naifeh, J. A., Sampson, N. A., Schoenbaum, M., Zaslavsky, A. M., Kessler, R. C., & the Army STARRS Collaborators. (2014). Prevalence and correlates of suicidal behavior among soldiers: Results from the Army Study to Assess Risk and Resilience in Servicemembers (Army STARRS). *JAMA Psychiatry*, *71*(5), 514–522. https://doi.org/10.1001/jamapsychiatry.2014.30

Nock, M. K., Ursano, R. J., Heeringa, S. G., Stein, M. B., Jain, S., Raman, R., Sun, X., Chiu, W. T., Colpe, L. J., Fullerton, C. S., Gilman, S. E., Hwang, I., Naifeh, J. A., Rosellini, A. J., Sampson, N. A., Schoenbaum, M., Zaslavsky, A. M., Kessler, R. C., & the Army STARRS Collaborators. (2015). Mental disorders, comorbidity, and pre-enlistment suicidal behavior among new soldiers in the U.S. Army: Results from the Army Study to Assess Risk and Resilience in Servicemembers (Army STARRS). *Suicide & Life-Threatening Behavior*, *45*(5), 588–599. https://doi.org/10.1111/sltb.12153

Novaco, R. W. (1994). Anger as a risk factor for violence among the mentally disordered. In J. Monahan & H. J. Steadman (Eds.), *Violence and mental disorder: Developments in risk assessment* (pp. 21–59). University of Chicago Press.

Novaco, R. W. (2010). Anger and psychopathology. In M. Potegal, G. Stemmler, & C. Spielberger (Eds.), *International handbook of anger: Constituent and concomitant biological, psychological, and social processes* (pp. 465–497). Springer. https://doi.org/10.1007/978-0-387-89676-2_27

Novaco, R. W. (2016). Anger. In G. Fink (Ed.), *Stress: Concepts, cognition, emotion, and behavior* (pp. 285–292). Academic Press.

Novaco, R. W., & Chemtob, C. M. (2002). Anger and combat-related posttraumatic stress disorder. *Journal of Traumatic Stress*, *15*(2), 123–132. https://doi.org/10.1023/A:1014855924072

Novaco, R. W., & Chemtob, C. M. (2015). Violence associated with combat-related posttraumatic stress disorder: The importance of anger. *Psychological Trauma: Theory, Research, Practice and Policy*, *7*(5), 485–492. https://doi.org/10.1037/tra0000067

Novaco, R. W., Swanson, R. D., Gonzalez, O. I., Gahm, G. A., & Reger, M. D. (2012). Anger and postcombat mental health: Validation of a brief anger measure with U.S. soldiers postdeployed from Iraq and Afghanistan. *Psychological Assessment*, *24*(3), 661–675. https://doi.org/10.1037/a0026636

Office of the Under Secretary of Defense. (2018). *Report to Congress: Mental health assessments for members of the Armed Forces.* https://urldefense.com/v3/__https://www.health.mil/Reference-Center/Congressional-Testimonies/2019/01/11/Mental-Health-Assessments-for-Members-of-the-Armed-Forces__;!!HgxT5Xd5qx1T!B4o1NfzvHS3VbBef6Sm4MYDQ3hnco2ut2CIt3Pi-jE4FBfetim3ix2SK-pJ4FA$

Office of the Under Secretary of Defense, Personnel and Readiness. (2017). *Population Representation in the Military Services: Fiscal Year 2017 Summary Report*. https://www.cna.org/pop-rep/2017/summary/summary.pdf

O'Keefe, V. M., & Reger, G. M. (2017). Suicide among American Indian/Alaska Native military service members and veterans. *Psychological Services*, *14*(3), 289–294. https://doi.org/10.1037/ser0000117

Olatunji, B. O., Ciesielski, B. G., & Tolin, D. F. (2010). Fear and loathing: A meta-analytic review of the specificity of anger in PTSD. *Behavior Therapy*, *41*(1), 93–105. https://doi.org/10.1016/j.beth.2009.01.004

O'Neill, O. A., Vandenberg, R. J., Dejoy, D. M., & Wilson, M. G. (2009). Exploring relationships among anger, perceived organizational support, and workplace outcomes. *Journal of Occupational Health Psychology, 14*(3), 318–333. https://doi.org/10.1037/a0015852

Oquendo, M. A., Waternaux, C., Brodsky, B., Parsons, B., Haas, G. L., Malone, K. M., & Mann, J. J. (2000). Suicidal behavior in bipolar mood disorder: Clinical characteristics of attempters and nonattempters. *Journal of Affective Disorders, 59*(2), 107–117. https://doi.org/10.1016/S0165-0327(99)00129-9

Orth, U., & Wieland, E. (2006). Anger, hostility, and posttraumatic stress disorder in trauma-exposed adults: A meta-analysis. *Journal of Consulting and Clinical Psychology, 74*(4), 698–706. https://doi.org/10.1037/0022-006X.74.4.698

Pennington, M. L., Ylitalo, K. R., Lanning, B. A., Dolan, S. L., & Gulliver, S. B. (2021). An epidemiologic study of suicide among firefighters: Findings from the National Violent Death Reporting System, 2003–2017. *Psychiatry Research, 295*, 113594. https://doi.org/10.1016/j.psychres.2020.113594

Perales, R., Gallaway, M. S., Forys-Donahue, K. L., Spiess, A., & Millikan, A. M. (2012). Prevalence of childhood trauma among U.S. Army soldiers with suicidal behavior. *Military Medicine, 177*(9), 1034–1040. https://doi.org/10.7205/MILMED-D-12-00054

Perlis, R. H., Smoller, J. W., Fava, M., Rosenbaum, J. F., Nierenberg, A. A., & Sachs, G. S. (2004). The prevalence and clinical correlates of anger attacks during depressive episodes in bipolar disorder. *Journal of Affective Disorders, 79*(1–3), 291–295. https://doi.org/10.1016/S0165-0327(02)00451-2

Pruitt, L. D., Smolenski, D. J., Bush, N. E., Skopp, N. A., Edwards-Stewart, A., & Hoyt, T. V. (2017). *DoDSER: Department of Defense suicide event report: Calendar year 2016 annual report.* https://www.dspo.mil/Portals/113/Documents/DoDSER%20CY%202016%20Annual%20Report_For%20Public%20Release.pdf?ver=2018-07-02-104254-717

Regehr, C. (2005). Bringing the trauma home: Spouses of paramedics. *Journal of Loss and Trauma, 10*(2), 97–114. https://doi.org/10.1080/15325020590908812

Reger, M. A., Pruitt, L. D., & Smolenski, D. J. (2018). Lessons from the latest US military suicide surveillance data. *Journal of Clinical Psychiatry, 79*(1), 17l11790.

Reilly, P. M., & Shopshire, M. S. (2000). Anger management group treatment for cocaine dependence: Preliminary outcomes. *The American Journal of Drug and Alcohol Abuse, 26*(2), 161–177. https://doi.org/10.1081/ADA-100100598

Reyes, V. A., & Hicklin, T. A. (2005). Anger in the combat zone. *Military Medicine, 170*(6), 483–487. https://doi.org/10.7205/MILMED.170.6.483

Rice, S. M., Oliffe, J. L., Kealy, D., & Ogrodniczuk, J. S. (2018). Male depression subtypes and suicidality: Latent profile analysis of internalizing and externalizing symptoms in a representative Canadian sample. *The Journal of Nervous and Mental Disease, 206*(3), 169–172. https://doi.org/10.1097/NMD.0000000000000739

Richmond, R. L., Wodak, A., Kehoe, L., & Heather, N. (1998). How healthy are the police? A survey of life-style factors. *Addiction, 93*(11), 1729–1737. https://doi.org/10.1046/j.1360-0443.1998.9311172910.x

Riviere, L. A., & Merrill, J. C. (2011). The impact of combat deployment on military families. In A. B. Adler, P. D. Bliese, & C. A. Castro (Eds.), *Deployment psychology: Evidence-based strategies to promote mental health in the military* (pp. 125–149). American Psychological Association. https://doi.org/10.1037/12300-005

Rona, R. J., Jones, M., Hull, L., MacManus, D., Fear, N. T., & Wessely, S. (2015). Anger in the UK Armed Forces: Strong association with mental health, childhood antisocial behavior, and combat role. *The Journal of Nervous and Mental Disease, 203*(1), 15–22. https://doi.org/10.1097/NMD.0000000000000228

Rosellini, A. J., Heeringa, S. G., Stein, M. B., Ursano, R. J., Chiu, W. T., Colpe, L. J., Fullerton, C. S., Gilman, S. E., Hwang, I., Naifeh, J. A., Nock, M. K., Petukhova, M., Sampson, N. A., Schoenbaum, M., Zaslavsky, A. M., & Kessler, R. C. (2015). Lifetime prevalence of *DSM-IV* mental disorders among new soldiers in the U.S. Army: Results from the Army Study to Assess Risk and Resilience in Servicemembers (Army STARRS). *Depression and Anxiety, 32*(1), 13–24. https://doi.org/10.1002/da.22316

Rosellini, A. J., Monahan, J., Street, A. E., Heeringa, S. G., Hill, E. D., Petukhova, M., Reis, B. Y., Sampson, N. A., Bliese, P., Schoenbaum, M., Stein, M. B., Ursano, R. J., & Kessler, R. C. (2016). Predicting non-familial major physical violent crime perpetration in the US Army from administrative data. *Psychological Medicine, 46*(2), 303–316. https://doi.org/10.1017/S0033291715001774

Rosellini, A. J., Monahan, J., Street, A. E., Petukhova, M. V., Sampson, N. A., Benedek, D. M., Bliese, P., Stein, M. B., Ursano, R. J., & Kessler, R. C. (2017). Predicting sexual assault perpetration in the U.S. Army using administrative data. *American Journal of Preventive Medicine, 53*(5), 661–669. https://doi.org/10.1016/j.amepre.2017.06.022

Rosellini, A. J., Stein, M. B., Benedek, D. M., Bliese, P. D., Chiu, W. T., Hwang, I., Monahan, J., Nock, M. K., Sampson, N. A., Street, A. E., Zaslavsky, A. M., Ursano, R. J., & Kessler, R. C. (2018). Predeployment predictors of psychiatric disorder-symptoms and interpersonal violence during combat deployment. *Depression and Anxiety, 35*(11), 1073–1080. https://doi.org/10.1002/da.22807

Saffer, B. Y., & Klonsky, E. D. (2018). Do neurocognitive abilities distinguish suicide attempters from suicide ideators? A systematic review of an emerging research area. *Clinical Psychology: Science and Practice, 25*(1), Article e12227. https://doi.org/10.1111/cpsp.12227

Sayer, N. A., Noorbaloochi, S., Frazier, P., Carlson, K., Gravely, A., & Murdoch, M. (2010). Reintegration problems and treatment interests among Iraq and Afghanistan combat veterans receiving VA medical care. *Psychiatric Services, 61*(6), 589–597. https://doi.org/10.1176/ps.2010.61.6.589

Schlossberg, N. K., Waters, E. B., & Goodman, J. (1995). *Adults in transition: Linking practice with theory*. Springer Publishing Company.

Schoenbaum, M., Kessler, R. C., Gilman, S. E., Colpe, L. J., Heeringa, S. G., Stein, M. B., Ursano, R. J., Cox, K. L., & the Army STARRS Collaborators. (2014). Predictors of suicide and accident death in the Army Study to Assess Risk and Resilience in Servicemembers (Army STARRS): Results from the Army Study to Assess Risk and Resilience in Servicemembers (Army STARRS). *JAMA Psychiatry, 71*(5), 493–503. https://doi.org/10.1001/jamapsychiatry.2013.4417

Shen, Y. C., Cunha, J. M., & Williams, T. V. (2016). Time-varying associations of suicide with deployments, mental health conditions, and stressful life events among current and former US military personnel: A retrospective multivariate analysis. *The Lancet. Psychiatry, 3*(11), 1039–1048. https://doi.org/10.1016/S2215-0366(16)30304-2

Simpson, T. L., Stappenbeck, C. A., Varra, A. A., Moore, S. A., & Kaysen, D. (2012). Symptoms of posttraumatic stress predict craving among alcohol treatment seekers: Results of a daily monitoring study. *Psychology of Addictive Behaviors, 26*(4), 724–733. https://doi.org/10.1037/a0027169

Singer, M. (2004). Shame, guilt, self-hatred and remorse in the psychotherapy of Vietnam combat veterans who committed atrocities. *American Journal of Psychotherapy, 58*(4), 377–385. https://doi.org/10.1176/appi.psychotherapy.2004.58.4.377

Sirratt, D., Ozanian, A., & Traenkner, B. (2012). Epidemiology and prevention of substance use disorders in the military. *Military Medicine, 177*(8, Suppl.), 21–28. https://doi.org/10.7205/MILMED-D-12-00139

Springer, K. W., Sheridan, J., Kuo, D., & Carnes, M. (2007). Long-term physical and mental health consequences of childhood physical abuse: Results from a large population-based sample of men and women. *Child Abuse & Neglect, 31*(5), 517–530. https://doi.org/10.1016/j.chiabu.2007.01.003

Stahre, M. A., Brewer, R. D., Fonseca, V. P., & Naimi, T. S. (2009). Binge drinking among U.S. active-duty military personnel. *American Journal of Preventive Medicine, 36*(3), 208–217. https://doi.org/10.1016/j.amepre.2008.10.017

Stanley, I. H., Hom, M. A., Hagan, C. R., & Joiner, T. E. (2015). Career prevalence and correlates of suicidal thoughts and behaviors among firefighters. *Journal of Affective Disorders, 187*, 163–171. https://doi.org/10.1016/j.jad.2015.08.007

Stanley, I. H., Hom, M. A., & Joiner, T. E. (2016). A systematic review of suicidal thoughts and behaviors among police officers, firefighters, EMTs, and paramedics. *Clinical Psychology Review, 44*, 25–44. https://doi.org/10.1016/j.cpr.2015.12.002

Start, A. R., Allard, Y., Adler, A., & Toblin, R. (2019). Predicting suicide ideation in the military: The independent role of aggression. *Suicide & Life-Threatening Behavior, 49*(2), 444–454. https://doi.org/10.1111/sltb.12445

Stein, M. B., Campbell-Sills, L., Gelernter, J., He, F., Heeringa, S. G., Nock, M. K., Sampson, N. A., Sun, X., Jain, S., Kessler, R. C., Ursano, R. J., & the Army STARRS Collaborators. (2017). Alcohol misuse and co-occurring mental disorders among new soldiers in the U.S. Army. *Alcoholism, Clinical and Experimental Research, 41*(1), 139–148. https://doi.org/10.1111/acer.13269

Stein, M. B., Campbell-Sills, L., Ursano, R. J., Rosellini, A. J., Colpe, L. J., He, F., Heeringa, S. G., Nock, M. K., Sampson, N. A., Schoenbaum, M., Sun, X., Jain, S., Kessler, R. C., & the Army STARRS Collaborators. (2018). Childhood maltreatment and lifetime suicidal behaviors among new soldiers in the US Army: Results from the Army Study to Assess Risk and Resilience in Servicemembers (Army STARRS). *The Journal of Clinical Psychiatry, 79*(2), 70–77. https://doi.org/10.4088/JCP.16m10900

Sterud, T., Hem, E., Ekeberg, O., & Lau, B. (2007). Occupational stress and alcohol use: A study of two nationwide samples of operational police and ambulance, personnel in Norway. *Journal of Studies on Alcohol and Drugs, 68*(6), 896–904. https://doi.org/10.15288/jsad.2007.68.896

Struthers, C. W., Miller, D. L., Boudens, C. J., & Briggs, G. L. (2001). Effects of causal attributions on coworker interactions: A social motivational perspective. *Basic and Applied Social Psychology, 23*(3), 169–181. https://doi.org/10.1207/S15324834BASP2303_3

Swogger, M. T., You, S., Cashman-Brown, S., & Conner, K. R. (2011). Childhood physical abuse, aggression, and suicide attempts among criminal offenders. *Psychiatry Research, 185*(3), 363–367. https://doi.org/10.1016/j.psychres.2010.07.036

Taft, C. T., Street, A. E., Marshall, A. D., Dowdall, D. J., & Riggs, D. S. (2007). Posttraumatic stress disorder, anger, and partner abuse among Vietnam combat veterans. *Journal of Family Psychology*, *21*(2), 270–277. https://doi.org/10.1037/0893-3200.21.2.270

Tangney, J. P. (1991). Moral affect: The good, the bad, and the ugly. *Journal of Personality and Social Psychology*, *61*(4), 598–607. https://doi.org/10.1037/0022-3514.61.4.598

Teten, A. L., Schumacher, J. A., Bailey, S. D., & Kent, T. A. (2009). Male-to-female sexual aggression among Iraq, Afghanistan, and Vietnam veterans: Co-occurring substance abuse and intimate partner aggression. *Journal of Traumatic Stress*, *22*(4), 307–311. https://doi.org/10.1002/jts.20422

Thomas, J. L., Wilk, J. E., Riviere, L. A., McGurk, D., Castro, C. A., & Hoge, C. W. (2010). Prevalence of mental health problems and functional impairment among active component and National Guard soldiers 3 and 12 months following combat in Iraq. *Archives of General Psychiatry*, *67*(6), 614–623. https://doi.org/10.1001/archgenpsychiatry.2010.54

Tiesman, H. M., Konda, S., Hartley, D., Chaumont Menéndez, C., Ridenour, M., & Hendricks, S. (2015). Suicide in U.S. workplaces, 2003–2010: A comparison with non-workplace suicides. *American Journal of Preventive Medicine*, *48*(6), 674–682. https://doi.org/10.1016/j.amepre.2014.12.011

Ursano, R. J., Colpe, L. J., Heeringa, S. G., Kessler, R. C., Schoenbaum, M., Stein, M. B., & the Army STARRS Collaborators. (2014). The Army study to assess risk and resilience in servicemembers (Army STARRS). *Psychiatry*, *77*(2), 107–119. https://doi.org/10.1521/psyc.2014.77.2.107

Ursano, R. J., Heeringa, S. G., Stein, M. B., Jain, S., Raman, R., Sun, X., Chiu, W. T., Colpe, L. J., Fullerton, C. S., Gilman, S. E., Hwang, I., Naifeh, J. A., Nock, M. K., Rosellini, A. J., Sampson, N. A., Schoenbaum, M., Zaslavsky, A. M., & Kessler, R. C. (2015). Prevalence and correlates of suicidal behavior among new soldiers in the U.S. Army: Results from the Army Study to Assess Risk and Resilience in Servicemembers (Army STARRS). *Depression and Anxiety*, *32*(1), 3–12. https://doi.org/10.1002/da.22317

Ursano, R. J., Kessler, R. C., Heeringa, S. G., Cox, K. L., Naifeh, J. A., Fullerton, C. S., Sampson, N. A., Kao, T.-C., Aliaga, P. A., Vegella, P., Mash, H. H., Buckley, C., Colpe, L. J., Schoenbaum, M., Stein, M. B., & the Army STARRS Collaborators. (2015). Nonfatal Suicidal Behaviors in U.S. Army Administrative Records, 2004–2009: Results from the Army Study to Assess Risk and Resilience in Servicemembers (Army STARRS). *Psychiatry*, *78*(1), 1–21. https://doi.org/10.1080/00332747.2015.1006512

Ursano, R. J., Kessler, R. C., Naifeh, J. A., Herberman Mash, H., Fullerton, C. S., Bliese, P. D., Zaslavsky, A. M., Ng, T. H. H., Aliaga, P. A., Wynn, G. H., Dinh, H. M., McCarroll, J. E., Sampson, N. A., Kao, T.-C., Schoenbaum, M., Heeringa, S. G., Stein, M. B., & the Army Study to Assess Risk and Resilience in Servicemembers (STARRS) Collaborators. (2017). Risk of suicide attempt among soldiers in Army units with a history of suicide attempts. *JAMA Psychiatry*, *74*(9), 924–931. https://doi.org/10.1001/jamapsychiatry.2017.1925

Ursano, R. J., Kessler, R. C., Naifeh, J. A., Herberman Mash, H. B., Nock, M. K., Aliaga, P. A., Fullerton, C. S., Wynn, G. H., Ng, T. H. H., Dinh, H. M., Sampson, N. A., Kao, T.-C., Heeringa, S. G., & Stein, M. B. (2018). Risk factors associated with attempted suicide among U.S. Army soldiers without a history of mental health diagnosis. *JAMA Psychiatry*, *75*(10), 1022–1032. https://doi.org/10.1001/jamapsychiatry.2018.2069

Ursano, R. J., Kessler, R. C., Stein, M. B., Naifeh, J. A., Aliaga, P. A., Fullerton, C. S., Sampson, N. A., Kao, T.-C., Colpe, L. J., Schoenbaum, M., Cox, K. L., Heeringa, S. G., & the Army Study to Assess Risk and Resilience in Servicemembers Collaborators. (2015). Suicide attempts in the U.S. Army during the wars in Afghanistan and Iraq, 2004–2009. *JAMA Psychiatry*, *72*(9), 917–926. https://doi.org/10.1001/jamapsychiatry.2015.0987

Ursano, R. J., Kessler, R. C., Stein, M. B., Naifeh, J. A., Aliaga, P. A., Fullerton, C. S., Wynn, G. H., Vegella, P. L., Ng, T. H. H., Zhang, B. G., Wryter, C. L., Sampson, N. A., Kao, T.-C., Colpe, L. J., Schoenbaum, M., McCarroll, J. E., Cox, K. L., Heeringa, S. G., & the Army STARRS Collaborators. (2016). Risk factors, methods, and timing of suicide attempts among U.S. Army soldiers. *JAMA Psychiatry*, *73*(7), 741–749. https://doi.org/10.1001/jamapsychiatry.2016.0600

Ursano, R. J., Kessler, R. C., Stein, M. B., Naifeh, J. A., Nock, M. K., Aliaga, P. A., Fullerton, C. S., Wynn, G. H., Ng, T. H. H., Dinh, H. M., Sampson, N. A., Kao, T.-C., Schoenbaum, M., McCarroll, J. E., Cox, K. L., Heeringa, S. G., & the Army STARRS Collaborators. (2017). Medically documented suicide ideation among U.S. Army soldiers. *Suicide & Life-Threatening Behavior*, *47*(5), 612–628. https://doi.org/10.1111/sltb.12316

Ursano, R. J., Naifeh, J. A., Kessler, R. C., Gonzalez, O. I., Fullerton, C. S., Mash, H. H., Riggs-Donovan, C. A., Ng, T. H. H., Wynn, G. H., Dinh, H. M., Kao, T.-C., Sampson, N. A., Heeringa, S. G., & Stein, M. B. (2018). Nonfatal suicidal behaviors in the administrative records of activated U.S. Army National Guard and Army Reserve soldiers, 2004–2009. *Psychiatry*, *81*(2), 173–192. https://doi.org/10.1080/00332747.2018.1460716

Ursano, R. J., Stein, M. B., Herberman Mash, H. B., Naifeh, J. A., Fullerton, C. S., Zaslavsky, A. M., Ng, T. H. H., Aliaga, P. A., Wynn, G. H., Dinh, H. M., McCarroll, J. E., Sampson, N. A., Kao, T.-C., Schoenbaum, M., Heeringa, S. G., & Kessler, R. C. (2018). Documented family violence and risk of suicide attempt among U.S. Army soldiers. *Psychiatry Research*, *262*, 575–582. https://doi.org/10.1016/j.psychres.2017.09.046

Vigil, N. H., Grant, A. R., Perez, O., Blust, R. N., Chikani, V., Vadeboncoeur, T. F., Spaite, D. W., & Bobrow, B. J. (2019). Death by suicide: The EMS profession compared to the general public. *Prehospital Emergency Care*, *23*(3), 340–345. https://doi.org/10.1080/10903127.2018.1514090

Violanti, J. M. (2004). Predictors of police suicide ideation. *Suicide & Life-Threatening Behavior*, *34*(3), 277–283. https://doi.org/10.1521/suli.34.3.277.42775

Violanti, J. M., Gu, J. K., Charles, L. E., Fekedulegn, D., Andrew, M. E., & Burchfiel, C. M. (2011). Is suicide higher among separated/retired police officers? an epidemiological investigation. *International Journal of Emergency Mental Health*, *13*(4), 221–228.

Wang, J., Ursano, R. J., Gifford, R. K., Dinh, H., Farooq, S., Broshek, C. E., Cohen, G. H., Sampson, L., Galea, S., & Fullerton, C. S. (2020). Mental health and suicidality in separating U.S. reserve and national guard personnel. *Psychiatry*, *83*(2), 166–175. https://doi.org/10.1080/00332747.2020.1715162

Webb, R. T., Qin, P., Stevens, H., Mortensen, P. B., Appleby, L., & Shaw, J. (2011). National study of suicide in all people with a criminal justice history. *Archives of General Psychiatry, 68*(6), 591–599. https://doi.org/10.1001/archgenpsychiatry.2011.7

Webb, R. T., Shaw, J., Stevens, H., Mortensen, P. B., Appleby, L., & Qin, P. (2012). Suicide risk among violent and sexual criminal offenders. *Journal of Interpersonal Violence, 27*(17), 3405–3424. https://doi.org/10.1177/0886260512445387

Wilk, J. E., Bliese, P. D., Thomas, J. L., Wood, M. D., McGurk, D., Castro, C. A., & Hoge, C. W. (2013). Unethical battlefield conduct reported by soldiers serving in the Iraq war. *The Journal of Nervous and Mental Disease, 201*(4), 259–265. https://doi.org/10.1097/NMD.0b013e318288d302

Wilk, J. E., Quartana, P. J., Clarke-Walper, K., Kok, B. C., & Riviere, L. A. (2015). Aggression in US soldiers post-deployment: Associations with combat exposure and PTSD and the moderating role of trait anger. *Aggressive Behavior, 41*(6), 556–565. https://doi.org/10.1002/ab.21595

Williams, A., Hagerty, B. M., Andrei, A.-C., Yousha, S. M., Hirth, R. A., & Hoyle, K. S. (2007). STARS: Strategies to assist navy recruits' success. *Military Medicine, 172*(9), 942–949. https://doi.org/10.7205/MILMED.172.9.942

Witkiewitz, K., & Villarroel, N. A. (2009). Dynamic association between negative affect and alcohol lapses following alcohol treatment. *Journal of Consulting and Clinical Psychology, 77*(4), 633–644. https://doi.org/10.1037/a0015647

Worthen, M., Rathod, S. D., Cohen, G., Sampson, L., Ursano, R., Gifford, R., Fullerton, C., Galea, S., & Ahern, J. (2014). Anger problems and posttraumatic stress disorder in male and female National Guard and Reserve Service members. *Journal of Psychiatric Research, 55*, 52–58. https://doi.org/10.1016/j.jpsychires.2014.04.004

Wright, K. M., Foran, H. M., Wood, M. D., Eckford, R. D., & McGurk, D. (2012). Alcohol problems, aggression, and other externalizing behaviors after return from deployment: Understanding the role of combat exposure, internalizing symptoms, and social environment. *Journal of Clinical Psychology, 68*(7), 782–800. https://doi.org/10.1002/jclp.21864

Zimmermann, P., & Iwanski, A. (2014). Emotion regulation from early adolescence to emerging adulthood and middle adulthood: Age differences, gender differences, and emotion-specific developmental variations. *International Journal of Behavioral Development, 38*(2), 182–194. https://doi.org/10.1177/0165025413515405

Zouk, H., Tousignant, M., Seguin, M., Lesage, A., & Turecki, G. (2006). Characterization of impulsivity in suicide completers: Clinical, behavioral and psychosocial dimensions. *Journal of Affective Disorders, 92*(2–3), 195–204. https://doi.org/10.1016/j.jad.2006.01.016

8 CLINICAL INTERVENTIONS FOR PROBLEMATIC ANGER

LESLIE A. MORLAND, LISA H. GLASSMAN,
MARGARET-ANNE MACKINTOSH, AND PAULA P. SCHNURR

KEY POINTS

- Individuals working in occupations with high exposure to trauma are at greater risk for developing posttraumatic stress disorder and dysregulated anger; significant anger symptoms often persist even after posttraumatic stress disorder is successfully treated.
- Although several anger management interventions have been evaluated, including cognitive behavior therapy and mindfulness-focused interventions, research in this area is limited and has yet to establish evidence-based practices. However, interventions that reduce physiological arousal appear to be the most successful at improving anger regulation.
- Researchers should continue to develop novel methods for increasing the accessibility and engagement in current anger management protocols with the best evidence base; digital health platforms may be an effective modality for these interventions.

(continues)

https://doi.org/10.1037/0000244-009
Anger at Work: Prevention, Intervention, and Treatment in High-Risk Occupations,
A. B. Adler and D. Forbes (Editors)

KEY POINTS (*Continued*)

- Anger symptoms may need targeted attention over and above treatments for posttraumatic stress disorder and other comorbid conditions.
- Future research is necessary to establish an evidence base for the treatment of dysregulated anger and to develop assessment and treatment guidelines for clinicians who are likely to encounter high levels of anger.

Anger in the workplace can be personally and professionally disruptive, resulting in emotion dysregulation; an unpleasant work environment; decreased occupational performance; and, in extreme cases, workplace hostility and violence. Certain high-risk populations are more likely to experience heightened anger in the workplace because of intense occupational stressors, the traumatic nature of the work itself, or a broader acceptance of anger as part of the professional culture. Many of these individuals experience higher rates of mental health problems, such as posttraumatic stress disorder (PTSD), depression, anxiety, anger, and mood dysregulation. Rates of mental health problems for first responders, including firefighters and ambulance workers, are estimated to be between 8% and 32% (see Kleim & Westphal, 2011, for a review); interestingly, police officers may have a lower prevalence of mental health diagnoses when compared with other types of emergency workers (Kleim & Westphal, 2011; van der Velden et al., 2013). Although overall, military personnel appear to have similar prevalence of mental health problems when compared with civilians (e.g., Riddle et al., 2007), certain military occupational factors may result in an increased risk for psychological symptoms (e.g., combat, deployment; Fear et al., 2010; MacManus et al., 2015). These data highlight the relationship between different occupations and risks for mental health problems, and how specific roles or occupational experiences can drastically influence this dynamic.

Often, individuals with high levels of anger are referred for treatment for diagnosable mental health conditions, such as PTSD, major depressive disorder (MDD), or an anxiety disorder. However, in many cases, anger symptoms persist even after the primary or comorbid conditions are successfully treated (e.g., Larsen et al., 2019; Schnurr & Lunney, 2019). Furthermore, anger is considered to be a secondary symptom to these disorders, rather than a separate problem. Although high levels of anger can be a common symptom of other conditions, it can also be a stand-alone problem with unique deleterious effects. Cognitive behavioral, psychosocial interventions that focus on ameliorating dysregulated anger have been developed, and preliminary research suggests they can be effective at improving anger symptoms; unfortunately, additional efficacy data are needed to establish evidence-based treatment (EBT) guidelines for problematic anger.

This chapter reviews the current literature on anger treatment. We also discuss specific guidelines regarding the treatment of anger within the context of PTSD. Anger and PTSD commonly co-occur, especially in occupations with high exposure to trauma, and high levels of anger are predictive of greater PTSD symptom severity and poorer PTSD treatment outcomes. We provide specific suggestions for researchers and clinicians regarding how to best manage residual anger symptoms following PTSD intervention and identify clinical strategies for adapting existing interventions and develop new interventions for addressing anger at different stages of the care continuum.

ANGER TREATMENTS

Although several interventions have been developed to treat anger symptoms directly, more research is needed on the efficacy of specific anger management protocols. These interventions, which predominantly include cognitive behavior therapy (CBT), relaxation, and mindfulness-based techniques, can be delivered in individual or group formats. This section reviews the interventions' techniques that have been examined explicitly with regard to anger symptoms. Some of these interventions have been examined in populations with co-occurring psychological conditions (e.g., PTSD) and anger, but the majority were developed for use with a broad set of consumers. A list of the treatments outlined next can be seen in Table 8.1.

Anger Management Treatment

Anger management treatment (AMT; Reilly & Shopshire, 2002, 2019), a CBT-based intervention, is the most extensively studied anger-focused treatment. AMT has since been adopted by the Department of Veterans Affairs (VA) and implemented across VA hospitals (Greene et al., 2014; Mackintosh et al., 2017; Morland et al., 2016). AMT teaches participants to observe and record their anger, identify anger triggers, use deep breathing and progressive muscle relaxation strategies to relieve tension, practice conflict resolution, and develop a cognitive and behaviorally focused plan for controlling their anger. A similar protocol developed by the National Center for PTSD (Grace et al., 2015) includes CBT skills for managing anger in the context of having a PTSD diagnosis. Most AMT protocols start with motivational

TABLE 8.1. Anger Treatments

Treatment	Description
Cognitive behavior therapy (CBT)	CBT is an intervention that focuses on patients' thoughts and behaviors. CBT aims to teach patients how to identify and make changes to unhealthy patterns of thoughts and behaviors in order to alleviate symptoms and support better functioning.
Anger management treatment (AMT)	AMT is a CBT-based intervention that teaches patients to observe and record their anger, identify triggers, engage in deep breathing and muscle relaxation, and practice conflict resolution. During AMT patients also develop a cognitively and behaviorally engaged plan for controlling their anger.
Mindfulness-based treatment	Mindfulness-based treatments include interventions that combine various facets of mindfulness as well as manualized protocols such as Mindfulness-based stress reduction and mindfulness-based cognitive therapy. Mindfulness-based stress reduction focuses on intense and regular practice of mindfulness meditation through the teaching of formal meditation techniques. Additionally, patients are encouraged to practice informal mindfulness techniques.
Acceptance and commitment therapy	Acceptance and commitment therapy is a CBT-based intervention; however, it differs from traditional CBT as it teaches patients to mindfully accept whatever thoughts or feelings they are having so that they may experience these thoughts and feelings without having to act on them.
Exposure therapies	Exposure therapies repeatedly engage patients with imaginal (e.g., image, memory) or in vivo (e.g., location, object, situation) stimuli with a focus on tolerating distress.
Relaxation training	In relaxation training, patients are taught and practice various relaxation techniques such as progressive muscle relaxation and pleasant imagery. The relaxation techniques taught may vary based on the protocol, but their aim is to reduce the physiological arousal that comes with dysregulated anger.
Social skills training	Social skills training centers around assertive skills training and the practice of interpersonal strategies, such as asking questions, active listening, and assertiveness. The purpose of this training is to reduce interpersonal conflict and improve relationships.

interviewing techniques to address a person's ambivalence regarding the need to treat dysregulated anger and their commitment to change. These anger treatment protocols have been widely disseminated across VA settings, are used in both individual and group formats, and have demonstrated positive outcomes among individuals with high levels of anger; however, randomized controlled trials (RCTs) are needed to determine whether AMT can be considered an EBT for dysregulated anger.

Mindfulness-Based Treatment

Research on the direct treatment of anger has also included several mindfulness-based approaches (e.g., Galantino et al., 2005; Park & Choi, 2016; Speca et al., 2000). Although some of these interventions are formally manualized protocols (e.g., mindfulness-based stress reduction [MBSR], mindfulness-based cognitive therapy [MBCT]), other protocols blend different aspects of mindfulness together. MBSR centers on the intensive and regular practice of mindfulness meditation and teaches clients how to meditate formally (e.g., body scan, hatha yoga) for at least 45 minutes per day, 6 days a week. Clients are also encouraged to engage in informal mindfulness practices (e.g., greater awareness of pleasant and uncomfortable bodily sensations and feelings) as a part of their daily functioning. Mindfulness protocols also show promise in their potential to be incorporated into standard practice, but more research is needed to build confidence in their utility for problematic anger, especially across diverse populations.

Acceptance and Commitment Therapy

Acceptance and commitment therapy (ACT) has also been studied as an anger treatment approach. ACT is a third-wave CBT intervention and differs from traditional CBT in several key ways. Although cognitive restructuring is the cornerstone of traditional CBT, ACT techniques do not focus on identifying thoughts, recognizing biases, and changing cognitions. Instead, ACT therapists encourage clients to be mindfully accepting of whatever thoughts or emotions arise. Ultimately, the objective is for clients to be open and willing to experience anger without acting on anger-related thoughts and feelings. For example, instead of focusing energy on controlling or getting rid of angry thoughts and feelings, the ACT model encourages clients to change their reaction to anger by changing their behaviors when they feel angry (e.g., choosing to take a walk instead of yelling at a spouse). ACT also includes values clarification and often employs metaphors (e.g., tug-of-war with the monster) to promote the understanding and use of the ACT strategies.

Mindfulness exercises as just outlined are used to help clients become more in touch with the present moment and to learn to separate oneself from his or her emotions and thoughts. Only limited, uncontrolled research supports the use of ACT for improving anger symptoms, and one RCT suggests that ACT can improve aggression (Zarling et al., 2015).

Dialectical Behavioral Therapy

Several studies have examined the efficacy of dialectical behavior therapy (DBT) for reducing anger and aggression in populations such as people with borderline personality disorder (BPD). DBT is a CBT designed to treat emotional dysregulation and the behavioral difficulties associated with chronic mood dysregulation characteristic of BPD. Although DBT was designed to treat BPD, it is used more broadly to treat emotional dysregulation. A meta-analysis (Frazier & Vela, 2014) examined DBT outcomes for the treatment of anger and aggression; findings suggest that DBT can have a positive impact on both domains. However, the samples included in this review were small and predominantly included White women with BPD or forensic populations. Although these findings are promising, the current literature on DBT for treating anger is methodologically weak and narrow in its application. As such, no specific recommendations for the use of DBT to treat dysregulated anger can be made at this time.

Exposure Therapies

Exposure therapies, such as prolonged exposure, have been established as effective approaches for several psychological conditions (e.g., PTSD and MDD; U.S. Department of Veterans Affairs and Department of Defense, 2017). Exposure involves repeatedly engaging with stimuli, either in vivo (e.g., location, object, situation) or imaginal (e.g., image, memory), and focuses primarily on tolerating the distress. Although several studies have examined anger measures as secondary outcomes of PTSD EBTs, only a few pilot studies have tailored exposure therapy or systematic desensitization (a combination of relaxation and exposure to imaginal scenarios; Wolpe, 1973; Wolpe & Lazarus, 1966) for anger management and examined anger outcomes (e.g., D. R. Evans et al., 1973; Grodnitzky & Tafrate, 2000).

Relaxation Training

Relaxation therapy centers on the systematic practice of relaxation. Individuals practice relaxation techniques, including progressive muscle relaxation and pleasant imagery, and are encouraged to use these strategies whenever necessary. The specific relaxation strategies used can vary by protocol, but the focus is on reducing the physiological arousal that is associated with dysregulated anger. A small number of studies have examined the utility of relaxation training with promising results, but many of these studies lacked methodological rigor (e.g., use of convenience samples).

Social Skills Training

Social skills training focuses on assertive skills training and practicing interpersonal strategies (e.g., asking questions, active listening, assertiveness) to minimize interpersonal conflict and improve interpersonal relationships. These strategies also reduce anger by providing alternative ways to interact interpersonally. Research on the effect of social skills training on problematic anger has had mixed outcomes.

RESEARCH ON ANGER TREATMENT OUTCOMES

Overall, research suggests that anger-focused interventions improve problematic anger and result in moderate therapeutic gains (DiGiuseppe & Tafrate, 2003; Lee & DiGiuseppe, 2018). Individuals with anger problems who receive an anger-focused intervention also report significant increases in positive behaviors (e.g., problem-solving) when compared with their pretreatment symptom levels. For example, approximately 80% of individuals who receive a targeted anger intervention report improvement in symptoms, and 70% have better outcomes than individuals who did not receive therapy (see DiGiuseppe & Tafrate, 2003, and Lee & DiGiuseppe, 2018, for meta-analyses). Furthermore, aggression and symptoms of other conditions (e.g., PTSD) may also improve following anger therapy (DiGiuseppe & Tafrate, 2003).

CBT-based interventions have the most data supporting their use for the treatment of anger. Three meta-analyses of CBT treatment studies for anger reported that these interventions elicited medium-to-large effects on anger symptoms. Taken together, these meta-analyses reported that interventions that included exposure (d = 0.51–0.60), cognitive restructuring only (d = 0.51–0.83), CBT (0.60–0.68), behavioral skills training (e.g., social skills training; d = 0.73–0.85), relaxation (d = 0.67–0.90), and multicomponent therapies (d =0.76–0.93), all had moderate-to-large effects on anger for adults (see Lee & DiGiuseppe, 2018, for a review of meta-analyses). DiGiuseppe and Tafrate (2003) also included AMT in their meta-analysis, and AMT exhibited the largest effects (d = 1.33).

Despite the growing body of literature supporting the use of anger-focused treatments, there is much more work to be done. Improvements in symptoms, though moderate in magnitude, still fall short of gains reported by evidence-based interventions for anxiety, depression, and PTSD (DiGiuseppe & Tafrate, 2003; Lee & DiGiuseppe, 2018). More research is needed on these promising treatments to further improve anger outcomes, establish an evidence-based first-line treatment for anger dysregulation, and determine how anger protocols may be tailored to the needs of specific populations (e.g., women, first responders).

Next, we review outcomes for the anger interventions just discussed, with a focus on which treatments have been studied among individuals in high-risk occupations.

Research Among First Responders

Surprisingly, only one study has examined one of the established anger treatments among first responders. Bergman et al. (2016) tested a version of MBSR specifically tailored to the needs of law enforcement officers among 59 police officers working in the Pacific Northwest. Officers, on average, reported significant reductions in anger and occupational stress. Improvements in anger were associated with hypothesized mechanisms of action in MBSR, such as treatment-related improvements in nonjudgment of internal experiences and acting with awareness.

One additional study has examined anger treatment outcomes among first responders; Abernethy and Cox (1994) tested AMT among law enforcement officers. The study protocol was a 6-hour group-based training that included modules on psychoeducation, relaxation/meditation, defense mechanisms, and strategies for identifying and responding to anger-provoking situations. Outcomes were mixed: Individuals who received the anger-focused intervention reported reductions in the use of force when making arrests and in their overall angry mood when compared to controls. However, there were no differences between groups in state anger, trait anger, or other performance variables (e.g., felony arrests; Abernethy & Cox, 1994).

Research Among Veterans and Service Members

Despite the high levels of anger reported among veterans and service members (Biddle et al., 2002; Jakupcak et al., 2007; Worthen et al., 2014), only a few studies have focused on treating anger among veterans (e.g., Chemtob et al., 1997; Donahue et al., 2017; Morland et al., 2010). To date, there has been only one treatment study that has focused on improving anger symptoms among active duty service members (Cash et al., 2018). This lack of research is concerning because approximately 35% to 50% of active duty service members report high levels of anger, making it one of the most common and deleterious concerns reported by this population (e.g., Biddle et al., 2002; Worthen et al., 2014).

In one of the few studies on anger treatment conducted with veterans, AMT was found to be efficacious. Morland et al. (2010) delivered group-based AMT to 125 male combat veterans with comorbid anger and PTSD either in person or via video teleconferencing (VTC). Participants, on average, exhibited significant reductions in anger following AMT. Although individuals who received therapy in person reported a stronger therapeutic alliance, those in the VTC group experienced similar improvements in anger symptoms when compared with those who received in-person therapy. Furthermore, the authors reported a significant reduction in PTSD symptoms at posttreatment across groups. This study not only demonstrates that AMT can be effective in improving anger and PTSD symptoms in male individuals with co-occurring conditions but also establishes VTC as a noninferior way of delivering this intervention.

In a study of ACT, Donahue et al. (2017) delivered a 12-week group-based ACT intervention to 23 male veterans who reported problematic anger and aggression. Anger and aggression commonly co-occur, but they are not the same. Anger is an emotional state, and aggression is behavioral and may be an expression of anger. Treatment completers experienced improvements in trait physical aggression but did not report improvements in quality of life, anger reactivity, or verbal aggression.

A few additional studies have examined cognitive behavior treatments for anger management among veterans. These interventions often include psychoeducation about anger cues, problem-solving, coping strategies, and identification of biased thoughts; however, protocols are inconsistent between studies, and so interpretations must be made with caution. Overall, these studies reported positive gains in anger symptoms, and many studies included veterans who had PTSD and/or substance use comorbidities (e.g., Gerlock, 1994; Shea et al., 2013). A recent case series study with active duty service members examined the effectiveness of a 12-session CBT intervention. The treatment, which was developed specifically for treating anger in the context of combat-related PTSD (Cash et al., 2018), elicited a significant reduction in anger ($d = 1.56$) with 88% of participants exhibiting managing reduction in anger and 63% reporting meaningful reduction in PTSD symptoms. This is one of the few protocols that addresses anger in the context of PTSD.

Research Among Health Care Workers

Two studies examined the interventions described earlier in this chapter among health care workers. D. R. Evans et al. (1973) randomly assigned 20 female nursing students to two groups; one group received systematic desensitization training sessions, and the other group was a no-treatment control. Individuals who received systematic desensitization reported lower anger symptoms and reduced physiological arousal when compared with controls. Also, one open trial among health care workers reported a decrease in anger and hostility following 8 weeks of mindfulness classes (Galantino et al., 2005).

Research With Mixed Populations

The remaining research studies on anger-focused interventions have been conducted using samples recruited from community clinics, health care systems, university students, and other broad samples. These studies explore the utility of interventions in diverse populations across different occupations.

In broader populations, AMT has also been shown to reduce anger and substance use among individuals with substance use disorders (SUDs; Clark et al., 1996; Reilly & Shopshire, 2000; Reilly et al., 1999; Shopshire et al., 1996). Further, one study suggests that AMT may be effective among individuals with comorbid PTSD and SUD (Reilly et al., 1996). An early version of a group AMT protocol, delivered before the intervention was manualized, was tested among women with SUD. These female participants reported reductions in anger and improvements in anger control following treatment, and their outcomes were not significantly different from male participants in the study (Reilly & Shopshire, 2000).

Although not traditionally considered occupational samples, two studies have reported improvements in anger following ACT treatments among incarcerated inmates and community samples. Plambeck (2015) delivered eight sessions of ACT over 8 weeks to incarcerated men in a minimum-security prison. Postintervention results indicated that ACT was associated with decreases in trait anger and associated problematic behaviors, the latter of which continued to improve at a 1-month follow-up. Saavedra (2008) delivered an ACT-based protocol to a group of ethnic minority patients with comorbid anger and SUDs and reported improved problematic anger-related behaviors following treatment. Interestingly, higher baseline anger was associated with greater treatment gains.

There is also evidence that ACT can impact aggression outcomes. One RCT examined group-based ACT for the treatment of aggression among perpetrators of intimate partner aggression. After receiving 12 two-hour sessions of ACT, participants reported significantly greater improvements in physical and psychological aggression in comparison with the supportive control condition (Zarling et al., 2015). However, no anger outcomes were reported.

Evidence for the utility of systematic desensitization in decreasing anger symptoms dates back to the 1970s. Two studies found reductions in anger and reactivity in broader occupational samples (O'Donnell & Worell, 1973; Rimm et al., 1971). Importantly, these studies are old and have not been replicated with modern procedures and assessments.

In a more recent small pilot study, six adults referred from a community mental health clinic with problematic anger levels received nine sessions of group-based imaginal exposure (Grodnitzky & Tafrate, 2000). Participants recorded a scene related to their ongoing anger problems and listened to this audiotape every day outside of therapy. Participants exhibited statistically significant decreases with large effect sizes across several anger domains, including trait anger, duration of angry feelings, and interference with functioning. These improvements were maintained at a 15-month follow-up. Although these results are promising, more research is needed on the impact of exposure therapy on elevated anger.

Several studies have found that mindfulness may have indirect effects on the improvement of anger across broad samples. The majority of this research has been conducted using medical patients. Momeni et al. (2016) delivered eight sessions of MBSR to cardiac patients. When compared with a no-therapy control group, individuals who received MBSR reported reductions in stress and anger. Two separate studies also reported improvements in stress and state and trait anger following MBSR protocols (Park & Choi, 2016; Speca et al., 2000).

Several studies have examined the use of relaxation training and found that relaxation training improves subjective anger levels among students with high levels of driving-related anger (e.g., Deffenbacher et al., 2000, 2002). Unfortunately, these studies lacked validated assessments or included only convenience samples (e.g., college students), so these results must be interpreted with caution when applied to occupational groups or individuals with elevated levels of anger.

Summary

Although several studies have reported outcomes of anger-focused interventions, the available research spans across many treatment protocols and populations, and research supporting any single individual manualized intervention is still lacking; thus, it is hard to make confident conclusions regarding the utility of these treatments for specific populations. Comprehensive RCTs are desperately needed.

Despite these challenges, there is one important emerging theme. Therapeutic strategies that target physiological arousal may be a key, initial intervention point for the successful regulation of anger (see discussions in Brondolo et al., 1997; Mackintosh et al., 2014; Novaco, 2011). In fact, several interventions modalities, such as CBT (Reilly & Shopshire, 2002, 2019), relaxation training (Deffenbacher et al., 2000, 2002), ACT (Donahue et al., 2017; Plambeck, 2015; Zarling et al., 2015), and mindfulness-based protocols (Bergman et al., 2016; Galantino et al., 2005), all target the disruption of the physiological arousal cycle associated with the maintenance of anger and aggression. This targeting is consistent with Novaco's (2011) conceptualization of arousal as a "fundamental part of anger treatment, and it is unfortunately given insufficient attention by CBT therapists" (p. 253), and it is empirically supported by Mackintosh and colleagues' (2014) finding that increases in arousal calming skills during AMT predicted larger reductions in physiological arousal, cognitive, and behavioral anger-related symptoms. In addition, the Mackintosh et al. (2014) study found that veterans who reported larger gains in arousal calming skills also demonstrated greater development in other anger-regulation skills (e.g., cognitive coping and behavioral control skills), providing further evidence for the importance of targeting the disruption of the physiological arousal cycle.

NOVEL DEVELOPMENTS IN ANGER INTERVENTIONS

The advent of new modalities of care provides an opportunity for the broad dissemination of psychological treatment and increases accessibility for a diverse group of individuals who would benefit from intervention. In particular, two interventions recently developed for anger management leverage telehealth modalities to maximize efficiency and accessibility.

In light of the limited availability of evidence-based anger management interventions across the VA health care systems, VA investigators developed a cognitive behavioral web-based intervention that focuses on anger management, Anger and Irritability Management Skills course (AIMS; Greene et al., 2014). AIMS is based on the AMT Substance Abuse and Mental Health Services Administration protocol (Reilly & Shopshire, 2002, 2019) and is tailored to veterans. It consists of eight modules that use videos, practice assignments, homework, and interactive content to encourage skill development and use in daily life. AIMS is an anonymous, self-paced program;

this platform may be particularly appealing to individuals who have elevated anger symptoms and difficulty accessing AMT, cannot attend standard in-person modalities of care, or are reluctant or skeptical of "therapy" (Weingardt & Greene, 2015). Although the AMT protocol from which AIMS was developed has a small body of research supporting its efficacy, to date there have been no published trials of the efficacy of the AIMS platform in reducing anger.

Using smartphone-based mobile applications (mobile apps) is another digital method for extending AMT, which has a small research base. For example, the Remote Exercises for Learning Anger and Excitation Management program (RELAX; Mackintosh et al., 2017; Morland et al., 2016) was a multifaceted system complementing the AMT protocol and provided users with anger monitoring tools (e.g., anger meter, anger log), anger management tools (e.g., guided breathing, cognitive restructuring), the ability to send app information to their treatment team, and a clinician dashboard. The goal of the RELAX system is to provide integrated support for individualized, anger-focused skills development with access to personalized information and tools whenever needed for individuals with elevated anger.

To date, one research study has examined the efficacy of the RELAX system. These researchers randomized 58 veterans to AMT plus the RELAX System or AMT alone (Mackintosh et al., 2017). Although there were no significant differences in anger or PTSD outcomes between the two conditions, military veterans reported that they were satisfied with the RELAX system, and individuals in this condition were about one third as likely to drop out of treatment, though the difference was not statistically significant. Furthermore, most treatment gains were maintained at a 3-month follow-up (Mackintosh et al., 2017). Although considerably more research is needed on mobile app-supported AMT as an adjunctive or stand-alone intervention, app-based technology provides the opportunity for a discrete, convenient, continuous, and effective method of delivering psychological interventions.

PTSD TREATMENT AND ANGER

As mentioned previously, individuals engaged in certain occupations are at increased risk for the development of PTSD. By way of comparison, approximately 6.1% of the general population will have PTSD at some point in their lifetime (Goldstein et al., 2016). Although the lifetime prevalence of PTSD for veterans is comparable with that for the general population (6.9%), veterans younger than age 29 (15.3%; Smith et al., 2016) and active duty service members (up to 17%; see Gates et al., 2012, for a review) report higher rates of PTSD. The prevalence of PTSD among first responders (e.g., firefighters, paramedics) may also be higher than in the general population; a meta-analysis determined that the prevalence of PTSD worldwide among first responders is 10% (Berger et al., 2012).

It is important to consider the prevalence of PTSD in understanding anger because anger is a common symptom of PTSD, and one that is predictive of higher PTSD symptom severity and poorer treatment outcomes in civilian and veteran populations. Prominent symptoms of anger immediately following a trauma are also predictive of the subsequent development of PTSD (Koenen et al., 2003; Morland et al., 2012; Orth & Wieland, 2006). Individuals with PTSD and anger report impaired judgment, attention, decision making, and physical and mental health, as well as high levels of occupational stress (see Morland et al., 2012, for a review). Given the prevalence of this comorbidity, effective interventions that improve both elevated anger and PTSD are critically important.

Several effective interventions have been developed to treat PTSD. The VA/DoD Clinical Practice Guideline for Management of Posttraumatic Stress (U.S. Department of Veterans Affairs and Department of Defense, 2017) recommends several trauma-focused psychotherapies, including cognitive processing therapy (CPT), prolonged exposure (PE), and eye movement desensitization and reprocessing. On average, these treatments have large effect sizes for PTSD symptoms and moderate effect sizes for depression (see Cusack et al., 2016, for a systematic review and meta-analysis). However, effects for PTSD related to combat trauma or in veterans may not be as strong (Steenkamp et al., 2015; Watts et al., 2013). Evidence on the comparative effectiveness of these EBTs for PTSD remains insufficient, especially when anger levels are taken into account (Cusack et al., 2016; Watts et al., 2013).

Trauma Adaptive Recovery Group Education and Therapy (TARGET) is a CBT-based PTSD treatment that teaches emotion regulation techniques (e.g., recognizing and evaluating emotions, identifying triggers) to help patients manage their physiological symptoms. In one small RCT with military combat veterans, TARGET was comparable with PE with regard to posttreatment improvement in PTSD symptoms, trait anger, and emotion regulation, and TARGET had a higher treatment completion rate (Ford et al., 2018). Although this study had a small sample size and a relatively low average pretreatment anger symptom severity, TARGET results are promising and should be further examined.

Despite the effects of PTSD EBTs on overall symptoms, reductions in anger levels following these interventions are modest; many patients report residual anger symptoms following PTSD treatment (Larsen et al., 2019; Schnurr & Lunney, 2019; Stapleton et al., 2006; Zayfert & DeViva, 2004). For example, in two studies of CPT, 55% to 78% of patients still had dysfunctional levels of anger at posttreatment (Mackintosh et al., 2015), and similar results were found for other PTSD interventions (e.g., PE, present-centered therapy; Schnurr & Lunney, 2019). Furthermore, one study found that increased levels of anger at the beginning of treatment were associated with more severe PTSD presentations (Elliott et al., 2005) and with increased rates of treatment dropout (Foa et al., 1995; Forbes et al., 2003; Koenen et al., 2003; Lloyd et al., 2014).

High levels of anger may also interfere with PTSD treatment process and response (Forbes et al., 2008; Lloyd et al., 2014); however, research has yet to develop a clear understanding of these relationships. Research and theory support some possible mechanisms, including fear of anger (e.g., belief that he or she will do something regrettable, fear that he or she will lose control) and substance misuse (Forbes et al., 2008), reductions in social support (Forbes et al., 2003), overall poor emotion regulation skills (Cloitre et al., 2004; Frewen & Lanius, 2006), smaller reductions in cognitive distortions during CPT (Mackintosh et al., 2016), and avoidance of other more vulnerable emotions (Foa et al., 1995). Still, two studies did not find support for the negative impact of anger on therapeutic alliance (Forbes et al., 2008; Mackintosh et al., 2016).

Taken together, this research highlights the need for greater attention to anger symptoms, whether it be in the context of PTSD-focused interventions or as separate therapy protocols. More research is needed to understand the impact of PTSD treatments on anger and to improve treatment guidelines for this population.

CLINICAL CONSIDERATIONS FOR ASSESSMENT AND TREATMENT OF ANGER

Mild, transient experiences of irritability or anger are common among those working in professions with frequent exposure to traumatic events, including many public health and public safety workers and military populations (e.g., Benedek et al., 2007; Morland et al., 2012). In their review, Benedek et al. (2007) concluded that first responders experiencing transient symptoms of anger may return to baseline without treatment, or may benefit from less intensive interventions, such as psychoeducation or community-level support.

As the intensity, frequency, or duration of anger episodes increase, or if aggression develops, immediate assessment is warranted; frequent symptoms of irritability, anger, and aggression may indicate underlying PTSD, depression, and other mental health concerns and may suggest a higher risk for violence (e.g., occupational, domestic; American Psychiatric Association, 2013; Elbogen et al., 2014). Assessing anger and helping individuals develop adaptive coping skills is key for psychological, social, and occupational functioning (S. Evans et al., 2006). However, it is important that clinicians treating individuals who work in high-risk environments avoid reinforcing common stigmatizing myths, including those that suggest that individuals with PTSD, other mental health diagnoses, or military personnel or veterans are likely to be explosive, dangerous, or disruptive in workplaces (Stone & Stone, 2015).

Several assessment tools are commonly used to evaluate anger and aggression (for more on survey-based assessment, see Osgood & Quartana, Chapter 1, this volume). Structured, clinician-administered, diagnostic interviews for PTSD and other potential comorbid conditions, such as the Clinician-Administered PTSD Scale (Weathers et al., 2013) and the Structured Clinical Interview for *DSM* (First et al., 2016), assess irritability and anger symptoms as part of their PTSD and mood disorder assessments. However, these assessments collect little information on the complex dynamics of anger and irritability, as they do not assess anger control skills; anger-related problems; aggression; and the physiological, emotional, and cognitive components of anger. Nevertheless, they can help identify whether comorbid conditions (e.g., PTSD, anxiety, depression) are present.

Self-report measures are also frequently used in the assessment of anger, but self-reports can be biased by workers' beliefs about the benefits of angry outbursts (e.g., maintaining social isolation, confirming the problem as external) rather than recognizing how their thoughts and behaviors contribute to negative outcomes in response to frustrating, frightening, or ambiguous situations (Morland et al., 2012; Schwarz, 2007). The State–Trait Anger Expression Inventory (Spielberger, 1999), the Novaco Anger Scale (Novaco, 2003), and the Multidimensional Anger Inventory (Siegel, 1986) provide comprehensive assessments of anger symptoms, coping skills, and other characteristics (e.g., hostility). The Dimensions of Anger Reactions–5 is a screening questionnaire for recent experiences of anger, as well as for the effects of anger expression on relationships and functioning (Forbes et al., 2004, 2014). Other scales provide more detailed analyses of psychological and physical aggression, including the Conflict Tactics Scale (Straus et al., 1996) and the Aggression Questionnaire (Buss & Perry, 1992).

Although a variety of assessment practices and treatment interventions may be used, clinicians must consider both the therapeutic and iatrogenic consequences of the assessment context (e.g., workers compensation evaluation) or clinical environment (e.g., onsite therapist, employer-paid treatment) on responses (Kilgour et al., 2015; Lippel, 1999). Workers may experience confusion navigating procedures for addressing behavioral health issues in work settings, feeling stigmatized about injuries and ongoing symptoms, needing social support and advocacy to support successful return to work, and feeling victimized by the system evaluating them (Beardwood et al., 2005; MacEachen et al., 2007). As in other contexts, clinicians need to clearly define their role in the process of evaluation and treatment, limits of confidentiality, implications of assessment procedures, and intervention goals.

Treatment Timing

The timing of the delivery of AMT remains an unanswered empirical question. Some research on timing interventions among individuals with comorbid anger and PTSD may help to guide these decisions. Jakupcak et al. (2007) recommended intervening early to address dysregulated anger and posttraumatic stress symptoms among individuals with both conditions. A meta-analysis found that the relationship between anger/hostility and PTSD strengthened as time since traumatic exposure increased (Orth & Wieland, 2006). This relationship is particularly important among individuals with "military war experience" (Orth & Wieland, 2006), as the meta-analysis indicated that the relationship between anger and other PTSD symptoms was stronger in this group. These points are important for two reasons. First, they further highlight the need to help individuals develop effective coping skills to address anger issues before they become entrenched. Second, as many military veterans serve in public service positions after leaving the military, additional evaluation is needed to determine whether the stronger relationship between anger and PTSD symptoms in these populations is a risk factor for poorer occupational and social functioning in subsequent jobs.

Among individuals with severe PTSD, anger interacts with PTSD symptoms and predicts poorer response to treatment when compared with those with less severe presentations (Forbes et al., 2013; Owens et al., 2008). This interaction is an essential clinical consideration regarding treatment timing. Clients with extreme levels of anger may need to learn anger management skills to effectively engage in other types of treatment. For example, poor anger control skills could interfere with PTSD treatment by patients avoiding the processing of natural emotions of anger (e.g., CPT), exposure to anger-inducing events (e.g., PE and other exposure protocols), and cognitive restructuring (e.g., CPT and cognitive therapies). Enhanced anger control skills may also help workers marshal needed social support resources (Morland et al., 2012). Also, research that increases in arousal calming skills can help workers develop other types of skills (e.g., cognitive coping and behavioral control skills; Mackintosh et al., 2014).

Summary of Clinical Implications

Mild and transient anger may be common among individuals with exposure to trauma in the workplace; however, increases in intensity, frequency, and duration of anger episodes, as well as the presence of aggression, should be carefully considered when determining whether clinical assessment and treatment are necessary. Anger, aggression, and risk for violence should all be adequately assessed when PTSD or another condition is suspected or present. When indicated, EBT should be delivered as soon as possible. Further, clinicians should be cognizant of the negative impacts that dysregulated anger and poor anger control skills can have on treatment engagement and behavior change processes.

Unfortunately, the research base supporting treatments for dysregulated anger remains underdeveloped. This clinical gap is particularly important because problematic anger symptoms may remain after the completion of PTSD EBTs (e.g., Schnurr & Lunney, 2019), and clinicians lack clear guidance regarding how to treat these residual symptoms. Although interventions for anger exist, including CBT (e.g., AMT, ACT, TARGET) and mindfulness-based (i.e., MBSR, MBCT) therapies, the majority of research on these protocols consists of small pilot studies or open trials. Researchers must conduct RCTs among individuals with increased need, especially those who work in specific high-risk occupations, to establish evidence-based protocols that can be delivered either in conjunction with or independent from PTSD treatment. Once EBTs have been established for anger, more information on the timing of PTSD/anger interventions and the patient characteristics associated with residual symptoms can be obtained and disseminated.

FUTURE DIRECTIONS

There are many avenues for future research on the treatment of anger. As noted earlier, large well-controlled studies are needed, as are treatment mechanism studies that examine the importance of disrupting the physiological arousal cycle. Furthermore, additional attention should be given to the development of novel treatment and implementation methods, especially those that can be easily disseminated to diverse patient populations who may have barriers to traditional in-person psychological care (e.g., "9-to-5" jobs). Many health care workers, first responders, and military personnel—those at increased risk for anger and PTSD—often work long hours outside of conventional standards or are hired as shift workers. Intervention designers should consider leveraging technology to create accessible and effective treatments; web-based and mobile app-based platforms hold promise as potentially effective telehealth interventions for anger. This line of research will allow for the delivery of personalized and effective psychotherapy to individuals with anger.

Once anger EBTs are established, researchers should address questions related to the timing of anger treatment in the context of PTSD and other comorbid conditions. Although we expect that this is a complex clinical decision that depends on patient characteristics (e.g., extreme anger, effective coping skills), clinicians need research-based guidance to determine whether patients with this comorbidity would benefit from concurrent anger and PTSD interventions, or whether one should be offered before the other. Importantly, this information must be effectively disseminated to providers across clinical settings.

Finally, researchers must ensure that samples are representative of the broad populations who experience problematic anger in response to challenging work environments. Most of the information collected on anger treatment outcomes are from male veterans and first responder populations. More research on treatment outcomes is critically needed across a broader range of high-risk occupations and occupational systems, as well as among female workers. This research should also focus on identifying other specific occupations or individuals that may be at higher risk of anger and related comorbidities, examining the relationship between occupational violence and anger, establishing treatment targets specifically oriented toward workplace sources of anger/frustration, and evaluating organizational-level initiatives (e.g., self-care, stress management programs) to determine any impact on workplace violence or anger.

Future research on the treatment of anger will significantly improve the state of the literature, as well as support the development of evidence-based guidelines for the assessment and treatment of problematic anger. Unfortunately, the studies recommended are in-depth, time-consuming, and expensive; thus, significant change in these areas will take time. Until then, clinicians working with individuals in any occupation should approach the assessment and treatment of dysregulated anger as potentially representing deficits across several domains of functioning (e.g., emotion regulation, social functioning, physiological reactivity), and implemented intervention strategies should be evaluated based on the frequency, duration, and challenges experienced by workers because of anger issues.

IMPLICATIONS

- Anger is a prominent concern among some individuals in high-risk occupations that are exposed to trauma.
- Even though dysregulated anger can exist independently, it is often conceptualized as part of PTSD, anxiety, or depression, and individuals with high levels of anger are usually referred to treatment for another condition. This is problematic because, although anger and PTSD commonly co-occur, research indicates that anger symptoms often persist even following successful PTSD treatment and are associated with higher rates of attrition and worse outcomes.
- Clinicians must comprehensively assess anger independently of other conditions (e.g., PTSD) to determine if a targeted anger management treatment is warranted and to consider appropriate clinical options.

REFERENCES

Abernethy, A. D., & Cox, C. (1994). Anger management training for law enforcement personnel. *Journal of Criminal Justice, 22*(5), 459–466. https://doi.org/10.1016/0047-2352(94)90036-1

American Psychiatric Association. (2013). *Diagnostic and statistical manual of mental disorders* (5th ed.). https://doi.org/10.1176/appi.books.9780890425596

Beardwood, B. A., Kirsh, B., & Clark, N. J. (2005). Victims twice over: Perceptions and experiences of injured workers. *Qualitative Health Research, 15*(1), 30–48. https://doi.org/10.1177/1049732304268716

Benedek, D. M., Fullerton, C., & Ursano, R. J. (2007). First responders: Mental health consequences of natural and human-made disasters for public health and public safety workers. *Annual Review of Public Health, 28*(1), 55–68. https://doi.org/10.1146/annurev.publhealth.28.021406.144037

Berger, W., Coutinho, E. S. F., Figueira, I., Marques-Portella, C., Luz, M. P., Neylan, T. C., Marmar, C. R., & Mendlowicz, M. V. (2012). Rescuers at risk: A systematic review and meta-regression analysis of the worldwide current prevalence and correlates of PTSD in rescue workers. *Social Psychiatry and Psychiatric Epidemiology, 47*(6), 1001–1011. https://doi.org/10.1007/s00127-011-0408-2

Bergman, A. L., Christopher, M. S., & Bowen, S. (2016). Changes in facets of mindfulness predict stress and anger outcomes for police officers. *Mindfulness, 7*(4), 851–858. https://doi.org/10.1007/s12671-016-0522-z

Biddle, D., Elliott, P., Creamer, M., Forbes, D., & Devilly, G. J. (2002). Self-reported problems: A comparison between PTSD-diagnosed veterans, their spouses, and clinicians. *Behaviour Research and Therapy, 40*(7), 853–865. https://doi.org/10.1016/S0005-7967(01)00084-5

Brondolo, E., DiGiuseppe, R., & Tafrate, R. C. (1997). Exposure-based treatment for anger problems: Focus on the feeling. *Cognitive and Behavioral Practice, 4*(1), 75–98. https://doi.org/10.1016/S1077-7229(97)80013-2

Buss, A. H., & Perry, M. (1992). The aggression questionnaire. *Journal of Personality and Social Psychology, 63*(3), 452–459. https://doi.org/10.1037/0022-3514.63.3.452

Cash, R., Varker, T., McHugh, T., Metcalf, O., Howard, A., Lloyd, D., Costello, J., Said, D., & Forbes, D. (2018). Effectiveness of an anger intervention for military members with PTSD: A clinical case series. *Military Medicine, 183*(9–10), e286–e290. https://doi.org/10.1093/milmed/usx115

Chemtob, C. M., Novaco, R. W., Hamada, R. S., & Gross, D. M. (1997). Cognitive-behavioral treatment for severe anger in posttraumatic stress disorder. *Journal of Consulting and Clinical Psychology, 65*(1), 184–189. https://doi.org/10.1037/0022-006X.65.1.184

Clark, H. W., Reilly, P. M., Shopshire, M. S., & Campbell, T. A. (1996). Anger management treatment in culturally diverse substance abuse patients. In L. S. Harris (Ed.), *Problems of Drug Dependence, 1995: Proceedings of the 57th Annual Scientific Meeting, The College on Problems of Drug Dependence, Inc.* (p. 225). National Institute on Drug Abuse.

Cloitre, M., Stovall-McClough, K. C., Miranda, R., & Chemtob, C. M. (2004). Therapeutic alliance, negative mood regulation, and treatment outcome in child abuse-related posttraumatic stress disorder. *Journal of Consulting and Clinical Psychology, 72*(3), 411–416. https://doi.org/10.1037/0022-006X.72.3.411

Cusack, K., Jonas, D. E., Forneris, C. A., Wines, C., Sonis, J., Middleton, J. C., Feltner, C., Brownley, K. A., Olmsted, K. R., Greenblatt, A., Weil, A., & Gaynes, B. N. (2016). Psychological treatments for adults with posttraumatic stress disorder: A systematic review and meta-analysis. *Clinical Psychology Review, 43*, 128–141. https://doi.org/10.1016/j.cpr.2015.10.003

Deffenbacher, J. L., Filetti, L. B., Lynch, R. S., Dahlen, E. R., & Oetting, E. R. (2002). Cognitive-behavioral treatment of high anger drivers. *Behaviour Research and Therapy, 40*(8), 895–910. https://doi.org/10.1016/S0005-7967(01)00067-5

Deffenbacher, J. L., Huff, M. E., Lynch, R. S., Oetting, E. R., & Salvatore, N. F. (2000). Characteristics and treatment of high-anger drivers. *Journal of Counseling Psychology, 47*(1), 5–17. https://doi.org/10.1037/0022-0167.47.1.5

DiGiuseppe, R., & Tafrate, R. C. (2003). Anger treatment for adults: A meta-analytic review. *Clinical Psychology: Science and Practice, 10*(1), 70–84. https://doi.org/10.1093/clipsy.10.1.70

Donahue, J. J., Santanello, A., Marsiglio, M. C., & Van Male, L. M. (2017). Acceptance and commitment therapy for anger dysregulation with military veterans: A pilot study. *Journal of Contemporary Psychotherapy, 47*(4), 233–241. https://doi.org/10.1007/s10879-017-9361-z

Elbogen, E. B., Johnson, S. C., Wagner, H. R., Sullivan, C., Taft, C. T., & Beckham, J. C. (2014). Violent behaviour and post-traumatic stress disorder in US Iraq and Afghanistan veterans. *The British Journal of Psychiatry, 204*(5), 368–375. https://doi.org/10.1192/bjp.bp.113.134627

Elliott, P., Biddle, D., Hawthorne, G., Forbes, D., & Creamer, M. (2005). Patterns of treatment response in chronic posttraumatic stress disorder: An application of latent growth mixture modeling. *Journal of Traumatic Stress, 18*(4), 303–311. https://doi.org/10.1002/jts.20041

Evans, D. R., Hearn, M. T., & Saklofske, D. (1973). Anger, arousal, and systematic desensitization. *Psychological Reports, 32*(2), 625–626. https://doi.org/10.2466/pr0.1973.32.2.625

Evans, S., Giosan, C., Patt, I., Spielman, L., & Difede, J. (2006). Anger and its association to distress and social/occupational functioning in symptomatic disaster relief workers responding to the September 11, 2001, World Trade Center disaster. *Journal of Traumatic Stress*, *19*(1), 147–152. https://doi.org/10.1002/jts.20107

Fear, N. T., Jones, M., Murphy, D., Hull, L., Iversen, A. C., Coker, B., Machell, L., Sundin, J., Woodhead, C., Jones, N., Greenberg, N., Landau, S., Dandeker, C., Rona, R. J., Hotopf, M., & Wessely, S. (2010). What are the consequences of deployment to Iraq and Afghanistan on the mental health of the UK armed forces? A cohort study. *The Lancet*, *375*(9728), 1783–1797. https://doi.org/10.1016/S0140-6736(10)60672-1

First, M. B., Williams, J. B. W., Karg, R. S., & Spitzer, R. L. (2016). *Structured Clinical Interview for DSM-5 Disorders, Clinician Version (SCID-5-CV)*. American Psychiatric Publishing.

Foa, E., Riggs, D. S., Massie, E. D., & Yarczower, M. (1995). The impact of fear activation and anger on the efficacy of exposure treatment for posttraumatic stress disorder. *Behavior Therapy*, *26*(3), 487–499. https://doi.org/10.1016/S0005-7894(05)80096-6

Forbes, D., Alkemade, N., Hopcraft, D., Hawthorne, G., O'Halloran, P., Elhai, J. D., McHugh, T., Bates, G., Novaco, R. W., Bryant, R., & Lewis, V. (2014). Evaluation of the Dimensions of Anger Reactions-5 (DAR-5) scale in combat veterans with posttraumatic stress disorder. *The Journal of Anxiety Disorders*, *28*(8), 830–835. https://doi.org/10.1016/j.janxdis.2014.09.015

Forbes, D., Creamer, M., Hawthorne, G., Allen, N., & McHugh, T. (2003). Comorbidity as a predictor of symptom change after treatment in combat-related posttraumatic stress disorder. *Journal of Nervous and Mental Disease*, *191*(2), 93–99. https://doi.org/10.1097/01.NMD.0000051903.60517.98

Forbes, D., Hawthorne, G., Elliott, P., McHugh, T., Biddle, D., Creamer, M., & Novaco, R. W. (2004). A concise measure of anger in combat-related posttraumatic stress disorder. *Journal of Traumatic Stress*, *17*(3), 249–256. https://doi.org/10.1023/B:JOTS.0000029268.22161.bd

Forbes, D., McHugh, T., Chemtob, C. M., & Fernandez, E. (2013). Regulating anger in combat-related posttraumatic stress disorder. In E. Fernandez (Ed.), *Treatments for anger in specific populations: Theory, application, and outcome* (pp. 52–73). Oxford University Press. https://doi.org/10.1093/med:psych/9780199914661.003.0004

Forbes, D., Parslow, R., Creamer, M., Allen, N., McHugh, T., & Hopwood, M. (2008). Mechanisms of anger and treatment outcome in combat veterans with posttraumatic stress disorder. *Journal of Traumatic Stress*, *21*(2), 142–149. https://doi.org/10.1002/jts.20315

Ford, J. D., Grasso, D. J., Greene, C. A., Slivinsky, M., & DeViva, J. C. (2018). Randomized clinical trial pilot study of prolonged exposure versus present centred affect regulation therapy for PTSD and anger problems with male military combat veterans. *Clinical Psychology & Psychotherapy*, *25*(5), 641–649. https://doi.org/10.1002/cpp.2194

Frazier, S. N., & Vela, J. (2014). Dialectical behavior therapy for the treatment of anger and aggressive behavior: A review. *Aggression and Violent Behavior*, *19*(2), 156–163. https://doi.org/10.1016/j.avb.2014.02.001

Frewen, P. A., & Lanius, R. A. (2006). Toward a psychobiology of posttraumatic self-dysregulation: Reexperiencing, hyperarousal, dissociation, and emotional numbing. *Annals of the New York Academy of Sciences, 1071*(1), 110–124. https://doi.org/10.1196/annals.1364.010

Galantino, M. L., Baime, M., Maguire, M., Szapary, P. O., & Farrar, J. T. (2005). Association of psychological and physiological measures of stress in health-care professionals during an 8-week mindfulness meditation program: Mindfulness in practice. *Stress and Health, 21*(4), 255–261. https://doi.org/10.1002/smi.1062

Gates, M. A., Holowka, D. W., Vasterling, J. J., Keane, T. M., Marx, B. P., & Rosen, R. C. (2012). Posttraumatic stress disorder in veterans and military personnel: Epidemiology, screening, and case recognition. *Psychological Services, 9*(4), 361–382. https://doi.org/10.1037/a0027649

Gerlock, A. A. (1994). Veterans' responses to anger management intervention. *Issues in Mental Health Nursing, 15*(4), 393–408. https://doi.org/10.3109/01612849409006916

Goldstein, R. B., Smith, S. M., Chou, S. P., Saha, T. D., Jung, J., Zhang, H., Pickering, R. P., Ruan, W. J., Huang, B., & Grant, B. F. (2016). The epidemiology of *DSM-5* posttraumatic stress disorder in the United States: Results from the National Epidemiologic Survey on Alcohol and Related Conditions–III. *Social Psychiatry and Psychiatric Epidemiology, 51*(8), 1137–1148. https://doi.org/10.1007/s00127-016-1208-5

Grace, M., Niles, B. L., & Quinn, S. (2015). *Managing anger: A treatment for those with PTSD.* National Center for PTSD.

Greene, C. J., Reilly, P. M., Niles, B. L., Mackintosh, M.-A., Morland, L. A., Watson, P., Prins, A., Lai, W. P., & Weingardt, K. R. (2014). Anger and irritability management skills (Version 1.0) [Web-based self-help course]. http://www.VeteranTraining.va.gov/aims

Grodnitzky, G. R., & Tafrate, R. C. (2000). Imaginal exposure for anger reduction in adult outpatients: A pilot study. *Journal of Behavior Therapy and Experimental Psychiatry, 31*(3–4), 259–279. https://doi.org/10.1016/S0005-7916(01)00010-6

Jakupcak, M., Conybeare, D., Phelps, L., Hunt, S., Holmes, H. A., Felker, B., Klevens, M., & McFall, M. E. (2007). Anger, hostility, and aggression among Iraq and Afghanistan War veterans reporting PTSD and subthreshold PTSD. *Journal of Traumatic Stress, 20*(6), 945–954. https://doi.org/10.1002/jts.20258

Kilgour, E., Kosny, A., McKenzie, D., & Collie, A. (2015). Interactions between injured workers and insurers in workers' compensation systems: A systematic review of qualitative research literature. *Journal of Occupational Rehabilitation, 25*(1), 160–181. https://doi.org/10.1007/s10926-014-9513-x

Kleim, B., & Westphal, M. (2011). Mental health in first responders: A review and recommendation for prevention and intervention strategies. *Traumatology, 17*(4), 17–24. https://doi.org/10.1177/1534765611429079

Koenen, K. C., Stellman, J. M., Stellman, S. D., & Sommer, J. F., Jr. (2003). Risk factors for course of posttraumatic stress disorder among Vietnam veterans: A 14-year follow-up of American Legionnaires. *Journal of Consulting and Clinical Psychology, 71*(6), 980–986. https://doi.org/10.1037/0022-006X.71.6.980

Larsen, S. E., Fleming, C. J. E., & Resick, P. A. (2019). Residual symptoms following empirically supported treatment for PTSD. *Psychological Trauma: Theory, Research, Practice and Policy, 11*(2), 207–215. https://doi.org/10.1037/tra0000384

Lee, A. H., & DiGiuseppe, R. (2018). Anger and aggression treatments: A review of meta-analyses. *Current Opinion in Psychology, 19*, 65–74. https://doi.org/10.1016/j.copsyc.2017.04.004

Lippel, K. (1999). Therapeutic and anti-therapeutic consequences of workers' compensation. *International Journal of Law and Psychiatry*, *22*(5–6), 521–546. https://doi.org/10.1016/S0160-2527(99)00024-2

Lloyd, D., Nixon, R. D. V., Varker, T., Elliott, P., Perry, D., Bryant, R. A., Creamer, M., & Forbes, D. (2014). Comorbidity in the prediction of Cognitive Processing Therapy treatment outcomes for combat-related posttraumatic stress disorder. *Journal of Anxiety Disorders*, *28*(2), 237–240. https://doi.org/10.1016/j.janxdis.2013.12.002

MacEachen, E., Kosny, A., & Ferrier, S. (2007). Unexpected barriers in return to work: Lessons learned from injured worker peer support groups. *Work*, *29*(2), 155–164.

Mackintosh, M. A., Morland, L. A., Frueh, B. C., Greene, C. J., & Rosen, C. S. (2014). Peeking into the black box: Mechanisms of action for anger management treatment. *Journal of Anxiety Disorders*, *28*(7), 687–695. https://doi.org/10.1016/j.janxdis.2014.07.001

Mackintosh, M. A., Niehaus, J., Taft, C. T., Marx, B. P., Grubbs, K., & Morland, L. A. (2017). Using a mobile application in the treatment of dysregulated anger among veterans. *Military Medicine*, *182*(11), e1941–e1949. https://doi.org/10.7205/MILMED-D-17-00063

Mackintosh, M. A., Willis, E., & Morland, L. A. (2015, November). Anger reductions in response to evidence-based psychotherapy for PTSD. In the *International Society for Traumatic Stress Studies Annual Meeting*. Paper presented at the 30th annual meeting of the International Society for Traumatic Stress Studies, New Orleans, LA.

Mackintosh, M. A., Willis, E. A., & Morland, L. A. (2016, November). *Effects of dysregulated anger on cognitive processing therapy outcomes* [Paper presentation]. International Society for Traumatic Stress Studies 31st Annual Meeting, Dallas, TX, United States.

MacManus, D., Rona, R., Dickson, H., Somaini, G., Fear, N., & Wessely, S. (2015). Aggressive and violent behavior among military personnel deployed to Iraq and Afghanistan: Prevalence and link with deployment and combat exposure. *Epidemiologic Reviews*, *37*(1), 196–212. https://doi.org/10.1093/epirev/mxu006

Momeni, J., Omidi, A., Raygan, F., & Akbari, H. (2016). The effects of mindfulness-based stress reduction on cardiac patients' blood pressure, perceived stress, and anger: A single-blind randomized controlled trial. *Journal of the American Society of Hypertension*, *10*(10), 763–771. https://doi.org/10.1016/j.jash.2016.07.007

Morland, L. A., Greene, C. J., Rosen, C. S., Foy, D., Reilly, P., Shore, J., He, Q., & Frueh, B. C. (2010). Telemedicine for anger management therapy in a rural population of combat veterans with posttraumatic stress disorder: A randomized noninferiority trial. *The Journal of Clinical Psychiatry*, *71*(7), 855–863. https://doi.org/10.4088/JCP.09m05604blu

Morland, L. A., Love, A. R., Mackintosh, M. A., Greene, C. J., & Rosen, C. S. (2012). Treating anger and aggression in military populations: Research updates and clinical implications. *Clinical Psychology: Science and Practice*, *19*(3), 305–322. https://doi.org/10.1111/cpsp.12007

Morland, L. A., Niehaus, J., Taft, C., Marx, B. P., Menez, U., & Mackintosh, M. A. (2016). Using a mobile application in the management of anger problems among veterans: A pilot study. *Military Medicine*, *181*(9), 990–995. https://doi.org/10.7205/MILMED-D-15-00293

Novaco, R. W. (2003). *The Novaco Anger Scale and Provocation Inventory (NAS-PI)*. Western Psychological Services.

Novaco, R. W. (2011). Perspectives on anger treatment: Discussion and commentary. *Cognitive and Behavioral Practice, 18*(2), 251–255. https://doi.org/10.1016/j.cbpra.2010.11.002

O'Donnell, C. R., & Worell, L. (1973). Motor and cognitive relaxation in the desensitization of anger. *Behaviour Research and Therapy, 11*(4), 473–481. https://doi.org/10.1016/0005-7967(73)90106-X

Orth, U., & Wieland, E. (2006). Anger, hostility, and posttraumatic stress disorder in trauma-exposed adults: A meta-analysis. *Journal of Consulting and Clinical Psychology, 74*(4), 698–706. https://doi.org/10.1037/0022-006X.74.4.698

Owens, G. P., Chard, K. M., & Cox, T. A. (2008). The relationship between maladaptive cognitions, anger expression, and posttraumatic stress disorder among veterans in residential treatment. *Journal of Aggression, Maltreatment & Trauma, 17*(4), 439–452. https://doi.org/10.1080/10926770802473908

Park, J. M., & Choi, I. R. (2016). The effect of K-MBSR program on stress, stress coping style, depression, anger and sleep of middle aged women. *Journal of Korean Academy of Nursing, 46*(2), 194–206. https://doi.org/10.4040/jkan.2016.46.2.194

Plambeck, K. L. (2015). *Acceptance and commitment therapy (ACT) treatment groups targeting the reduction of problematic anger-related behaviors and psychological inflexibility in incarcerated men: A pilot study* (Publication No. 3664509) [Doctoral dissertation]. ProQuest Dissertations and Theses Global.

Reilly, P. M., Clark, H. W., Shopshire, M. S., & Delucchi, K. L. (1996). Anger management, posttraumatic stress disorder, and substance abuse. In L. S. Harris (Ed.), *Problems of Drug Dependence, 1995: Proceedings of the 57th Annual Scientific Meeting, The College on Problems of Drug Dependence, Inc.* (p. 322). National Institute on Drug Abuse.

Reilly, P. M., & Shopshire, M. S. (2000). Anger management group treatment for cocaine dependence: Preliminary outcomes. *The American Journal of Drug and Alcohol Abuse, 26*(2), 161–177. https://doi.org/10.1081/ADA-100100598

Reilly, P. M., & Shopshire, M. S. (2002). *Anger management for substance abuse and mental health clients: A cognitive behavioral therapy manual.* Center for Substance Abuse Treatment, Substance Abuse and Mental Health Services Administration.

Reilly, P. M., & Shopshire, M. S. (2019). *Anger management for substance abuse and mental health clients: A cognitive-behavioral therapy manual.* Center for Substance Abuse Treatment, Substance Abuse and Mental Health Services Administration.

Reilly, P. M., Shopshire, M. S., & Clark, H. (1999). An anger management treatment for cocaine dependent patients. In L. S. Harris (Ed.), *Problems of drug dependence, 1998: Proceedings of the 60th Annual Scientific Meeting, The College on Problems of Drug Dependence.* (p. 226). Lane Rockville, MD: National Institute on Drug Abuse.

Riddle, J. R., Smith, T. C., Smith, B., Corbeil, T. E., Engel, C. C., Wells, T. S., Hoge, C. W., Adkins, J., Zamorski, M., Blazer, D., & the Millennium Cohort Study Team. (2007). Millennium Cohort: The 2001–2003 baseline prevalence of mental disorders in the U.S. military. *Journal of Clinical Epidemiology, 60*(2), 192–201. https://doi.org/10.1016/j.jclinepi.2006.04.008

Rimm, D. C., deGroot, J. C., Boord, P., Heiman, J., & Dillow, P. V. (1971). Systematic desensitization of an anger response. *Behaviour Research and Therapy, 9*(3), 273–280. https://doi.org/10.1016/0005-7967(71)90013-1

Saavedra, K. (2008). *Toward a new Acceptance and Commitment Therapy (ACT) treatment of problematic anger for low income minorities in substance abuse recovery: A randomized controlled experiment* [Unpublished doctoral dissertation]. Wright Institute.

Schnurr, P. P., & Lunney, C. A. (2019). Residual symptoms following prolonged exposure and present-centered therapy for PTSD in female veterans and soldiers. *Depression and Anxiety*, *36*(2), 162–169. https://doi.org/10.1002/da.22871

Schwarz, N. (2007). Retrospective and concurrent self-reports: The rationale for real-time data capture. In A. A. Stone, S. Schiffman, A. A. Atienza, & L. Nebeling (Eds.), *The science of real-time data capture: Self-reports in health research* (pp. 11–26). Oxford University Press.

Shea, M. T., Lambert, J., & Reddy, M. K. (2013). A randomized pilot study of anger treatment for Iraq and Afghanistan veterans. *Behaviour Research and Therapy*, *51*(10), 607–613. https://doi.org/10.1016/j.brat.2013.05.013

Shopshire, M. S., Reilly, P. M., & Ouaou, R. (1996). Anger management strategies associated with decreased anger in substance abuse patients. In L. S. Harris (Ed.), *Problems of Drug Dependence, 1996: Proceedings of the 58th Annual Scientific Meeting, The College on Problems of Drug Dependence, Inc.* (p. 226). National Institute on Drug Abuse.

Siegel, J. M. (1986). The Multidimensional Anger Inventory. *Journal of Personality and Social Psychology*, *51*(1), 191–200. https://doi.org/10.1037/0022-3514.51.1.191

Smith, S. M., Goldstein, R. B., & Grant, B. F. (2016). The association between posttraumatic stress disorder and lifetime *DSM-5* psychiatric disorders among veterans: Data from the National Epidemiologic Survey on Alcohol and Related Conditions-III (NESARC-III). *Journal of Psychiatric Research*, *82*, 16–22. https://doi.org/10.1016/j.jpsychires.2016.06.022

Speca, M., Carlson, L. E., Goodey, E., & Angen, M. (2000). A randomized, wait-list controlled clinical trial: The effect of a mindfulness meditation-based stress reduction program on mood and symptoms of stress in cancer outpatients. *Psychosomatic Medicine*, *62*(5), 613–622. https://doi.org/10.1097/00006842-200009000-00004

Spielberger, C. D. (1999). *STAXI-2: State–Trait Anger Expression Inventory-2: Professional manual*. Psychological Assessment Resources.

Stapleton, J. A., Taylor, S., & Asmundson, G. J. (2006). Effects of three PTSD treatments on anger and guilt: Exposure therapy, eye movement desensitization and reprocessing, and relaxation training. *Journal of Traumatic Stress*, *19*(1), 19–28. https://doi.org/10.1002/jts.20095

Steenkamp, M. M., Litz, B. T., Hoge, C. W., & Marmar, C. R. (2015). Psychotherapy for military-related PTSD: A review of randomized clinical trials. *Journal of the American Medical Association*, *314*(5), 489–500. https://doi.org/10.1001/jama.2015.8370

Stone, C., & Stone, D. L. (2015). Factors affecting hiring decisions about veterans. *Human Resource Management Review*, *25*(1), 68–79. https://doi.org/10.1016/j.hrmr.2014.06.003

Straus, M. A., Hamby, S. L., Boney-McCoy, S. U. E., & Sugarman, D. B. (1996). The Revised Conflict Tactics Scales (CTS2). *Journal of Family Issues*, *17*(3), 283–316. https://doi.org/10.1177/019251396017003001

U.S. Department of Veterans Affairs and Department of Defense. (2017). *VA/DOD clinical practice guideline for the management of posttraumatic stress disorder and acute stress disorder*.

van der Velden, P. G., Rademaker, A. R., Vermetten, E., Portengen, M. A., Yzermans, J. C., & Grievink, L. (2013). Police officers: A high-risk group for the development of mental health disturbances? A cohort study. *BMJ Open*, *3*(1), e001720. https://doi.org/10.1136/bmjopen-2012-001720

Watts, B. V., Schnurr, P. P., Mayo, L., Young-Xu, Y., Weeks, W. B., & Friedman, M. J. (2013). Meta-analysis of the efficacy of treatments for posttraumatic stress disorder. *The Journal of Clinical Psychiatry*, *74*(6), e541–e550. https://doi.org/10.4088/JCP.12r08225

Weathers, F. W., Blake, D. D., Schnurr, P. P., Kaloupek, D. G., Marx, B. P., & Keane, T. M. (2013). The clinician-administered PTSD scale for *DSM-5* (CAPS-5). https://www.ptsd.va.gov/professional/assessment/adult-int/caps.asp#obtain

Weingardt, K. R., & Greene, C. J. (2015). New electronic tools for veterans. *North Carolina Medical Journal*, *76*(5), 332–334. https://doi.org/10.18043/ncm.76.5.332

Wolpe, J. (1973). *The practice of behavior therapy*. Pergamon.

Wolpe, J., & Lazarus, A. A. (1966). *Behavior therapy techniques: A guide to the treatment of neuroses*. Pergamon.

Worthen, M., Rathod, S. D., Cohen, G., Sampson, L., Ursano, R., Gifford, R., Fullerton, C., Galea, S., & Ahern, J. (2014). Anger problems and posttraumatic stress disorder in male and female National Guard and Reserve Service members. *Journal of Psychiatric Research*, *55*, 52–58. https://doi.org/10.1016/j.jpsychires.2014.04.004

Zarling, A., Lawrence, E., & Marchman, J. (2015). A randomized controlled trial of acceptance and commitment therapy for aggressive behavior. *Journal of Consulting and Clinical Psychology*, *83*(1), 199–212. https://doi.org/10.1037/a0037946

Zayfert, C., & DeViva, J. C. (2004). Residual insomnia following cognitive behavioral therapy for PTSD. *Journal of Traumatic Stress*, *17*(1), 69–73. https://doi.org/10.1023/B:JOTS.0000014679.31799.e7

9 COGNITIVE BIAS INTERVENTIONS

GAL ARAD AND YAIR BAR-HAIM

KEY POINTS

- Some of the mechanisms fueling anger and aggressive behavior are related to biased attention and interpretation processes.
- These processes are largely automatic and are associated with the initiation and preservation of anger and aggression.
- Although attention and interpretation are not under direct volitional control, it is possible to measure and modify anger-related biases through mechanized interventions.
- Cognitive bias modification techniques show promise in the treatment of various psychopathologies but are still only scantly applied to anger. Extant evidence indicate promise for such techniques in moderating anger. Future application in the workplace context is warranted.

https://doi.org/10.1037/0000244-010
Anger at Work: Prevention, Intervention, and Treatment in High-Risk Occupations,
A. B. Adler and D. Forbes (Editors)

In this chapter, we review the literature on anger-related cognitive biases, as well as cognitive bias modification and its effectiveness as applied to different components of anger and aggressive behavior. Although this topic has been widely researched in various contexts, and mainly in relation to anxiety and traumatic stress, anger-related cognitive biases and their manifestation in the workplace have not been directly explored. However, the extant information can offer meaningful insights for anger in the workplace and for high-risk occupations in particular, in which high stress and exposure to extreme and potentially traumatic events are routine. We also review data on the interplay between anger and cognitive biases and on their potential influence on functioning in the workplace.

COGNITIVE MODELS OF ANGER

Appraisal theories of emotion (e.g., Arnold, 1960; Frijda, 1988; Lazarus, 1991; Scherer, 1984) view cognitive processes as precursors of all emotions, including anger. Such theories postulate that one's subjective cognitive evaluations of a given situation, rather than the situation itself, will determine whether an emotion is evoked and which emotion will be evoked (Roseman & Smith, 2001).

Accordingly, people rapidly determine which stimuli in their environment are relevant for processing. This rapid determination includes directing selective attention to information that is significant for well-being, current goals, needs, or concerns. Attended information is then evaluated on the basis of past experience, motivations, and other idiosyncratic factors that determine which emotions are experienced (Wranik & Scherer, 2010). Although appraisals may consist of effortful, conscious, and controlled cognitive processes, most theories presume that appraisals often occur automatically, based on schematic structures acquired from previous experience, without requiring effortful thinking (Roseman & Smith, 2001).

Within this framework, trait anger can be understood in terms of higher accessibility or activation levels of particular evaluations, leading to more frequent or intense experiences of anger under certain circumstances. For example, anger is related to appraisals of goal obstruction, others' hostility, or blameworthiness and injustice. Thus, enhanced attention to and biased evaluations of others' hostile intentionality may be linked to dysfunctional anger. Moreover, from this perspective, because anger is caused by certain appraisal tendencies, changes in appraisal may lead to changes in anger. This presumption is reflected in treatments for anger that commonly include cognitive restructuring, as cognitive restructuring involves altering attentional focus and modifying anger-provoking appraisals (e.g., A. T. Beck, 1999; Deffenbacher & McKay, 2000).

One example of attention and interpretation processes in anger expression is the association between anger and combat-related posttraumatic stress disorder (PTSD; Chemtob et al., 1994; Novaco & Chemtob, 2002; Sakusic et al., 2010). Anger control problems were found to be the most prevalent readjustment problem among war veterans (Sayer et al., 2010), influencing mental and physical health as well as psychosocial functioning (Novaco et al., 2012). Chemtob and colleagues (1988) suggested that individuals with combat-related PTSD are engaged in survival mode behaviors in inappropriate circumstances and that less evidence of threat is required to induce survival mode action in these individuals (Novaco & Chemtob, 2002). Biased activation of threat schemas in PTSD may increase vigilance and potentiate anger, a combination that can facilitate aggressive and harmful behaviors in benign contexts. Indeed, anger, alienation, and hostility are widely evidenced among soldiers returning home from combat (Adler et al., 2011; Novaco & Chemtob, 2002; Pardeck, 1982), as are high levels of aggressive and violent behavior (Adler et al., 2011; Killgore et al., 2008; McCarroll et al., 2000).

Several specific models have been proposed to describe the ways by which different cognitive processes relate to anger and aggression. One influential example is social information processing theory (Crick & Dodge, 1994). According to this theory, the first steps of cognitive processing create mental representations of social situations. These steps include focusing attention on particular cues in the environment, encoding them, and interpreting them using schemata based on previous experience. Biased processing at either stage (elevated attention to potentially hostile cues or hostile attribution biases) may predispose an individual toward increased anger and reactive aggression. Another model—the integrative cognitive model of trait anger and reactive aggression (Wilkowski & Robinson, 2008, 2010)—suggests that individuals with high trait anger are predisposed to automatically interpret ambiguous situations in a hostile manner, tend to engage their attention on such hostile information, and fail to use effortful control resources to modulate these automatic tendencies.

Overall, appraisal theories of emotion, as well as more specific models of trait anger and reactive aggression (Roseman & Smith, 2001), postulate that both attention and interpretation processes reflect initial stages of information processing that are biased in anger prone individuals. Empirical support for the associations between trait anger and biased attention and interpretation is emerging. This literature is reviewed in the following sections.

ATTENTION PROCESSES

Empirical data support an association between trait anger and biased processing of anger-related information at the attentional level (for reviews, see Owen, 2011; Schultz et al., 2010). Three main tasks have been used to study attentional bias: emotional Stroop, visual search, and dot probe. In the following subsections, we describe these tasks and how they have revealed evidence of attentional bias related to anger.

Emotional Stroop

Essentially, the emotional Stroop task models one's ability to perform a task involving certain features of a target while ignoring other potentially distracting features. This task assesses anger-related biased processing by quantifying the interference exerted by anger-related stimuli on reaction time or accuracy while performing an unrelated task. The emotional Stroop task displays words of different valence printed in different colors. Color-naming latency is compared between trials presenting threat-related words (e.g., "fight") and trials presenting neutral words (e.g., "chair"; see Figure 9.1). In a faces-based variation of the emotional Stroop, participants view faces

FIGURE 9.1. Emotional Stroop Task

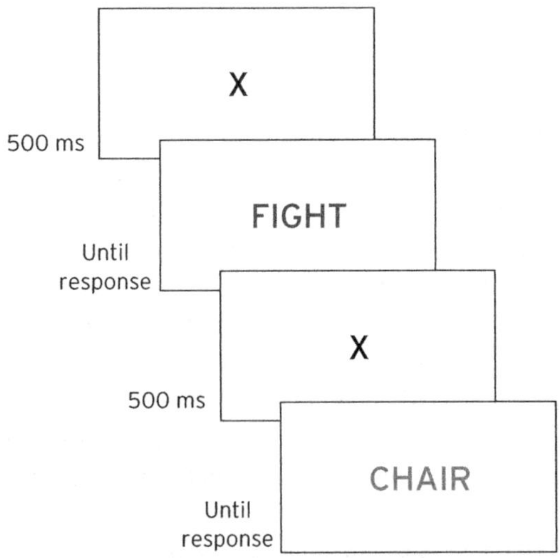

Note. Participants are asked to name the color of the word in each trial, with word valence being anger-related (first trial) or neutral (second trial).

displaying either threatening or neutral expressions and are required to name the color that is superimposed on the face picture. Studies in clinical populations indicate that patients are slower in naming stimuli with a content that matches their clinical status. For instance, anxious participants are slower to name the color of threat relative to neutral words, a bias not observed in nonanxious participants.

A common explanation for this effect is that biased attention toward trait-relevant but task-irrelevant stimuli hinders performance, causing longer reaction times (Bar-Haim et al., 2007; MacLeod, 1991; Williams et al., 1996). In the context of anger, negative words and angry faces have been found to induce greater cognitive interference (reflected in longer response times) relative to neutral stimuli on the emotional Stroop task in participants with high relative to low trait anger (Van Honk, Tuiten, De Haan, et al., 2001; Van Honk, Tuiten, Van den Hout, et al., 2001). Individuals high in revenge-planning, an anger-related behavior, also demonstrate greater interference by angry facial expressions in the Stroop task even when these are presented subconsciously (Crowe & Wilkowski, 2013). Furthermore, when anger was experimentally induced in participants, similar effects were found with longer color naming latencies after anger induction relative to baseline (Eckhardt & Cohen, 1997).

Visual Search

This task models one's capacity to continue visual scanning of the environment in the presence of anger-related or hostile detractions. In visual search tasks, participants are required to identify the location of a target (e.g., the neutral word "chair") among several visual distractors of a different valence (e.g., threat-related words such as "scared"), competing for attention (see Figure 9.2). In this task, *interference* is defined as the increase in time or decrease in accuracy for trials with threat-related distractors as opposed to neutral or positive distractors. Two studies applying a visual search tasks have shown that participants high in trait anger (Cohen et al., 1998) and violent offenders (Smith & Waterman, 2004) display greater interference (i.e., slower times to detect a neutral target while ignoring hostile distractors) than participants low in trait anger.

The Dot-Probe Task

The dot-probe task models spatial attention patterns to anger-related versus neutral stimuli when these compete for attention resources. In this task (MacLeod et al., 1986), two stimuli are presented simultaneously: one

FIGURE 9.2. Visual Search Task

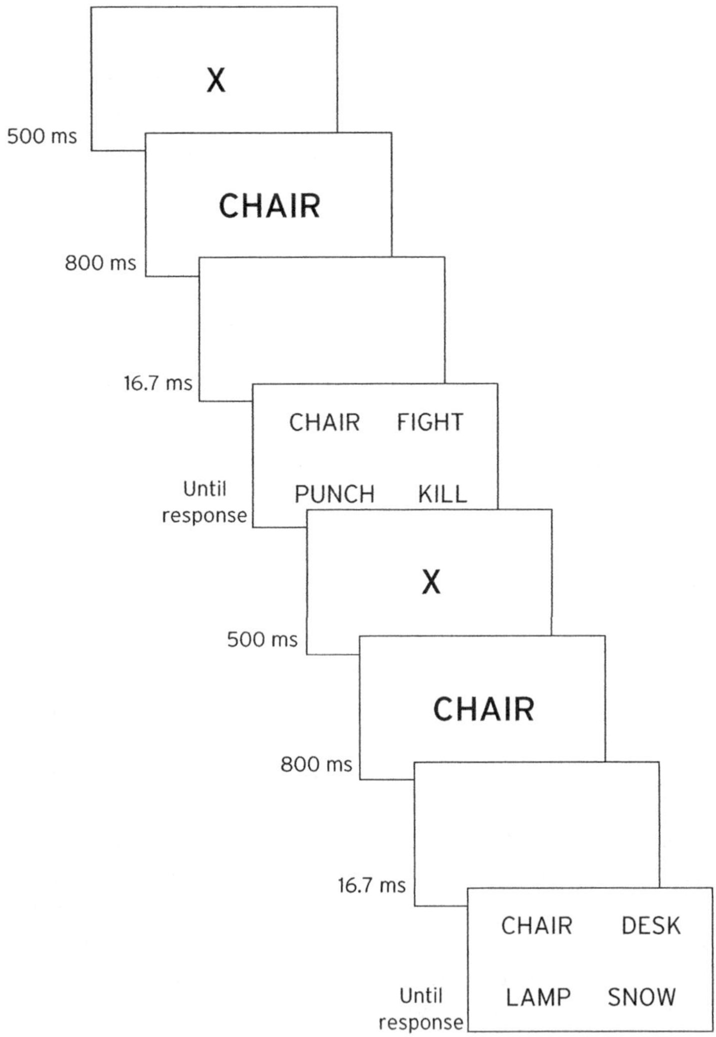

Note. Participants are asked to identify the location of a neutral target word within an array of either anger-related (first trial) or neutral (second trial) words.

neutral and one suspected to incur attention bias (e.g., disgusted faces for social anxiety, threat-related words for PTSD, anger-related words for anger prone individuals).

After the display of these two stimuli, they disappear and in the place of one of them appears a target probe to which participants are asked to respond (see Figure 9.3). Faster reaction times when target probes appear at the location of the threat-related stimulus rather than the neutral stimulus are thought to reflect vigilance, or an attention bias toward threat. This task has been widely used to assess attentional biases in anxiety (Cisler & Koster, 2010) depression (Peckham et al., 2010), eating disorders (Aspen et al., 2013), and addiction (Field & Cox, 2008). Two studies used this task to assess anger-related attention biases in clinical populations and demonstrated

FIGURE 9.3. Dot-Probe Task

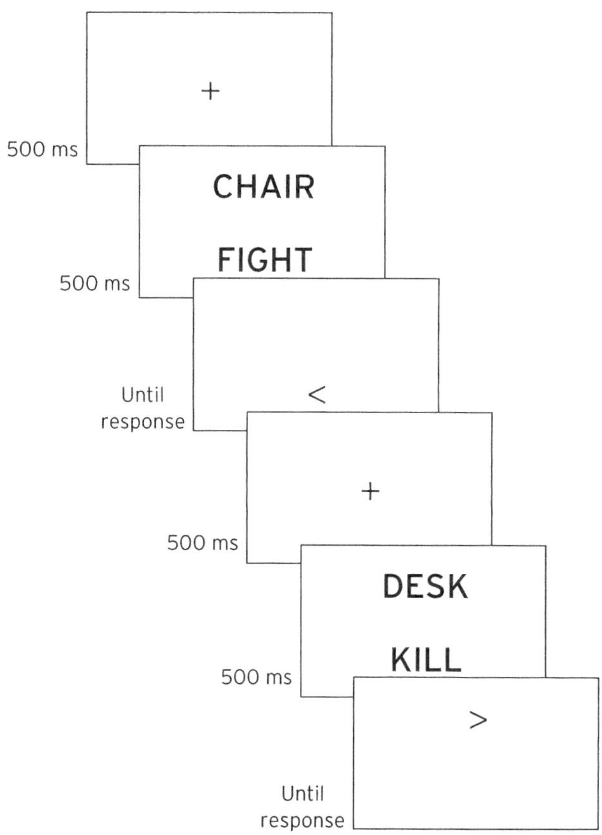

Note. Participants are asked to identify the direction of an arrow probe appearing at the location of either anger-related (first trial) or neutral (second trial).

attention biases toward aggression-related words and faces in a sample of violent offenders (Smith & Waterman, 2003) and in youth with severe mood dysregulation, a condition characterized by high levels of irritability and anger (Hommer et al., 2014).

In nonselected samples, higher trait anger had been associated with enhanced attention to aggressively themed words (Smith & Waterman, 2003) and with an attention bias toward angry faces (Maoz et al., 2017). More specifically, Maoz et al. (2017) found that attention bias toward angry faces was associated with lower ability to control anger expression but not with anger expression per se, suggesting that anger-related attention bias influences aggressive behavior via processes of anger regulation rather than anger expression (Maoz et al., 2017).

The exact mechanisms through which attention deployment affects anger and aggression are not fully understood. Van Honk and colleagues (Van Honk & Schutter, 2007; Van Honk, Tuiten, De Haan, et al., 2001) proposed a dominance-based explanation for the association between increased attention to threat/anger-related stimuli and aggression and anger. These authors suggested that to maintain dominance within their social environments, angry individuals might be keen to detect anger and potential aggression threats as quickly as possible. That is, when presented with potential anger/threat cues, individuals high in trait anger may more readily perceive these as a challenge to their social status and allocate more processing resources toward such stimuli. This possibility is partially supported by neurocognitive findings indicating that elevated attention bias to angry faces is associated with higher levels of testosterone (for a review, see Van Honk & Schutter, 2007), a hormone related to dominance, aggression, and anger (Peterson & Harmon-Jones, 2012). More research is needed to determine the exact mechanisms linking biased attention and anger, and whether these associations reflect a causal mechanism in anger or a mere by-product of anger.

Summary and Workplace Applications

Attention biases toward anger-related stimuli have been shown to negatively influence functioning. In the workplace, this bias can have extensive implications for professional functioning but also on the workplace atmosphere, teamwork, and efficiency, as indicated by both emotional contagion and emotional cycle theories (Barsade, 2002; Elfenbein, 2014; Gibson & Callister, 2010; Hareli & Rafaeli, 2008). For example, in a professional environment, disagreements are a common occurrence. An employee with an anger-related attention bias may be more sensitive or vulnerable to distractions because of potentially mild anger cues. They may find it difficult to stay "on task" when a coworker expresses their opinion more aggressively or when a colleague shows signs of disagreement. This can also affect specific relationships within the workplace. A relationship may involve many interactions with a colleague, most of which are benign but may also at times be argumentative or competitive. An employee with an attentional bias toward anger-related information may experience such interactions as more salient, fueling aggressive or retaliatory behaviors. Such behaviors, fueled by biased attention patterns, could be highly disruptive for both the employee and their environment (Cheshin et al., 2011; Geddes & Stickney, 2011; Gibson et al., 2009). The impact of anger-related attentional biases can be exacerbated in high-risk workplaces because of both higher exposure to aggression-related cues and the severe consequences of inappropriate or incompatible reactions. For example, when performing crowd control during a protest, police officers are often exposed to hostility from protesters. Officers with an anger-related attention bias may be more sensitive to cues of potential aggression, particularly during periods of stress. As a result, such an officer may respond more quickly and aggressively than necessary, leading to undue violence. Another example comes from deploying soldiers. Anger-related attentional vigilance may serve an adaptive function in combat but could be deleterious and anxiety provoking upon reintegration into a civilian environment.

INTERPRETATION PROCESSES

High trait anger and anger arousal have also been associated with biased interpretation of ambiguous information, typically attribution of anger, hostility, and negative intent to others, as well as more negative interpretation of ambiguous events and stimuli (for reviews, see Owen, 2011; Schultz et al., 2010).

The tendency of anger-prone or aggression-prone individuals to automatically infer hostile intent in a benign situation is often referred to as *hostile interpretation bias*. For example, Hazebroek et al. (2001) showed video clips of social interactions to individuals high and low in trait anger. Although all video clips depicted a negative outcome, half showed clear deliberate intent and half showed ambiguous intent. Relative to individuals with low trait anger, individuals high in trait anger more readily identified another person as an antagonist, tended to put more blame on the antagonist, identified negative events as more relevant to their own interests, and responded more angrily to the events. Furthermore, these biases were more prominent when the intentionality of the provoking event was ambiguous. In a different study, participants with high trait anger were more likely to select anger-related explanations for ambiguous events relative to anxious participants and nonangry and nonanxious participants (Wenzel & Lystad, 2005). Such aggressive attributions appear to start early in life. For example, following a frustrating negative outcome caused by a peer, aggressive and nonaggressive children differed in their reaction only under conditions of ambiguous intentionality, with aggressive children responding as if the peer's intent was hostile (Dodge, 1980). Aggressive children, adolescents, and adults also demonstrate hostile attribution of intent to ambiguous facial expressions or actions (e.g., Barazzone & Davey, 2009; Wilkowski & Robinson, 2012), and this result has been replicated in many studies, using different procedures and with various populations including normal, clinical, and forensic samples (Dodge, 2006; for a meta-analysis, see Orobio de Castro et al., 2002).

Similar biases emerge regarding interpretation of facial expressions (for a review, see Mellentin et al., 2015), where increasing levels of self-reported aggression correlate with an increased tendency to mislabel different emotions as anger (e.g., Hall, 2006) and to infer hostility from neutral faces (e.g., Burt et al., 2009). One task used to detect interpretation biases of ambiguous emotional stimuli is the emotion perception task (Figure 9.4). In this task, two distinct facial expressions at either end of an emotion continuum (e.g., angry-to-happy) are morphed to generate ambiguous facial stimuli along the continuum (Jusyte & Schönenberg, 2014). Maoz (2017) asked undergraduate participants to label the emotion displayed by such morphed ambiguous faces ranging from positive (happy) to negative (angry) emotion. The propensity to quickly interpret ambiguous faces as angry was associated with greater anger expression and with lower anger control.

Using the same paradigm, youth with disruptive mood dysregulation disorder (DMDD), characterized by high irritability and anger regulation difficulties, showed a greater tendency than their healthy peers to classify ambiguous faces as angry than as happy (Stoddard et al., 2016). Similarly, children who were rated as angry by their teachers and peers demonstrated more anger attribution biases when interpreting ambiguous facial expressions as well as ambiguous social situations (Schultz et al., 2004). Studies on violent offenders and psychiatric patients characterized with heightened hostility found that compared with healthy or nonviolent controls, they tended to interpret ambiguous facial expressions as hostile and to overrate anger intensity (Jusyte & Schönenberg, 2014; Smeijers et al., 2017; Wegrzyn et al., 2017). These empirical examples suggest that anger-prone individuals are biased toward hostile interpretations of social information, in line with the aforementioned cognitive models of anger.

FIGURE 9.4. Emotion Perception Task

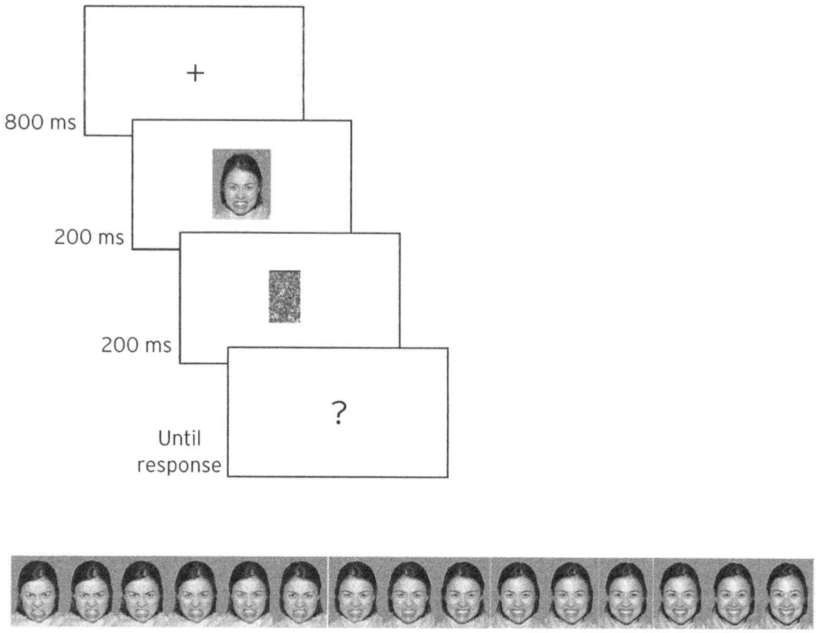

Note. Participants are asked to label the emotion displayed by an ambiguous face ranging from a happy to an angry emotion. Faces were taken from the NimStim set. From "The NimStim Set of Facial Expressions: Judgments From Untrained Research Participants," by N. Tottenham, J. W. Tanaka, A. C. Leon, T. McCarry, M. Nurse, T. A. Hare, D. J. Marcus, A. Westerlund, B. J. Casey, and C. Nelson, 2009, *Psychiatry Research, 168*(3), pp. 242–249, model 18 (https://doi.org/10.1016/j.psychres.2008.05.006). Copyright 2009 by Elsevier. Adapted with permission.

In summary, people high in anger and aggressive tendencies misinterpret social situations as more volatile, deliberate, and aggressive and respond accordingly. Most often, this occurs in situations of ambiguity. Many workplaces routinely offer ambiguous social and professional circumstances. When faced with ambiguous facial expressions during a workgroup meeting or with undesirable work-related results, employees higher in aggression or anger might more readily attribute negative intentionality and emotions to their workmates. Such negatively biased attributions can instigate disputes and grudges that can derail professional goals and productive teamwork. For example, an employee may discover a mistake made by a colleague. If this employee is high in trait anger or aggression, they are more likely to assume that the spotted mistake was not innocent but rather made with malicious intent. They might openly blame their coworker for the mistake and possibly interpret their coworker's offended response as hostile or aggressive. Such interactions may result in an unnecessary crisis at the workplace. Although interpretation biases are often automatic and in no way intentional, they can exert great influence on a workplace's professional processes and interpersonal ambience (Barsade, 2002; Elfenbein, 2014; Gibson & Callister, 2010; Hareli & Rafaeli, 2008).

In a high-risk workplace, interpretation biases can be dangerous. Police officers, soldiers, and firefighters are constantly required to work under ambiguous conditions and make life-and-death decisions based on incomplete and missing information. Interpreting benign or vague situations as hostile and therefore dangerous can have devastating implications. For example, a police officer answering a call is often required to quickly and accurately identify the offender and victim in the situation. High trait anger may cause misinterpretation of fear, confusion, agitation, or shock as aggression and threat, and cause an officer to respond based on this misinterpretation. Such biased interpretations might lead to misdirected professional aggression in situations that could otherwise be resolved peacefully.

COGNITIVE BIAS MODIFICATION

Cognitive bias modification (CBM) refers to the process designed to modify cognitive biases in patients with psychological disorders such as anxiety, depression, and addiction for which the presence of specific cognitive biases has been established. CBM includes a variety of training and treatment protocols targeting specific cognitive aberrations such as attention biases, interpretation biases, and approach/avoidance biases. CBM research in the context of anger and aggression is still in its early days. In this context, it may be useful to refer to the process model of emotion regulation proposed by Gross (1998, 2013; Gross & Thompson, 2007), describing the involvement of distinct stages in the process of emotion generation that, in turn, offer potential windows for intervention and regulation.

In his model, Gross outlined an emotion-generative cycle with four distinct stages—situation, attention, appraisal, and response—that could be adapted to the emotion of anger (see Figure 9.5). Gross portrayed opportunities for emotion regulation that correspond to these four stages of emotion generation: (a) One can select to avoid certain anger-provoking situations (e.g., Joe, a police officer, knows he tends to respond aggressively during arrests; he may therefore ask for a desk job that doesn't require this type of interactions—*situation selection*), (b) one could alter a situation to better

FIGURE 9.5. Process Model of Emotion Regulation

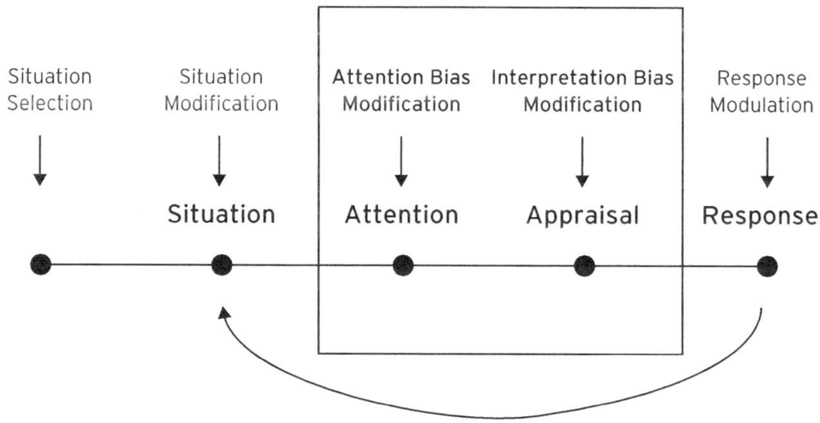

Note. Adapted from "Emotion Regulation: Taking Stock and Moving Forward," by J. J. Gross, 2013, *Emotion, 13*(3), p. 360 (https://doi.org/10.1037/a0032135). Copyright 2013 by the American Psychological Association.

regulate their emotions (e.g., Joe could ask his partner to make the arrest while he provides backup so he has more time to assess and respond—*situation modification*), (c) one could attempt to regulate anger by paying more or less attention to certain aspects of a situation (*attentional deployment*), (d) one could attempt to appraise situations in manners that promote emotion regulation (*appraisal*), and (e) people can attempt to modulate their emotional response once evoked (e.g., if Joe found himself in an overly aggressive arrest, he could attempt to suppress his anger and respond more moderately, or ask his partner to help him to do so—*response modulation*). The first four regulation windows reflect antecedent-focused strategies; they refer to actions taken to alter a potentially anger-evoking situation. The last regulation option of the model refers to response-focused strategies, that is, actions taken once anger has been incurred. Importantly, the model takes into account the fact that one's response to the situation influences and creates new situations.

Most extant anger interventions focus on top-down processes involved in situation selection, situation modification, and response modulation (R. Beck & Fernandez, 1998; Deffenbacher, 2011). Interventions encouraging conscious efforts at the attention and appraisal stages have also shown some promise, using cognitive reappraisal strategies (Lazarus & Alfert, 1964; Ray et al., 2008; Szasz et al., 2011). However, attention and interpretation processes often reflect rapid and automatic actions not readily accessible to conscious control (Amir et al., 1998; Barry et al., 2015; Carretié et al., 2004; Roseman &

Smith, 2001). As such, biased attention and interpretation processes might be difficult to modify through conscious effort and may be more effectively targeted through specialized CBM techniques (Lazarov et al., 2018; Shechner et al., 2014; White et al., 2017). Next, we describe such bottom-up intervention procedures targeting biases at the attention and appraisal stages of emotion generation.

In most cases, the tasks used for CBM are similar to the cognitive tasks used to evaluate these biases at the trait level at baseline (Figures 9.1–9.4). However, in CBM protocols, specific in-task contingencies between emotional valence of the presented stimuli and task demands are varied so as to encourage the desirable alternation in cognitive processing (Bar-Haim, 2010; Koster et al., 2009). For instance, in dot-probe-based CBM interventions for anxiety designed to reduce vigilance toward threat, target probes are placed more frequently at neutral stimuli locations rather than threat-related locations. This pattern gradually trains participants to allocate attention away from threat and toward neutral stimuli, thereby rectifying an original attention bias toward threat and reducing anxiety. Randomized controlled trials of CBM suggest efficacy in reducing symptoms of generalized anxiety disorder (Amir, Beard, Burns, & Bomyea, 2009; Hazen et al., 2009), social anxiety disorder (Amir, Beard, Taylor, et al., 2009; Amir et al., 2008, 2010; Pergamin-Hight et al., 2016; Schmidt et al., 2009), dysphoric and depressive symptoms (Blackwell & Holmes, 2010; Lang et al., 2012; Watkins et al., 2009; Wells & Beevers, 2010), and PTSD symptoms (Badura-Brack et al., 2015; Wald et al., 2017). Meta-analyses indicate a medium effect size for clinical efficacy in anxiety (Hakamata et al., 2010; Linetzky et al., 2015) and smaller effects in depression (Hallion & Ruscio, 2011; Mogoaşe et al., 2014) and addictions (Christiansen et al., 2015; Cristea et al., 2016). Unfortunately, much less CBM work exists in the field of anger and aggression, but the processes should be similarly affected by bias modification techniques.

CBM in the context of anger-related therapeutics may hold several advantages. First, most current anger treatments rely on verbal dialogue, psychoeducation, and explicit attempts to change or control one's information-processing biases. However, as just indicated, cognitive biases are often automatic and are not under simple volitional control. Thus, a more direct alternative to modify such processes via repeated practice in cognitive computerized tasks that require rapid processing may be more effective (Beard, 2011). Second, although current anger treatments usually focus on altering cognitive processing of situations or events, CBM may target more basic components of these complex situations, such as the processing of facial expressions, a fundamental element in understanding of basic human interactions. Third, current anger treatments tend to suffer from high attrition rates (e.g., Hird et al., 1997; Linkh & Sonnek, 2003; Siddle et al., 2003). Computerized interventions may improve treatment compliance, as they are cheaper, less time-consuming, and more accessible. CBM interventions carry a large potential for dissemination and could therefore be advantageous not only for patients who suffer from current anger-related problems but also as means for preventing excessive anger in populations at risk for developing maladaptive anger (e.g., soldiers with a history of traumatic combat experiences, first responders dealing with high stress, workers with a history of violence or anger management difficulties). Last, there may be an advantage for interventions targeting anger that are nonconfrontational in nature and where patients will not feel judged or misunderstood for their (mis)interpretations of hostile or angering situations. In conventional therapy, anger-prone patients often resent a therapist's suggestion that they have misinterpreted certain situations or that they, rather than others, are at fault for the way they feel (DiGiuseppe & Tafrate, 2003; Gorenstein et al., 2007; Siddle et al., 2003). Therefore, treatments that reduce anger-related cognitive biases but also offer some emotional distance may provide some relief, even as a basis for improving effectiveness of future psychotherapy. Next, we review findings from preliminary implementations of CBM to anger-related issues.

ATTENTION BIAS MODIFICATION

Although biased threat-related attention appears to be linked to both anxiety and anger, the vast number of computerized attention bias modification (ABM) training studies have been applied to anxiety symptoms (Bar-Haim, 2010; Beard, 2011; Hakamata et al., 2010; Hallion & Ruscio, 2011; Koster et al., 2009), whereas implementation in the context of anger is scant. ABM uses computer-based protocols to implicitly modify biased attentional patterns (Bar-Haim, 2010). Clinical ABM trials indicate that training anxious patients to attend away from threat reduces self-reported as well as clinician-evaluated anxiety levels (Hakamata et al., 2010; Heeren et al., 2015). In addition, studies with nonclinical high-anxious participants show that ABM training typically reduces stress vulnerability in the face of lab-induced (Amir et al., 2008; Bar-Haim et al., 2011; MacLeod et al., 2002) or real-life (See et al., 2009) stressors. To our knowledge, only one study has attempted to research the efficacy of ABM in reducing self-reported and expressed anger. In a randomized controlled trial (Maoz, 2017), participants high in trait anger were randomized to receive four sessions of either ABM training or a placebo training condition. Following training, participants in the ABM group, compared with the placebo training group, demonstrated less displaced retaliation toward an "innocent" player in the context of an ultimatum game. However, no detectable changes in self-reported anger, or physiological response (skin conductance) to anger-inducing situations, were found as a function of training type. These results suggest weak evidence of an effect of ABM on trait anger and aggression and may be due to the use of a nonclinical population or ineffective training variants. More research is required to determine the value of ABM as an intervention for anger and aggression issues.

INTERPRETATION BIAS MODIFICATION

The predisposition to interpret ambiguous information and stimuli in a negative or hostile manner is a key cognitive precursor of high trait anger and reactive aggression. Unlike with ABM, where evidence is scant, several studies have attempted to examine how to moderate anger and aggressive behavior by influencing basic processes of interpretation. Penton-Voak et al. (2013) used a computerized feedback-based training to modify participants' interpretations of ambiguous facial expression to be more positive oriented and less hostile oriented. The paradigm was based on the face-morphing task described earlier (Figure 9.1). For each participant, a balance point between angry and happy expression recognition was attained during a measurement phase, reflecting an estimate of the point in the morphed sequence in which a participant's interpretation shifted from happy to angry interpretation. In the training phase, feedback (a message saying "correct"/ "incorrect") appeared. Feedback was given in relation to the participant's balance point, but with correct responses shifted two morphed faces positions so that the two faces closest to the balance point and classified as angry would receive feedback indicating that "happy" was the correct response. This feedback was designed to shift the balance point of the participant away from "angry" interpretations. One session (180 trials) of this task resulted in reduced anger in a sample of undergraduate students as well as less aggressive behavior recorded by independent evaluators in a sample of frequently aggressive adolescents at risk for criminal behavior (Penton-Voak et al., 2013).

Two additional studies have tested this procedure in multiple training sessions. In one study, two sessions of training reduced perception of anger and speeded perceptions of happy faces compared with sham training in participants with high levels of trait anger. These effects also generalized to novel ambiguous faces, not used during training. Training also reduced displaced retaliatory behavior in a consecutive Ultimatum Game but did not influence direct retaliatory behavior or levels of trait anger (Maoz, 2017). In another study, Stoddard et al. (2016) delivered four daily training session over 4 days using the same task, which again resulted in a shift of the balance point toward the happy end of the continuum in both healthy participants and youth with DMDD. This shift in interpretation remained stable after 2 weeks without additional training. In the DMDD sample, this training regimen also led to a reduction in irritability, a major characteristic of the disorder, closely related to trait anger.

Other studies have attempted to influence interpretive biases by using verbal stimuli rather than faces. In this type of interpretation bias modification, participants are presented with scenarios describing daily social interactions with a potential for hostile or benign interpretations (e.g., a person bumps into you at the supermarket) and asked to imagine themselves in these scenarios. The presentation of each scenario is followed by a sentence resolving the ambiguity in either a positive way (the other person was clumsy) or a negative way (the other person was aggressive). In each of these sentences, one of the letters in the key word is omitted (e.g., clum_y/aggres_ive), and participants are requested to fill it in. Then the benign or hostile interpretation is reinforced by asking the participants comprehension questions ensuring that they answer according to their training condition (e.g., "Did the other person intend to bump into you?"). Such positive interpretation training was found to alter anger-related interpretation biases as well as decrease anger and irritation following an insult, compared with a control condition (Hawkins & Cougle, 2013).

In a similar study conducted with 10- to 12-year-olds high in aggressive behavior, a three-session intervention led to a decrease in hostile attributions as well as decrease in aggressive behavior and in self-reported anger scores compared with a group of nontrained controls (Vassilopoulos et al., 2015). This treatment protocol also showed encouraging results when administered online over eight sessions in a sample of adults with high trait anger and alcohol use disorder. Although treatment did not lead to decreases in alcoholism relative to a control group, it did lead to improvements in interpretation bias at posttreatment that was maintained after 1 month and to decreases in anger expression compared with the control group. These reductions in interpretation bias also mediated a larger decrease in trait anger for this active training group (Cougle et al., 2017).

Taken together, these findings point to interpretation biases in trait anger as being malleable to change and relevant targets for treatment. Various attempts to treat anger and anger-related pathologies using interpretation bias modification have shown promise across a range of clinical and nonclinical populations. Between one and eight sessions of treatment, using social situations or facial expressions managed to alter interpretations of ambiguous stimuli as well as anger, irritability, and retaliatory behaviors. These interventions show promise on several fronts. First, they are promising for individuals dealing with problematic anger following stressful or traumatic work-related experiences (e.g., soldiers postdeployment, first responders). Second, they are promising for individuals in jobs that routinely and frequently involve exposure to high stress and aggression (e.g., prison guards, soldiers, police officers). Last, these interventions may be helpful for individuals prone to problematic anger who are facing the type of work environment that may be stressful and anger provoking. The efficacy of such intervention for anger and aggression in these different contexts, the appropriate time frame for intervention, and optimal training dosages must await further systematic research.

CONCLUSION

Anger and aggression are a natural part of the human experience. Societies and individuals are preoccupied with managing the consequences of aggression and with regulating anger expression on a daily basis. At times, anger is upregulated to achieve certain goals, and at times, anger is downregulated to achieve social acceptability. In the workplace, the need for anger management interventions arises when professional functioning of a certain worker is hindered, affecting both the individual suffering from anger issues and their work environment. In such contexts, interventions typically aim to manage extreme forms of anger and aggression. This is especially true when the stakes are high in occupations such as law enforcement, first responder, military personnel, or emergency medicine. In these fields, clouded judgment and poor decision making due to cognitive biases may impede team cohesion, affect task performance, and potentially cost lives. When competent and skilled workers are concerned, it is important to separate the anger issues from the individual's professional skills and to provide effective interventions to get things back on track. Ideally, these treatments should be affordable, accessible, and time sensitive—CBM carries great promise on these accounts.

The primary focus of most anger management interventions has been on behavior modification: response modulation, or targeting unacceptable behaviors stemming from angry emotions; and situation selection and modification, or targeting the circumstances leading to angry outbursts. More recent interventions have introduced therapeutic components that are also directed at effortful cognitive control aimed to help patients consciously reevaluate potentially anger-evoking situations to make these less angering. Although automatic biases in attention and interpretation have been implicated in anger and aggression, until recently these processes remained out of reach for clinical targeting. However, technological and conceptual advancements in the past 2 decades led to the development of effective tools for measurement of anger-related attention and interpretation biases and preliminary tools for intervention.

Studies suggest that biases at the attention and interpretation levels play a role in the activation and maintenance of anger. Preliminary attempts to leverage these basic findings into attention and interpretation bias modification treatments are scant, with particular promise emerging for interpretive bias modification protocols. However, larger and better-controlled studies are necessary to substantiate clinical efficacy and unraveling the underlying mechanisms of therapeutic change. Future studies could also test the utility of CBM procedures as adjuvants to extant evidence-based treatments for anger and aggression. In sum, evidence-based CBM interventions hold promise for effective, easily disseminated, and acceptable interventions for individuals with excessive anger. These types of interventions may be especially relevant for workers in high-risk occupations, where stress, aggression, and ambiguity are common and split-second decisions have critical consequences. However, it is important to keep in mind that research into the clinical implementation of CBM protocols is still in its infancy. Future research will determine CBM's feasibility, acceptability, and clinical efficacy in the context of anger and aggression.

IMPLICATIONS

- Anger and aggression in the workplace can negatively influence relationships, hinder teamwork, and reduce productivity.
- Aggressive, hostile, or retaliatory behaviors are often addressed directly, though they may stem from anger-related biases. Attention bias toward anger-related cues can lead to higher vulnerability to social behaviors or situations implying hostility or aggression (i.e., facial expression, choice of words), causing unwarranted aggressive reactions. Interpretation bias can cause wrongful or exaggerated attribution of malicious intent or hostility, making benign situations appear more anger provoking and resulting in an aggressive response.
- Most anger management interventions focus on the situation leading to anger and the aggressive behavior following it. Cognitive bias modification, however, aims to modify and normalize attention and interpretation processes to reduce anger. These evidence-supported interventions are short, cost-effective, and nonconfrontational.

REFERENCES

Adler, A. B., Britt, T. W., Castro, C. A., McGurk, D., & Bliese, P. D. (2011). Effect of transition home from combat on risk-taking and health-related behaviors. *Journal of Traumatic Stress*, *24*(4), 381–389. https://doi.org/10.1002/jts.20665

Amir, N., Beard, C., Burns, M., & Bomyea, J. (2009). Attention modification program in individuals with generalized anxiety disorder. *Journal of Abnormal Psychology*, *118*(1), 28–33. https://doi.org/10.1037/a0012589

Amir, N., Beard, C., Taylor, C. T., Klumpp, H., Elias, J., Burns, M., & Chen, X. (2009). Attention training in individuals with generalized social phobia: A randomized controlled trial. *Journal of Consulting and Clinical Psychology*, *77*(5), 961–973. https://doi.org/10.1037/a0016685

Amir, N., Bomyea, J., & Beard, C. (2010). The effect of single-session interpretation modification on attention bias in socially anxious individuals. *Journal of Anxiety Disorders*, *24*(2), 178–182. https://doi.org/10.1016/j.janxdis.2009.10.005

Amir, N., Foa, E. B., & Coles, M. E. (1998). Automatic activation and strategic avoidance of threat-relevant information in social phobia. *Journal of Abnormal Psychology*, *107*(2), 285–290. https://doi.org/10.1037/0021-843X.107.2.285

Amir, N., Weber, G., Beard, C., Bomyea, J., & Taylor, C. T. (2008). The effect of a single-session attention modification program on response to a public-speaking challenge in socially anxious individuals. *Journal of Abnormal Psychology*, *117*(4), 860–868. https://doi.org/10.1037/a0013445

Arnold, M. B. (1960). *Emotion and personality*. Columbia University Press.

Aspen, V., Darcy, A. M., & Lock, J. (2013). A review of attention biases in women with eating disorders. *Cognition and Emotion*, *27*(5), 820–838. https://doi.org/10.1080/02699931.2012.749777

Badura-Brack, A. S., Naim, R., Ryan, T. J., Levy, O., Abend, R., Khanna, M. M., McDermott, T. J., Pine, D. S., & Bar-Haim, Y. (2015). Effect of attention training on attention bias variability and PTSD symptoms: Randomized controlled trials in Israeli and U.S. combat veterans. *The American Journal of Psychiatry*, *172*(12), 1233–1241. https://doi.org/10.1176/appi.ajp.2015.14121578

Barazzone, N., & Davey, G. C. L. (2009). Anger potentiates the reporting of threatening interpretations: An experimental study. *Journal of Anxiety Disorders*, *23*(4), 489–495. https://doi.org/10.1016/j.janxdis.2008.10.007

Bar-Haim, Y. (2010). Research review: Attention bias modification (ABM): A novel treatment for anxiety disorders. *Journal of Child Psychology and Psychiatry, and Allied Disciplines*, *51*(8), 859–870. https://doi.org/10.1111/j.1469-7610.2010.02251.x

Bar-Haim, Y., Lamy, D., Pergamin, L., Bakermans-Kranenburg, M. J., & van IJzendoorn, M. H. (2007). Threat-related attentional bias in anxious and nonanxious individuals: A meta-analytic study. *Psychological Bulletin*, *133*(1), 1–24. https://doi.org/10.1037/0033-2909.133.1.1

Bar-Haim, Y., Morag, I., & Glickman, S. (2011). Training anxious children to disengage attention from threat: A randomized controlled trial. *Journal of Child Psychology and Psychiatry, and Allied Disciplines*, *52*(8), 861–869. https://doi.org/10.1111/j.1469-7610.2011.02368.x

Barry, T. J., Vervliet, B., & Hermans, D. (2015). An integrative review of attention biases and their contribution to treatment for anxiety disorders. *Frontiers in Psychology*, *6*, Article 968. https://doi.org/10.3389/fpsyg.2015.00968

Barsade, S. G. (2002). The ripple effect: Emotional contagion and its influence on group behavior. *Administrative Science Quarterly*, *47*(4), 644–675. https://doi.org/10.2307/3094912

Beard, C. (2011). Cognitive bias modification for anxiety: Current evidence and future directions. *Expert Review of Neurotherapeutics*, *11*(2), 299–311. https://doi.org/10.1586/ern.10.194

Beck, A. T. (1999). *Prisoners of hate: The cognitive basis of anger, hostility, and violence.* HarperCollins Publishers.

Beck, R., & Fernandez, E. (1998). Cognitive-behavioral therapy in the treatment of anger: A meta-analysis. *Cognitive Therapy and Research*, *22*(1), 63–74. https://doi.org/10.1023/A:1018763902991

Blackwell, S. E., & Holmes, E. A. (2010). Modifying interpretation and imagination in clinical depression: A single case series using cognitive bias modification. *Applied Cognitive Psychology*, *24*(3), 338–350. https://doi.org/10.1002/acp.1680

Burt, S. A., Mikolajewski, A. J., & Larson, C. L. (2009). Do aggression and rule-breaking have different interpersonal correlates? A study of antisocial behavior subtypes, negative affect, and hostile perceptions of others. *Aggressive Behavior*, *35*(6), 453–461. https://doi.org/10.1002/ab.20324

Carretié, L., Hinojosa, J. A., Martín-Loeches, M., Mercado, F., & Tapia, M. (2004). Automatic attention to emotional stimuli: Neural correlates. *Human Brain Mapping*, *22*(4), 290–299. https://doi.org/10.1002/hbm.20037

Chemtob, C. M., Hamada, R. S., Roitblat, H. L., & Muraoka, M. Y. (1994). Anger, impulsivity, and anger control in combat-related posttraumatic stress disorder. *Journal of Consulting and Clinical Psychology*, *62*(4), 827–832. https://doi.org/10.1037/0022-006X.62.4.827

Chemtob, C. M., Roitblatt, H. L., Hamada, R. S., Carlson, J. G., & Twentyman, C. T. (1988). A cognitive action theory of Post-Traumatic Stress Disorder. *Journal of Anxiety Disorders*, *2*(3), 253–275. https://doi.org/10.1016/0887-6185(88)90006-0

Cheshin, A., Rafaeli, A., & Bos, N. (2011). Anger and happiness in virtual teams: Emotional influences of text and behavior on others' affect in the absence of non-verbal cues. *Organizational Behavior and Human Decision Processes*, *116*(1), 2–16. https://doi.org/10.1016/j.obhdp.2011.06.002

Christiansen, P., Schoenmakers, T. M., & Field, M. (2015). Less than meets the eye: Reappraising the clinical relevance of attentional bias in addiction. *Addictive Behaviors*, *44*, 43–50. https://doi.org/10.1016/j.addbeh.2014.10.005

Cisler, J. M., & Koster, E. H. (2010). Mechanisms of attentional biases towards threat in anxiety disorders: An integrative review. *Clinical Psychology Review*, *30*(2), 203–216. https://doi.org/10.1016/j.cpr.2009.11.003

Cohen, D. J., Eckhardt, C. I., & Schagat, K. D. (1998). Attention allocation and habituation to anger-related stimuli during a visual search task. *Aggressive Behavior*, *24*(6), 399–409. https://doi.org/10.1002/(SICI)1098-2337(1998)24:6<399::AID-AB1>3.0.CO;2-I

Cougle, J. R., Summers, B. J., Allan, N. P., Dillon, K. H., Smith, H. L., Okey, S. A., & Harvey, A. M. (2017). Hostile interpretation training for individuals with alcohol use disorder and elevated trait anger: A controlled trial of a web-based intervention. *Behaviour Research and Therapy*, *99*, 57–66. https://doi.org/10.1016/j.brat.2017.09.004

Crick, N. R., & Dodge, K. A. (1994). A review and reformulation of social information-processing mechanisms in children's social-adjustment. *Psychological Bulletin, 115*(1), 74–101. https://doi.org/10.1037/0033-2909.115.1.74

Cristea, I. A., Kok, R. N., & Cuijpers, P. (2016). The effectiveness of cognitive bias modification interventions for substance addictions: A meta-analysis. *PLOS ONE, 11*(9), Article e0162226. https://doi.org/10.1371/journal.pone.0162226

Crowe, S. E., & Wilkowski, B. M. (2013). Looking for trouble: Revenge-planning and preattentive vigilance for angry facial expressions. *Emotion, 13*(4), 774–781. https://doi.org/10.1037/a0032252

Deffenbacher, J. L. (2011). Cognitive-behavioral conceptualization and treatment of anger. *Cognitive and Behavioral Practice, 18*(2), 212–221. https://doi.org/10.1016/j.cbpra.2009.12.004

Deffenbacher, J. L., & McKay, M. (2000). *Overcoming situational and general anger: A protocol for the treatment of anger based on relaxation, cognitive restructuring, and coping skills training*. New Harbinger Publications.

DiGiuseppe, R., & Tafrate, R. C. (2003). Anger treatment for adults: A meta-analytic review. *Clinical Psychology: Science and Practice, 10*(1), 70–84. https://doi.org/10.1093/clipsy.10.1.70

Dodge, K. A. (1980). Social cognition and children's aggressive behavior. *Child Development, 51*(1), 162–170. https://doi.org/10.2307/1129603

Dodge, K. A. (2006). Translational science in action: Hostile attributional style and the development of aggressive behavior problems. *Development and Psychopathology, 18*(3), 791–814. https://doi.org/10.1017/S0954579406060391

Eckhardt, C. I., & Cohen, D. J. (1997). Attention to anger-relevant and irrelevant stimuli following naturalistic insult. *Personality and Individual Differences, 23*(4), 619–629. https://doi.org/10.1016/S0191-8869(97)00074-3

Elfenbein, H. A. (2014). The many faces of emotional contagion: An affective process theory of affective linkage. *Organizational Psychology Review, 4*(4), 326–362. https://doi.org/10.1177/2041386614542889

Field, M., & Cox, W. M. (2008). Attentional bias in addictive behaviors: A review of its development, causes, and consequences. *Drug and Alcohol Dependence, 97*(1–2), 1–20. https://doi.org/10.1016/j.drugalcdep.2008.03.030

Frijda, N. H. (1988). The laws of emotion. *The American Psychologist, 43*(5), 349–358. https://doi.org/10.1037/0003-066X.43.5.349

Geddes, D., & Stickney, L. T. (2011). The trouble with sanctions: Organizational responses to deviant anger displays at work. *Human Relations, 64*(2), 201–230. https://doi.org/10.1177/0018726710375482

Gibson, D. E., & Callister, R. R. (2010). Anger in organizations: Review and integration. *Journal of Management, 36*(1), 66–93. https://doi.org/10.1177/0149206309348060

Gibson, D. E., Schweitzer, M. E., Callister, R. R., & Gray, B. (2009). The influence of anger expressions on outcomes in organizations. *Negotiation and Conflict Management Research, 2*(3), 236–262. https://doi.org/10.1111/j.1750-4716.2009.00039.x

Gorenstein, E. E., Tager, F. A., Shapiro, P. A., Monk, C., & Sloan, R. P. (2007). Cognitive-behavior therapy for reduction of persistent anger. *Cognitive and Behavioral Practice, 14*(2), 168–184. https://doi.org/10.1016/j.cbpra.2006.07.004

Gross, J. J. (1998). The emerging field of emotion regulation: An integrative review. *Review of General Psychology, 2*(3), 271–299. https://doi.org/10.1037/1089-2680.2.3.271

Gross, J. J. (2013). Emotion regulation: Taking stock and moving forward. *Emotion, 13*(3), 359–365. https://doi.org/10.1037/a0032135

Gross, J. J., & Thompson, R. A. (2007). Emotion regulation: Conceptual foundations. In J. J. Gross (Ed.), *Handbook of emotion regulation* (pp. 3–24). Guilford Press.

Hakamata, Y., Lissek, S., Bar-Haim, Y., Britton, J. C., Fox, N. A., Leibenluft, E., Ernst, M., & Pine, D. S. (2010). Attention bias modification treatment: A meta-analysis toward the establishment of novel treatment for anxiety. *Biological Psychiatry, 68*(11), 982–990. https://doi.org/10.1016/j.biopsych.2010.07.021

Hall, C. W. (2006). Self-reported aggression and the perception of anger in facial expression photos. *The Journal of Psychology, 140*(3), 255–267. https://doi.org/10.3200/JRLP.140.3.255-267

Hallion, L. S., & Ruscio, A. M. (2011). A meta-analysis of the effect of cognitive bias modification on anxiety and depression. *Psychological Bulletin, 137*(6), 940–958. https://doi.org/10.1037/a0024355

Hareli, S., & Rafaeli, A. (2008). Emotion cycles: On the social influence of emotion in organizations. *Research in Organizational Behavior, 28*, 35–59. https://doi.org/10.1016/j.riob.2008.04.007

Hawkins, K. A., & Cougle, J. R. (2013). Effects of interpretation training on hostile attribution bias and reactivity to interpersonal insult. *Behavior Therapy, 44*(3), 479–488. https://doi.org/10.1016/j.beth.2013.04.005

Hazebroek, J. F., Howells, K., & Day, A. (2001). Cognitive appraisals associated with high trait anger. *Personality and Individual Differences, 30*(1), 31–45. https://doi.org/10.1016/S0191-8869(00)00007-6

Hazen, R. A., Vasey, M. W., & Schmidt, N. B. (2009). Attentional retraining: A randomized clinical trial for pathological worry. *Journal of Psychiatric Research, 43*(6), 627–633. https://doi.org/10.1016/j.jpsychires.2008.07.004

Heeren, A., Mogoaşe, C., Philippot, P., & McNally, R. J. (2015). Attention bias modification for social anxiety: A systematic review and meta-analysis. *Clinical Psychology Review, 40*, 76–90. https://doi.org/10.1016/j.cpr.2015.06.001

Hird, J. A., Williams, P. J., & Markham, D. M. H. (1997). Survey of attendance at a community-based anger control group treatment programme with reference to source of referral, age of client and external motivating features. *Journal of Mental Health, 6*(1), 47–54. https://doi.org/10.1080/09638239719030

Hommer, R. E., Meyer, A., Stoddard, J., Connolly, M. E., Mogg, K., Bradley, B. P., Pine, D. S., Leibenluft, E., & Brotman, M. A. (2014). Attention bias to threat faces in severe mood dysregulation. *Depression and Anxiety, 31*(7), 559–565. https://doi.org/10.1002/da.22145

Jusyte, A., & Schönenberg, M. (2014). Threat processing in generalized social phobia: An investigation of interpretation biases in ambiguous facial affect. *Psychiatry Research, 217*(1–2), 100–106. https://doi.org/10.1016/j.psychres.2013.12.031

Killgore, W. D. S., Cotting, D. I., Thomas, J. L., Cox, A. L., McGurk, D., Vo, A. H., Castro, C. A., & Hoge, C. W. (2008). Post-combat invincibility: Violent combat experiences are associated with increased risk-taking propensity following deployment. *Journal of Psychiatric Research, 42*(13), 1112–1121. https://doi.org/10.1016/j.jpsychires.2008.01.001

Koster, E. H. W., Fox, E., & MacLeod, C. (2009). Introduction to the special section on cognitive bias modification in emotional disorders. *Journal of Abnormal Psychology, 118*(1), 1–4. https://doi.org/10.1037/a0014379

Lang, T. J., Blackwell, S. E., Harmer, C. J., Davison, P., & Holmes, E. A. (2012). Cognitive bias modification using mental imagery for depression: Developing a novel computerized intervention to change negative thinking styles. *European Journal of Personality, 26*(2), 145–157. https://doi.org/10.1002/per.855

Lazarov, A., Marom, S., Yahalom, N., Pine, D. S., Hermesh, H., & Bar-Haim, Y. (2018). Attention bias modification augments cognitive-behavioral group therapy for social anxiety disorder: A randomized controlled trial. *Psychological Medicine, 48*(13), 2177–2185. https://doi.org/10.1017/S003329171700366X

Lazarus, R. S. (1991). Progress on a cognitive-motivational-relational theory of emotion. *The American Psychologist, 46*(8), 819–834. https://doi.org/10.1037/0003-066X.46.8.819

Lazarus, R. S., & Alfert, E. (1964). Short-circuiting of threat by experimentally altering cognitive appraisal. *Journal of Abnormal Psychology, 69*(2), 195–205. https://doi.org/10.1037/h0044635

Linetzky, M., Pergamin-Hight, L., Pine, D. S., & Bar-Haim, Y. (2015). Quantitative evaluation of the clinical efficacy of attention bias modification treatment for anxiety disorders. *Depression and Anxiety, 32*(6), 383–391. https://doi.org/10.1002/da.22344

Linkh, D. J., & Sonnek, S. M. (2003). An application of cognitive-behavioral anger management training in a military/occupational setting: Efficacy and demographic factors. *Military Medicine, 168*(6), 475–478. https://doi.org/10.1093/milmed/168.6.475

MacLeod, C. M. (1991). Half a century of research on the Stroop effect: An integrative review. *Psychological Bulletin, 109*(2), 163–203. https://doi.org/10.1037/0033-2909.109.2.163

MacLeod, C., Mathews, A., & Tata, P. (1986). Attentional bias in emotional disorders. *Journal of Abnormal Psychology, 95*(1), 15–20. https://doi.org/10.1037/0021-843X.95.1.15

MacLeod, C., Rutherford, E., Campbell, L., Ebsworthy, G., & Holker, L. (2002). Selective attention and emotional vulnerability: Assessing the causal basis of their association through the experimental manipulation of attentional bias. *Journal of Abnormal Psychology, 111*(1), 107–123. https://doi.org/10.1037/0021-843X.111.1.107

Maoz, K. (2017). *Cognitive bias modification (CBM) tools to reduce anger levels and anger susceptibility* [Unpublished doctoral dissertation]. Tel Aviv University.

Maoz, K., Adler, A. B., Bliese, P. D., Sipos, M. L., Quartana, P. J., & Bar-Haim, Y. (2017). Attention and interpretation processes and trait anger experience, expression, and control. *Cognition and Emotion, 31*(7), 1453–1464. https://doi.org/10.1080/02699931.2016.1231663

McCarroll, J. E., Ursano, R. J., Liu, X., Thayer, L. E., Newby, J. H., Norwood, A. E., & Fullerton, C. S. (2000). Deployment and the probability of spousal aggression by U.S. Army soldiers. *Military Medicine, 165*(1), 41–44. https://doi.org/10.1093/milmed/165.1.41

Mellentin, A. I., Dervisevic, A., Stenager, E., Pilegaard, M., & Kirk, U. (2015). Seeing enemies? A systematic review of anger bias in the perception of facial expressions among anger-prone and aggressive populations. *Aggression and Violent Behavior, 25*(Pt. B), 373–383. https://doi.org/10.1016/j.avb.2015.09.001

Mogoaşe, C., David, D., & Koster, E. H. (2014). Clinical efficacy of attentional bias modification procedures: An updated meta-analysis. *Journal of Clinical Psychology, 70*(12), 1133–1157. https://doi.org/10.1002/jclp.22081

Novaco, R. W., & Chemtob, C. M. (2002). Anger and combat-related posttraumatic stress disorder. *Journal of Traumatic Stress*, *15*(2), 123–132. https://doi.org/10.1023/A:1014855924072

Novaco, R. W., Swanson, R. D., Gonzalez, O. I., Gahm, G. A., & Reger, M. D. (2012). Anger and postcombat mental health: Validation of a brief anger measure with U.S. soldiers postdeployed from Iraq and Afghanistan. *Psychological Assessment*, *24*(3), 661–675. https://doi.org/10.1037/a0026636

Orobio de Castro, B., Veerman, J. W., Koops, W., Bosch, J. D., & Monshouwer, H. J. (2002). Hostile attribution of intent and aggressive behavior: A meta-analysis. *Child Development*, *73*(3), 916–934. https://doi.org/10.1111/1467-8624.00447

Owen, J. M. (2011). Transdiagnostic cognitive processes in high trait anger. *Clinical Psychology Review*, *31*(2), 193–202. https://doi.org/10.1016/j.cpr.2010.10.003

Pardeck, J. T. (1982). Veterans and aggression: An empirical test of two rival theoretical models. *The International Journal of Social Psychiatry*, *28*(3), 223–229. https://doi.org/10.1177/002076408202800309

Peckham, A. D., McHugh, R. K., & Otto, M. W. (2010). A meta-analysis of the magnitude of biased attention in depression. *Depression and Anxiety*, *27*(12), 1135–1142. https://doi.org/10.1002/da.20755

Penton-Voak, I. S., Thomas, J., Gage, S. H., McMurran, M., McDonald, S., & Munafò, M. R. (2013). Increasing recognition of happiness in ambiguous facial expressions reduces anger and aggressive behavior. *Psychological Science*, *24*(5), 688–697. https://doi.org/10.1177/0956797612459657

Pergamin-Hight, L., Pine, D. S., Fox, N. A., & Bar-Haim, Y. (2016). Attention bias modification for youth with social anxiety disorder. *Journal of Child Psychology and Psychiatry, and Allied Disciplines*, *57*(11), 1317–1325. https://doi.org/10.1111/jcpp.12599

Peterson, C. K., & Harmon-Jones, E. (2012). Anger and testosterone: Evidence that situationally-induced anger relates to situationally-induced testosterone. *Emotion*, *12*(5), 899–902. https://doi.org/10.1037/a0025300

Ray, R. D., Wilhelm, F. H., & Gross, J. J. (2008). All in the mind's eye? Anger rumination and reappraisal. *Journal of Personality and Social Psychology*, *94*(1), 133–145. https://doi.org/10.1037/0022-3514.94.1.133

Roseman, I. J., & Smith, C. A. (2001). Appraisal theory: Overview, assumptions, varieties, controversies. In K. R. Scherer, A. Schorr, & T. Johnstone (Eds.), *Appraisal processes in emotion: Theory, methods, research* (pp. 3–19). Oxford University Press.

Sakusic, A., Avdibegovic, E., Zoricic, Z., Pavlovic, S., Gaspar, V., & Delic, A. (2010). Relationship between anger, alcoholism and symptoms of posttraumatic stress disorders in war veterans. *Medicinski Arhiv*, *64*(6), 354–358.

Sayer, N. A., Noorbaloochi, S., Frazier, P., Carlson, K., Gravely, A., & Murdoch, M. (2010). Reintegration problems and treatment interests among Iraq and Afghanistan combat veterans receiving VA medical care. *Psychiatric Services*, *61*, 589–597. https://doi.org/10.1176/ps.2010.61.6.589

Scherer, K. R. (1984). On the nature and function of emotion: A component process approach. In K. R. Scherer & P. Ekman (Eds.), *Approaches to emotion* (pp. 293–317). Lawrence Erlbaum Associates, Inc.

Schmidt, N. B., Richey, J. A., Buckner, J. D., & Timpano, K. R. (2009). Attention training for generalized social anxiety disorder. *Journal of Abnormal Psychology*, *118*(1), 5–14. https://doi.org/10.1037/a0013643

Schultz, D., Grodack, A., & Izard, C. E. (2010). State and trait anger, fear, and social information processing. In M. Potegal, G. Stemmler, & C. Spielberger (Eds.), *International handbook of anger: Constituent and concomitant biological, psychological and social processes* (pp. 311–325). Springer. https://doi.org/10.1007/978-0-387-89676-2_18

Schultz, D., Izard, C. E., & Bear, G. (2004). Children's emotion processing: Relations to emotionality and aggression. *Development and Psychopathology*, *16*(2), 371–387. https://doi.org/10.1017/S0954579404044566

See, J., MacLeod, C., & Bridle, R. (2009). The reduction of anxiety vulnerability through the modification of attentional bias: A real-world study using a home-based cognitive bias modification procedure. *Journal of Abnormal Psychology*, *118*(1), 65–75. https://doi.org/10.1037/a0014377

Shechner, T., Rimon-Chakir, A., Britton, J. C., Lotan, D., Apter, A., Bliese, P. D., Pine, D. S., & Bar-Haim, Y. (2014). Attention bias modification treatment augmenting effects on cognitive behavioral therapy in children with anxiety: Randomized controlled trial. *Journal of the American Academy of Child & Adolescent Psychiatry*, *53*(1), 61–71. https://doi.org/10.1016/j.jaac.2013.09.016

Siddle, R., Jones, F., & Awenat, F. (2003). Group cognitive behaviour therapy for anger: A pilot study. *Behavioural and Cognitive Psychotherapy*, *31*(1), 69–83. https://doi.org/10.1017/S1352465803001073

Smeijers, D., Rinck, M., Bulten, E., van den Heuvel, T., & Verkes, R. J. (2017). Generalized hostile interpretation bias regarding facial expressions: Characteristic of pathological aggressive behavior. *Aggressive Behavior*, *43*(4), 386–397. https://doi.org/10.1002/ab.21697

Smith, P., & Waterman, M. (2003). Processing bias for aggression words in forensic and nonforensic samples. *Cognition and Emotion*, *17*(5), 681–701. https://doi.org/10.1080/02699930302281

Smith, P., & Waterman, M. (2004). Role of experience in processing bias for aggressive words in forensic and non-forensic populations. *Aggressive Behavior*, *30*(2), 105–122. https://doi.org/10.1002/ab.20001

Stoddard, J., Sharif-Askary, B., Harkins, E. A., Frank, H. R., Brotman, M. A., Penton-Voak, I. S., Maoz, K., Bar-Haim, Y., Munafò, M., Pine, D. S., & Leibenluft, E. (2016). An open pilot study of training hostile interpretation bias to treat disruptive mood dysregulation disorder. *Journal of Child and Adolescent Psychopharmacology*, *26*(1), 49–57. https://doi.org/10.1089/cap.2015.0100

Szasz, P. L., Szentagotai, A., & Hofmann, S. G. (2011). The effect of emotion regulation strategies on anger. *Behaviour Research and Therapy*, *49*(2), 114–119.

Tottenham, N., Tanaka, J. W., Leon, A. C., McCarry, T., Nurse, M., Hare, T. A., Marcus, D. J., Westerlund, A., Casey, B. J., & Nelson, C. (2009). The NimStim set of facial expressions: Judgments from untrained research participants. *Psychiatry Research*, *168*(3), 242–249. https://doi.org/10.1016/j.psychres.2008.05.006

Van Honk, J., & Schutter, D. (2007). Vigilant and avoidant responses to angry facial expressions. *Social Neuroscience: Integrating Biological and Psychological Explanations of Social Behavior*, 197–223.

Van Honk, J., Tuiten, A., De Haan, E., Van den Hout, M., & Stam, H. (2001). Attentional biases for angry faces: Relationships to trait anger and anxiety. *Cognition and Emotion*, *15*(3), 279–297. https://doi.org/10.1080/0269993004200222

Van Honk, J., Tuiten, A., Van den Hout, M., Putman, P., De Haan, E., & Stam, H. (2001). Selective attention to unmasked and masked threatening words: Relationships to trait anger and anxiety. *Personality and Individual Differences*, *30*(4), 711–720. https://doi.org/10.1016/S0191-8869(00)00160-4

Vassilopoulos, S. P., Brouzos, A., & Andreou, E. (2015). A multi-session attribution modification program for children with aggressive behaviour: Changes in attributions, emotional reaction estimates, and self-reported aggression. *Behavioural and Cognitive Psychotherapy*, *43*(5), 538–548. https://doi.org/10.1017/S1352465814000149

Wald, I., Bitton, S., Levi, O., Zusmanovich, S., Fruchter, E., Ginat, K., Charney, D. S., Pine, D. S., & Bar-Haim, Y. (2017). Acute delivery of attention bias modification training (ABMT) moderates the association between combat exposure and posttraumatic symptoms: A feasibility study. *Biological Psychology*, *122*, 93–97. https://doi.org/10.1016/j.biopsycho.2016.01.005

Watkins, E. R., Baeyens, C. B., & Read, R. (2009). Concreteness training reduces dysphoria: Proof-of-principle for repeated cognitive bias modification in depression. *Journal of Abnormal Psychology*, *118*(1), 55–64. https://doi.org/10.1037/a0013642

Wegrzyn, M., Westphal, S., & Kissler, J. (2017). In your face: The biased judgement of fear-anger expressions in violent offenders. *BMC Psychology*, *5*(1), 16. https://doi.org/10.1186/s40359-017-0186-z

Wells, T. T., & Beevers, C. G. (2010). Biased attention and dysphoria: Manipulating selective attention reduces subsequent depressive symptoms. *Cognition and Emotion*, *24*(4), 719–728. https://doi.org/10.1080/02699930802652388

Wenzel, A., & Lystad, C. (2005). Interpretation biases in angry and anxious individuals. *Behaviour Research and Therapy*, *43*(8), 1045–1054. https://doi.org/10.1016/j.brat.2004.02.009

White, L. K., Sequeira, S., Britton, J. C., Brotman, M. A., Gold, A. L., Berman, E., Towbin, K., Abend, R., Fox, N. A., Bar-Haim, Y., Leibenluft, E., & Pine, D. S. (2017). Complementary features of attention bias modification therapy and cognitive-behavioral therapy in pediatric anxiety disorders. *The American Journal of Psychiatry*, *174*(8), 775–784. https://doi.org/10.1176/appi.ajp.2017.16070847

Wilkowski, B. M., & Robinson, M. D. (2008). The cognitive basis of trait anger and reactive aggression: An integrative analysis. *Personality and Social Psychology Review*, *12*(1), 3–21. https://doi.org/10.1177/1088868307309874

Wilkowski, B. M., & Robinson, M. D. (2010). The anatomy of anger: An integrative cognitive model of trait anger and reactive aggression. *Journal of Personality*, *78*(1), 9–38. https://doi.org/10.1111/j.1467-6494.2009.00607.x

Wilkowski, B. M., & Robinson, M. D. (2012). When aggressive individuals see the world more accurately: The case of perceptual sensitivity to subtle facial expressions of anger. *Personality and Social Psychology Bulletin*, *38*(4), 540–553. https://doi.org/10.1177/0146167211430233

Williams, J. M. G., Mathews, A., & MacLeod, C. (1996). The emotional Stroop task and psychopathology. *Psychological Bulletin*, *120*(1), 3–24. https://doi.org/10.1037/0033-2909.120.1.3

Wranik, T., & Scherer, K. R. (2010). Why do I get angry? A componential appraisal approach. In M. Potegal, G. Stemmler, & C. Spielberger (Eds.), *International handbook of anger: Constituent and concomitant biological, psychological and social processes* (pp. 243–266). Springer. https://doi.org/10.1007/978-0-387-89676-2_15

PART IV FUTURE DIRECTIONS

10 ADVANCING ANGER RESEARCH

DAVID FORBES AND AMY B. ADLER

The challenge posed by problematic anger in the context of occupations that carry a high potential risk of mental or physical harm is rapidly becoming the focus of increasing organizational, clinical, and research attention. The performance of personnel in these high-risk roles, such as military, policing and firefighting, can mean the difference between life and death. High-arousal states, including anger, that mobilize threat engagement potentially play a unique and prominent part in the critical situations faced by those in high-risk roles (Adler & Forbes; Introduction, this volume). The chapters in this volume have explored the different lenses through which anger is examined at phenomenological, etiological, mechanistic, and manifested levels, both within organizational contexts and following the person's transition out of that role. The increased focus by researchers, clinicians, and the organizations themselves on anger in these high-risk organizations represents

---

Material has been reviewed by the Walter Reed Army Institute of Research. There is no objection to its presentation and/or publication. The opinions or assertions contained herein are the private views of the authors and are not to be construed as official, or as reflecting true views of the Department of the Army or the Department of Defense.

https://doi.org/10.1037/0000244-011
Anger at Work: Prevention, Intervention, and Treatment in High-Risk Occupations, A. B. Adler and D. Forbes (Editors)

an exciting area of emerging scientific and practical endeavor. This body of work is critical not only for optimizing operational performance but also for the health, well-being, and safety of the personnel who serve (and have served) in these potentially dangerous occupations.

The preceding chapters have outlined the nature and experience of anger and its consequences at individual and organizational levels. They have described recent developments in the measurement of anger, as well as the role of anger as a mechanism in influencing adaptive and maladaptive individual and organizational responses. Finally, they have explored the current status of a range of intervention paradigms that aim to ameliorate problematic anger and its consequences. Each chapter also highlighted key directions for future research in that particular area. This chapter seeks to integrate those ideas with a view to forging a road map for a program of research designed to optimally progress this area of significant need.

PHENOMENOLOGY AND MEASUREMENT

As highlighted by Britt et al. in Chapter 2 of this volume, the field of anger from both the clinical and research perspectives is currently notable for the heterogeneity with which it is conceptualized and assessed. It is plagued by variations in definitions, including the conflation of emotion and action, resulting in a lack of consistency in measurement. These variations and conflations are a major impediment to progress. Consistent, universally agreed-upon definitions, construct operationalization, and valid assessment instruments are critically important for the advancement of any field. Anger presents an intriguing challenge in this endeavor: It is important to focus not only on maladaptive expressions of anger but also on the conceptualization and assessment of its adaptive expression. In high-risk organizational contexts, these potentially adaptive functions of anger may include factors such as group bonding, collective response to injury, and prompts for organizational and social change. A critical role for future research, therefore, will be to establish a more fine-grained phenomenological lens around both adaptive and maladaptive anger, leading to improved assessment strategies at individual, group, and organizational levels.

There is a clear benefit to researchers across the world adopting the same measures in their anger research. Not only does this facilitate more meaningful and valid comparisons across studies, it also has the potential to allow data sets to be combined to produce numbers that allow the use of highly sophisticated statistical analysis and exploratory techniques such as machine learning. To this end, a valuable future research program would aim to generate an empirically validated, consensus-driven assessment battery—a minimum data set that can be used internationally to facilitate the development of a consolidated anger evidence base across multiple organizational contexts. This goal may be best achieved through the formation of an international expert consensus panel to provide advice not only regarding the initial measurement approaches but also about modifications required over time to address developments in the science of anger. Considerations for this panel may include optimal anger measures for inclusion in organizational screening, both for preenlistment and routine periodic psychological health assessments over the course of the person's career. The panel should also consider optimum measures for inclusion in treatment outcome trials to facilitate collation of empirical evidence on intervention effectiveness from multiple studies. Although there are good candidate measures that could be considered for adoption (e.g., including brief measures such as the Dimensions of Anger Reactions–5 [Forbes et al., 2014] and more extensive measures such as the State–Trait Anger Expression Inventory–2 [Spielberger, 1999]), less work has been conducted in developing measures of adaptive anger.

A key factor for consideration will be the domains in which such measurement and assessment is conducted (including, e.g., clinician-rated, self-report symptom checklists, physiological measures). As outlined by Britt et al. (Chapter 2) and described in-depth by Osgood and Quartana (Chapter 1), real-time contemporaneous methods such as experience sampling methods and ecological momentary assessment are used increasingly to assess anger experiences. These strategies offer a more "real-time" understanding of the experience of anger in multiple settings across a person's life. They provide the capacity to capture variations in frequency, intensity, and duration throughout the day, as well as cognitions, triggers and provocations, and associations with aggressive and other high-risk behaviors. The potential also exists to augment these sampling methods by combining them with data drawn from passive data collection options such as smartphones and smartwatches. This wealth of data significantly enhances the sophistication with which we can measure, map, and understand the experience of anger in real time. As such, in terms of clinical intervention, they offer a unique opportunity to deliver "just-in-time" interventions.

A lack of consistency in measurement strategies has also contributed to the paucity of research on rates of problematic anger (i.e., anger that is elevated, prolonged, and destructive) within these high-risk organizations. The establishment of universally agreed-upon cutoff scores on well-validated measures of problematic anger, linked with clearly defined indices of functional impairment, would aid in determining baseline rates of problematic anger across organizations. Systematic mapping of the extent of the problem would allow for identification of variations in anger expression; examination of organizational factors that may uniquely contribute to these expressions; and the development and evaluation of intervention options targeted at the organization, the unit, or the individual. The question also remains as to whether there is merit in the introduction of an anger-specific disorder into diagnostic nomenclatures such as the *Diagnostic and Statistical Manual of Mental Disorders* or the *International Classification of Diseases* that represents problematic anger that causes extensive distress and impairment. Anger is currently represented transdiagnostically (Fernandez & Johnson, 2016; Owen, 2011) through diagnoses of intermittent explosive disorder, which is related but narrow in its phenotype, and others such as posttraumatic stress disorder (PTSD), borderline personality disorder, bipolar disorder, and agitated depression. Future research could examine the degree to which problematic anger is present in the absence of, or in a manner not explained by, these other disorders and hence warrants being considered as a disorder in its own right akin with problematic anxiety and mood.

ETIOLOGY AND MECHANISMS

Another critical area for future research in high-risk organizations is the role played by anger in the development and maintenance of high-prevalence mental health problems such as PTSD, suicidal thoughts, suicide attempts, and other risk-related behaviors. As discussed by Lawrence-Wood et al. (Chapter 6) and Naifeh et al. (Chapter 7), anger appears to play an important role in the development and maintenance of these phenomena. As Naifeh et al. indicate, we need to better understand the "when, where, and why" of maladaptive anger over the course of the person's career in a high-risk organization. For example, for military personnel this would be from enlistment through, training, postings, deployment, and following separation. Future research should attempt to determine which factors contribute to the shift in anger from a transitory emotional state to one that is consolidated, impairing adaptive processing and increasing the consequential risk.

Likewise, Osgood and Quartana (Chapter 1), in their in-depth examination of theoretical models of anger, emphasize the need for future research to advance understanding of potential moderators of the relationship between anger at work and workplace aggression, particularly moderators such as trait anger, gender, and status within the organizational hierarchy. They also introduce sleep as an important psychological moderator that warrants further examination. Their work, as well as the work of Lawrence-Wood et al. and Naifeh et al., points to the need for future research needs to explore the neurobiological underpinnings of the anger response, recognizing that this response may be enhanced by high states of arousal associated with the occupational context and these high states of arousal are incrementally compounded by repeated exposure to potentially traumatic experiences.

Preexisting characteristics may also place individuals at risk for the development of problematic anger. We need to explore the role that preexisting anger regulation and vulnerabilities play, over and above or in combination with service life, in the development of subsequent disorder and risk for suicidal thoughts and behavior. We also need to better understand biological alterations that occur following exposure to high stress or adversity. As highlighted by Naifeh et al. (Chapter 7), there is also a potential role for algorithms generated through machine learning to help us better understand the confluence of anger with other risk factors in contributing to mental health problems and risk to self and others. The large numbers required for these kinds of analyses, of course, may be possible only if we can agree upon a universally accepted minimum data set. Such research, however, has enormous potential. For example, it could illuminate the degree to which factors such as age, gender, role, length of service, nature of operations, and number of exposures can assist us in better identifying the risk for problematic anger as a concern in its own right and its contribution to the development of other mental health problems like suicidality.

This research has the potential to improve identification of the mechanisms by which anger plays a differential role across the manifestations of suicidality—ideation, attempts, and completion—each of which is likely to be driven by different risk algorithms. It would help us understand how much of the variance is driven by personality vulnerabilities, neurobiological responses, and manifested phenotypic expressions. This research approach would allow us to explore whether variations in anger expression—for example, the explosive anger characteristic of intermittent explosive disorder compared with the persisting high trait but low expressed simmering anger—are important in predictable and identifiable ways. It is clear from the preceding chapters that considerable work is already underway in these areas. Substantially more methodologically rigorous and, ideally, collaborative research is required, however, to better understand the etiological, mechanistic role of anger in the development of problematic conditions and behaviors, as well as its longitudinal course among those who serve in our high-risk organizations.

INTERVENTIONS

The ultimate purpose of generating improved definitions, measurement strategies, and risk identification is to improve our capacity to intervene in order to minimize risk and suffering and to maximize functioning and performance. Achievement of this goal will require consideration of interventions at both clinical and organizational levels.

Clinical Interventions

As highlighted by Morland et al. in Chapter 8 of this volume, there is currently a paucity of research on anger in personnel from high-risk organizations and an urgent need to increase the evidence base around interventions for problematic and dysregulated anger in this population. This research will require focused randomized controlled trials, with careful consideration as to how the intervention protocols may be tailored to the specific needs of the target populations. Interventions may, for example, need to be tailored according to gender, nature of the role or service, time in service, or serving versus ex-service populations. Building on this increasing sophistication, there is potential to distill the most effective ingredients of these interventions to refine both efficacy and efficiency. There is also an opportunity to explore the degree to which interventions that target dysregulated anger should be offered as augmentations to existing evidence-based treatments for common mental health conditions in these populations such as PTSD and depression. In the case of PTSD, for example, and particularly in military-related PTSD, anger is often a highly prominent and significant associated feature. We need to better understand how to augment evidence-based treatments for PTSD with specific and efficient use of interventions targeting anger. In achieving this goal, an important consideration requiring empirically driven guidance is timing. Given the evidence around the attenuation effect of anger on PTSD treatment outcomes—particularly in military veterans, in whom it has been most closely studied (e.g., Lloyd et al., 2014)—there is a pressing need to determine the optimal timing of interventions targeting anger. In particular, should they be delivered prior to, or concurrently with, trauma-focused treatments?

In our search for more effective interventions, it is important to remember the multifactorial, transdiagnostic nature of high trait anger (Owen, 2011). Thus, we need to consider interventions that address not only the emotional dysregulation and high arousal components but also the cognitive and attentional biases that generate and maintain problematic anger and that probably also contribute to other comorbid clinical conditions. Innovative research by Arad and Bar-Haim (Chapter 9) has identified the potential therapeutic role of interventions designed to modify attention and cognitive bias in anger, either as stand-alone or as augmentation to interventions alongside evidence-based cognitive behavior therapy (CBT). As with other anger interventions, Arad and Bar Haim also raise the important question of timing: Should these attentional and cognitive bias modifications be delivered prior to, concurrently with, following, or even instead of CBT anger interventions and trauma-focused treatments for PTSD and related conditions?

An important challenge for large high-risk organizations is how best to reach significant numbers of members with effective preventive and treatment interventions. One part of the solution, and an approach that likely appeals to those who prefer self-management (Adler et al., 2015) or who may be concerned about stigma or a negative impact on their career, is to consider "self-delivered" approaches. These may be delivered through online programs, mobile apps, protocol manuals, and workbooks. As interventions for problematic anger become more refined, there is considerable potential to explore how best to deliver the essential ingredients in a self-delivered form and to compare the effectiveness with practitioner-delivered anger interventions.

When considering anger-related interventions for personnel from high-risk organizations, the field typically focuses on PTSD, depression, and other mental health disorders. Phelps et al. (Chapter 3), however, also flag the need for research to consider anger as part of the expression of moral injury. Phelps and colleagues note that potentially morally injurious events that involve transgression of one's moral code can lead to powerful emotions such as shame and betrayal, and individuals working in high-risk occupations may be likely to encounter these events. The potential mental health impact of these morally challenging events requires a more comprehensive form of intervention. There is a pressing need for research into the links between moral injury and anger, exploring betrayal, injustice, and shame as mediating factors. Such research would not only help to further our understanding of the development and maintenance of anger problems associated with moral injury but also guide the development of effective therapeutic approaches. In addressing anger in the context of moral injury, it seems likely that we will need to leverage the evidence base for problematic anger more broadly, outlined by Morland et al. (Chapter 8), as well as the evidence base for effective treatment of PTSD (Forbes et al., 2020). Future research, however, may also highlight the need for a more tailored, differentiated approach that targets the specific clinical presentation of anger in the context of moral injury. In short, we still need to learn much about the nature and treatment of moral injury, particularly for those with a strong anger component to their clinical presentation.

A final consideration regarding clinical interventions is whether the development of more effective intervention protocols also has the potential to empower clinicians, hopefully enhancing their confidence to engage with, and actively treat, angry and aggressive patients. The importance of this confidence and comfort is highlighted by evidence that these patients are often the most likely to drop out of treatment (Berkout et al., 2019; Howells & Day, 2003), to be referred elsewhere (Deffenbacher, 2011), or to induce reluctance in therapists to adhere to protocol-driven treatment for other comorbid presenting problems (Boswell et al., 2013). It would be interesting to determine whether arming clinicians with more effective anger treatments would go some way to addressing these shortfalls in treatment delivery.

Organizational Interventions

Although individual interventions for anger play a central role in targeting problematic anger, effectively addressing anger within high-risk organizations also needs to consider the organizational context, such as how anger is manifested at team and organizational levels. O'Neill (Chapter 4) and Hammer et al. (Chapter 5) both highlight that organizations vary in their emotional cultures around the experience and expressions of anger, including the levels of anger that are tolerated and potentially expressed adaptively or, indeed, maladaptively.

In discussing anger and emotional culture in high-risk organizations, O'Neill (Chapter 4) emphasizes the need for greater sophistication in identifying distinctions between various manifestations of cultural anger, including differing intensities and functionalities (e.g., anger directed toward organizational change vs. contempt toward others). O'Neill also discusses the need for research to generate a more tailored approach in which interventions can be differentially targeted at various groups, accommodating for intensity and with clearly identified functional outcomes in mind.

Hammer et al. (Chapter 5) also highlight that an organizational focus on anger needs to consider leadership and supervisory actions given that supervisor behaviors provide a model across the organization. The significance of these leadership behaviors becomes magnified when the individual or team is operating in high-stress, high-stakes situations. Research should guide a systematic approach to addressing anger typologies in high-risk organizations at individual, team, and organizational levels, with an emphasis on informed and targeted leadership interventions. For example, which forms of leadership interact with which forms of anger expression in employees and under what conditions to produce the most positive operational outcomes?

Hammer and colleagues (Chapter 5) encourage the study of team norms for anger expression, how work units within the same organization differ in norms regarding anger expression, and how these norms influence individual and team functioning. Not only do we need to understand how anger expression operates at the team level, but we also need to build on the evidence in relation to how the experience and expression of anger among employees in high-risk occupations can spill over to colleagues or family members. This is particularly important given the known benefits of social support in mental health more broadly.

In terms of anger, research needs to consider the potential benefits of harnessing or enhancing organizationally driven social support, as well as social support drawn from important networks in the member's life outside the organization. If done properly, this social support may help to mitigate problematic anger, offering balance and potential stability both during and following the person's career in the high-risk role.

CONCLUSION

As the chapters in this volume attest, the issue of dysregulated and problematic anger is now emerging from the shadows. Its impact on the mental health, well-being, and functioning of the individuals themselves, their significant others, their colleagues, and the organizations in which they serve is now becoming evident. Quite rightly, the field has become the focus of increased attention from a mental health and quality-of-life perspective, as well as from the perspective of organizational functioning and operational effectiveness. This volume addresses key issues for consideration across a broad array of lenses relating to anger in high-risk organizations. In this final chapter, our goal is to identify a road ahead to improve the understanding and amelioration of problematic anger at individual, group, familial, and organizational levels. Collectively, this volume represents a "call to action" to elevate issues of problematic anger and encourage those working in this area to collaborate (see Table 10.1 for a summary of key takeaways). Ultimately, the field needs a seismic shift to bring the study of dysregulated and problematic anger to the forefront, where it can serve as a focal point for improving the health and functioning of those operating in high-risk occupations.

TABLE 10.1. Priorities for Future Research on Anger in High-Risk Occupations

Category	Specific research targets
Phenomenology and measurement	Develop consistent, universally agreed-upon definitions and construct operationalization, and shared use of validated assessment measures for defined purposes
	Understand both adaptive and maladaptive anger
Etiology and mechanisms	Determine factors contributing to the shift in anger from a transitory emotional state to one that impairs adaptation and increases risk
	Explore the neurobiological underpinnings of the anger response and the role of high states of arousal associated with the occupational context
	Identify preexisting risk factors in developing problematic anger and how they interact with the occupational context
Clinical interventions	Increase evidence base around interventions for problematic and dysregulated anger
	Determine treatment as a possible augmentation to existing evidence-based treatments for high prevalence disorders such as PTSD
	Address timing of anger interventions relative to other evidence-based interventions
	Consider cognitive and attentional bias modification
	Test "self-delivered" interventions
	Examine role of moral injury in development of problematic anger and implications for intervention
	Improve provider confidence and efficacy
Organizational interventions	Establish distinctions between manifestations of cultural anger
	Consider group norms in expressing anger
	Develop leadership interventions for managing anger

Note. PTSD = posttraumatic stress disorder.

REFERENCES

Adler, A. B., Britt, T. W., Riviere, L. A., Kim, P. Y., & Thomas, J. L. (2015). Longitudinal determinants of mental health treatment-seeking by US soldiers. *The British Journal of Psychiatry, 207*(4), 346–350. https://doi.org/10.1192/bjp.bp.114.146506

Berkout, O. V., Tinsley, D., & Flynn, M. K. (2019). A review of anger, hostility and aggression from an ACT perspective. *Journal of Contextual Behavioral Science, 11*, 34–43. https://doi.org/10.1016/j.jcbs.2018.12.001

Boswell, J. F., Gallagher, M. W., Sauer-Zavala, S. E., Bullis, J., Gorman, J. M., Shear, M. K., Woods, S., & Barlow, D. H. (2013). Patient characteristics and variability in adherence and competence in cognitive-behavioral therapy for panic disorder. *Journal of Consulting and Clinical Psychology*, *81*(3), 443–454. https://doi.org/10.1037/a0031437

Deffenbacher, J. L. (2011). Cognitive-behavioral conceptualization and treatment of anger. *Cognitive and Behavioral Practice*, *18*(2), 212–221. https://doi.org/10.1016/j.cbpra.2009.12.004

Fernandez, E., & Johnson, S. L. (2016). Anger in psychological disorders: Prevalence, presentation, etiology and prognostic implications. *Clinical Psychology Review*, *46*, 124–135. https://doi.org/10.1016/j.cpr.2016.04.012

Forbes, D., Alkemade, N., Mitchell, D., Elhai, J. D., McHugh, T., Bates, G., Novaco, R. W., Bryant, R., & Lewis, V. (2014). Utility of the Dimensions of Anger Reactions–5 (DAR-5) scale as a brief anger measure. *Depression and Anxiety*, *31*(2), 166–173. https://doi.org/10.1002/da.22148

Forbes, D., Bisson, J. I., Monson, C., & Berliner, L. (Eds.). (2020). *Effective treatments for PTSD: Practice guidelines from the International Society for Traumatic Stress Studies* (3rd ed.). Guilford Press.

Howells, K., & Day, A. (2003). Readiness for anger management: Clinical and theoretical issues. *Clinical Psychology Review*, *23*(2), 319–337. https://doi.org/10.1016/S0272-7358(02)00228-3

Lloyd, D., Nixon, R. D. V., Varker, T., Elliott, P., Perry, D., Bryant, R. A., Creamer, M., & Forbes, D. (2014). Comorbidity in the prediction of Cognitive Processing Therapy treatment outcomes for combat-related posttraumatic stress disorder. *Journal of Anxiety Disorders*, *28*(2), 237–240. https://doi.org/10.1016/j.janxdis.2013.12.002

Owen, J. M. (2011). Transdiagnostic cognitive processes in high trait anger. *Clinical Psychology Review*, *31*(2), 193–202. https://doi.org/10.1016/j.cpr.2010.10.003

Spielberger, C. D. (1999). *State–Trait Anger Expression Inventory-2 (STAXI-2): Professional manual*. Psychological Assessment Resources.

Index

A

B

D

P

R

T

U

V

About the Editors

Amy B. Adler, PhD, is a clinical research psychologist and senior scientist with the Center for Military Psychiatry and Neuroscience at the Walter Reed Army Institute of Research. She studies stress and performance in high-risk occupations, focusing on training innovation in managing emotions within teams, optimizing leadership, and enhancing resilience. She also co-leads the U.S. Army's research on unit-level behavioral health, resilience, and readiness. Dr. Adler has extensive experience conducting research with operational units and spent more than 20 years working for the U.S. Army overseas. Besides serving as a U.S. representative to NATO research groups, Dr. Adler has published more than 160 articles and chapters and coedited six books. She has also led the development of an array of knowledge and training products that are designed to support behavioral health under high-stress conditions. She served as an associate editor of the *Journal of Occupational Health Psychology*, is a recipient of the Distinguished Service Award from The Military Health Systems Research Symposium, and is a fellow of the American Psychological Association.

David Forbes, PhD, is director of Phoenix Australia, Centre for Posttraumatic Mental Health and professor in the Department of Psychiatry, University of Melbourne. He is a clinical psychologist specializing in the assessment and treatment of mental health problems in trauma survivors, with a particular focus on anger and mental health in military, veteran, and high-risk populations. He led the development of the inaugural Australian Guidelines for the Treatment of Posttraumatic Stress Disorder (PTSD) approved by the National Health and Medical Research Council, was vice chair of the International PTSD Guidelines, and was lead editor on the seminal *Effective Treatments for PTSD, Third Edition* (2020). Dr. Forbes has a strong track record in the conduct of research in the areas of anger and trauma-related mental health across the lifespan. He is also a leading expert in the provision of policy and service development advice to government and agencies responsible for the care of those occupationally exposed to trauma and community members exposed to trauma and disaster, and the provision of training in evidence-based treatments for trauma-related disorders. He has published over 180 scientific papers and invited book chapters and sits on many Commonwealth government policy and scientific advisory panels and academic journal editorial boards.